The Northern Ireland Question
Perspectives on Nationalism and Unionism

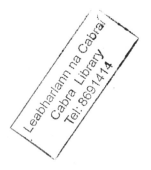

Also by Brian Barton

The Secret Court Martial Records of the Easter Rising

A History of St Peter's Parish, Antrim Road, Belfast

Northern Ireland, 1920-1945 in A New History of Ireland, Volume VII, Ireland 1921-1984

Brookborough: The Making of a Prime Minister

Northern Ireland in the Second World War

The Blitz: Belfast in the War Years

The Easter Rising (*co-author with Michael Foy*)

A Pocket History of Ulster

The Northern Ireland Question: Myth and Reality
(*co-edited with Patrick J. Roche*)

The Northern Ireland Question: Perspectives and Policies
(*co-edited with Patrick J. Roche*)

The Northern Ireland Question: Nationalism, Unionism and Partition
(*co-edited with Patrick J. Roche*)

The Northern Ireland Question: The Peace Process and the Belfast
Agreement (*co-edited with Patrick J. Roche*)

The Northern Ireland Question

Perspectives on Nationalism and Unionism

Edited by

Patrick J. Roche and Brian Barton

**Wordzworth
Publishing**

First published in 2020
by Wordzworth
www.wordzworth.com

ISBN 978-1-78324-145-3

British Library Cataloguing in Publication Data.
A catalogue record for this book is available from the British Library.

Cover photograph supplied by Pacemaker Press

Contents

Acknowledgements

As editors we wish to express our gratitude to the contributors for their co-operation, enthusiasm and patience. The expertise they have deployed in their contributions to this book makes an original and invaluable addition to an understanding of the history and politics of Northern Ireland and specifically provides a challenge to conventional understanding of the cause of the conflict in Northern Ireland and what brought it to an end and how to deal with the 'past'.

We also wish to express our gratitude to our publisher, Wordzworth Publishing, for their hallmark high quality production.

Introduction

Brian Barton and Patrick J. Roche

In producing this volume, the editors have drawn on the expertise of aca-demics engaged in a wide range of specialisms – Irish history, political philosophy, economics, politics and counter-terrorism. They have each pro-vided original and insightful contributions which will deepen and enrich the reader's understanding in relation to a wide range of vitally import-ant topics. These include: the genesis and establishment of a functioning government in Northern Ireland in the context of Ireland's turbulent, revo-lutionary period; the treatment of Protestants in the Free State/Republic of Ireland post-1921; the experience and practice of devolution in Northern Ireland, and its contemporary relevance within the United Kingdom; a consideration of the logic of Irish nationalist ideology and the moral legit-imacy of the republican resort to the use of physical force; an analysis of the political significance and validity of nationalist allegations of discrimination in relation to public housing allocation and employment; an examination of the republican contribution to the origins and nature of the civil rights movement and an investigation into the economic viability of Irish uni-fication. In a study of the historical background to, and the dynamics of, the terrorist campaign that engulfed Northern Ireland for thirty years, the decisive role of the security forces in bringing the conflict to an end is high-lighted. Other chapters in the book assess the operation post-1998 of the institutions of government in Northern Ireland and the political motiva-tions that have directed 'dealing with the past' within the terms of the 1998 Belfast Agreement. Finally, in view of the Johnson government's decision to withdraw Britain from the European Union, current post Brexit unionist and nationalist ' anxieties' and 'expectations' are explored.

Brian Barton's chapter sets the genesis of Northern Ireland in the context of Ireland's revolutionary period, beginning with the Easter

Rising and its repercussions over the seven years that followed. Its leaders became role models for generations of Irish youth. During Easter week 1916 they reaffirmed and rejuvenated the physical force tradition in Irish nationalism. They were uncompromising in pursuing and advocating their objective, a thirty-two county sovereign republic, and so helped define and elevate this as the primary goal of Irish nationalism. They were elitist, aware that their actions lacked popular support, but were nonetheless determined to ignore the wishes of the majority and fight for their conception of Irish freedom, convinced that they spoke for the country's deepest self. The Rising contributed to the rise of Sinn Fein, the initiation of the Anglo-Irish war and of the civil war. Those opposed to the Treaty regarded it as a betrayal of the martyrs of 1916, and of the republic they had proclaimed.

This background of cataclysmic violence and prolonged turbulence, 1916-23, did much to determine and permanently distort Northern Ireland's political structure. Pearse's irreconcilable spirit inspired the minds of the leaders of Sinn Fein. They refused to engage with the 1920 Act, did not accept the legitimacy of unionist opposition to unity and regarded partition as being unnatural and reversible. They were unwilling to recognize the Belfast parliament and were to deploy every means to destabilize and overthrow it. Their negative and belligerent attitude largely determined the nationalist minority's response to the Northern Ireland state after its formation in mid-1921. Its members adopted a strategy of passive resistance and civil disobedience, and of abstentionism by its elected representatives and, for a time, broadly endorsed the use of physical force. Michael Collins encouraged, organized and financed their negativism and obstructionism. Though Westminster retained its sovereignty, it failed to provide Craig's government with adequate support or any sense that its position was secure. After the truce British ministers were distracted by, and prioritized, reaching agreement with the southern leadership. During the Anglo-Irish negotiations it was evident that they regarded the new institutions in Belfast as being entirely dispensable, and that Irish unity was their preferred outcome. The 1921 Anglo-Irish treaty made provision (Article 12) for a Boundary Commission to revise the borders of the six counties if the northern parliament rejected all-Ireland institutions. This prospect alarmed unionists, whilst raising nationalist expectations and confirming them in their strategy of non-cooperation. In early 1922, the Dublin government increasingly focused its energies on the ending of Partition as a means of averting civil war. It sponsored a concerted IRA campaign aimed at making Northern Ireland ungovernable. The violence peaked in May/June 1922.

Though stretched to the limits of its resources, Northern Ireland survived this onslaught, and retained the powers and boundaries laid down in the 1920 Act. That it did so was mainly due to the stringent security measures taken by Craig's government and the outbreak of civil war in the south in mid-1922. A further factor was the dwindling level of support for the IRA campaign then being provided by northern nationalists. Their expectations of major border changes resulting from the adjudication of the Boundary Commission were to end in disappointment in December 1925. In the meantime their failure to engage with the new state had robbed them of any say in the future shape of its institutions and political culture, and this reinforced further their feelings of alienation.

The traumatic experience of these its most formative years left an indelible imprint on Northern Ireland's institutions and cohesion. In the policies they adopted after 1922 unionist politicians continued to display a siege mentality, even though the siege had by then largely been lifted. Their continuing sense of insecurity was rooted in apprehension regarding the substantial and alienated minority within the state, the sporadic recurrence of IRA campaigns, the undependable nature of the support they received from Westminster and the persistence of Dublin irredentism. It was only in the course of the recent Troubles that the main political parties in the south, and eventually Sinn Fein also, accepted the principle of unionist consent to Irish unity. But republican recalcitrants, who consider themselves to be the true heirs of the Easter Rising, remain. So, a century later, the malignant influence of Ireland's revolutionary period still endures and is used to justify murder, even though any perceived unfairness in the governance of the six counties has long since been extirpated.

In his chapter Graham Walker analyses Northern Ireland's experience of devolution, and also its contemporary relevance. He begins by pointing out that events after the 1920 Act did not transpire as some leading politicians had anticipated. No single devolved Irish parliament materialized, nor were federal institutions formed in other regions of the United Kingdom; there was no 'home rule all round'. Northern unionists accepted and implemented the legislation because it recognized Ulster as a distinctive entity with a democratic right to remain in the Union, at least for as long as the party's unity was maintained and it retained its position in power. A Belfast parliament was established, but there was a degree of ambiguity and confusion as to its precise status. Time and constitutional conventions set in 1925 and 1949 fed unionists' illusions of sovereignty, and this helps account for the strength of their objections to any threatened intervention from London.

Hard choices had to be made to preserve Unionist Party unity. Craig (and his immediate successors) elected to take a minimalist approach to the possibilities offered by devolution. He adopted a 'populist' policy, his objective being to maintain the same social security provision and welfare payments as in Great Britain. Northern Ireland could not afford the expenditure this entailed. It became feasible as a consequence of set-tlements reached with London, most notably the Colwyn Committee's decision regarding the Imperial Contribution and an agreement inte-grating the region into Britain's unemployment insurance scheme. Some in Craig's government circles ('anti-populists') deprecated his 'begging bowl' approach, arguing that it ran counter both to London's wish that Northern Ireland should be self-reliant and to the spirit of the 1920 Act. But Craig insisted that Northern Ireland had, like any other depressed area, a legitimate claim to its share of the United Kingdom's pool of resources, and that its citizens were fully entitled to the same state bene-fits as they paid taxes at the same rates as elsewhere. Unionists had long argued that the advantage of having UK citizenship and of being in the Union was that the resulting rights and privileges would apply equitably to all. He was perfectly content to regard Northern Ireland as a subordi-nate unit within the UK economy, and made no apology for its financial dependence. He considered that devolution had been a British govern-ment 'convenience', which it had introduced in an attempt to resolve the Irish question, and that it should therefore be prepared to pay the sums required to make it work. Ulster unionists had neither wished for nor sought it, and had themselves made sacrifices in order to bring about the 1921 settlement. For Craig a further advantage of his policy was that it affirmed Northern Ireland's place within the Union, bound the region more closely into the UK as the unit of democratic decision-making, and minimized the disjunctive impact of having a regional parliament. Moreover his 'populist' approach to social welfare was politically astute. For him not to have adopted it would have risked disaffecting working class party members and opening up class divisions within unionism, whilst it also took the ground from under the feet of the Northern Ireland Labour Party.

Walker points out that the impartial administration of welfare benefits which resulted from the 'step by step' policy could be used by unionists to refute some allegations of discrimination. He proceeds to examine the validity of nationalist claims of ill treatment, and of the mantra: 'fifty years of Unionist misrule.' On housing in the interwar period he suggests that the Northern Ireland government should have pressed its party members on local authorities to have been less partisan in their allocations. He notes that this grievance persisted post 1945, and helped fuel the civil rights movement, and he accepts that there were cases of egregious bias by unionists west of the Bann desperate to preserve their majorities on councils they controlled. But he stresses that the Housing Trust acted with scrupulous impartiality, and that the rigorous examination conducted by Rose concluded that, by and large, this was also the case in Belfast and to the east of the province. With regard to education, Walker argues that allegations of discrimination are weakened when the unconstructive role of the Catholic Church is acknowledged. It refused to become involved in the creation of a new educational system and was uncompromising in its insistence on running its own schools. Yet from the beginning all staff's salaries in these were fully funded by the state, as well as 50 per cent of school running costs. Moreover, under the 1947 Act, capital grants were increased to 65 per cent. This measure was indisputably fair and progressive, it benefited the minority and was formative in increasing opportunities to progress to third level institutions, an outcome which had significant political consequences. Education was not therefore one of the issues highlighted by the civil rights movement in the 1960s.

Walker then examines the role of the minority in the state and comments, for example, on: the inflexibility and sectarian outlook of many Catholic leaders and politicians; their abstention from the Belfast parliament until 1925 and their insistence until the 1960s that the constitutional question was the only one that mattered. He comments on the extreme views expressed by Cardinal MacRory and notes that, unlike some Protestant clerics, these have largely escaped censure. Though the IRA's border campaign failed partly because it lacked minority support, it did have unfortunate consequences. It kept sectarian tensions simmering, and helped prevent progressive unionist elements from attracting greater support for reform and the extension of a 'step by step' policy beyond social policy. Moreover, the palpable threat posed by militant republicans shaped how many Protestants viewed the civil rights movement. As Walker observes, Ulster unionists had a siege mentality but there were also besiegers.

In his conclusion Walker states that balanced and nuanced assessments of the unionist governance of Northern Ireland are rare. He argues that critical evaluations are unsurprising given the Party's mishandling of the civil rights movement in the 1960s, myopia regarding reform of the local government franchise and tolerance of council abuses. Its siege mentality and arrogance in regarding the six counties as being 'our place' prevented an inclusive reform programme. At the same time its success in preserving the unity of is members around the constitutional issue prevented the development of an effective opposition and of healthier politics. Walker notes that investigations into devolution in Northern Ireland conducted before the outbreak of the Troubles are generally more measured and more favourable.

Finally Walker stresses the importance of writing Northern Ireland properly into accounts of Britain's constitutional and political development, especially in view of the recent creation of separate parliaments in Scotland and Wales. The Belfast institution was the first instance of devolution, the 'pioneer.' It serves as a reminder that constitutional change has a long and complex history and did not just appear in the late twentieth century. The process also illustrates the internal diversity of the United Kingdom, and that it is the product of several past unions.

Patrick Roche's consideration of terrorism and Irish nationalism focuses on the 'one nation' claim common to constitutional nationalists and republicans. He stresses that this determines their understanding of unionism and Partition. Both assert that Ireland is 'one nation' and, consequently, assert that unionists, as a minority within the Irish nation, have no de jure right of veto over the achievement of Irish unity. They regard Partition as being an injustice against the Irish nation because it deprives the claimed nation of its right to 'self-determination' within the island of Ireland, which they understand to be the 'national territory'.

The perennial problem for nationalists is how to induce unionist consent to Irish unity. Republicans choose to resort to physical force which was directed at compelling Britain to withdraw from Northern Ireland and at breaking the will of Ulster unionists to remain within the Union. Roche argues that this raises a fundamental moral question regarding the legitimacy of the IRA/Sinn Fein resort to terrorism. He notes that republicans operate with a tacit appeal to the jus ad bellum (rightness of resort to the use of force) dimension of the just war tradition.

To justify the use of force there are two crucial ad bellum requirements. The first prerequisite is that of 'just cause' and the republican position is that this is met by the claimed 'injustice of Partition'. The second is that of 'right authority' – the requirement for competent authority to authorize resort to the use of force. Republicans claim that the IRA derives this from the First Dail (1919-1921) which they consider to be the legitimate parliament of the republic proclaimed by Pearse on 24 April 1916. Roche argues that this understanding of 'right authority' is rooted in a combination of historical and political fantasy (the republic proclaimed in 1916 was never a sovereign state) reinforced by what Conor Cruise O'Brien referred to in *Ancestral Voices* as the 'ghosts that call for blood'.

As noted, the nationalist claim that Partition is an 'injustice' is rooted in the 'one nation' thesis. Roche proceeds by examining the legitimacy of this position, and he raises the crucial question: is there a single nation on the island of Ireland? He argues that the 'objective' and 'subjective' criteria of national identity traditionally used by Irish nationalists do not establish the 'one nation' claim. These considerations mean therefore that the resort to physical force on the part of IRA/Sinn Fein does not meet the 'right authority' and 'just cause' ad bellum requirements. Furthermore he states that the thirty years of violence unleashed during the Troubles was an extreme form of terrorism and was therefore contrary to the in bello requirement that the use of force must not involve intentional and indiscriminate killing directed towards, quite literally, the terrorizing of a population in order to achieve a political objective.

Roche considers that the moral character of the terrorism indulged in by the IRA ought never to be eclipsed. Yet, despite their heinous actions, he brings into focus the fact that the 'peace process' of the 1990s elevated the leadership and active members of the republican movement (IRA/ Sinn Fein) to the status of 'peace makers' and, moreover, that the terms of the 1998 Belfast Agreement placed them in the seat of government in Northern Ireland and that in the post-1998 period republicans and their 'fellow travellers' have focused on a re-writing of the history of the conflict directed at the moral exoneration of the IRA and the obscuring the fact that IRA's thirty-year campaign ended in abject failure. He makes the obvious point that the IRA failed to secure its primary political objective of 'Irish unity' and argues that it was militarily defeated.

Andrew Charles and Patrick Roche explore the genesis and legacy of the civil rights movement in Northern Ireland. Their chapter sets out two diametrically opposed understandings of the civil rights movement. The first is that support for the civil rights movement, and specifically the republican involvement in it during the 1960s, marked at least a tacit acceptance of the constitutional status quo. The second is that republican and left wing radical involvement in the civil rights movement was driven by the understanding that Northern Ireland required anti-Catholic discrimination in order to survive with the import for nationalists that the elimination of discrimination would ineluctably lead to the end of Partition.

An understanding that the eradication of alleged discrimination in Northern Ireland would result in the ending of Partition was deeply implanted in the thinking of those Marxists and republicans whom Charles and Roche designate as being the 'early ideologues'. The key figures they include in this category are Greaves, Coughlin and Johnston who were the intellectual leaders of the Wolfe Tone Societies, and who influenced the thinking of the 1960s Marxist orientated, IRA leader Cathal Goulding. The Goulding strategy for achieving Irish unity was informed by his conviction that the 1956-62 IRA campaign had failed for lack of sufficient backing from the public. In essence his view was that the mobilization of popular support to end Partition must be embedded in a socialist transformation of Ireland and that this must involve the elimination of discrimination within the six counties without which, in Goulding's understanding, Partition would not survive.

The first two marches authorized by the Northern Ireland Civil Rights Association (NICRA) confirmed and reinforced the unionist perception that the civil rights movement was inspired by the objectives of Irish nationalism. The first of these, from Coalisland to Dungannon on 24 August 1968, was an overt display of nationalist disposition, and was described by Simon Prince in Northern Ireland's '68 as an 'Irish nationalist parade'. Though the second, on 5 October 1968, was authorized by NICRA, it had actually been organized by the Derry Housing Action Committee (DHAC) with the deliberate intention of provoking confrontation with the RUC. Unfortunately it did precipitate an over-reaction by the police, and subsequently this became the focus of international media attention whilst causing nationalist outrage.

The events of 5 October led directly to the formation of People's Democracy on 9 October 1968, an organization directed by a combination of Irish republicans and radical socialists. It was this body which organized the infamous 'long march' from Belfast to Londonderry on 1 January 1968, the outcome of which was the intensification of political instability and violence in Northern Ireland exemplified by the 'battle of the Bogside' in Londonderry on 12 August 1969. NICRA then authorized widespread demonstrations outside Belfast to draw the police away from Londonderry. Wherever these occurred they resulted in violence. This was particularly the case in west Belfast; the eruption of disorder there provoked a loyalist backlash on 14-15 August. This descent into inter-communal conflict occasioned the deployment of the British army in Belfast and Londonderry on 14 August 1969 and, in January 1970, the Provisional IRA (PIRA) came into existence. By then the era of mass civil rights protests and demonstrations had effectively ended and three decades of IRA terrorism were about to begin.

In his chapter Graham Gudgin highlights the political significance of nationalist allegations of discrimination made against the unionist majority in Northern Ireland. The fact that these were widely accepted internationally meant that the cause of violence post-1969 was understood in terms of, and attributed to, unionist sectarian discrimination against Catholics. The growth of this perception was facilitated by the intellectual inability of unionists to effectively counter such claims and by the highly pejorative treatment unionism has historically received. The result was that a broad consensus emerged in both London and Dublin that majority based government was not appropriate for Northern Ireland. To a significant degree this perception determined the nature of the mandatory power-sharing institutions which were required by the 1998 Belfast Agreement.

With regard to discrimination, Gudgin focuses on the allegations of discrimination relating to public housing allocation and employment. After an exhaustive analysis of the relevant statistical data he concludes that, contrary to the claims that have routinely been made, in fact 'Catholics were over-represented, not under-represented, in social housing at the end of the unionist regime in 1971'. His examination of allegations of anti-Catholic discrimination with regard to employment effectively undermines: firstly, the suggestion that a persistent high Catholic/Protestant unemployment ratio is 'proof' of discrimination and, secondly, the assertion made in the New Ireland Forum report that regional patterns of Catholic/Protestant employment indicate Catholics were 'deprived of the means of social and economic development'. He argues that the persistent demand for 'Irish unity' made by the nationalist minority created and sustained a culture of grievance. But he also states that unionists failed to 'take what opportunities they had to bring the nationalists into the political system and to reform the outmoded system of local government'. Nonetheless, he concludes that whatever level of discrimination had existed in Northern Ireland it provided 'no moral justification for violence or the threat of violence for political ends in Ireland'.

William Matchett documents the counter-insurgency strategies directed against republican and loyalist terrorism, and he identifies three phases: the react phase (1969-75); the adjust phase (1976-82) and the mature phase (1982-98). The distinctive characteristic of this third phase was the primacy of the RUC and, in particular, the crucial role played by RUC Special Branch in 'intelligence-led policing'. During this period Special Branch penetrated the IRA to an extent which a former leading IRA activist acknowledged was both 'colossal and fatal'. Matchett considers that as a consequence of its success there was, by the late 1980s, an 'historic opportunity to defeat the IRA'. Howver, after the resignation of Thatcher in 1990, this auspicious moment was not seized by Major or Blair. Instead, both prioritized the 'peace process', which eventually resulted in the 1998 Belfast Agreement.

Matchett argues that the terms of the Belfast Agreement have provided the basis for the ongoing 'scapegoat phase.' This, he states, began in 1998 with, firstly, the establishment of the Patten Commission which resulted in the destruction of the RUC and, secondly, the creation of a police ombudsman with powers to retrospectively investigate the actions taken by members of the force. The Agreement also created a framework for the pursuit of a continuing and destructive 'lawfare' against the RUC conducted by Sinn Fein and republican 'fellow travellers'. This focuses on claims of 'collusion' and of a 'dirty war syndrome' within the security forces, and its object is morally and legally to exonerate republican terrorism and shift the blame for violence on to the security forces, specifically the RUC and Special Branch. The import of Matchett's contribution is that the clerics and politicians and other assorted 'peaceniks', who have since 1998 arrogated to themselves the role of peace-makers, have in fact 'reaped the peace that others had sown in a long intelligence war'.

Cillian McGrattan's deeply insightful and carefully articulated thesis is that political decision-making in Northern Ireland has been 'calibrated' towards the perceived exigency of 'bringing violent republicans into the political process'. He argues that this 'predisposition' has imposed on the specific and vital area of 'legacy issues' an 'implicit ideological bias'. He writes that this 'bias' has 'facilitated the representation of "legacy issues" as primarily transitional to an end state [the transcending of an illegitimate Northern state] as distinct from them being about culpability for the injustices and violence of the past'. This ideologically determined utilization of the past has in effect become a re-writing of history. McGrattan argues that 'truth recovery in the Provisional republican mode ought to be understood as truth creating'. With respect to legacy issues this process of 'truth creating' is cynically directed to the 'disarticulation of unionist memory', to the 'cutting off' or effacing or obliteration or 'creation of an oblivion relating to the Protestant experience of the conflict'.

Arthur Aughey's contribution is a sophisticated consideration of 'syndromes', or patterns of thought relating to history and politics that mark the nationalist and unionist 'expectations and anxieties' that characterized their responses to Brexit. He detects in the northern nationalist reaction to Brexit a 'dynamic concurrence' of two distinct patterns of thought. First was the nationalist reaction of 'outrage at the betrayal of [their] expectations'. This response was rooted in their understanding that the EU project and UK membership of the EU were historical continuities providing a perceived protective framework that shaped nationalist identity (while allowing northern nationalists to enjoy the benefits of UK citizenship) and a guarantee that the 'EU train' would lead to their desired goal of Irish unity. Brexit shattered this nationalist expectation of historical and political continuity within the EU framework.

Aughey argues that paradoxically this mood of anxiety and unfulfilled expectation has been combined in the northern nationalist mind with a more deterministic understanding of an immediate 'irresistible movement towards Irish unity' consequent upon Brexit. The traditional deterministic dimension of Irish nationalist thought – the assumed inevitability of Irish unity – is reinforced for nationalists by the expectation that the adverse economic repercussions of Brexit will persuade erstwhile unionists to opt to join the Republic as a means of retaining the perceived benefits of EU membership. But Aughey considers that this perception lacks the merits of historical skepticism and does not allow for the contingency of events. The Brexit that is now used to reinforce nationalist determinism and notions of political inevitability with respect to the unification of Ireland was itself an unforeseen contingency, and the economic 'self-harm' that nationalists predict will be its consequence is more than counteracted and negated by the economic 'self-harm' that Irish unity would inflict on Ireland.

Aughey notes the essentially conservative character of unionism: 'its ideological vocation is to maintain Northern Ireland within the Union'. This defensive 'ideology' is rooted in an understanding that any historical/political change which impacts on unionism is pregnant with risk and danger; it is the unionist version of a form of historical determinism. This mindset is the root cause of the 'pessimism' that is a marked feature of the unionist disposition which, in turn, generates the expectation of 'betrayal'. This is also combined, however, with 'hope in the effectiveness of resistance' to halt the impact of change, or a belief that 'the impact of change can be sufficiently tamed in order to render it either acceptable or manageable'.

Despite their characteristic 'pessimism' unionists, specifically the DUP, paradoxically greeted the prospect of Brexit with political complacency. They assumed that the continuity of the status quo with respect to the border would remain unchanged. They adopted this position even though it was evident that Brexit would 'change everything in the UK's relationship with the EU and with the rest of the world'. Their complacent response did not allow for the unexpected and the contingent – the prospect that the negotiation of a withdrawal agreement would fracture the economic integrity of the UK, isolate Northern Ireland within the EU single market and customs union and create an entirely new context for the age-old conflict between unionism and nationalism. Paraphrasing Shakespeare, Aughey concludes on a note of historical skepticism, writing: 'we are afloat on a full sea and where the present tide of affairs will take us, I fear we cannot tell'.

Esmond Bernie's chapter on the economics of nationalism and unionism provides a critical appraisal of a number of current positive arguments regarding the viability of Irish unity. These arguments are set within the context of Brexit and the contemporary performance of the Republic's economy. Collectively they deploy the German experience of unification as a relevant theoretical template for Ireland combined with the argument that a significant amount of the annual Westminster subvention to Northern Ireland (currently £9 billion per annum) would not be required in the post-unification situation or that Britain would continue the subvention for a number of decades post-unification.

The Brexit dimension of the pro-Irish unity argument is the presumption that Britain's withdrawal from the EU will deliver a 'shattering blow to the Northern Ireland economy' with the result that erstwhile unionists will opt for unification in order to secure and preserve their position within the EU. On the basis of a detailed examination of these arguments Bernie concludes that there is still a strong case for the Union but he considers that it would be strengthened if the Northern Ireland economy was to become more productive, and he argues that this should be the primary orientation of unionist economic policy.

Robin Bury's chapter presents a formidable challenge to the 'myth of a Protestant sanctuary' within the post-1921 Free State/Republic of

Ireland. He covers in detail the intimidation and attacks experienced by southern Protestants between 1919-1923, ranging from sectarian murder in the Bandon Valley in April 1922 to the burning of 'big house' throughout these years. This varied pattern of violence resulted in an accelerating exodus of up to 48,000 Protestants between 1911 and 1926. Those who opted to remain in southern Ireland post-independence were subjected to: further violent outrages in 1935; legislation on contraception, divorce and censorship whose content and tone was determined by the demands of Catholic moral values; the ne temere decree which imposed the repressive content of the Church's canon law on mixed marriages and the blight of compulsorily learning Irish as part of their primary and secondary school education (this was unsuccessfully resisted by the Church of Ireland).

Over subsequent decades Protestants in the Free State/Republic of Ireland have been enclosed within a society dominated by a nationalist understanding of history and a violent foundational mythology of the state. As a consequence of the identification of being authentically Irish with being Catholic, they lived in what was virtually a theocratic state, which was marked under de Valera by a further retreat from modernity. Bury recognizes that much has changed in contemporary Ireland with the emergence of a more secular and multicultural society. Nevertheless he suggests that a residual Anglophobia remains, and that this was evidenced by the stance taken over Brexit by the Varadkar-led, Fine Gael government in 2019. He also asserts that there has been a failure fully to acknowledge the 'ethnic cleansing' of Protestants that occurred, and the consequent loss to the new state of the 'energy, intransigence and fierce radicalism' of the Protestant tradition in the south.

The implementation of the Belfast Agreement from 1998 has coincided with, and exacerbated, the polarization of politics in Northern Ireland. The core issue explored by Dennis Kennedy is the extent to which the Agreement directly contributed to this polarization and the instability which resulted, despite the claim made by its proponents that it had secured a 'final resolution' of an 'intractable source of political conflict'. The initial expectation of its supporters was that the Agreement would consolidate the 'moderate' middle ground in Northern Ireland politics which had for decades been occupied by the UUP and the SDLP. But the opposite of this has occurred. By 2003 the DUP and Sinn Fein were dominant within unionism and nationalism respectively. Unsurprisingly the Executive was by then in suspension.

Kennedy examines how the appeasement of the IRA, which had characterized the entire 'peace process', was reinforced by the terms of the Belfast Agreement which required the release of terrorist prisoners, and by the implementation of the Agreement which resulted in the destruction of the RUC. The entirely predictable electoral consequence of these developments was to strengthen Sinn Fein at the expense of the SDLP, and to weaken the UUP to the advantage of the DUP. Though the Executive was reinstated in 2007 on the basis of the St Andrews Agreement, this was accepted by the DUP and Sinn Fein for mutually incompatible political reasons and for divergent strategic calculations. Moreover, the inherently unstable institutional framework which was established by the Agreement has remained. Its terms mandatorily require that a coalition must be formed between parties with diametrically opposed political objectives and social policies. In addition, as a result of the interdependent, dual structure of the Department of the First and Deputy First Minister if either resigns from office, and the relevant party refuses to nominate a replacement, the entire edifice of government collapses; this is what happened in 2017.

Kennedy sets his exploration of the polarization and instability of the Agreement's institutional structures within an analysis of the national policies pursued by the British and Irish governments. This entailed a consideration of the impact on Northern Ireland of changing external circumstances. Much of Kennedy's focus is on Brexit which he considers has altered the operational context of the Agreement and, as a result, diminished further its capacity to provide an effective framework of government. He notes that the inappropriate institutional requirements which the Agreement imposed, and which made possible the suspension of the Executive and Assembly, from January 2017 to January 2020 were left basically intact in the *New Decade, New Approach* agreement which ended the suspension. He cautions that the provisions in this document which relate to the Irish language may well provide the grounds for a future existential crisis for the Belfast Agreement.

1

The birth of Northern Ireland in Ireland's revolutionary period

Brian Barton

The Easter Rising, and its repercussions during the seven turbulent years which followed, largely determined the context for the genesis of Northern Ireland. It helped ensure that when, in mid June 1921, the leaders of the Unionist Party sought to establish a functioning government in Belfast they were confronted by problems which stretched their resources to the limit. For a time it was unclear whether or not they would succeed in sustaining the powers and boundaries that had been laid down in the 1920 Government of Ireland Act. They did so, but the traumatic experience of this formative period left an indelible mark on the institutions and cohesion of the state.

The 1916 insurrection was commonly referred to as the Sinn Fein Rising, but its real, secret spring was a small, underground, revolutionary organization, the Irish Republican Brotherhood (IRB). Within it, a clandestine and dynamic group emerged and, in August 1915, its members formed the IRB Military Council. It was eventually composed of seven members: Thomas Clarke, Sean MacDermott, Patrick Pearse, Eamonn Ceannt, Joseph Plunkett, James Connolly and Thomas MacDonagh. These men conceived, planned and guided the Rising to fruition. They shared a passionate desire to establish a sovereign Irish republic, and an unshakeable conviction that this could only be achieved by force. Their intention was covertly to infiltrate the numerically strong Irish Volunteer Force (IVF) for use as their strike force. The IRB was too small and too secretive by habit and instinct to attempt openly to precipitate a large-scale rising.

The roots of the Rising go back to the 1880s. Its causal factors include: the emergence of a new nationalism in Ireland; disillusionment with the Parliamentary Party which over a period of over forty years had failed to achieve self-government and the Boer War which dispelled assumptions of Britain's military invincibility. The militancy of Ulster unionists and, in particular, the formation of the Ulster Volunteer Force (UVF) in 1912 was also significant. But rather than 'bringing the gun back into Irish politics', this merely helped confirm the drift towards support for the use of physical force. The Fenian tradition was at least as profound and as formative an influence, with its litany of revolt dating back to Wolfe Tone. It emphasized the inadequacy of relying on constitutional methods and the necessity for force of arms to win genuine independence. The centenary of the 1798 rebellion served to remind a new generation of the old faith. The outbreak of war in Europe was seized on by militant nationalists as an opportune moment to strike, acting on the old adage that 'England's difficulty is Ireland's opportunity.'

The members of the Military Council were also motivated by the idea of a 'blood sacrifice.' They were convinced that Ireland's national spirit was dying and that through a rising, and their own death and martyrdom, militant Irish nationalism could be revived and the republican tradition rejuvenated. Moreover they considered that their willingness to die for their country would in itself prove Ireland's right to freedom, that it was 'worthy of the august destiny to which it was called.'[1] For romantic nationalists like Pearse, religion and nationalism fused. Consciously emulating Christ's redemptive sacrifice on the cross, he believed that through his death he himself would help redeem the Irish nation. But undue emphasis on the 'blood sacrifice' interpretation of the Rising with its implication that its leaders from its inception regarded it as a doomed enterprise is misleading. Pearse, and the others who shared his romantic mindset (Plunkett and later MacDonagh), were junior partners in the entire revolutionary enterprise. Clarke was its 'true leader.'[2] Both he and MacDermott, with whom he forged an unbreakable bond, were hardheaded, calculating, manipulative republican zealots. Documentary evidence, particularly the Ireland Report, reveals the far-reaching nature of the Military Council's initial plans, and the scale of military operations it had anticipated. This source indicates that its clear objective was military victory to be achieved by means of an insurrection in Dublin, supported by substantial German aid. This was to include 12,000 troops and 40,000 rifles to be landed on Ireland's west coast, and U Boat cover to block off Ireland's east coast from British military reinforcements. However, this assistance failed to materialize. Thus, in practice, the 'blood sacrifice' was a gambit hastily concocted at the end of Easter week, when the Rising had disintegrated. Facing inevitable defeat and the slaughter of many of their number, the deal its leaders hoped to strike was that they should be executed, and that their sacrifice would enable the rank and file to go free, and fight again another day. It was designed not to redeem Ireland but to perform the practical task of saving the lives of their men.

Several members of the Military Council had close links to Ulster (Thomas Clarke, Sean MacDermott, James Connolly), but they developed little in the way of a strategy regarding Ulster unionism. Clarke believed that the connection with England, perfidious Albion, was the 'source of Ireland's woes, [and] he gave little thought to the political shape Ireland might take after it was broken.'[3] For all seven the priority was to proceed with the Rising; they regarded the Ulster question as an issue best dealt with later. They had, however, no doubt that the Irish nation was geographically, politically and culturally indivisible from the island of Ireland, the 'national territory.' They were therefore unwilling to concede that a substantial majority in one region of the country had as much right to remain in the British state as they had to secede from it. At the time nationalists expressed various improbable, often incompatible, theories and viewpoints with regard to the troubling phenomenon of Ulster unionism. To some industrial Belfast was like a creeping disease, Anglicized, alien, materialistic, corrupting and degraded; for decades, they had displayed a 'partitionist mentality' by referring pejoratively to the 'black North.'[4] During 1912-14 unionists were widely dismissed as 'bluffers' who, despite their rhetoric, would eventually recognize the futility of opposing Irish independence. Others thought of them as having been duped into supporting Crown, Empire and Union, as having been manipulated by conservatives in Britain or Belfast's commercial elite or the local reactionary feudal aristocracy. It was assumed that in time they would recognize their true Irish identity. Conversely, unionists were also projected as being a model for Irish nationalism, a 'splendid example', as they had 'led the way'[5] in opposing Westminster legislation, the third home rule bill. Clarke held the naïve belief that the UVF and IVF were 'brothers under different skins'[6], and had hopes of all creeds joining together against England. There was a pragmatic reason for militant Irish separatists to admire Ulster's belligerence; the formation of the UVF provided them with a plausible pretext for forming the Irish Volunteers in 1913. In general, nationalists were slow to grasp that the emergence of this force in the north was symptomatic of a genuine, mass radicalization of grassroots unionism. Few were willing or able to acknowledge the fact that this was the real obstacle to them securing greater self-government for a thirty-two county Ireland – this, rather than the Conservative Party or English politicians.

The Rising did not proceed as planned. It was to have taken place on Easter Sunday, 23 April, when it was to have been masked behind well-publicized and apparently routine, Irish Volunteer manoeuvres arranged for that day. Disaster threatened when Eoin MacNeill, the IV Chief of Staff who opposed an insurrection, heard of what was intended, and issued a last-minute, countermand order cancelling them. Undeterred, the Military Council met on the Sunday morning, 23 April, and decided to proceed at noon next day with whatever forces it could muster. In the meantime, on Friday, 21 April, the ship bearing German arms had been captured and Roger Casement been arrested. As a result of these multiple setbacks the insurrection was confined almost entirely to Dublin, and the number of rebels mobilized, roughly 1,000, was much lower than had been anticipated. Nonetheless, given the element of surprise, the buildings and outposts which they had identified in the city were occupied virtually without opposition, and they initially faced just 400 troops. The General Post Office (GPO) served as their HQ, and it was from there that Pearse read the Proclamation at 12.45 pm on Easter Monday. It proclaimed the establishment of an Irish Republic and of a Provisional Government, and stated that: 'In the name of God and of the dead generations ... Ireland through us ... strikes for her freedom ... Having organized and trained her manhood ... she strikes in full confidence of victory.'[7]

The British military authorities responded purposefully, competently and speedily: troop reinforcements were dispatched, strategic locations defended, information gathered on the rebels' positions and strength and a military cordon put in place around the city. By Wednesday, most significant insurgent-held outposts had been taken and, during Thursday and Friday, the remaining strongholds, the GPO and the Four Courts, were encircled and isolated. The GPO was then deluged with incendiary shells, resulting in massive conflagrations in O'Connell Street, and forcing Volunteers in the building to scatter into Moore Street. At noon on Saturday, 29 April, the leaders accepted the only terms on offer, unconditional surrender. Though the rising was brief, the number of fatalities was considerable. British troops sustained losses of 116 officers and other ranks, and twenty-three policemen and sixty-two insurgents were killed. It was the citizens of Dublin who suffered most. Of the 590 persons who died, over 370 of them were civilians, including thirty-eight children. They also experienced much dislocation – forced evacuation from homes, destruction of property, shortages of essentials, disruption of gas, transport and mail services and the closure of businesses, shops and places of entertainment.

The evidence is conflicting as to how the people of Dublin viewed the Rising at the time. Undoubtedly much hostility was felt towards the rebels – anger at the number of deaths, the scale of destruction and distress, and at its timing when a home rule act was on the statute book and the country prosperous. Individual bishops, the most influential body of opinion in nationalist Ireland, denounced it as irrational, futile, sinful. Relatives of Irishmen in military service regarded it as an act of treachery and cowardice and, with few exceptions, the Irish regiments deployed in Dublin obeyed their orders to suppress it. There were bitter confrontations with hostile crowds when the insurgents surrendered at the College of Surgeons and at Jacob's Bakery and, afterwards, the garrisons were taunted by furious onlookers while being escorted to Richmond Barracks. During Easter week the houses of presumed loyalists were singled out by Volunteers and their cars and arms seized and, immediately after it was over, a Church of Ireland rector records that 'an exodus' of his congregation began. They were 'frightened by what had taken place'; one of them said that they 'would not stay another winter amongst the Sinn Feiners.'[8]

But public attitudes were by no means uniformly hostile. At the South Dublin Union and Boland's Bakery the surrendering Volunteers were heartened by the friendly reception they received. In some areas civilians actively helped them, most notably the medical staff at Richmond Hospital and the Capuchin Fathers, Church Street. A number of the insurgents expressed the view that sympathy for their cause had grown as the week progressed, and there is evidence to support this. According to one diarist, by Thursday, the 'ancient hatred of England [had begun] ... to revive.' It was rekindled by the perceived arrogance of the English soldiers in Dublin, the devastation their artillery had caused to property in the city and, above all, by reports that unarmed civilians had suffered as a result of their ill-discipline. The shooting of Francis Sheehy Skeffington by military firing squad caused outrage, and it was widely believed that troops 'massacred' fifteen innocent and unarmed men in North King Street, near the Four Courts. There was a feeling too that the rebels had fought a disciplined and clean fight with courage and conviction and had shown genuine concern for the distress their actions had caused the city's citizens. There was admiration for the fact that with their motley collection of rifles and revolvers they had held out for a week against the resources of an empire. After the surrender, one Dublin diarist wrote: 'This ends the last attempt for poor old Ireland. What noble fellows! The cream of the land. None of your corner-boy class.'[9]

Major General Sir John Maxwell was appointed GOC, British troops in Ireland on 27 April, and it was he who was the main architect of the government's response to the Rising. He was appalled by the death and destruction it had caused and by evidence of the rebels' treasonable collaboration with Germany, and he was also convinced by police reports that Ireland had 'narrowly missed the most serious rebellion.'[10] He believed that it had its roots in the government's weakness and prevarication during the Home Rule crisis before the war, and that revolutionary nationalism must now be crushed, not least because this would help deter further acts of violence by extremists. Those rebels thought to have played the most prominent role in the insurrection were therefore court-martialed (187 in total). Each faced the same central charge: that they 'did take part in armed rebellion ... with the intention ... of assisting the enemy.' The trials of the fifteen men who were executed took place between 2 and 9 May and, in all but one case, their bodies were taken to Arbour Hill Detention Barracks, Dublin, for burial. All of them faced death with fortitude and courage, proud of their achievements, convinced of the rightness of their cause and legitimacy of their actions, believing that these would stimulate further bids for Irish freedom which would ultimately prove successful. MacDermott confidently predicted that: 'our blood will re-baptize and reinvigorate the old land.'[11]

At the time some thought that the executions were fully justified. The Dublin press depicted the rebels as criminals, fanatics, traitors, fools. After twelve had faced the firing squad, on 10 May, the *Irish Independent* declared: 'let the worst of the ringleaders be singled out and dealt with as they deserve.' Britain's military leaders considered that they themselves were 'exceptionally restrained' in their response to the Rising. Herbert Asquith, the Prime Minister, declared that he was 'perfectly satisfied with the manner in which he [Maxwell] has discharged' his duties, adding that he had 'shown ... discretion ... humanity.' Eighty-eight rebels were sentenced to 'death by being shot', and he had commuted this verdict in 73 cases. Amongst those he had reprieved was Countess Markievicz, 'solely and only on account of her sex.'[12] This contrasts with the treatment of nurse Edith Cavell; she was executed by German troops in October 1915 for helping allied prisoners escape from occupied Belgium. In her case the German Under-Secretary for Foreign Affairs asserted that she had been 'judged justly', and he asked: 'What would happen to a state, particularly in war, if it left crimes aimed at the safety of its armies go unpunished because committed by women?'[13]

Within nationalist Ireland, however, there was no perception that the military authorities had exercised restraint. The secret nature of the trials made a deep impression on Irish popular opinion. They were held 'in camera'; Maxwell had been advised by legal opinion that 'in certain cases the evidence is not too strong ... far from conclusive.'[14] That it was often circumstantial, misleading and inaccurate was inevitable given the haste with which the cases were heard, the deficiencies in Dublin Castle's intelligence and the numbers accused. In some instances the proceedings lasted no more than ten minutes and defendants were tried in batches of three. There was frequently a heavy reliance on one prosecution witness who knew little or nothing about the prisoner being charged. The seven signatories of the Proclamation and three of the four Volunteer Officers Commanding in Dublin were amongst those executed but, apart from these, the pattern is haphazard. De Valera, commandant at Boland's Bakery, escaped the death sentence as did all his garrison, even though British forces sustained their heaviest losses in this command area. Three of those shot had served in Jacob's Factory which had seen very little fighting during Easter week. Willie Pearse, Michael O'Hanrahan and John MacBride faced the firing squad even though they had taken a much less active part than many others who had done so. The physical condition of several of those who were shot evoked much sympathy, in particular, Connolly, Plunkett and McDermott. Warren B Wells, a journalist, attempted to explain to his English readership the impact of the executions on the Irish public. He stated that they read of them 'with something of the feeling of helpless rage with which one would watch a stream of blood dripping from under a closed door.'[15] Arthur Griffith graphically described his response, writing: 'Something of the primitive man awoke in me. I clenched my fists with rage, and I longed for vengeance.'[16]

As the trials and executions dragged on they quickly generated a culture of rebel martyrdom and national victimhood. In early May John Dillon, the nationalist MP, stated in the Commons that the government's actions were 'washing out our whole life work in a sea of blood.'[17] Soon ballads and poems celebrated the rebels' actions, and crowds flocked to requiem masses where those executed were venerated like Catholic martyrs. In consequence, physical force republicanism fused with populist faith, and the Rising was made to appear more Catholic than it had been; Clarke had refused the sacraments and 'died unreconciled to the Catholic Church.'[18] Prisoner welfare organizations also provided an outlet for public expressions of support, there being as yet no political party through which this commitment could be channelled. Prior to Easter week, many nationalists had opposed violence for purely pragmatic reasons rather than on grounds of principle, and this helps account for the speed with which the popular mood changed. They had regarded violence as futile and counter-productive, and home rule as all that could realistically be achieved, not as the fulfillment of their aspirations. The Rising shattered these assumptions because within weeks Asquith's government had hastily initiated negotiations and offered Home Rule as soon as terms could be agreed. It appeared that, as Maxwell phrased it, 'out of rebellion more had been got than by constitutional methods.'[19] This humiliated the Irish Party, and it was damaged further by its willingness during these talks to accept partition, albeit temporarily. A cause is hallowed by those who die for it, but other issues apart from the Rising and executions helped shape the popular mood, and convert public sympathy for the rebels into something more tangible. In particular, the mass deportations and internments initiated by the British government after Easter week fuelled and spread Irish disaffection, and increased popular sympathy for the use of force to achieve independence and for an Irish republic. Between 1916 and 1918, British government policy, driven as it was by its own domestic necessities, veered unhappily between coercion and conciliation.

Pearse stated in February 1914 that he did 'not know how nationhood is achieved except by armed men.'[20] The most significant legacy of the Rising was, as its leaders had intended, that it reaffirmed and rejuvenated the physical force tradition in Irish nationalism. Before his execution Clarke asked his wife, Kathleen, to memorize his final message to the Irish people. It was a 'clarion call to resume' the armed struggle and win through to final victory. It read: 'I believe we have struck the first successful blow for freedom ... Between this and freedom Ireland will go through Hell, but she will never lie down again until she has attained full freedom.'[21] The rebels of Easter week became the role models for future generations of Irish youth. What they used as justification for their actions were those of the Military Council whose 'sanctified' members were 'retrospectively legitimized and elevated to the status of founding fathers of the new state.'[22] In this process the struggles, achievements and sacrifices of constitutional nationalists were traduced and denigrated. In 1966 Father Francis Shaw wrote in *Studies*: 'The Irishman of today is asked to disown his own past. He is expected to censure as unpatriotic the common Irishmen who were not attracted by the new revolutionary ideas. [They] ... are invited at least implicitly to apologize for their fellow-countrymen who accepted loyally the serious guidance of the Church. [They]... must despise as unmanly those of their own county who preferred to solve problems, if possible, by peaceful rather than by violent means.'[23]

The leaders of the Rising were uncompromising in advocating and pursuing their objective, a thirty-two county sovereign Irish republic.

They did so in a spirit of self-sacrifice, valuing this cause more than life itself, and this too was an important part of their legacy. When leaving the GPO Connolly had commented: 'We're going out to be slaughtered'[24] and, during Easter week Clarke readily accepted that 'of course, we shall all be wiped out.'[25] They and the others were driven by, and consumed with, a belief in their own rightness, a hallmark of physical force nationalism that had been lauded throughout the decades of the IRB's existence. Nicholas Mansergh wrote of Easter week that it was 'above all a challenge to those Irishmen who believed in compromise.'[26] Pearse said 'the national demand of Ireland is fixed and determined ... we have not the right to alter it.'[27] In his view, anyone who settled for anything less than complete separation from England was 'guilty of so immense a crime against the Irish nation ... that it were better for that man ... that he had not been born.'[28] Connolly stated emphatically that 'the British government has no right in Ireland ... Never can have any right in Ireland.'[29] As Ruth Dudley Edwards stated: 'it was such thinking that would ... keep violence going for another century.'[30]

That the Rising was also elitist added to the potency of its legacy. It was brought about by the seven members of the Military Council, which operated as a clique within the IRB, which was itself a clique within the Irish Volunteers. At most 1,800 men and women participated in the events of Easter week, whilst some 200,000 Irishmen fought in the First World War and, of these, 35,000 made the supreme sacrifice. The 16th (Irish) Division lost 570 men at the battle of Loos during the same week as the insurrection. Its leaders recognized that it lacked popular support, and anticipated that many would condemn it. They were fully aware that it did not meet the church's criteria for a just war. They had no electoral mandate, and a democratic path to independence was available; a home rule measure had been enacted. Nonetheless they were determined to ignore the electorate's repeated endorsement of the Irish Parliamentary Party, and instead fight a war for their conception of Irish freedom and ally themselves with Germany. The Military Council made the elitist claim in the Proclamation that through themselves, a small, self-appointed group of revolutionaries, the people of Ireland were being summoned into violent action. This sprang from its authors' overpowering conviction that they spoke for the country's deepest self, that complete freedom was essential for Ireland's wellbeing as a nation, and that it was only through their actions that the national spirit could be rekindled. Pearse stated: 'we have done right', though conceding that 'people will say hard things of us now.'[31] Clarke found solace in the belief that: 'shedding blood had always raised the Irish people's spirit.'[32] In hindsight it was to become evident that the Great War was not the final opportunity to resurrect the Irish nation, and that national identity was not then facing extinction by the forces of imperialism either in Ireland or in Europe.

In mid June Maxwell commented that 'there is a danger'[33] the Parliamentary Party will lose the next election. But there was a widespread sense of disillusionment with constitutional nationalism long before an alternative arose to replace it, and the shift occurring in public opinion could find political expression. Its opponents were fragmented, whilst the widespread arrests after Easter week left them leaderless and directionless. Sinn Fein benefited from its association with the insurrection, from Westminster's repressive response to the growing support for republicanism, as well as the failure of more moderate politicians to deliver tangible results during the negotiations held between 1916 and 1918. It attracted an amalgam of physical force nationalists and republicans, disillusioned members of the IPP, Volunteers, Gaelic enthusiasts, socialists and opportunists. At its *Ard Fheis* in October 1917 these disparate elements coalesced into a fragile coalition. The party that was then emerging was not a reinvigorated version of its pre war incarnation but a new revolutionary movement. It was now formally committed in its constitution to using 'every means available' to achieve an 'independent Irish republic.'[34] De Valera, its newly elected president, described this objective as 'a monument to the brave men [of 1916]'[35] and it was the Rising that had brought it from the margins of national politics into the mainstream. Easter week had also revived the physical force tradition, but an open, and potentially divisive, commitment to the use of violence was avoided at this convention. Four months later, in early 1918, it was the prospect that Britain might impose conscription on Ireland that sealed Sinn Fein's popularity. The party's close collaboration with the Catholic Church when organizing resistance to this measure imbued it with a new respectability. Its membership soared, as did enlistment to the Volunteers.

At the general election (14 December 1918), Sinn Fein benefited from the recent reform of the franchise which had trebled the Irish electorate to two million, (extending the vote to the working class, agricultural workers, and women over thirty), and from new constituency boundaries which boosted urban representation. Whilst the Home Rule Party stood primarily on its past achievements, Sinn Fein offered voters the 'path to national salvation', a thirty-two county republic. De Valera asserted that it would complete this 'holy task', so that the 'Irish race' would be 'permitted to build up the great nation which God intended it to be.'[36] Its heavily censored manifesto stated that its successful candidates would abstain from Westminster, establish a national government in Dublin and appeal to the post war peace conference that it recognize Irish independence. Though its leaders condemned Redmond for having accepted partition during the wartime negotiations, they offered no coherent alternative policy. They projected the Ulster question as being due to the British presence in Ireland and unionists as having been duped, and blandly asserted that once independence was achieved the problem would resolve itself. They would effect a reconciliation. There was no suggestion that they had accepted the principle of unionist consent. De Valera described the Protestants in the northeast as 'planters,' 'an alien garrison' and threatened that if they were obstructive 'we will have to kick them out ... Ulster must be coerced if she stood in the way.' Likewise Arthur Griffiths said that Ulster unionists 'must make up their minds to throw in their lot with the Irish nation [and, if not] ... the Irish nation must deal with them.'[37]

The results were declared on 28 December. They revealed that Sinn Fein had triumphed with 485,000 votes (47 per cent) and 73 successful candidates out of the 105 Ireland returned to Westminster, compared with the Irish Parliamentary Party's 237,400 votes (22 per cent), and six seats. It had won all but three of the constituencies in Leinster, Munster and Connacht. Its success represented a mandate for an Irish republic, for a separatist rather than devolutionist version of Ireland's future. Discounting the outcome in Ulster, de Valera declared: 'no people on earth ever agreed so overwhelmingly on a great issue.'[38] They had not, however, endorsed a renewal of the armed struggle. This had not appeared in the party's election literature. It was the 'latent threat of force, but not its actual application'[39], which it had offered the electorate.

On 21 January 1919 the victorious Sinn Fein candidates still at liberty assembled in Dublin as the first Dail and, regarding themselves as being the sovereign national authority, proceeded to endow Ireland with the trappings of an independent state. They declared the establishment of an Irish republic, claiming authority over the whole island, so essentially ratifying the Republic proclaimed by Pearse in 1916. They also elected a cabinet, adopted a provisional constitution, demanded Britain's evacuation from all thirty-two counties and selected delegates to attend the post war peace conference. The Westminster government was preoccupied with post war peacemaking and it initially marked time, but it could not have stood back indefinitely and watched its authority being eradicated and displaced. The resumption of fighting in Ireland was – as with the Rising – due to the 'action of a small and unrepresentative minority'[40] who 'took the instructions of the dead generations seriously'[41], most recently those of 1916, and had a 'militaristic contempt for Sinn Fein's timidity.'[42] Cathal Brugha (Vice Commandant at the South Dublin Union during Easter week) was confident that, if given a strong lead, the people would follow. It was Michael Collins who provided that leading role.

After serving at the GPO in Easter week Collins had rapidly emerged as a major republican figure: he was a member of the Sinn Fein executive, and of the IRB Supreme Council and, by 1919, *de facto* leader of the Irish Volunteers and Dail Minister of Finance. He had no doubt that 'the fight for freedom must be continued, the Rising to count as the first blow', and that the 'armed truce' after the December election was 'doomed to collapse when the British were ready to crush the republican movement.' He believed that the nation therefore faced a 'stark choice' between the total 'obliteration of its legitimately formed government and an Anglo-Irish war.'[43] At first most republicans neither desired nor expected a renewal of the armed struggle. But after the peacemakers at Versailles had refused to acknowledge Ireland's right to self-determination, and British ministers had taken the decision to suppress the Dail, their attitudes changed and hardened. Collins regarded the latter as a declaration of war and responded accordingly. Over the next two years the initially sporadic acts of violence escalated into a brutal pattern of terror, counter-terror and reprisal. In these unpromising circumstances Britain's attempted solution to the Irish question, the Government of Ireland Act (December 1920), was a dead letter outside the northeast. Under its terms Ireland was to be partitioned and provision was made for the establishment of two states (six-county 'Northern Ireland' and twenty-six county 'Southern Ireland'), each with home rule powers. It was too little and too late for Irish nationalists and brought no abatement in the conflict. In contrast, Ulster unionists proceeded to amend and implement the measure, and set up the state of Northern Ireland.

By the time the terms of the truce had been agreed (11 July 1921) the Anglo-Irish war had resulted in 1,400 deaths, including 550 members of the IRA. After protracted negotiations Sinn Fein and the British government signed the Anglo-Irish Treaty (6 December 1921) which granted the twenty-six counties dominion status. Though this fell short of the republic proclaimed in 1916, and reaffirmed by the Dail in 1919, it did provide for a substantially greater level of self-government than the three previous home rule measures had done. Partition remained but the Irish delegates were convinced that in its Article 12 they had won 'essential unity.' It had been included because Lloyd George, the prime minister, had been concerned that the issue of Northern Ireland was going to wreck any prospect of a settlement; it was his means of circumventing this prospect. It stated that, if the Belfast parliament refused to accept assimilation into the 'Irish Free State', the boundary of the six counties would be revised by a Boundary Commission. Though the criteria the commissioners were to apply were ambiguous, the Sinn Fein negotiators anticipated that the outcome would be to reduce the partitioned area to so small a residual rump that it would no longer be politically viable; Michael Collins asserted that: 'majorities must rule.'[44] In any case their priority throughout the negotiations was to maximize the extent of Ireland's independence rather than achieve unity. Sinn Fein continued to regard partition as being due to Britain's duplicity and inherent colonialism. Their belief was that 'if England would stand aside, there would be no difficulty.' Lloyd George summarized Griffith's view as 'Ulster would come in if we let her alone', whilst de Valera asserted that 'the difficulty is not the Ulster question. As far as we are concerned this is a fight between Ireland and England.'[45]

The Treaty's most contentious clauses were those that preserved southern Ireland's link with the Crown through an oath of allegiance and, to a lesser extent, the fact that under its terms Britain would have continued use of the 'treaty ports' and Ireland would be obligated to contribute to its war debt. The agreement was ratified by the Dail cabinet and the Dail, and supported by a majority of the electorate (by a ratio of 4:1 in the 'Treaty election', 20 May 1922). The Catholic church also approved it, as did the press, farmers and business interests, the Supreme Council and higher ranks of the IRB and the Irish Volunteers' HQ staff and its Dublin Brigade. Those favouring its acceptance, advanced arguments based on pragmatism, stating that it was the best that could be obtained, that it would ultimately lead to full independence, and that to reject it would result in further bloodshed. Some leading republican figures bitterly opposed it, however, including de Valera, and also a 2:1 majority of IRA members. They had sworn an oath not to achieve an Irish republic but to defend the living one proclaimed during the Rising. At a convention (March 1922) they reaffirmed their allegiance to the republic as established in 1916. Whether or not they should proceed to establish a military dictatorship was referred to their executive. Opponents of the Treaty challenged its moral and spiritual legitimacy. They claimed that it was a 'betrayal of the dead martyrs of 1916'[46], and appealed to the sanctity of the republic for which a minority had sacrificed and inflicted so much, and on which there could be no possibility of compromise. They did so despite their failure to achieve victory in the Anglo-Irish war which was the only way this goal could have been attained. Though in a minority, those who shared this perspective regarded themselves as being the 'guardian of the morals of … the authentic Irish nation.'[47] De Valera said that they stood for the 'unbought, indomitable soul of Ireland.'[48] He succinctly expressed their elitist approach when frequently declaring: 'the majority have no right to do wrong.' He warned that the IRA 'would have to wade through Irish blood … and through perhaps the blood of some of the members of the government to get Irish freedom.' In his view the 'principles which republicans are defending are by their nature irreducible and not open to compromise.'[49]

That the Treaty proved to be so divisive was not due to Partition. Both sides believed that Article 12 would deliver unity; thus the north was virtually ignored in the course of the Dail debates. WT Cosgrave could justifiably claim that 'no one here [in the Dail] has suggested any better way of dealing with them [Ulster Unionists] than that laid down.'[50]

When de Valera initially put forward his alternative to the document the Irish delegates had signed (his Document No 2), it retained the Boundary Commission clauses *verbatim*. Though in his second draft he asserted that no part of Ireland could be excluded from Dail authority, Partition was not the cause of his opposition to the Treaty. The split had its roots in the Rising; amongst the most vehement opponents of the terms were the relatives of those who had fought during Easter week. It was caused primarily by the oath of loyalty, and the sanctity of constitutional symbols. As a result of the insurrection and its aftermath the goal of a sovereign Irish republic had been elevated to more than a mere political objective. The civil war which followed (June 1922-June 1923) has been depicted as having been a conflict between: idealists and pragmatists, majority right and divine right, the will of the people and dictatorship. The eventual triumph of pro-Treaty forces might be regarded as a victory for the democratic Irish tradition of the Parliamentary Party over that of IRA militarism and the IRB. It came at considerable cost: between 1,500 and 2,000 Irishmen died, a generation of Ireland's most talented leaders was lost, including Collins and Griffith, whilst it imposed a heavy financial burden on the new state.

Overall, the Rising influenced profoundly the flow of events in southern Ireland from 1916 to 1923. It ensured that the process of transition during these years was both bloody and divisive. It helped to define and sanctify the primary goal of Irish nationalism as a thirty-two county, independent republic and, more than that, one that was Gaelic in culture and Catholic in ethos. It regenerated and legitimized the physical force tradition in Irish political culture. It also provided both the precedent and inspiration for a violent, uncompromising elitist minority to strike to achieve its vision of Ireland's future and ignore the wishes of the majority. It had a formative and enduring impact on the north of Ireland as well, as it was in the context of this revolutionary period that Ulster unionists attempted to establish a functioning government in the six counties.

Ulster unionism had emerged in the 1880s in opposition to the first home rule bill which would have established an all-Ireland parliament in Dublin. By 1900 it had become a strong, united, mass movement, with a broad social base. Its members supported the Union for a variety of reasons. They shared an acute sense of being different from Ireland's nationalist population in religion, ethnic origins and culture, as well as political aspirations. They felt an instinctive loyalty towards Britain which, in their view, embodied civil and political liberty and valued the security of belonging to its Protestant majority. They feared that home rule would result in 'Rome rule', a state in which the Catholic Church would exercise pervasive political and social influence, and they would experience religious discrimination and exclusion from public life. They were convinced that the region's rapid economic growth was dependent on having continued access to Britain's markets, raw materials, capital, skilled labour, and entrepreneurs. Moreover they considered that Irish nationalism lacked genuine popular support, and that it had been manufactured by manipulative political leaders and priests who had exploited the ignorance and greed of the peasantry and labouring classes.

Unionists faced their gravest challenge in 1912 when the Liberal administration introduced the third home rule bill, legislation which seemed certain to pass through parliament. Initially they organized protest rallies and demonstrations, including, on 28 September 1912, 'Covenant Day', when the 450,000 signatories of the 'Covenant' swore that they were willing to use 'all means ... to defeat the present conspiracy to set up a Home Rule parliament in Ireland.'[51] But Herbert Asquith, the prime minister, ignored their opposition and, meanwhile, his measure continued to make steady un-amended progress through Westminster. In December 1912, therefore, the unionist leadership began to recruit a paramilitary force, the Ulster Volunteer Force (UVF) and, on 24-5 March 1914, imported 140 tons of rifles from Germany to arm them; by the summer of that year 90,000 men had enlisted. These provocative initiatives boosted their morale and confidence, while narrowing the policy options open to the prevaricating and inert British government. Irish nationalists responded by forming and arming the Irish Volunteer Force. Meanwhile, the plausibility of the Parliamentary Party's strategy of abject reliance on the Liberals to deliver all-Ireland self-government was being undermined.

The impact of the unionists' campaign was enhanced by having the sympathy and backing of the Conservative Party. Its leaders thought it unjust to expel one million loyal citizens from the Union, and were concerned that home rule would lead to complete Irish separation and possibly the dismemberment of the Empire as well as compromising Britain's strategic position. They also believed that the issue would have electoral appeal nationally, and could be exploited to drive the Liberals from office. The unionists attracted support from other elevated elements in British public life. King George V threatened not to sign the home rule bill and urged Asquith to compromise. The army's attitude to the Irish question was clarified by the 'Curragh Mutiny' (20 March 1914) when fifty-seven out of seventy cavalry officers indicated that they would resign their commissions rather than obey orders to impose all-Ireland institutions on Ulster. As a consequence the prime minister could no longer extract concessions from opponents of Irish self-government by credibly threatening military intervention to suppress them.

Gradually the principle that special provision should be made for Ulster became firmly established at Westminster. By mid-1913 both Ulster unionists and Conservatives were reconciled to the inevitability of home rule, and were arguing for a solution based on partition. However, after an all-party conference at Buckingham Palace (21-24 July 1914) failed to reach agreement on the area to be excluded, civil war seemed inevitable. That this outcome was avoided was due to the outbreak of the First World War, after which Sir Edward Carson and John Redmond agreed to support Britain's war effort, and to postpone the resolution of the Irish question until after hostilities had ceased. On 18 September 1914 the home rule bill was placed on the statute book, but its operation was suspended until the end of the conflict. At the time, Asquith stated unequivocally that the coercion of Ulster was 'absolutely unthinkable'[52], and that he would introduce an amending bill before the act was put into effect.

During the First World War the political position of the Ulster unionists became stronger. At Westminster, Asquith provided ineffective leadership – his was the last Liberal administration in British history – and, in December 1916, a coalition government was formed under Lloyd George. The new prime minister was dependent on Conservative Party support and its capacity to help its unionist allies increased with its powers (Sir Edward Carson became First Lord of the Admiralty, and later Minister without Portfolio). By then, however, its members were doing so out of a sense of obligation to honour past pledges, rather than current conviction.

Moreover, they no longed needed Ulster as a 'patriotic issue which might help them back into office.'[53] Earlier that year, unionists had viewed the Easter Rising 'quite complacently, even gleefully.'[54] They had applauded the imposition of martial law. In common with influential opinion in Britain they regarded the insurrection as an act of treachery and treason, as a 'stab in the back' struck when the nation was in grave peril. They could cite it as an illustration of the untrustworthiness of Irish nationalists, and contrast it with their own loyalty and fidelity. Subsequently, in June 1916, when Lloyd George hastily initiated negotiations in a despairing bid to resolve the Irish question, their 'solidarity and sense of righteousness … enabled them to resist'[55] powerful pressures to compromise and demand exclusion. The terms Britain eventually offered Carson were that Ireland would be granted home rule, but that the six north eastern counties would be excluded and would continue to be governed from Westminster. The talks collapsed because the Irish Parliamentary Party demanded that this arrangement should last for no more than three to six years. Nonetheless, it was a significant milestone as both sides had for the first time reached agreement on the area to be partitioned, and on terms which foreshadowed those of the Government of Ireland Act.

The Irish republican tradition had been re-ignited and rejuvenated by the Rising and, less than three months later, the pride and conviction of northern unionists was reaffirmed by a defining episode amid the slaughter of the Western Front; it was to become deeply etched into their shared communal memory. In 1914 the War Office had formed the 36th (Ulster) Division specifically to encourage UVF members to enlist in the armed forces. On 1-2 July, the first two days of the Battle of the Somme, it sustained 5,500 casualties. Afterwards WJ Lynas, a 27-year-old soldier from Belfast's dockland, wrote home to his wife with a pride and passion comparable to that of Pearse's effusive correspondence after Easter week. He extolled the 'gallantry of our boys' who, he said, had 'made a name for Ulster that will never die in the annals of history … doing their duty for King and Country.'[56] Historians agree that as a consequence of their collective sacrifice unionists attained a 'new credibility within British political life'[57], and that subsequently 'no British government would ever force [them] … to accept Dublin rule.'[58] In effect, the Union had been sealed in blood.

The Government of Ireland Act (December 1920) reflected the broad consensus on the Irish question that had emerged amongst British politicians in wartime. Lloyd George considered that in its partitioning of Ireland and making provision for the establishment of parliaments in Belfast as well as Dublin, the legislation was honouring past imperial commitments to Ulster unionists. He also believed that these arrangements would assuage northern nationalists who, he assumed, would resent direct rule from London more than being governed by their fellow-countrymen. At the same time they would enable Westminster to disengage from Irish affairs, while still protecting its vital interests; it retained its sovereign authority. The prime minister hoped that the two states would remain closely bound to Britain and would eventually unite. Under the terms of the legislation additional 'reserved' powers would be transferred to them if their institutions merged. A Council of Ireland was to be formed to discuss matters of common concern 'with a view to the eventual establishment of a parliament for the whole of Ireland'[59], and it was envisaged that a Lord Lieutenant would be appointed to represent the crown throughout all thirty-two counties. Thus the measure was 'slanted towards Irish unity.'[60] At the same time future decisions on this issue were 'thrown wholly onto Irish shoulders.'[61] Though unionist MPs abstained from voting on the bill as it passed through the commons, they recognized that it was the most favourable they were likely to be offered. Its provisions recognized the reality of the bitter divisions in Ireland, it was based on the principle of unionist consent to unity and it would provide them with greater security than direct rule from Westminster. They distrusted the Labour Party, which had demanded self-determination for 'all subject peoples within the British Commonwealth'[62] in the 1918 election, and were cognizant of the fact that the Conservatives had lost much of their earlier enthusiasm for their cause. To enhance their domination of 'Northern Ireland' they amended the measure in parliament, thereby reducing the partitioned area from the nine counties it proposed to six.

The Act came into operation on 3 May 1921, elections for the fifty-two seats in the new house of commons in Belfast were held on 24 May (under proportional representation). All forty unionist candidates were successful, winning a 67 per cent share of the poll. Sinn Fein and the nationalist party received one-third of the vote and won six seats each. Sir

James Craig, who had succeeded Sir Edward Carson as Unionist Party leader in January 1921, became the state's first premier. When King George V formally opened the Northern Ireland parliament on 22 June there seemed grounds for optimism. In his speech he implored Irishmen to 'stretch out the hand of forbearance and conciliation, to forgive and forget.'[63] Its content had been suggested by Jan Smuts, the South African premier, and approved by the British cabinet. The favourable response it elicited was followed by the truce less than three weeks later and the end of the Anglo-Irish war. Also, under the terms of the 1920 Act, the Belfast administration was to be responsible for 'peace, order and good government', and Craig's public statements suggested an awareness of the opportunity to break the mould of sectarian division and conflict in the north. He stated that he would 'look to the people as a whole' and be 'absolutely fair'[64], and appealed for cooperation and friendship with the South. Guided by Westminster it seemed possible that these intentions and aspirations would be realized.

But defects in the provisions of the 1920 Act itself made this task more difficult. The institutional structures it established replicated those at Westminster, and these were ill-suited to the political realities and needs of the region. Simple majority rule was to be the foundation of a fifty-year monopoly of power by the Unionist Party. The rights of the minority were inadequately protected. With insufficient tax-raising powers Craig and his colleagues were unable to implement a coherent legislative programme relevant to the context of social and economic deprivation (90 per cent of Northern Ireland's tax revenue was paid direct to the British exchequer). In addition, short of imposing direct rule, British ministers had no effective means of supervising how the regional government functioned. In any case, after the truce, they were distracted by, and prioritized, reaching an agreement with the Sinn Fein leadership. It soon became evident that in this pursuit they regarded Northern Ireland as being entirely dispensable. Craig had mistakenly assumed that its institutions were sacrosanct.

Northern Ireland's birth, at a time of cataclysmic change and prolonged turbulence in Ireland, did much to determine and permanently distort its political structures; its first two years were the most formative in its history. Craig's inexperienced cabinet faced problems which were grave, possibly insoluble, and these demanding circumstances reinforced the unionists' sense of paranoia, their siege mentality. They had found it difficult to reach an accommodation with John Redmond and his constitutionalist, gradualist Parliamentary Party, which valued the Empire, esteemed Westminster's parliamentary institutions, had supported Britain's war effort and had accepted temporary partition in return for limited self-government. They were now confronted by the Sinn Fein Party with its radical nationalist objectives, and extreme republican elements who were prepared to use force rather than compromise. As Mansergh states: Pearse's 'irreconcilable spirit still ... inspired the minds'[65] of its leaders. They had refused to engage with the Government of Ireland Act and, as a consequence, the Council of Ireland was stillborn; Bryan Follis suggests that it was this which 'achieved real partition.'[66] From their perspective the Ulster question was due to the British presence in Ireland. They did not accept the legitimacy of unionist opposition to unity, and regarded Partition as being unnatural and reversible. They refused to recognize the Belfast parliament, increasingly focused their energies on the north, deployed every means available to destabilize and overthrow it and attempted to use the issue to raise public sympathy in Britain and the United States.

To a large extent Sinn Fein's negative and belligerent attitude was to 'dictate the level of the Catholic minority's engagement'[67] with the Northern Ireland state. Compared with the rest of Ireland, the northeast had been relatively peaceful up until late 1919. Northern nationalists had taken little part in the Rising. From the outset the IRB Military Council made clear its intention that Ulster should play only a limited role. It was aware that any action taken there would likely ignite sectarian conflict, and that the Irish Volunteers were a negligible force in Belfast, and had little presence elsewhere in the province. Denis McCullough, the IRB President and IV leader in the city, met Connolly and Pearse in Dublin in early 1916 and was told of their plans. He was informed that: 'I was to mobilize my men ... convey them to Tyrone, joining the Tyrone men mobilized there and proceed with all possible haste to join [Liam] Mellows in Connacht'; once there they were to assist in holding the line of the River Shannon. He responded by 'pointing out the length of the journey ... the type of country and population we had to pass through, and how sparsely armed my men were.' He therefore suggested that while marching south they should attack RIC barracks to obtain arms on the way. At this point he records that Connolly 'got quite cross and almost shouted at me: 'you will fire no shot in Ulster. You will proceed with all possible speed to join Mellows ... If we win through we will then deal with Ulster ... You will observe that as an order and obey it strictly ... Pearse "nodded", and said: "yes, that's an order."'

McCullough dutifully assembled about one hundred Belfast Volunteers and, by Saturday 22 April, they had been transported to Coalisland. They were equipped with forty ancient rifles, and had two days rations. The local men from Tyrone refused pointblank to move outside their own district, and most of them ridiculed the idea of marching to Galway, both because of the distance and the fact that their journey would 'mostly [be] through hostile territory.' Several aired their suspicions that the insurrection had not been planned by the Volunteers at all, but was a 'socialist Rising ... inspired by Connolly.' With news filtering through that the arms dispatched from Germany had been captured and Casement had been arrested, McCullough took the decision that those under his command should simply demobilize and return home. So, next morning, they marched to Cookstown to board a train back to Belfast. While proceeding there they were attacked at Stewartstown, which McCullough described as being a 'hotbed of Orangeism.' He states that the incident could easily have developed into a full-scale 'sectarian riot to the disadvantage and disgrace of the whole movement.' He felt vindicated, observing that 'if we had marched to Connacht ... similar scenes would have developed at every Protestant village and townland we passed through in Fermanagh and Tyrone.'[68]

The northern Catholic population remained quiescent throughout the First World War, and conservative, even loyal, in its attitudes. Roughly 8,000 Belfast Catholics had joined the British army by the end of the conflict, a total which represented one-quarter of those who enlisted from the city. Moreover, their political affiliation underwent less change than elsewhere in Ireland. In contrast to other provinces, Sinn Fein failed to become the dominant nationalist party in Ulster in the 1918 election. This was because of the personal appeal of Joe Devlin in Belfast and northeastern counties, and the organizational strength of constitutional nationalism, reinforced by the pervasive influence of the Catholic

Church. Also in most districts the IRA remained numerically small and weak owing to the disinterested response from its own community, a dearth of competent leadership and the difficulties involved in operating amid a large, hostile unionist population.[69]

However, from late 1919 levels of tension in the North rose sharply and, in mid 1920, the region experienced its first explosion of mass violence. This was partly due to the heavily politicized atmosphere which emanated from the looming prospect of Partition. On 13 February 1920, Devlin warned Bishop Patrick O'Donnell that the area to be excluded would probably be the six northeastern counties. In his view this would be 'the worst form' it could take, as Catholics would become a 'permanent minority, with all the sufferings and tyranny of the present day continued only in worse form.'[70] The local government elections, conducted under proportional representation in January and June 1920, added further to the excitement. The nationalist and Labour parties both made substantial advances, the former gaining control of Tyrone and Fermanagh county councils, Omagh, Enniskillen, Strabane, Newry and Londonderry City. These results boosted the confidence of its supporters, especially those in the west of the province, that they would soon be living under Dublin rule. The likelihood of inter-communal conflict was also heightened by the context of deepening recession, the irresponsible interventions made by the local press and by political leaders and the region's long and unenviable record of sectarian confrontation.

During the period 1920 to 1922, the peak levels of disorder coincided with the major political milestones – the passing of the 1920 Act, the setting up of the regional parliament and the impact of significant events in southern Ireland. Michael Laffan states that: 'the Anglo-Irish war was fought in the twenty-six counties.'[71] Certainly the northern IRA was little involved until its final stages. Nonetheless the conflict spilt over into the north where a pattern of violence quickly emerged: IRA activity on the border or elsewhere would precipitate a loyalist response, reprisals and widespread sectarian clashes. The murder in Cork of an RIC officer from Banbridge, Colonel Gerald Smith, on 17 July, was followed by riots in a number of northern towns. It also led to the expulsion of 8,000 Catholics from Belfast shipyards and engineering works, though this was partly a retaliatory response to Protestant workers having recently been driven out of the dockyards in Londonderry. The Dail reacted by instigating a boycott of goods from the northeast which served to further embitter North/South relations and also to partition the Irish economy. A similar incident, on Sunday 22 August the murder of Oswald Swanzy, an RIC District Inspector, outside Lisburn cathedral by IRA members from Cork, resulted in Catholics being expelled from the city.

These incidents and the escalating conflict in the south increased concern over security provision in Ulster; from June 1920 the UVF began to revive. The initial radical impulse to form and arm the organization (1912-14) had come from rank and file unionists, and their leaders had felt obliged to act upon it. Now, this pattern was repeated as units of the force mushroomed up spontaneously and independently throughout much of the northeast. Their function remained to protect property, to defend the Union and to preserve unionist discipline. They were symptomatic of the unease felt at the growth in local support for Sinn Fein and at the 'general spread of lawlessness'[72], and fears that the IRA campaign would spread to the province. It was doubted that Dublin Castle had the capacity or will to preserve order, there were widespread suspicions regarding the reliability of the RIC and it was thought likely that British troops based in the north would be transferred elsewhere as the Anglo-Irish war intensified. In response to unionist pressure and to release military personnel for service in other parts of Ireland, on 8 September 1920, the British government agreed to recruit an official police force, the Special Constabulary, from the ranks of the reinvigorated UVF. Its members were universally detested by northern Catholics. The *Fermanagh Herald* described them as being the 'dregs of the Orange Lodges'[73], and Joseph Devlin claimed that Westminster was 'arming pogromists ... to murder the Catholics.'[74] However, as Robert Lynch states: '[it was] in this force more than any other, that the Northern IRA would find its most severe opposition.'[75]

The IRA in Ulster was also transformed as a consequence of the Anglo-Irish war. In February 1921 its northern units were reorganized and formed into divisions; this restructuring has been described as the 'birth of the Northern IRA.'[76] It was initiated by IRA headquarters in Dublin which had begun to prioritize the province more. Its intention was to spread destruction and instability to the northeast as a means of easing the pressure being applied by Crown forces in Leinster, Munster and Connacht. It also regarded the region as being an important bridge-head and conduit for British troops and supplies entering Ireland, and was seeking to counteract and disrupt this flow. As a consequence of this change, the IRA units based in the north became more professional and aggressive, and more closely linked to their southern leadership. They were to play an integral role in the political and military strategy developed by Sinn Fein during the following months.

The high level of excitement in Northern Ireland is evidenced by the 90 per cent turnout in the parliamentary elections in May 1921. The results were not only a triumph for the Unionist Party, but also revealed how much political loyalties had changed within the northern minority since 1918. Sinn Fein won a 20 per cent share of the vote (Arthur Griffith topping the poll in Fermanagh and Tyrone) compared with 12 per cent for the nationalist party. Outside Devlin's west Belfast Sinn Fein had become the dominant force in the northeast. Its virulent opposition to Partition contributed to its electoral appeal, as well as the hope that its leaders in the Dail would eventually deliver a united self-governing Ireland. The truce in July reinforced this shift towards support for greater militancy. Its terms were applied to the six counties without Craig being consulted despite the fact as a result the Special Constabulary was stood down, the activities of the RIC curtailed and army units virtually confined to barracks. Furthermore, they conferred full official recognition and legal status on the IRA; it appointed liaison officers to implement them, and was free to organize openly, set up training camps and recruit. This brought it increased prestige, respect and unprecedented popularity. Its membership in Northern Ireland rose from less than 2,200 in July 1921 to 4,000 by October. Seamus Woods, Officer Commanding Northern Division, estimated that before the truce just 25 per cent of the Catholic population supported them but that, after it, 'believing for the moment that we had been victorious and that the Specials and UVF were beaten, practically all flocked to our standard.'[77] In Craig's view, these developments 'gravely imperiled the position of Ulster.'[78]

Northern nationalists also expressed their bitter hostility towards the new state by constitutional means. They supported a strategy of passive resistance and civil disobedience, and of abstentionism by their elected representatives. In late 1921 public bodies on which they held majorities, including Fermanagh and Tyrone county councils, pledged allegiance to Dail Eireann as their *de facto* government. Michael Collins acted and was acknowledged as their spokesperson, assisted by an advisory council drawn from their number. He encouraged, organized and financed their negative and obstructionist responses. For example, assured of his support, 270 (roughly one-third) elementary schools and also twenty-three secondary schools under Catholic management refused to recognize the Northern Ireland education department. For the Church's hierarchy this was a 'political rather than a religious issue.'[79] From February to October 1922, the Dublin government paid the salaries of staff in the institutions affected at an estimated cost of £18,000 per month.

Meanwhile, progressively, the feelings of optimism and expectation shared by unionists in June 1921 had been replaced by a deepening sense of betrayal and disillusionment, isolation and vulnerability. They feared that the rejuvenated IRA might launch a full-scale campaign in Northern Ireland, and distrusted the Westminster government which, after the truce, was entering into discussions with the Sinn Fein leadership. Leading Conservative politicians were members of Lloyd George's negotiating team and, though against Ulster's coercion, they argued that unionists should make concessions to secure the settlement, and also for the sake of the Empire. From late July Craig came under intense pressure to accept the sovereignty of an all-Ireland Dublin parliament. British ministers made it clear that they would welcome unity. So as not to prejudice the outcome of the talks, they refused to transfer any of the powers provided for in the 1920 Act to the Belfast parliament until 22 November 1921. Prior to this, the Northern premier and his colleagues were impotent, 'a glorified pressure group'[80], their popularity plummeted, and tensions rose. Rioting in Belfast on 14 July caused twenty-one deaths and in further civil disorder in the city, between 19-25 November, twenty-seven people lost their lives. Over the course of these months Protestant paramilitary organizations proliferated reaching an estimated membership of 21,000. In discussions with the British government Craig 'stressed the danger of the loyalist element getting out of hand' and he 'pressed for firm security measures.'[81]

The Anglo-Irish Treaty (December 1921) did nothing to assuage unionist anxieties, especially Article 12 which made provision for a

Boundary Commission. It had strong cross-party support amongst Westminster politicians, and they urged Craig to accept it, emphasizing that Sinn Fein had compromised on its goal of a thirty-two county republic. He protested that unionists had already made concessions both by accepting a regional parliament and by abandoning three of Ulster's nine counties. He also argued that he was under no obligation to cooperate with the Commission because his government had not been engaged in the negotiations which had agreed to it. Whilst the prospect of border revision terrified unionists, conversely, it boosted northern nationalist expectations. They had hopes that the process would result in Northern Ireland no longer being viable, and it encouraged them in their strategy of non-recognition of the Belfast parliament, and in their efforts to destabilize the putative state.

During early 1922, the level of violence in Northern Ireland reached unprecedented levels. Political uncertainty as well as deepening recession fomented traditional sectarian tensions (68 per cent of IRA members in Belfast were unemployed in July 1921[82]). The decisive factor, however, was the deterioration in North/South relations. Three meetings took place between Craig and Collins (25 January, 2 February and 22 March), at which shipyard expulsions, the Belfast boycott, the IRA campaign and boundary revision were discussed. But they ended in total breakdown. Collins' involvement in six county affairs reflected his genuine sympathy for the position of northern nationalists. However, an increasingly important motivation was his determination to arrest the deepening split in southern Ireland over the treaty by diverting attention to the perceived iniquity of Partition. He hoped to exploit the issue as a means of uniting moderate and hard-line elements within Sinn Fein.

Collins adopted various strategies which were aimed at undermining the northern state. To disrupt its administration he impeded the transfer of civil servants and government records from Dublin to Belfast. He launched a propaganda campaign alleging that Craig's government was brutally suppressing the Catholic minority, and he encouraged its members not to cooperate with the Belfast parliament. Above all he covertly sponsored and orchestrated an IRA campaign aimed at causing such mayhem and instability in Northern Ireland as to make it ungovernable. In January 1922 he set up the 'Ulster Council.' It was comprised of the

IRA's northern divisional commanders and its purpose was to enable them to coordinate their activities in the province more effectively; covertly they each received salaries from the southern state. Two months later he established the 'Belfast City Guard.' It was composed of sixty members from each of the city's four IRA battalions, and its function was to supervise and integrate their operations. The northern IRA had been revitalized during the truce, and been strengthened further by the Treaty as a result of which Britain released all republican internees. With the backing of the Dublin administration, it was now able to establish its headquarters and organize training camps across the border, and it was given active support by units drawn from the pro and anti Treaty IRA.[83]

The northern IRA's campaign in early 1922 was a 'largely Belfast and border affair'[84]; its 'intention' was to 'demonstrate the inability of the unionists to control'[85] the city. Its members were under orders to be ruthless, were to carry out reprisals and shoot informers, and some of their targets were 'blatantly sectarian.'[86] Two major incidents occurred. On 14 January, the 'Monaghan footballers' – an IRA squad from Monaghan disguised as footballers – were arrested in Dromore. They were *en route* to release three republican prisoners awaiting execution in Londonderry gaol (they were reprieved by the British government on 7 February). Collins' response was to order southern IRA units to kidnap over forty unionist notables in Fermanagh and Tyrone who were to be held in exchange. Craig's reaction was fully to mobilize the Special Constabulary for the first time since they had been stood down after the truce, the terms of which he simply ignored. The 'Clones Incident' (11 February) was a more ominous and violent occurrence. Nineteen Special Constables, most of them unarmed, were being transferred by rail from Newtownards, their training depot, to Enniskillen where they were to reinforce the security forces. Their train journey entailed crossing the border at Clones and, whilst they were waiting at the station there, they were attacked by a local unit of the IRA. Four of them were killed in the ensuing gun battle, as well as one of their assailants. To unionists it was a 'massacre', to nationalists an 'invasion.' During this period the IRA also carried out attacks on police barracks and personnel, Orange halls, commercial property and 'big houses.' As before its offensive provoked riots, reprisals, shootings and bombings especially in Belfast where thirty-one people died between 12 and 16 February. March proved to be the most brutal month of the 'troubles' so far with fifty-nine killings, including five members of the McMahon family (on 23-24 March); they were Catholics and lived in the north of the city.

Northern Ireland ministers were fully aware of the role of the Dublin government and of southern republicans in the IRA's campaign. This was confirmed when, on 10 March, a police raid on St Mary's hall, Belfast, uncovered documents which proved their collusion, as well as lists of the names and ranks of local IRA members, and details regarding their training camps. During these months the sustained military and political pressure and unreliable nature of the support received from Westminster, accentuated the Ulster unionist laager mentality. Craig and his embattled colleagues responded by expanding the security forces under their control and extending their emergency powers so that, independently of London, they could cope with any disorder short of southern invasion. Their agreed priorities were: 'the safety of Ulster ... to maintain the confidence of our people' and 'to bring the British government with us.'[87] They had to retain Westminster's sympathy and goodwill as it remained the irreplaceable source of money, troops and ultimately of power (by 1925 it had provided grants of £6.8 million to cover the cost of the Special Constabulary[88]). In early 1922 the number of Specials was increased – the force continued to bear the main burden of security work – and, on 7 April, the Civil Authorities (Special Powers) Act (Northern Ireland) became law. In essence this measure replicated the terms of the Restoration of Order in Ireland Act, 1920, which applied to Britain's armed forces and was passed to assist them restore the rule of law. Though less far-reaching than this, it empowered the Ministry of Home Affairs 'to take all such steps ... as may be necessary for preserving the peace and maintaining order.'[89] It could, for example, impose the death penalty and sentences of flogging for specified offences, imprison without trial, prohibit inquests and convene non-jury courts.

In London these initiatives were regarded with profound unease, especially the expansion of the Special Constabulary, which had been constituted, equipped and funded by Westminster. Its members were almost exclusively Protestant, their discipline was regarded as question-able and it was possible that they could in the future clash violently with crown forces (for example, in the event of a dispute over boundary revision). But no alternative policy was open to Craig. The twenty battalions of troops then stationed in the province had been relegated to a minor peacekeeping role. Lloyd George hesitated to deploy them either in Belfast or on the border, fearing that Collins might regard this as a breach of the truce, and that it could potentially undermine the Treaty. Also to do so might well lead to a confrontation with the IRA and a renewal of the Anglo-Irish war. Moreover, he was anxious to avoid giving any impression that Partition was being militarily imposed. The fact that Britain had unilaterally decided to disband the RIC (with effect from 31 May 1922) further restricted the options available to the authorities in the six counties. When the Royal Ulster Constabulary became operational on 1 June it had just 1,100 members, and no adequate system of intelligence. In these circumstances the Northern Ireland government had to rely on the Special Constabulary to restore and maintain order. The force was never likely to attract many recruits from members of the minority, given their bitter opposition to the state. Any who did enroll faced the prospect of social ostracism and retribution by the IRA who regarded them as 'traitors to the Republic.'[90] Furthermore, had northern Catholics joined in significant numbers, it would have compromised, possibly undermined, the nationalist position before the Boundary Commission. In any case, the Ministry of Home Affairs regarded their failure to do so with little more than indifference.

The level of violence peaked during May-June 1922, reaching a point where the two Irish states were 'to all intents and purposes openly at war.'[91] On 14 April anti-Treaty forces had seized the Four Courts in Dublin and, as a result, civil conflict in the south seemed imminent. Desperate to avoid this outcome, Collins launched a 'shared crusade'[92] aimed at crushing Northern Ireland, the ending of Partition being the only issue on which there was substantive agreement between the pro and anti-Treaty sides. In any case by then this objective had become for him a personal obsession. In a bid to achieve Irish unity, an 'Army of the North' was formed. Pro-Treaty IRA units supplied it with rifles, sub-machine guns, revolvers, grenades and mines, and anti- Treaty forces provided its leadership. The northern IRA, which had been preparing for an all-out offensive since March, was to furnish the manpower, supplemented by well-armed republicans who crossed the border. Craig's government estimated that by May it had over 8,000 members, double its strength nine months earlier and, secretly, a number of them were given commissions in the army of the Provisional Government.[93]

Eoin O'Duffy, one of Collins' deputies and pro-Treaty IRA Chief of Staff, was given responsibility for coordinating the 'army's' operations which amounted to a 'virtual full-scale invasion of Northern Ireland.'[94] Much of the violence which erupted was opportunistic and sectarian. Persistent sniping along the border was combined with full-scale guerilla attacks. Inside the six counties, RIC barracks and members of the police forces were targeted (ninety-seven of them lost their lives, 1920-22). At the same time an all-out incendiary campaign was waged against commercial premises, the railway system, bridges, 'big houses' (Shanes Castle was burnt to the ground on 20 May), Orange halls and property belonging to unionists and police personnel. This provoked riots, bitter inter-communal conflict and reprisals, as well as retaliatory action by unruly, loyalist mobs. On 18 May Musgrave RIC barracks in Victoria Street, Belfast, was attacked and one constable killed, sparking vicious clashes in the streets to the west of the city which persisted for over a month. On 17 June, the IRA killed six Protestants in cold blood at Altnaveigh near Newry. In May, over 600 violent incidents were recorded in the six counties (there had been 500 in April), and claims for compensation arising from malicious injuries spiraled to £800,000; the June figure was £760,000. During 1922 alone, damage amounting to £3 million was caused to property.[95]

From a security viewpoint the gravest incident occurred on 27 June, when an estimated 600 IRA members loyal to Collins occupied a salient in Fermanagh, which included the villages of Belleek and Pettigo. The area was cut off by Lower Lough Erne, and had no road access from within Northern Ireland. Over sixty Special Constables were dispatched to drive the invaders out, crossing the lake by pleasure boat, but their expedition failed and two of them were killed. More in hope than expectation, Craig requested that the Westminster government send in troops. Lloyd George hesitated but Churchill, Colonial Secretary, threatened resignation if they were not dispatched. He stated: 'we could not meet the House of Commons … with the admission that we did not know what was going on in a British village and did not dare to find out.'[96] This view prevailed and, by 8 June, the republican force had been expelled by soldiers, whose use of artillery proved decisive. It was a response fraught with peril, however, as it was the first direct confrontation between British troops and the IRA since the truce, and risked a renewal of the Anglo-Irish war. It reinforced Lloyd George's concerns over the persistently high level of disorder in Northern Ireland, despite the considerable sums expended by the Treasury. Meanwhile, Collins had been claiming that a 'pogrom' was taking place north of the border, and pleading for a judicial enquiry, even a declaration of martial law.

During June 1922 law and order was gradually restored and, by the autumn, it seemed to Craig that a 'land of promise, peace and happiness'[97] was beckoning. In large part this was due to the stringent, security measures taken by the regional government. By then the police services had been strengthened to the point where there was one member of the Special Constabulary or RUC for every six families living in Northern Ireland. Over the weekend, 20/21 May, there were fourteen more victims of the 'troubles' and, on the 22 May, William Twaddell, a unionist MP, was murdered in Belfast city centre. These deaths, and his concern that pro and anti-Treaty elements were uniting in the South (on 20 May Collins and de Valera agreed an electoral pact), prompted Craig's cabinet immediately to invoke its emergency powers. Over a 24-hour period 500 mainly republican suspects were interned, and a further 230 during the following months[98]. This was effective as the documents seized during the raid on St Mary's hall in March could be used to identify those arrested. Meanwhile the IRA and various republican organizations were proscribed (IRB, Cumann na mBan), a curfew was imposed throughout the six counties and additional border roads were closed.

The violent implosion in southern Ireland in late June also made a significant contribution to the restoration of order, though Follis claims that by then the northern IRA campaign 'had already proved a dismal failure.'[99] The final action ordered by Collins in his military assault on Northern Ireland was the murder of Field Marshall Sir Henry Wilson on 22 June. After retiring as Chief of Imperial General Staff, he had become unionist MP for North Down in February 1922, as well as Craig's 'security advisor.' His assassination led to intense British pressure on the Dublin government to expel the anti-Treaty garrison occupying the Four Courts.

This was a key factor in its decision to launch a bombardment of the building six days later and this was, in effect, the first act in the Irish civil war. Subsequently it ordered that IRA members 'cease all operations in the six counties' and that 'no troops from the 26 counties ... should be permitted to invade'[100] the area, it exchanged intelligence with the northern authorities and a number of IRA members in Belfast and those in anti-Treaty forces were arrested and their arms seized. With Collins' death three months later (22 August), the northern IRA lost 'the one sympathetic supporter'[101] it had within Sinn Fein's leadership. Cahir Healy was to complain that local republicans had been 'abandoned to Craig's mercy.'[102] WT Cosgrave, Collins successor, abandoned his policy of destabilizing the north, ceased paying the salaries of Catholic teachers refusing to recognize the regional education department, ended the press campaign against Partition and, in 1923, erected customs posts along the border. His priority was the implementation of the Treaty for which many had fought and sacrificed so much.

Largely as a result of these developments, by June 1922, the northern IRA's campaign had disintegrated along with its hopes of ending Partition. Its morale was shattered as a result of the impact of internment, the provisional government's abrupt reversal of policy and the outbreak of civil war which led to men and arms flowing south across the border. It has been estimated that 360 of its members joined the Free State army. Robert Lynch states that before the end of 1923, 'to all intents and purposes, [it] ... no longer existed' and that it was to make 'no serious attempt ... to challenge the northern state again for the next fifty years.'[103] A significant additional reason for its ignominious defeat was the collapse in its support from within its own nationalist community. This is evidenced by the increasing volume of confidential information it began passing on to the security forces. Seamus Woods observed forlornly that the position was 'hopeless' and the 'national spirit ... practically dead. [They would be] ... compelled to mete out capital punishment amongst the Catholic civilian population'[104] if they persisted with their operations. The northern minority was war weary and exhausted, wished for nothing more than an end to violence and secure employment and had come to 'regard republicans as attempting the impossible, and as a menace to their peace'[105]; Bishop Joseph MacRory personally appealed to de Valera to 'call away his gunmen.'[106] Its members had suffered most during the 'troubles.' Follis states that between December 1921 and late May 1922, 147 Catholics were killed in Northern Ireland and 166 wounded, whilst eighty-nine Protestants and members of the security forces had died, and 180 been wounded. Lynch calculates that during the entire course of the 'troubles', between June 1920 and June 1922, 366 Catholics died (including thirty-five IRA members), and 278 Protestants (including eighty-two policemen though this figure underestimates the number of their fatalities). He also estimates that in this same period 8,500 members of the minority were expelled from their workplaces, and 23,000 from their homes, and that as many as 50,000 may have fled from the six counties altogether. Their outward migration peaked during the IRA's all-out offensive in May-June 1922.[107]

For northern nationalists Article 12 of the Treaty seemed their best hope. The Free State came into existence on 6 December 1922; next day the Northern Ireland parliament opted out of its jurisdiction and, as a consequence, its border became subject to review by a Boundary Commission. This body first met on 6 November 1924. The prolonged delay was mainly due to the civil war in the South. Also Craig prevaricated over appointing a representative to it, and successive elections in Britain and for the two parliaments in Ireland held up the process. Richard Feetham, a respected judge from South Africa who was in later years an ardent critic of apartheid, was appointed as its chairman though he had no experience of border disputes and no knowledge of Ireland. But in any case the task was always going to be a difficult and controversial one. The wording of Article 12 was ambiguous: the border was to be amended 'in accordance with the wishes of the inhabitants so far as may be compatible with economic and geographic conditions.' Moreover nationalists and unionists held diametrically opposing views as to what criteria should be applied, and what adjudication they would regard as equitable. The Commission received submissions from the Unionist Party and the Free State's 'North East Boundary Bureau', as well as various interested groups and individuals. It held public meetings and toured the borders of Fermanagh and Tyrone, though it did not visit their heartlands. The Dublin government's position was that the boundary must be made to reflect the wishes of the population, and it therefore anticipated that the land area of Northern Ireland would be reduced by at least one-third and its population by one-fifth. Ulster unionists bitterly opposed any modification of the boundary. On 23 May 1922, Craig had declared in the Commons: 'what we have we hold', and he had fought an election in 1924 on the slogan: 'not an inch.'[108] He argued that none of the territory of the six counties could be sacrificed after so much blood had been shed in its defence, and warned that if the Commission's recommendations were unacceptable he would resign, and that there was a likelihood of violent upheaval in the north. Unionists also asserted that geographical and economic factors, such as property ownership, should be taken into consideration. They produced figures claiming that Protestants paid 75 per cent of the rates in Fermanagh and 68 per cent in Tyrone.

Throughout the investigation Feetham adopted a narrowly legalistic approach, and took into account economic, geographical and historical considerations, not just the wishes of the population. Above all, he was convinced that the *status quo* must be preserved and that nothing should be done that would weaken or undermine the position of Northern Ireland. After all, by the time he and his Commissioners had begun their deliberations Partition was well established and Ireland, north and south, was stable. He recommended only minor modifications of the border; these would have shortened it by fifty miles, and transferred 31,000 people to the south, and 7,500 to the north. Eventually, on 3 December 1925, the three governments signed an agreement that the boundary would remain unchanged. Craig had always hoped for this outcome. British ministers were equally satisfied; owing to the dilatoriness with which the Free State had implemented the terms of the treaty their sympathies, and those of the English press and public, lay with the Ulster Unionists.

The settlement has been described as WT Cosgrave's 'darkest hour' and a 'fiasco', but that he was able to 'ride the storm with ease'[109], helped by the fact that members of de Valera's opposition party had not yet taken their seats in the Dail. Various factors induced him to ratify it. Unlike Collins, he had no need to appease anti- partitionist radical elements at home. He was determined that the south should lose no territory, as any other adjudication could well have resulted in political instability. He was keen to foster better relations with the north, which he believed would end partition more quickly than covert attempts to destabilize it.

In any case, it is evident that his 'concentration [was] … on the Free State and its interests'[110], on national sovereignty rather than unity. Under the terms agreed the Dublin administration benefited financially because its liability to contribute over £8 million towards Britain's war debt (Article 5 of the Treaty) was written off. Furthermore Cosgrave accepted that the Council of Ireland should be formally abandoned and that its powers relating to the six counties should be transferred to the Northern Ireland government. He failed to consult northern nationalists before signing the document, and they alone gained nothing from it. Instead their hopes that the Commission would deliver unity were dashed, and they faced the prospect of 'partition forever.'[111] They felt isolated, impotent and betrayed by southern politicians; in Cahir Healy's words, they had been 'thrown to the wolves.'[112]

The failure of northern nationalists to engage with the Northern Ireland state during these turbulent formative years 'robbed them of any say in the future shape of its institutions or political culture'[113], and reinforced their feelings of alienation. Their strategy of non-recognition and abstentionism was evident from the outset. When Cardinal Michael Logue, the Catholic Primate, was invited to attend the opening of the Belfast parliament he declined, whilst the twelve nationalist MPs elected in May refused to take their seats. The new government immediately proceeded to initiate a range of measures which were to have far-reaching, long-term implications, but these were distorted and emasculated as a consequence of the minority's lack of engagement. When the RUC was being formed in 1922, Craig's government had envisaged it having an establishment of 3,000 members, and had determined that one-third of these should be drawn from the Catholic community, preference being given to those who had served in the RIC. However laudable this target was, it was never a realistic prospect given the attitudes prevailing at the time. In 1936 the force had an 83 per cent Protestant enrollment.

A similar pattern arose regarding the reform of local government and education. The Northern Ireland government inherited seventy-five local authorities elected in 1920 under proportional representation, and 32 per cent of these were either nationalist or Labour party controlled. After the Belfast parliament was established, many of the former passed motions pledging allegiance to Dail Eireann. Utilizing his devolved powers, Craig had suspended twenty of these by March 1922. In May, he introduced legislation to abolish proportional representation in council elections and redraw the polling district boundaries. Its timing was related to the apprehension felt, especially amongst unionists living near the border, that the votes cast by those recalcitrant councils unwilling to recognize the Northern Ireland government might influence the findings of the Boundary Commission. However, the measure was 'not aimed primarily against the nationalists.'[114] Craig's main concern was that Labour and independent unionist candidates might attract so many Protestant working class votes that the Unionist Party would lose its majority position, and the Union might therefore be imperilled. When the unionist leadership proceeded to organize public enquiries as a preliminary to redrawing local government boundaries, the minority generally boycotted the hearings; only in Ballycastle and Irvinestown did it 'help shape the new electoral arrangements', a process completed locally without controversy. Its negative response was mainly due to its concern that its participation would jeopardize its claim to transfer to the Free State before the Boundary Commission. As a result, the changes made were 'virtually dictated'[115] by local unionists. Northern nationalists also refused to take part in the subsequent elections, so reducing them to a farce. By 1927 non-unionist parties controlled just twelve councils, half the number they had held in 1920.

Meanwhile, in September 1921, the Catholic hierarchy had refused to nominate representatives to the Ministry of Education's Lynn committee. The department had convened this body in preparation for the legislation enacted in 1923. In this measure the department showed both vision and ambition. It aimed to establish an efficient, non-sectarian, democratically accountable educational system in which children from both traditions would be taught together, and no religious instruction provided within compulsory hours of attendance. But this initiative was still born. The Catholic Church refused to transfer the institutions it administered to public control, whilst Protestant clergy, who were well organized and lobbied zealously, agitated for amendments. These were passed between 1925-1930, and totally undermined the intention of the original bill. As a consequence, state schools became, in effect, Protestant schools.

During Ireland's revolutionary period the recourse to the use of physical force by republicans did produce tangible results. From 1870, for over forty years, constitutional nationalism had failed to achieve any measure of self-government. Though it had clearly expressed the will of the Irish people as evidenced by its successive election victories, this was not acted upon by Westminster. In contrast, the violence of Easter week, and again during the Anglo-Irish war, concluded with a treaty in which Britain granted Ireland dominion status, a significantly greater level of independence than had been envisaged in the three previous home rule bills. This progress towards self-government came at a heavy price, however.

Republican violence polarized Irish society and, as a consequence, the process of establishing functioning administrations in Northern Ireland and in the twenty-six counties was costly both in terms of lives lost, and financially. It exacerbated tribal hatred on the island and culminated in the formation of two mutually hostile states, each economically retarded, and harbouring deep suspicions towards its minority populations. Lynch states that by 1923 the total strength of their combined security forces totaled over 120,000. In that year the Free State's national debt stood at £26 million, whilst the raising of the Special Constabulary had cost the northern Ministry of Finance £7.4 million by 1925. Between the Rising and late 1922, 5,000 Irishmen died as a direct result of internal civil conflict, and up to 80,000 had been forced to flee from their homes as refugees. Between 1911 and 1926 over one-third of the Protestants living in southern Ireland were driven out or opted to leave. In this same period, the number of Catholics resident in the six counties fell by 10,000. Joe Devlin estimated that there were 20,000 fewer of his co-religionists living in Belfast in 1922 than in 1920.[116]

The violence between 1916 to 1923 deepened the divisions within southern Ireland. Laffan writes that it was left 'poorer and uglier ... crippled and poisoned', and that its politics were affected 'for generations.'[117] The impact of these years was prolonged by the fact that, until the 1970s, it was led by politicians who were veterans of the civil war, during which both its major parties had emerged. Nonetheless, as events in 1932 dramatically illustrated, democracy survived. 'The people's will had triumphed'[118] then when politicians who were pro-Treaty peacefully handed power over to those who had opposed it. Vital to its survival, however, was the willingness of the southern Irish leaders to ruthlessly suppress republican irreconcilables. The Free State executed over seventy of them, Cosgrave being determined, as he phrased it, to 'enforce and carry out the law of God'[119] in Ireland. De Valera dealt with recalcitrant IRA members equally harshly by means of internment and mass imprisonment; three of those arrested died on hunger strike and six were hanged. Meanwhile, from 1923 onwards, southern politicians progressively removed the symbols sacrificed in the Treaty, a process that culminated with the establishment of a republic in 1949. But independence did not bring about a realization of the objectives cherished by the rebel leaders in Easter week. It did not lead to either a united Ireland or a Gaelic republic, and women and socialists were marginalized in favour of a socially conservative, nationalist vision of 1916. Between 1924 and 1927, 100,000 citizens of southern Ireland emigrated mostly to North America and Australia. Through future generations this haemorrhaging of its youth was to stand out as both a feature of the state and an indictment of its politicians.

In late December 1921 there is evidence that some unionist businessmen became more receptive to the prospect of an all-Ireland parliament. The views they expressed then were, of course, influenced by the context of civil disorder in Belfast, acute political and economic instability, uncertainty resulting from the treaty negotiations and also by a feeling that they had been 'betrayed by English Tories.'[120] What they sought were assurances from Sinn Fein regarding its future policies particularly on the role of the Catholic Church in education, on the promotion of the Irish language by the state and on taxation and trade. But above all they wanted the Party to show 'a genuine desire to adopt a friendly, fraternal attitude towards the Ulster people' and that 'Ulstermen will be welcome to assist in the task of building a new Ireland.'[121] No such assurances were forthcoming, no hand of friendship was reached out. The expression of these sentiments was short-lived and rapidly overshadowed by events. In similar vein the boundary agreement, which both Irish governments signed in December 1925, committed each of them 'to aid one another in a spirit of neighbourly comradeship.'[122] Once again there was to be no such reconciliation. In the policies they prioritized, southern leaders made no attempt to appeal to or appease, let alone attract, Ulster unionists, and this contributed to a 'widening gulf' between the two states and partition becoming ever more deeply entrenched.

From the outset Cosgrave strove to bring about the 'Gaelicization ... of our whole culture.'[123] In his 1922 constitution Irish was declared to be the national language of the Free State, and strenuous efforts were made to promote it despite the fact that just 18 per cent of the population claimed to speak it in the 1926 census. De Valera suggested repeatedly that its 'restoration' was a 'more urgent national issue than partition.' He was convinced that 'Irish nationality would wither if the language revival failed', and he stated emphatically that he 'would not tomorrow for the sake of a united Ireland give up the policy of trying to make this a really Irish-Ireland – not by any means.'[124] Similarly, from the outset, southern leaders set about constructing a confessional Catholic state. Cosgrave's government farmed out a number of its responsibilities to the Church particularly in health and education. In education Buckland claims that it 'carved out for itself more extensive control ... than in any other country in the world', and that its 'influence ... was all pervasive.'[125] Divorce was not permitted, birth control outlawed, literature advocating contraception banned, and films and books were censored to such an extent that 'independent Ireland [became] an object of international ridicule for the next forty years.'[126] In his 1937 constitution, de Valera endowed the Catholic Church with a 'special position' in the state (Article 44). When it was suggested to him that this would hinder Irish unity, he responded: 'we can only take these things as they come.'[127] It was not until the early 1970s that an effort was made to construct a more pluralistic 'new' Ireland, one that would have greater appeal to northern unionists. At the time Garret FitzGerald, the driving force behind this policy, was rebuked by Pope Paul VI. The Pontiff stated uncompromisingly that 'Ireland was a Catholic country – perhaps the only one left – and should stay that way.'[128]

Despite pursuing these policies, Articles 2 and 3 of the 1937 constitution also asserted the Dublin government's claim to jurisdiction over the entire island. Its leaders continued to regard Partition as irrational and reversible, and generally to encourage the northern minority not to cooperate with the Northern Ireland state. This approach was broadly 'based on the deeply flawed dogma ... that Unionists could be coerced into unity.'[129] After becoming Taoiseach in 1932, de Valera confessed: 'I

see no immediate solution'[130] to the northern issue. Throughout his political career, he asserted the South's 'unabated' claim to sovereignty over all
thirty-two counties, its 'natural boundary', discounted the 'two nations'
theory and considered that in time unity was inevitable; it was an Irish
version of 'manifest destiny.' After some early belligerent speeches, unlike
some in his party, he rejected the use of force. This was not because he
held a 'pacifist position'; if he had 'thought force could unite the island he
would support it.'[131] He believed that 'it would be impossible to dislodge
British troops' and also, in the mid 1950s, he rejected a motion by his
own party calling on his government to take action against the IRA. But
when a Fianna Fail committee then suggested increasing the Republic's
links with the north, and reassuring unionists that their rights would be
respected in a united Ireland, he again refused to do so. He considered
that such an initiative would generate 'serious controversy', possibly cause
'confusion' amongst the northern minority. He himself favoured a policy
of non-cooperation. When speaking to the British ambassador in 1954,
he was still referring to the 'occupation' of the six counties by English
soldiers, complaining that their presence was a 'provocation' and alleging that they were there to hold the local population in 'subjection.'[132]
According to Bowman, his 'fixed view' was that the problem could only
be solved in the 'larger general play of English interest'[133], and he hoped
that the Westminster government would commit itself to the unification
of Ireland. Overall southern politicians failed 'to either adapt to or confront the realities of partition'[134], and to recognize and accept the depth
and intensity of the sense of British identity shared by unionists. This perspective enabled them to absolve themselves for their continuing failure
to achieve unity, and place the blame on Britain, rather than work con-
structively to resolve the widening divisions between north and south.
De Valera's only gesture to Northern Ireland was his decision not declare
a republic; he described this 'as necessary bait for Ulster Unionists.'[135]

Within the six counties the collapse of the IRA campaign in mid
1922 did not lead to any new sprit of reconciliation between unionists
and nationalists. The long-serving ministers in the Northern Ireland
government continued to display a siege mentality even after the siege
had lifted. That their mental attitudes did not change is evident: republican suspects interned in 1922 were not released until early 1926; the

Special Powers Act was made permanent and remained law until 1978; in 1929 proportional representation was abolished in elections for the northern parliament and the Special Constabulary was an important backbone of the security forces till March 1970. Their ongoing sense of insecurity was rooted in: apprehension regarding the alienated minority present within the state; the recurrence of IRA campaigns and the persistence of Dublin irredentism. Moreover, though Westminster retained its sovereignty, it failed to supervise or guide them and continued to be an unreliable partner, 'often careless of [Northern Ireland's] ... condition.'[136] As a result of its niggardliness during the interwar years social services in the region lagged behind those in Britain, and for most of this period roughly one-quarter of Northern Ireland's workforce was unemployed. In 1940 British ministers once again pressurized Craig to accept Irish unity.

Ulster unionists have been described as the 'only clear winners'[137] to emerge in Ireland over the period 1886 to 1925. Their achievement was the formation of a functioning Northern Ireland state, and the fact that it survived with its 1920 boundaries unchanged and its powers intact. But it still confronted formidable and enduring internal problems. By far the gravest of these was its substantial Catholic minority. Its members had bitterly opposed the creation of the state, and their negative responses had robbed them of any say in shaping its structures. In an account sympathetic to the unionist position, Follis observes that their sense of alienation was reinforced during 1920-1922 by the 'sectarian attacks made [on them] by elements of the Protestant community.' He includes in this the 'outrages committed by certain elements' in the Special Constabulary though these, he notes, were 'localized and unauthorized.' He considers that this violence 'scarred the minority's collective consciousness ... The fragile peace which existed between two hostile communities ... was shattered.' He concludes that it was 'highly regrettable that they [the Ulster unionists] did not later seek to improve relations', and 'offer nationalists greater participation' in the state. As a result of their failure to do so, he writes, 'problems were being stored up for the future.'[138] It is difficult to refute the verdict that successive unionist leaders lacked vision and magnanimity, too readily resigned themselves to the perception that the internal divisions they faced were immutable, and were too responsive to the claims of their own supporters and overly concerned that a liberalizing initiative would jeopardize party unity, their majority and ultimately the Union.

The Northern Ireland state has experienced sporadic eruptions of republican violence throughout its history. Until August 1969, when British troops were deployed, it coped with these using its police forces and emergency powers; just one IRA member was executed. When conducting its campaigns, the IRA has felt legitimized and inspired by the methods and objectives of the Easter Rising, and has regarded the eradication of Partition as the main item of 'unfinished business.' Their actions have been 'built on the illusory possibility of political unity without compromise'[139] achieved through the use of physical force. Its premise has been that the Irish republic was entitled to the allegiance of every Irishman and Irishwoman, including unionists and constitutionalists, just as the men of 1916 had insisted. Ruairí Ó'Brádaigh, IRA Chief of Staff, highlighted the significance of the fiftieth commemoration of Easter Week in 1966 in relation to the violence that followed. He stated that 'the national rethink which sprang, particularly among the youth, from [this event] ... was in some measure responsible for the developments in the North since 1969.'[140] Irish-Americans then provided money and arms to help young militants ignore the will of the Irish people, and once again kill and die for Ireland, because they believed themselves commanded to do so by the dead generations. Between 1969 and 1994 there were 3,518 fatalities in Northern Ireland, Southern Ireland, Britain and Germany: 59 per cent of the killings were inflicted by republicans, 29 per cent by loyalists and 10 per cent by the security forces; 58 per cent of those who died were civilians, of whom 186 were aged under sixteen, and 60 per cent were Catholic.[141] Fewer than 15 per cent of the deaths resulted in criminal convictions.

The twenty-five years of the Troubles forced southern politicians to reassess their views on the Rising because the IRA sought to legitimize its campaign by claiming its legacy. They were also obliged to re-evaluate their policy towards the six counties. Though the unionist parties were not consulted during the negotiations that led to the Anglo-Irish Agreement in 1985, Article 1 was included specifically for their reassurance. In it the Taoiseach, Garret FitzGerald (Fine Gael), formally endorsed the proposition that Northern Ireland could not be coerced into a united Ireland (Article 1), and that there could be no change in its constitutional status unless and until a majority of its citizens agreed to join the Republic. Following the Good Friday Agreement, 1998, the then Taoiseach, Bertie Ahern (Fianna Fail), signed a declaration amending Articles 2 and 3 of the Irish constitution, thereby implicitly recognizing that Northern Ireland was part of the United Kingdom's sovereign territory. After the collapse of the IRA's campaign, Sinn Fein agreed to and ratified the 1998 Agreement as well, thus accepting the principle of unionist consent to the unification of Ireland. So, despite condemning and sometimes murdering nationalist rivals as traitors for accepting Partition, it had been obliged to do the same; it proved to have no more solution to the problem than the constitutional parties had.

Republican irreconcilables, who perceive themselves as being the true heirs of the Rising, remain at large in Ireland. Sinn Fein's leaders, now members of the Stormont executive, denounce these dissidents. But they respond by arguing that if a tiny cabal could kill people in Easter week, and the Provisional IRA did so for almost thirty years, then why should they not now. If violence by a minority without a democratic mandate was legitimate and acceptable in 1916, then why not in 2020. Thus, more than a century later, the malign legacy from Ireland's revolutionary period lingers on and is used to justify murder.[142] This despite the fact that any perceived inequity in Northern Ireland's governance has long since been eradicated.

Notes

[1]   1916 Proclamation. For analysis of the Easter Rising, see Michael Foy and Brian Barton, *The Easter Rising* (Stroud: Sutton Publishing, 1999), *passim.*

[2]   Michael Foy, *Tom Clarke: The True Leader of the Easter Rising* (Dublin: The History Press, 2014).

[3]   *Ibid.,* p. 245.

[4]   Bryan A Follis, *A State under Siege: The Establishment of Northern Ireland, 1920-25* (Oxford: Clarendon Press, 1995), p. 187.

[5]   Gerard MacAtnasney, *Sean MacDiarmada: The Mind of the Revolution* (Manorhamilton: Drumlin Publications, 2004), pp. 69-70.

[6]   Foy, *Clarke, op. cit.,* p. 245.

7   1916 Proclamation.

8   Rev. H Cameron Lyster, *An Irish Parish in Changing Times* (London: Francis Griffiths, 1933), pp. 117-8.

9   Both diary quotes are in Brian Barton, *The Secret Court Martial Records of the Easter Rising* (Stroud: The History Press, 2010), p. 27.

10 *Ibid.*, pp. 60-63.

11 Foy and Barton, *Easter Rising, op. cit.*, p. 238.

12 Barton, *Secret Court Martial Records, op. cit.*, pp. 98, 101.

13 Ruth Dudley Edwards, *The Seven: The Lives and Legacies of the Founding Fathers of the Irish Republic* (London: Oneworld Publications, 2017), p. 365.

14 Barton, *Secret Court Martial Records, op. cit.*, pp. 38-9.

15 Charles Townshend, *Easter 1916: The Irish Rebellion* (London: Penguin Books, 2006), p. 306.

16 Fearghal McGarry, *The Rising: Ireland, Easter 1916* (Oxford: Oxford University Press, 2010), p. 280.

17 *Ibid.*, p. 285.

18 Foy, *Clarke, op. cit.*, p. 241.

19 Barton, *Secret Court Martial Records, op. cit.*, p. 107.

20 Foy, *Clarke, op. cit.*, p. 156.

21 *Ibid.*, p. 241.

22 Dudley Edwards, *Seven, op. cit.*, p. 353.

23 *Ibid.*, p. 349.

24 Barton, *Secret Court Martial Records, op, cit.*, p. 332.

25 Foy, *Clarke, op. cit.*, p. 220.

26 John Bowman, *De Valera and the Ulster Question, 1917-1973* (Oxford: Clarendon Press, 1982), p. 18.

27 Dudley Edwards, *Seven, op. cit.*, p. 371.

28 Bowman, *De Valera, op. cit.*, p. 3.

29 Dudley Edwards, *Seven, op. cit.*, p. 367.

30 *Ibid.*, p. 353.

31 Barton, *Secret Court Martial Records, op. cit.*, p. 125.

32 Foy, *Clarke, op. cit.*, p. 219.

33 Barton, *Secret Court Martial Records, op. cit.*, p. 105.

[34] Joseph M Curran, *The Birth of the Irish Free State* (Alabama: University of Alabama, 1980), pp. 17-18.

[35] McGarry, *The Rising, op. cit.*, p. 286.

[36] Robert Lynch, *The Partition of Ireland, 1918-1925* (Cambridge: Cambridge University Press, 2019), pp. 41, 46.

[37] Both quotes in Robert Lynch, *Revolutionary Ireland, 1912-25* (London: Bloomsbury, 2015), p. 58.

[38] Bowman, *De Valera, op. cit.*, p. 40.

[39] Paul Bew, *Ireland and the Politics of Envy, 1789-2006* (Oxford: Oxford University Press, 2007), p. 392.

[40] *Ibid.*, p. 395.

[41] Dudley Edwards, *Seven, op. cit.*, p. 367.

[42] Michael Foy, *Michael Collins' Intelligence War: The Struggle between the British and the IRA* (Stroud: The History Press, 2006), p. 20.

[43] *Ibid., op. cit.*, pp. 7, 21, 26.

[44] Brian Barton, 'Northern Ireland, 1920-25' in *A New History of Ireland, VII*, edited by JR Hill (Oxford: Oxford University Press, 2003), p. 173.

[45] Both quotations given in Lynch, *Revolutionary Ireland, op. cit.*, pp. 103-4.

[46] Curran, *Irish Free State, op. cit.*, p. 172.

[47] Lynch, *Revolutionary Ireland, op. cit.*, p. 88.

[48] Curran, *Irish Free State, op. cit.*, p. 234.

[49] Quotations given in David McCullagh, *De Valera, Volume I: Rise, 1882-1932* (Dublin: Gill Books, 2017), pp. 272-3, 305.

[50] Michael Laffan, *Judging WT Cosgrave* (Dublin: Royal Irish Academy, 2014), p. 198.

[51] Patrick Buckland, *Irish Unionism 2: Ulster Unionism and the Origins of Northern Ireland, 1886 to 1922* (Dublin: Gill and Macmillan, 1973), pp. 55-56.

[52] *Ibid.*, p. 104.

[53] Follis, *State under Siege, op. cit.*, p. 24.

[54] Buckland, *Irish Unionism, op. cit.*, p. 105.

[55] *Ibid*, p.111.

[56] Foy and Barton, *Easter Rising, op. cit.*, p. 244.

[57] Bew, *Ireland, op. cit.*, p. 382.

[58] Buckland, *Irish Unionism, op. cit.*, p. 104.

[59] Laffan, *Cosgrave, op. cit.*, p. 198.

[60] Follis, *State under Siege, op. cit.*, p. 186.

[61] Lynch, *Partition, op. cit.*, p. 73.

[62] *Ibid.*, p. 41.

[63] Follis, *State under Siege, op. cit.*, p. 50.

[64] *Belfast Telegraph*, 24 December 1920; 23 June 1921, *Hansard NI (Commons) i*, cols. 36-37.

[65] Bowman, *De Valera, op. cit.*, p. 17.

[66] Follis, *State under Siege, op. cit.*, p. 186.

[67] Robert Lynch, *The Northern IRA and the Early Years of Partition, 1920-1922* (Dublin: Irish Academic Press, 2006), p. 99.

[68] Account given by Denis McCullough, Witness Statement WS 915, Bureau of Military History, Irish Military Archives.

[69] Based on Lynch, *Northern IRA, op. cit.*, p. 12.

[70] Eamon Phoenix, *Northern Nationalism: Nationalist Politics, Partition and the Catholic Minority in Northern Ireland, 1890-1940* (Belfast: Ulster Historical Foundation, 1994), p. 76.

[71] Quoted in Lynch, *Northern IRA, op. cit.*, p. 43.

[72] Brian Barton, *Brookeborough: The Making of a Prime Minister* (Belfast: Institute of Irish Studies, 1988), p. 31, and *passim*, pp. 29-59.

[73] Lynch, *Revolutionary Ireland, op. cit.*, p. 101.

[74] Michael Farrell, *Arming the Protestants: The Formation of the Ulster Special Constabulary and the Royal Ulster Constabulary, 1920-27* (London: Pluto Press Ltd., 1983), pp. 48-9.

[75] Lynch, *Northern IRA, op. cit.*, p. 35.

[76] *Ibid.*, p. 47.

[77] *Ibid.*, p. 79.

[78] Barton, *New History of Ireland, op. cit.*, p. 167.

[79] *Ibid.*, p. 195.

[80] Follis, *State under Siege, op. cit.*, pp. 55-6.

[81] Barton, *New History of Ireland, op. cit.*, p. 168.

[82] Lynch, *Northern IRA, op. cit.*, p. 72.

[83] *Ibid.*, p. 100, and *passim*, pp. 165-173.

[84] *Ibid.*, p. 125.

85 Fergus Whelan, 'Belfast Battalion: A History of the Belfast IRA, 1922-1969' in *History Ireland*, November-December 2019, vol. 7, no. 6.

86 Lynch, *Northern IRA, op. cit.*, p. 88.

87 Barton, *A New History of Ireland, op. cit.*, p. 172.

88 Follis, *State under Siege, op. cit.*, p. 131.

89 Text of Act given in Lynch, *Northern IRA, op. cit.*, p. 223.

90 Barton, *New History of Ireland, op. cit.*, p. 165.

91 Follis, *State under Siege, op. cit.*, p. 93.

92 Lynch, *Northern IRA, op. cit.*, p. 126.

93 *Ibid.*, pp. 207, 81 and 165-175, *passim*.

94 *Ibid.*, p. 140.

95 Statistics given in Follis, *State under Siege, op. cit.*, pp. 98-9.

96 Barton, *Brookeborough, op. cit.*, p. 50.

97 Barton, *New History of Ireland, op. cit.*, p. 185.

98 Follis, *State under Siege, op. cit.*, p. 99. Also Lynch, *Northern IRA, op. cit.*, p. 124.

99 Follis, *State under Siege, op. cit.*, p. 107.

100 Lynch, *Northern IRA, op. cit.*, pp. 187, 189.

101 *Ibid.*, p. 194.

102 Lynch, *Revolutionary Ireland, op. cit.*, p. 114.

103 Lynch, *Northern IRA, op. cit.*, p. 177.

104 *Ibid.*, pp. 179-180.

105 *Ibid.*, p. 208.

106 Barton, *New History of Ireland, op. cit.*, p. 183.

107 Statistics given in Lynch, *Northern IRA, op. cit.*, p. 227 and Follis, *State under Siege, op. cit.*, pp. 93-4.

108 *Ibid.*, pp. 176, 101.

109 Eunan O'Halpin, 'Politics and the State, 1922-32' in *A New History of Ireland, op. cit.*, p. 108.

110 Laffan, *Cosgrave, op. cit.*, p. 209.

111 Lynch, *Partition, op. cit.*, p. 213.

112 Follis, *State under Siege, op. cit.*, p. 180.

113 Lynch, *Northern IRA, op. cit.*, p. 210.

[114] Patrick Buckland, *The Factory of Grievances: Devolved Government in Northern Ireland, 1921-1939* (Dublin: Gill and Macmillan, 1979), p. 235.

[115] *Ibid.*, pp. 238-9.

[116] Statistics drawn from: Lynch, *Partition, op. cit.*, pp. 110, 158, 169, 176, 196; Laffan, *Cosgrave, op. cit.*, p. 172; Follis, *State under Siege, op. cit.*, p. 131.

[117] Laffan, *Cosgrave, op. cit.*, pp. 127-8.

[118] *Ibid.*, p. 275.

[119] *Ibid.*, p. 124.

[120] See Diarmaid Fawsitt's 'Special Mission to Belfast', first report, dated 3 December 1921, NAI DE/2/304/13 (National Archives, Dublin). Fawsitt was an advisor to the Irish Treaty delegation and to the Dail cabinet, and undertook five missions to Belfast between November 1921 and January 1922 to ascertain attitudes in Northern Ireland regarding the acceptability of an all-Ireland parliament. Also letter to *Irish Times*, 13 August 2019, by Julitta Clancy, Fawsitt's granddaughter. Fawsitt's papers have been deposited in Cork City and County Archives, Cork.

[121] *Ibid.*.

[122] Follis, *State under Siege, op. cit.*, p. 182.

[123] Laffan, *Cosgrave, op. cit.*, p. 184.

[124] Bowman, *De Valera, op. cit.*, pp. 18, 127, 311.

[125] Patrick Buckland, *A History of Northern Ireland* (Dublin: Gill and Macmillan, 1981), p. 59.

[126] Laffan, *Cosgrave, op. cit.*, p. 261.

[127] Bowman, *De Valera, op. cit.*, p. 152.

[128] Dermot Keogh, 'Ireland, 1972-84' in *A New History of Ireland, op. cit.*, p. 369.

[129] Lynch, *Northern IRA, op. cit.*, p. 211.

[130] David McCullagh, *De Valera, volume 1, op cit.*, p. 406.

[131] Bowman, *De Valera, op. cit.*, p. 305.

[132] Quotations given in David McCullagh, *De Valera, Volume 2: Rule, 1932-1975* (Dublin: Gill Books, 2018), pp. 341-3. Also McCullagh, *De Valera, Volume 1; Rise, op. cit.*, p. 406.

[133] Bowman, *De Valera, op. cit.*, pp. 302-3.

[134] Lynch, *Northern IRA, op. cit.*, p. 211.

[135] Bowman, *De Valera, op. cit.*, p. 268.

[136] Follis, *State under Siege, op. cit.*, p. 182.

THE BIRTH OF NORTHERN IRELAND

137   *Ibid.*, pp. 181, 192.

138   *Ibid.*, pp. 113, 115, 190, 193, 194.

139   Lynch, *Northern IRA, op. cit.*, p. 211.

140   Brian Hanley, 'Burnt Out: How the Troubles Began' in *History Ireland*, September-October 2019, vol. 7, no. 5. See also *Sunday Times*, 27 October 2019.

141   David McKittrick et al, *Lost Lives: The Stories of the Men, Women and Children who died as a Result of the Northern Ireland Troubles* (Edinburgh and London: Mainstream Publishing, 1999), Tables 1, 6, 16, pp. 1473-1482

142   Dudley Edwards, *Seven, op. cit.*, p. 371.

2

Northern Ireland: devolution pioneers

Graham Walker

The political entity of Northern Ireland was the outcome of the Government of Ireland Act of 1920. It is a rather prosaic point, although one often forgotten, that this piece of legislation was drawn up to provide a very different settlement of the 'Irish question' than what actually transpired: it was envisaged that there would be two 'home rule' (or devolved) parliaments in Ireland – one for the six county North, and one for the rest of the country. It was, in effect, a fourth Irish home rule scheme, following the precedents of 1886, 1893, and 1912.[1]

The 1920 Act also provided for a Council of Ireland through which both devolved administrations could work co-operatively on issues of mutual concern, with the expectation of an eventual merger into one devolved parliament and government for the whole of Ireland within the United Kingdom (UK). The Government of Ireland Act is frequently referred to as the 'partition act', and the Council of Ireland as a cosmetic gesture. However, it is more plausible to argue that the Long Committee (which devised the legislation) was non-partitionist in its intentions and that the Council was proof of its desire to keep avenues to unity open. The scheme arguably involved a dynamic towards unity: it was probable, for example, that had North and South worked the Act and presented a common front, then more powers, including taxation, would have been devolved.[2] All this, moreover, was consistent with a quasi-federal line of thought which had come to be adopted by Walter Long (Chairman of the Committee) himself[3]: Ireland (in the shape of one unit or two) might simply be the first to receive devolutionary powers later to be distributed throughout the UK. Gradually, the 'home rule all round' thinking of the era of 1880 to 1920 had been brought to bear on policy-making, and the arguments – long rehearsed and fitfully entertained even by Ulster unionist leader Sir Edward Carson[4] – that it might reconcile the different aspirations of the two parts of Ireland commensurate with British/UK coherence and security, accepted at government level.

As it turned out the Council of Ireland never sat, while the parliament meant for Dublin proved to be a dead letter in the context of the War of Independence between 1919 and 1921, and the decimation of the Irish Parliamentary Party at the general election of 1918 and its eclipse by Sinn Fein. The Anglo-Irish treaty of December 1921 led to the establishment of an Irish Free State with Dominion Status for the twenty-six counties. While guerrilla warfare raged in the south, the Ulster unionists, led now by James Craig, moved quickly to set up Northern Ireland as a functioning political unit; the unionist urge to make a material reality of the 1920 Act overrode any consideration of the potential problems it posed. The first elections to the Northern Ireland parliament were held in May 1921, and the parliament officially opened the following month. Nevertheless, the treaty of December 1921 required Northern Ireland to vote herself out of the new Irish Free State within one month of the treaty's ratification, and the consequence of doing so was the setting up of a Boundary Commission to determine the border between Northern Ireland and the rest of Ireland.[5] Unionist anxieties regarding the outcome of the Commission, although quelled by the joint decision on the part of the British, Irish Free State, and Northern Ireland governments to leave the border in practical terms unaltered, nonetheless shaped significantly the early politics of the new state.

Perhaps unsurprisingly, given the political turmoil in Ireland at the time of partition, there was a degree of ambiguity and confusion about Northern Ireland's constitutional status. The influence of 'federal' thinking around the 'home rule all round' idea has been noted, and there seems to have been a perception on the part of important political figures in both London and Belfast that this was the spirit if not the letter of the 1920 Act. For example, in a leaflet published by the Ulster Unionist Council the first Minister of Education for Northern Ireland, Lord Londonderry, remarked as follows: 'As a measure of Federation within the United Kingdom, Ulster has a Parliament of her own which is competent to deal with her purely local problems.'[6] Other important figures such as the first Minister of Finance, Hugh Pollock, and Sir Wilfrid Spender, head of the new Northern Ireland civil service, quickly took the hint that London desired Northern Ireland to be as self-reliant as possible, and British politics to be no longer troubled by the 'Irish question' in any form. There was little doubt that the British public, as well as all political parties, had wearied of the issue by the 1920s, and Ulster certainly could not count on the sympathetic hearing she had received in the pre First World War years. Later Ulster unionist objections to the threat of London intervention or dictation in the 1960s as the Troubles loomed, and to the eventual suspension of Stormont in 1972, centred on the notion of Northern Ireland possessing 'squatters' rights' earned through time and constitutional convention, and on such developments as the 1925 agreement over the border which was ratified as an international treaty and involved Northern Ireland as a participating government.[7] There was also, in this respect, the matter of the Ireland Act of 1949, which stipulated that Northern Ireland could only cease to be part of the UK with the consent of the Northern Ireland (Stormont) parliament. This may not have theoretically cancelled out the ultimate right, enshrined in article 75 of the 1920 Act, of London to trump Belfast in any constitutional dispute. Nevertheless, it understandably fed illusions of sovereignty on the part of Ulster unionists and bolstered the claims of those who were inclined in the 60s and 70s to regard Northern Ireland's relationship to the rest of the UK as 'de facto' federalism.[8] These points of constitutional dispute and debate may be said to have acquired a fresh significance with the advent of devolved institutions for Scotland, Wales, and Northern Ireland at the end of the twentieth century.

Craig in some respects wished to be 'left alone', chiefly in the business of securing Northern Ireland as an entity and providing for its indefinite inclusion in the UK. This translated into the practical steps required to maintain Unionist Party unity and the party's grip on local power. The way unionists were inclined to view the establishment of Northern Ireland (which, it needs to remembered, was never their preferred goal) was as their slice of a settlement that of the Irish question which would be permanent. Unionists believed that they had compromised significantly to arrive at such an outcome, particularly around the sacrifice of their fellow unionists in the border counties of Donegal, Cavan, and Monaghan, and that nothing more should be asked of them. Craig could contemplate the nationalist opposition within the new Northern Ireland with equanimity provided unionism stood firm and together.

The task of ensuring unionist unity was nonetheless a challenging one, and it involved Craig and his government – the Unionist Party won the first Northern Ireland election emphatically – in some hard choices. The choices made were to ensure the adoption for the first nineteen years of Northern Ireland's existence under Craig's guidance, of a minimalist approach to the possibilities offered by devolution.[9] Indeed, Craig's approach was in essence followed by his successors, John M. Andrews and Basil Brooke, and it was not until the 1960s with the accession to the premiership of Terence O'Neill that a more expansive and adventurous approach to the use of devolved powers can be discerned.[10] The reasons for this lie mainly in the management of divisions around social class within unionism.

Besides being drawn up in anticipation of a very different outcome, the terms of the Government of Ireland Act were also devised in the middle of a post First World War trading boom which benefited Ulster's staple heavy industries. This boom gave way to slump, and it became clear, early in the life of Northern Ireland's first parliament, that the revenue resources would not be sufficient to cover expenditure. Northern Ireland controlled only a number of minor taxes, the major ones such as income tax and customs and excise being reserved to the central Exchequer in London which decided on the Province's share. The 1920 Act also specified the payment to the Treasury of the cost of reserved services and a so-called Imperial Contribution to cover Northern Ireland's share of defence and Empire management costs. The burden of this, combined with the cost of providing for the Province's own needs and services which in the early years involved a significant policing and security outlay, raised the prospect of the UK's first devolution experiment foundering on the rock of bankruptcy.

The Northern Ireland Minister of Finance, Pollock, set out to reduce the Imperial Contribution while the Minister of Labour, Andrews, with the crucial backing of Craig, pursued indefatigably the objective of maintaining the level of welfare services such as unemployment and health insurance and old age pensions in line with the rest of the UK. Andrews and Craig were determined that devolution would not mean lower standards of social security for Northern Ireland and they recognised the potential damage of such a development to the Unionist Party in the form of the disaffection of its working class supporters. Indeed, an Ulster Unionist Labour Association (UULA) had been integrated into the wider party organisation since 1918 for the express purpose of addressing working class concerns.

Tough negotiations with the British government resulted in an arbitration process chaired by Lord Colwyn. The Colwyn Committee verdict in 1925 was that the Imperial Contribution should be made a final rather than a first charge on the Northern Ireland exchequer. Parallel with this an Unemployment Re-Insurance agreement was reached which integrated Northern Ireland with the UK unemployment insurance fund.[11] Craig and Andrews's 'populist' line prevailed and the 'step by step' policy, as it was to be colloquially known, was put firmly in place in respect of both social security and welfare benefits, and the re-production (often only marginally adjusted) of legislation passed at Westminster aimed at improving the social and economic conditions of the mass of workers. This was trumpeted by Craig as evidence of the Northern Ireland government getting what was due for its citizens on the basis that they paid the same rate of the major taxes as the rest of the UK population. The tendency within Northern Ireland governing circles dubbed 'anti-populist' by Bew, Gibbon and Patterson in their seminal work on the Northern Ireland state[12], and epitomised by Pollock and Spender, deprecated what they saw as the 'begging bowl' aspect to Belfast-London relations which resulted from the 'step by step' line. This, after all, was not, in their view, in the spirit of the Government of Ireland Act nor calculated to meet with London's approval. A variation on the populist/ anti-populist theme might be to characterise the Pollock/Spender tendency as one of distancing Northern Ireland from the view of London; on the other hand, Craig and Andrews represented an intimate tendency concerning Northern Ireland's place in the UK scheme of things.

This internal Ulster unionist debate and its outcome should be recognised as a significant moment in the UK's devolution history. What Craig and his fellow advocates of 'step by step' were insisting upon was the right of Northern Ireland still to be part of the broader UK 'pool' when it came to the sharing of resources and assistance in troubled times. Craig was arguing that Northern Ireland still had the right to be treated in the manner of other parts of the UK that were economically depressed. For Craig, this insistence was a matter of citizenship rights and nothing to be ashamed of. Indeed, this episode can be linked to the much later debate in Scotland during the independence referendum of 2014 about the continuing value of the Union. It was the former Labour Prime Minister Gordon Brown's dramatic intervention late in the campaign around this very idea of the 'pooling and sharing of resources' as the hallmark of a socially progressive Union that is widely believed to have killed off the 'Yes' campaign's chances of success.[13]

Craig was content to regard Northern Ireland strictly as a subordinate unit within the UK, and as much as possible a regional part of the UK economy. He made no apology for edging Northern Ireland into a financially dependent position vis-à-vis London. As far as Craig was concerned, devolution was a 'convenience' adopted by the British government to help them out of their Irish difficulties: as such the British government would have to pay for it, and no UK citizen in Northern Ireland, particularly if they were 'loyal', should be asked to accept less than a universal British/UK entitlement to whatever state benefits were provided. In a way what developed after the setting up of Northern Ireland as a devolved entity was the enactment in a real political context of the unionist arguments against Dublin rule that were expressed throughout the period of political controversies over the prospect of Irish home rule in the late nineteenth and early twentieth century. In that period the lines of argument used were first, that the unit of democratic decision-making should be the UK as a whole; and then, increasingly, the assertion of democratic rights as the alternative 'nation' in Ireland. Mapping on to these respective positions were inclusive arguments on the one hand about the benefits of UK citizenship for all; and, on the other, exclusivist claims of 'rights' for Ulster based on distinguishing ethnic characteristics, particularly that of Protestantism.[14] Ulster unionists ultimately felt justified in accepting the settlement of 1921-22 (imperfect as it was from their point of view), because it recognised 'Ulster' as a distinctive entity with the democratic right to remain in the UK; however, in working this settlement they sought to be faithful to their principles about the benefits of the Union applying across the whole UK.

The Colywn changes – copper-fastened by further agreements in 1938 and 1946 – produced a situation in which the financial basis of Northern Ireland's devolved arrangements shifted from being 'revenue-based' to being 'expenditure-based', something duly noted by the Royal Commission on the Constitution (1968-73) – the Kilbrandon Commission as it became known – in its findings. This commission's majority report published in 1973 recommended devolved assemblies for Scotland and Wales, with 'expenditure-based' (block grant) financial arrangements.[15] The critical commentaries of nationalists and others on successive unionist governments' handling of devolved powers and of Northern Ireland being a 'drain' on the British public purse tend not to address the question of how the alternative course of Northern Ireland relying strictly on its own resources would have affected the working class people of all creeds. Such commentaries also fail to appreciate how the UK has worked as a broad multi-national construct to 'pool and share' and redistribute resources to meet social and economic challenges. Downbeat assessments of Northern Ireland in relation to various – usually economic – indicators tend to rest on stark comparisons with overall British averages. A fairer picture emerges when 'Britain' is dis-aggregated and Northern Ireland is compared to, say, Scotland, Wales, or the North of England. As a Stormont Cabinet Office memorandum, in relation to criticisms of Northern Ireland being a 'drain' put it: 'Our line of argument should ... be that Northern Ireland is taxed on the same scale as the rest of the United Kingdom. Its inhabitants pay according to their means like everyone else and their contribution goes into the pool which finances the whole amalgam of Imperial Services in which we are entitled to share. Some of these Services take the form of subsidies etc., but it is wrong to single them out as an offset to the contribution.'[16]

The Craig governments – and those of Andrews and Brooke following him – used the constitutional arrangements unionists had been given primarily to affirm Northern Ireland's place in the Union. Hence the emphasis on 'step by step' in relation to social services as a means of minimising the disjunctive effects of devolution, namely the detachment of Northern Ireland politically from Westminster (notwithstanding the twelve MPs that the Province returned to that parliament) and from the British party system – none of the mainstream British parties, Conservative, Labour, or Liberal, organised or stood for election in Northern Ireland. However, 'step by step' also made political sense within the narrow confines of Ulster's political world: it took the ground from beneath a party like the Northern Ireland Labour Party (NILP) and made credible the unionist appeals for Protestant working class support. Moreover, the Craig government's decision to scrap the proportional representation (PR) electoral system for local government elections (in 1922) and parliamentary elections (in 1929) and replace it with the Westminster 'first past the post' system damaged Labour more than any other rival party.[17]

The Unionist Party, with its own Labour wing (UULA) headed by Andrews, was able to claim, more or less plausibly,[18] that every benefit won for working people at Westminster would be passed on to the workers of Northern Ireland. Hence the party's ability to maintain its cross-class appeal, despite occasional challenges from the NILP and, indeed, from independent unionists who campaigned against the government often on the basis of class grievances.[19] 'Step by step', in addition, could be cited by Craig and the unionists to refute at least some of the allegations of discrimination against the Catholic minority in the light of the impartial administration of welfare benefits. This factor's significance was to be greatly heightened in the post Second World War era when Northern Ireland fully shared in the Labour government's welfare stare measures including family allowances and the establishment of a national health service. The right wing political orientation of so many Ulster unionists made celebration of these social achievements politically problematic – they were too 'socialistic' for the Ulster Unionist Party in effect to 'own'; yet their implementation and the way that they further tied Northern Ireland into the UK even in a period when the Province was a devolutionary 'outlier' cannot be overlooked.

Claims of ill treatment by the minority centred on matters such as housing and employment, and the application of the Special Powers Act of 1922 that was brought in to meet the threat to the fledgling state posed by the IRA. In relation to the latter, it needs to be kept in mind that there was what the historian Tim Wilson has called a 'policing vacuum' in the early months of Northern Ireland's existence[20]: The old Royal Irish Constabulary (RIC) was run down and disbanded at the end of 1921 and the Royal Ulster Constabulary (RUC) not set up until the middle of 1922. In between it was left to the Ulster Special Constabulary (USC) to act as the counter-insurgency force against the IRA. The USC had been set up by the British government in controversial circumstances in 1920. The IRA attempted to exploit the opportunity which these muddled transitional measures offered to de-stabilise and destroy the new state. Not for the last time they were prepared to play fast and loose with the lives and security of the Catholic community in doing so. The unionist government felt constrained to recruit more 'Specials' in this period with all the additional financial outlay this entailed, and at the risk of admitting unsuitable and improperly-vetted candidates.[21]

The unionist governments of the 1920s and 1930s might have pressed local authorities to provide better standards and fairer allocations regarding housing and jobs, but such was the reluctance of the government to come into confrontation with its own supporters and fellow party members who controlled most of the councils that the sectarian agendas of many of the latter were permitted to flourish, and the policy of keeping down rates strictly followed. As Patrick Buckland has observed, the Northern Ireland government was 'uncomfortably sandwiched between the Imperial government with its exacting Treasury and congeries of parsimonious local authorities.'[22] The relationships between different layers of government were allowed to grow stale: London was content (tight control of the budget aside) to turn a blind eye to Belfast which in turn allowed local authorities in some cases to indulge in partisan conduct and sectarian priorities. These, it might be said, constituted 'varieties of neglect' that underlay problems of communal division. Inter-governmental relations in the broadest sense was one of the weakest aspects of Northern Ireland's governing arrangements; it is, however, salutary to note that there has been much criticism of the way inter-governmental relations have been conducted in the new devolutionary age across the UK in the twenty-first century.[23]

Nationalist grievances around housing allocation persisted after the Second World War and indeed fuelled the civil rights agitation of the 1960s. There were certainly cases of egregious bias as unionists strove to maintain control over certain councils west of the Bann. However, there has recently been acknowledgement of the progressive achievements and scrupulously fair record of the Housing Trust which was set up by the unionist government in the post-war era.[24] Furthermore, the American political scientist, Richard Rose, in his landmark book *Governing without Consensus* (1971) provided a detailed analysis of housing allocation and found that the provision of local authority housing in Belfast and other regions in the east of the Province to be fair.[25] Rose's work, despite its scholarly credentials, is seldom referred to in the often sweeping denunciations of 'fifty years of misrule' that are routinely made about the unionists.

Similarly, allegations that are regularly made of discrimination in education are weakened if there is due acknowledgement of the Catholic Church's refusal to be involved in creating a new education system for the state and its insistence on running its own school sector without any state representation on its governing boards. Nevertheless, Catholic schools still had all their staff costs and fifty percent of their running costs paid by the state from the beginning, arrangements that compared favourably with religious-based schools in many other countries including the USA. Capital grants to Catholic schools were increased to 65 percent in the Education Act of 1947 which, in common with the rest of the UK, guaranteed secondary level education for all. The significance of this Act today may be said to lie in its relationship to the dominant narrative of unionist rule in Northern Ireland. Like the Housing Trust measure, the 1947 act subverts that narrative: it was socially progressive, fair, and beneficial to the Catholic minority. The Act was socially transformative in that it opened up opportunities for those in less well-off circumstances to attend third level institutions, and it has been well noted that the new generation of political leaders of the civil rights era from the Catholic community were those, like Bernadette Devlin, John Hume, and Austin Currie, who had taken such opportunities.[26] It is pertinent to note that education did not feature in the catalogue of issues highlighted by the Northern Ireland Civil Rights Association (NICRA) in the 1960s, a clear point of contrast with the case of the USA – to which the Northern Ireland civil rights controversies have often been glibly related – where the de-segregation of schools was a key issue.

The Catholic Church prioritised control of its schools above all else in the new Northern Ireland. They were prepared, in effect, to pass on the costs there were to their adherents. The inflexibility and sectarian outlook of Church leaders such as Bishop (later Cardinal) MacRory,[27] and the policy of abstentionism pursued by the elected nationalist politicians to the Northern Ireland parliament in the 1921-25 period, contributed to the detachment of the Catholic community from the task of shaping the new state. MacRory later expressed admiration for Italy under Mussolini, seemed to have no preference between the Allies and the Axis powers during the war, and advised the American ambassador to Ireland, David Gray, that peace should be made with Hitler in October 1941; he also enjoyed friendly relations with leading IRA personnel at a time when the IRA was hopeful of a Nazi victory which would somehow undo partition.[28] In April 1943 MacRory speculated on an Axis victory in relation to Ireland saying that he had hopes that 'they would see the folly and absurdity of dividing or partitioning a small island like ours, made one by God'.[29] Certain Protestant clerical figures have been roundly condemned by historians and commentators for contributing to communal tensions in Northern Ireland; it is perhaps long past time for MacRory to receive the full assessment of his leadership qualities, and, arguably, failings that is his due.

Balanced and nuanced assessments of how Northern Ireland was governed from 1921 until the suspension of the Stormont parliament in 1972 have become increasingly rare as a blanket narrative of 'unionist misrule' has taken hold. In a way this is not surprising given unionist mishandling of the civil rights challenge of the 1960s, their myopic refusal to reform the local government franchise along the same lines as the rest of the UK until it was, in effect, too late, and the leadership's tolerance of abuses at local government level over decades. Yet it is seldom acknowledged that nationalist and republican politics in Northern Ireland were geared overwhelmingly to the narrow goal of anti-partitionism until the mid-1960s. Nationalists as much as unionists insisted upon the constitutional question being the only one that really counted. In the late 1940s and early 50s the campaign of the Anti-Partition League (APL), conducted on a global scale rallying the Irish Catholic diaspora, drew together the strands of both constitutional and physical force nationalism, along with the Catholic Church whose ant-Communist Cold War agenda was eagerly accommodated.[30] When the APL ran out of steam, the IRA stepped in to launch a 'border campaign' lasting from 1956 till 1962. It has been well observed that this campaign did not receive much support from the Catholic community, at least in urban areas; yet it served nonetheless to keep sectarian tensions in the Province simmering, and, in effect, prevented liberal elements within unionism from gaining sufficient support for the reforms that were urgently needed.[31] It can hardly be wondered at that Protestant and unionist perceptions of a continuing IRA threat were still very much alive a handful of years later to shape their view of the street politics of the civil rights movement. The unionist 'siege mentality' tends to be factored into analyses of Northern Ireland's history without due reference to the besiegers. Ultimately, it was a combination of this mentality with a certain arrogance that assumed this was 'our place to govern as we wish' that prevented the fulfilment of an inclusivist unionist programme; it prevented the extension of 'step by step' into the crucial areas of electoral practices (particularly the local government franchise and the drawing of boundaries), and of law and order. The 'step by step' approach should have been taken beyond those areas of social policy discussed above where the unionist record was a defensible one. Also, it was the very success of Ulster unionism in maintaining internal unity around the constitutional question which stymied the development of the kind of effective opposition that would have led to a healthier politics. Devolution in this sense was seriously harmed, and there are some suggestive parallels to be drawn in this respect with the current arrangements in Northern Ireland.

It is interesting to note that investigations of the workings of devolution in Northern Ireland prior to the outbreak of the Troubles generally provided measured evaluations about the strengths and weaknesses of the arrangements; and some studies concluded favourably.[32] The editor of a substantial collection of academic essays published in 1955 challenged the allegation that Northern Ireland was uniquely 'subsidised' while calling for Stormont to act more independently and for inter-governmental relations to be re-organised.[33] In 1968, just as civil unrest was brewing, the Labour MP and constitutional scholar John P. Mackintosh used the Northern Ireland case to support his call for broader de-centralisation in the UK, and to refute the anti-devolution argument that it would lead inevitably to separation.[34] Mackintosh anticipated that Scotland, like Northern Ireland, would seek no deviation from British standards of welfare and social security even with devolution. Significantly, in the Report of the Kilbrandon Commission in 1973 there was the following verdict on the Northern Ireland precedent: 'The general conclusion we reach is that, despite the great difference between the theory of home rule and its practical application, and despite the special difficulties inherent in the Northern Ireland situation, in many fields, notably those that were unaffected, or at least not dominated, by the community problem – the home rule experiment had considerable success.'[35] Despite the gathering condemnations of the Stormont system against the background of horrendous political violence in the early 1970s, the Royal Commission reported that the people of Northern Ireland (from across the community) they had consulted believed that 'substantial advantages' had been derived from the experiment.[36]

It is indeed important to write Northern Ireland properly into the constitutional and political history of the UK, and not compartmentalise it, in a facile way, as 'a place apart'.[37] This is especially so in the context of the contemporary UK with devolved institutions in Scotland, Wales, and Northern Ireland, and talk of 'devolution deals' for parts of England. The Northern Ireland example, for all the problems encountered during the 1921-72 period, highlighted the UK's internal diversity – some have said 'de facto federalist' character[38] – and the series of historic unions that underpinned it.[39] It serves as a reminder that devolution and constitutional change has a long, complex, and fascinating history, and did not just appear magically at the end of the twentieth century.

Notes

1.   Among many informative histories see A. Jackson, *Home Rule: An Irish History* (London: Allen Lane, 2003); and A. O'Day, *Irish Home Rule 1867-1921* (Manchester: Manchester University Press, 1998).

2.   See V. Bogdanor, *Devolution in the United Kingdom* (Oxford: Oxford University Press, 1979), ch.3.

3.   J. Kendle, *Walter Long, Ireland and the Union, 1905-20* (Dublin: Gill and Macmillan, 1992).

4.   See A. Jackson, *Judging Redmond and Carson* (Dublin: RIA, 2018), pp. 147-149.

5.   See D. Ferriter, *The Border* (London: Profile Books, 2019) for a recent scholarly account.

6.   Quoted in G. Walker, *A History of the Ulster Unionist Party* (Manchester: Manchester University Press, 2004), p.59; for Lord Londonderry's 'federal' outlook see I. Kershaw, *Making Friends with Hitler: Lord Londonderry and Britain's Road to War* (Penguin, 2005), pp. 14-15.

7.   See Walker, *History*, p. 223.

8.   See H. Calvert, *Constitutional Law in Northern Ireland* (London: Stevens, 1968); also discussion in G. Walker, 'Scotland, Northern Ireland and Devolution, 1945-79', *Journal of British Studies* 49, 1, 2010, pp. 117-142.

9.   See P. Buckland, *The Factory of Grievances* (Dublin: Gill and Macmillan, 1979); Bogdanor, *Devolution*, ch.3.

10.   See M. Mulholland, *Terence O'Neill* (Dublin: UCD Press, 2013), ch.2.

11.   See B. Follis, *A State under Siege: the Establishment of Northern Ireland* (Oxford: Oxford University Press, 1995), ch. 6 for a fully detailed and authoritative account of these changes.

12.   P. Bew, P. Gibbon and H. Patterson, *The State in Northern Ireland* (Manchester: Manchester University Press, 1979).

13.   See Brown's case for the Union as discussed in detail in his *My Scotland Our Britain* (London: Simon Schuster, 2014); for the 2014 campaign see P. Geoghegan, *The People's Referendum* (Edinburgh: Luath Press, 2015); also G. Walker, *The Labour Party in Scotland: Religion, the Union, and the Irish Dimension* (Palgrave, 2016), ch.3.

14.   Both forms of argument can be found in the landmark collection of Unionist essays in S. Rosenbaum (ed.), *Against Home Rule* (London, 1912).

15.   The Royal Commission on the Constitution 1969-1973, Cmnd. 5460, henceforth 'Kilbrandon Report'.

16.   PRONI, D3084/I/B/2/3. See discussion in G. Walker, 'Scotland, Northern Ireland, and Devolution: Past and Present', *Contemporary British History* 24, 2, 2010, pp. 235-256.

[17] See C.J.V. Loughlin, *Labour and the Politics of Disloyalty in Belfast, 1921-39* (Palgrave, 2018), ch.3 for a recent scholarly investigation.

[18] See Loughlin, *Labour*, pp. 108-114 for discussion of the case of the Trades Disputes Act.

[19] See Walker, *History*, pp. 70-75.

[20] T. Wilson, '"The most terrible assassination that has yet stained the name of Belfast": the McMahon murders in context', *Irish Historical Studies* 37, 145, 2010, pp. 83-106.

[21] Wilson's forensic work (see previous endnote) calls into question assumptions that murders carried out by Loyalists have historically been motivated by simple anti-Catholic hatred while murders carried out by the IRA have been motivated purely by political considerations.

[22] P. Buckland, *James Craig* (Dublin: Gill and Macmillan, 1980), p.90.

[23] See for example, A. Trench, 'The Practice of Multi-Level Government', in A. Trench (ed.), *The State of the Nations 2008* (Exeter: Imprint Academic, 2008).

[24] M. Elliott, *Hearthlands* (Belfast: Blackstaff Press, 2017); see also H. Patterson and E. Kaufmann, *Unionism and Orangeism since 1945* (Manchester: Manchester University Press, 2007), especially chs. 1 and 2.

[25] R. Rose, *Governing Without Consensus: An Irish Perspective* (Boston: Beacon Press, 1971), pp. 291-296.

[26] Elliot, *Hearthlands*; K. Bloomfield, *A Tragedy of Errors* (Liverpool: Liverpool University Press, 2007), p. 168.

[27] See Ferriter, *The Border*, p.22.

[28] O. Rafferty, *Violence, Politics and Catholicism in Ireland* (Dublin: Irish Academic Press, 2016), pp. 167-172.

[29] Quoted in Rafferty, *Violence*, p. 172.

[30] See discussion in Walker, *History*, pp. 100-104.

[31] See Patterson and Kaufmann, *Unionism*, pp.

[32] See discussion of this literature in Walker, 'Scotland, Northern Ireland and Devolution'.

[33] T. Wilson (ed.), *Ulster Under Home Rule* (Oxford: Oxford University Press, 1955).

[34] J. P. Mackintosh, *The Devolution of Power* (Penguin, 1968).

[35] Kilbrandon Report, p.54; see also J. Oliver, 'The Stormont Administration', in B. Barton and P. Roche (eds.), *The Northern Ireland Question: Myth and Reality* (Aldershot: Avebury, 1991)

36 Quoted in Oliver, 'Stormont Administration'.

37 See G. Walker, '"A Place Apart"? the interventions of John P. Mackintosh and Bernard Crick on Northern Ireland', *Contemporary British History* 31, 4, 2017, pp. 593-610.

38 Ibid. re Crick's writings on the UK as being informally federated.

39 See J. Mitchell, *Devolution in the UK* (Manchester: Manchester University Press, 2009), ch. 1; also I. McLean and A. MacMillan, *State of the Union* (Oxford: Oxford University Press, 2005). It should be stressed that Scotland's 'administrative devolution' arrangements from the establishment of the Scottish Office in 1885 through to the coming of legislative devolution in 1999, form another distinctive chapter in the UK's constitutional history – see Mitchell, *Devolution*, ch.2.

3

Terrorism and Irish nationalism

Patrick J. Roche

Introduction

Thirty years of conflict in Northern Ireland produced an extensive literature but virtually no substantive critical examination of Irish nationalism.
This uncritical stance was shared by both the Conservative and Labour
parties and shaped their policies on Northern Ireland. For example, the
Conservative government under John Major conducted the Brooke/
Mayhew talks[1] on the understanding that nationalism and unionism are of
'equal validity' or 'equal legitimacy'.[2] The implication of this understanding of 'equal validity' was that the then Conservative government was not
in principle committed to the constitutional and territorial integrity of the
United Kingdom. This implication was stated with indisputable clarity in
the 1993 *Downing Street Declaration*: the British government has 'no self-
ish strategic or economic interest in Northern Ireland'.[3] The Labour Party
since at least 1987 has gone beyond the neutrality of the 'equal validity'
thesis to a commitment to a coercive inducement of unionists consent
to Irish unity. This was stated with equal clarity in the 1988 Labour Party
policy document, *Towards a United Ireland* which contains the contradic-
tory statement that 'consent must by definition be freely given' but ' no
group [the obvious reference is to unionists] … can be allowed to veto
advance in that direction' – that is 'towards gaining a united Ireland'.[4] The
policy orientation of the two major British political parties was, therefore, based on the acceptance of the intellectual coherence and practical
(particularly economic) feasibility of the imperatives of Irish nationalism.

One nation in Ireland

That raises a fundamental question which has received too little attention. How coherent and feasible[5] is the nationalist case for Irish unity? The nationalist case for Irish unity and the claimed 'injustice' of Partition are fundamentally based on the claim that the inhabitants of the island of Ireland constitute a single nation. Constitutional nationalists and self-styled 'republicans' (IRA/Sinn Fein) are committed to the foundational belief that (to quote Garrett Fitzgerald) 'history has created in the island of Ireland one nation'.[6] Charles J. Haughey's advocacy of a politically united Ireland derived from the same belief: 'Ireland is an ancient nation whose roots and culture go back into the mists of time ... a nation that embraces all the people of Ireland'.[7] The core ideological commitment of all Irish nationalists was summarised by Gerry Adams in *The Politics of Irish Freedom* in which Adams claimed that Ireland is 'historically, culturally and geographically one single unit'.[8]

The ideological imperatives of Irish nationalism and the nationalist understanding of unionism are rooted in the 'one nation' claim. 'Territorial integrity' and 'self-determination' or 'self-government' are the core political imperatives of Irish nationalism. There is no diversity between republicans and constitutional nationalists on the validity of these claims and in particular on the identification of the island of Ireland as 'by geography and history' (to quote Garrett Fitzgerald) the 'national territory'.[9] The position of Fitzgerald (representative of the thinking of all contemporary Irish nationalists) is the root of what Clare O'Halloran in *Partition and the Limits of Irish Nationalism*[10] has described as the 'anachronistic' and 'tattered remnants' of an irredentism that has been central to Irish nationalism since Partition – even if since 1998 removed from the Irish constitution (Bunreach na hEireann). The claimed right of 'self-government' for the inhabitants of the island of Ireland is based on two propositions: (1) the inhabitants of the island of Ireland constitute a single nation and (2) nations have a right of self-determination. This position was clearly articulated by Haughey in *The Spirit of the Nation*: 'the Irish people [the reference is to the 'one nation'] have certain rights that belong to all nations, in particular the right to territorial integrity and self-determination'.[11]

Nationalist understanding of unionism and Partition

The one nation doctrine also determines the nationalist understanding of unionism and Partition. Nationalist discourse, particularly since the late 1970s, has emphasised the understanding of unionism as a 'tradition' within the Irish nation. This understanding of unionism as a 'tradition' within the claimed Irish nation originated with John Hume and was central to the discourse of the so-called peace process prior to the signing of the Belfast Agreement in 1998. The New Ireland Forum (1983-84) represented the thinking of constitutional nationalists. The Forum's understanding of unionism was accurately summarised by Dick Spring, leader of the Labour Party (1982-1997) in the Republic: 'The New Ireland Forum recognised the Irish nation as consisting of at least two traditions each with its own distinct cultural and political aspirations ... But are they not, both nationalist and unionist, members of the Irish nation.'[12] Spring's rhetorical question ('are they not both nationalist and unionist members of the Irish nation') is a textbook example of the logical fallacy of *petitio principii* or 'begging the question' – an instance of the logical deficiency of much nationalist argument.

The implication for nationalists of the understanding of unionism as a 'tradition' within the claimed single Irish nation is that unionism is a national minority viewpoint: Adams claimed in the *Politics of Irish Freedom* and *A Pathway to Peace* that 'loyalists are Irish' and consequently are a 'national minority'.[13] This is the basis of the nationalist claim that Partition is 'undemocratic' and 'artificial' – that is, Partition was not required by any legitimizing socio-political reality in Ireland. Garrett Fitzgerald underpinned the logic of this nationalist position (common to both republicans and constitutional nationalists) by advancing the extreme thesis that: 'Partition divided Irishmen rather than being caused by pre-existing division'.[14] The immediate political inference is that Partition is a denial of both 'territorial integrity' and the right of 'self government' and consequently an injustice against the 'one nation'.

The persistence of the 'failure' of unionists to politically regard themselves as part of an Irish nation is understood by constitutional nationalists and republicans to be the consequence of the British 'imposition' of Partition. The logic of this understanding is that (to quote Adams) 'unionism is a child of the British connection'[15] – an understanding of the genesis of unionism that carries (and is intended to carry) the connotation that unionism is an infantile and irrational politics and that the dependence of unionism on the 'British connection' is such that unionism as a political commitment would cease to exist in the context of Irish unity.[16] The political claims of unionists are understood from this perspective to express a 'false consciousness' – that is, a failure on the part of unionists as a minority of the claimed Irish nation to accept their real or authentic national and political identity. The nationalist understanding of what they perceive to be unionist 'false consciousness' (sustained by the 'British presence') is variously explained in nationalist anti-unionist polemic. For example, Adams in *Pathway to Peace* claimed that unionism and unionist self-differentiation from the Irish nation is rooted in the 'system of political, social and economic privilege' which makes unionists (according to Adams) the beneficiaries of Partition.[17]

The 1984 *Forum Report* in effect (prior to Adams) developed the logic of the 'child simile' – the understanding of unionism as rooted in irrationality. The emphasis in the *Forum Report* was on a pejorative psychology of unionists based, as pointed out by Clare O'Halloran, on an established nationalist stereotype of unionists – the 'fearful northern Protestant'.[18] The *Forum Report* presented unionism as essentially irrational – the psychological product of an amalgam of 'fears' and 'concerns' rooted in misrepresentations of 'reality' resulting in a failure on the part of unionists to perceive their true national identity and their consequent irrational (in nationalist understanding) opposition to the nationalist goal of 'Irish unity'.[19] The *Forum Report's* nationalist stereotypical understanding of unionism in fact represented a failure by Irish nationalists to undertake what D. George Boyce has referred to as 'the deep and possibly agonizing reappraisal of northern unionism and Irish nationalism in general required for a resolution of the Irish question'.[20]

This stereotypical denigration of unionists and unionism was reinforced by a morally pejorative presentation of unionism by historians engaged in anti-unionist polemic. For example, Joseph Lee in *Ireland: Politics and Society* grounded the unionist resistance to unification in a '*Herrenvolk* mentality'[21] – unionism, for Lee, is the political expression of nothing more commendable than a 'racial imperative'.[22] David Fitzpatrick in a contribution to *The Oxford History of Ireland* extended this racist stereotype to incorporate within unionism something like a latent genocidal intent: 'the rulers [the reference is to the post-1920 unionist leaders] regarded Catholics rather as Joshua and the chosen people regarded the unfortunate inhabitants of Jericho'.[23] Tim Pat Coogan in *Disillusioned Decades: Ireland 1966-87* plumbed the depths of polemic absurdity – he detected at the core of unionism an 'anti-feminism' suggestive of a 'repressed homosexuality'.[24] For these writers unionism is comprehensible by something akin to a collective psychoanalysis – a 'peeling of the attitudinal onion skins of seemingly mild mannered Protestant farmers' (to quote Coogan[25]) to disclose the disordered psychic roots of unionism. Apart from the issue of fact, the presentation of unionism in terms of an innate supremacist /racist mentality is a retreat from historical understanding by, in the examples considered, professional historians.[26] Lee and Fitzpatrick exemplify a failure to liberate the understanding of unionism and the politics of Northern Ireland from nationalist mythology and stereotype despite some decades of 'historical revisionism' in Ireland.

The retreat from historical understanding in the stereotypical and 'supremacist' presentations of unionism and unionists is rooted in a form of de-contextualized historiography in which hostility towards unionism precludes an empathetic examination of the historical context in which unionists had to consolidate their legitimate right to remain within the Union against a background of: bad faith shown by Westminster towards the 1920 Government of Ireland Act; the implacable hostility of Collins' provisional government to Northern Ireland; recurrent IRA terrorism in Northern Ireland after 1920; the active hopes of nationalists until 1925 that the revision of the boundary would prove fatal for Northern Ireland; the self-exclusion of northern nationalists from the devolved institutions of government established after 1921 and the rise to power of de Valera in 1932 culminating in the emergence of an anti-British, Catholic and (officially) Gaelic state. D. George Boyce has emphasized in *Nationalism in Ireland* that 'the failure to acknowledge the sustained Republican assaults on Northern Ireland in the early years of the state is at the root of the unwillingness of many modern commentators to allow that Ulster Unionists had much to fear from Irish nationalists'.[27]

The nationalist understanding of unionism and Partition is an inversion of historical reality rooted in the construction of what Clare O'Halloran has called 'artificial realities' required by nationalists to cope with the actual reality of Partition: 'nationalists in effect created an artificial northern landscape ... in an effort to minimize the unpalatable realities ... which were in conflict with their ideology'.[28] The Fitzgerald thesis (central to nationalist 'one nation' ideology) that 'Partition divided Irishmen rather than being caused by pre-existing division' is a classic example of nationalist historical inversion. Contrary to Fitzgerald, Partition was a recognition of pre-existing division: 'Partition was in fact no deep laid plot ... to divide Irishmen ... It was simply a recognition of reality'[29] – that is, a recognition of a reality that is an ideological imperative for Irish nationalists to deny. Irish nationalism is, with respect to its foundational ideological imperatives, a retreat from historical reality and consequently is an ideology of self-deception.[30] The presentation in nationalist polemic of the genesis of Partition and the roots of unionism is an exemplification of Renan's dictum that 'getting its history wrong is part of being a nation'.[31] The retreat from historical understanding in the Irish nationalist presentation of unionism and Partition facilitates a nationalist polemic, masquerading as history, which is intended to denigrate unionism as not only irrational but immoral and to present Partition as an injustice against a claimed Irish nation. The objective of this denigration of unionism is to ensure that the core demands of unionists for the maintenance of the Union are, as in the *Forum Report*, excluded from the category of 'legitimate right'.[32]

Unionist consent

These considerations raise the issue of the nationalist understanding of unionist consent. The total rejection of the legitimacy of unionist opposition to Irish unity is an absolute requirement of the imperatives of Irish nationalism – specifically of the core 'one nation' claim . Unionists are (for nationalists) a 'minority' within the Irish nation and therefore have no legitimate or *de jure* right to veto the right of 'self-determination' or self-government of the Irish nation. Hume and Adams agreed precisely on this point during the 1988 Sinn Fein/SDLP talks. However, nationalists are sufficiently realistic to concede that unionists have a *de facto* or what Hume referred to as a 'natural' veto on Irish unity. Hume in the 1988 talks with Adams drew attention to what he regarded as the 'harsh' reality of an actual or *de facto* unionist veto: 'the harsh reality is that unionists have a natural veto since their agreement is essential if unity is to be achieved'.[33] The SDLP recognition of a *de facto* unionist veto was shared by Sinn Fein. For example, Adams in *Pathway to Peace* conceded (in terms almost identical with section 5.8 of the 1984 constitutional nationalist *Forum Report*) that 'the consent of the northern Protestants is desirable' for constitutional arrangements to replace Partition.[34] The recognition from the late 1980s by republicans of a *de facto* unionist veto was misunderstood by even as severe a critic of the IRA as Cardinal Daly who, in a December 1993 House of Commons speech to Catholic parliamentarians, presented the Adams pronouncements as a 'new departure' of 'immense significance' which was due to the fact (claimed by the Cardinal) that the republican movement had 'embraced the desire for peace'.[35]

The problem with this presentation of change within the Republican movement (apart from the fact that it did not easily fit with the 23 October 1993 IRA Shankill bomb that killed nine innocent victims including two children a few weeks before the Cardinal's address) is that it presupposes that there was something new and significant in the recognition by republicans of a *de facto* unionist veto on unification and consequently on the politically pragmatic need to obtain unionist consent.[36] There has never been in nationalist understanding any contradiction between the acceptance of the pragmatic need for unionist consent to unification and the denial of a *de jure* unionist right of veto over constitutional change in Ireland. Adams stated the nationalist position on the issue of unionist veto and unionist consent at the 1994 Sinn Fein Ard Fheis: 'republicans have .. consistently demanded an end to the unionist veto, but we acknowledge that the consent and agreement of all sections of our people is necessary and essential in the building of an agreed and stable Ireland'.[37]

How is this unionist consent to be obtained? Nationalists operate with the notion of induced consent aimed at the liberation of unionists from what at the 1993 SDLP conference Hume referred to as the unionist 'classic Afrikaner mind-set' of 'holding all power in their own hands and excluding everyone else'.[38] For nationalists the key to this liberation of unionists was for the British government to end what they understood to be the unionist veto on government policy. For example, Hume in a 1989 contribution to the *London Review of Books* argued that the ending of 'the unjust unionist veto [here Hume is denying the legitimacy of the unionist veto while recognising its actual existence] on British policy' would 'break through the vicious circle which has paralysed all political development'[39] The nationalist argument presented by Hume was that the British acceptance of a unionist veto on unification, or on institutional developments compatible with the goal of unification, was a self-imposed immobilisation of British policy.

The implication of this understanding is that the end of the unionist veto (which exists only so long as it is accepted by Britain) is the necessary condition of both national self-determination (that is, the self-determination/self-government of the claimed Irish nation) and the effective inducement of unionists to accept the political unification of Ireland. The key to the inducement of unionist consent for both constitutional nationalists and Sinn Fein/IRA was to shift British policy from neutrality on the issue of unification to active support for the nationalist goal. The nationalist argument was that once the policy shift is clearly presented to unionists they will come to accept the inevitability of Irish unity and negotiate their status within the 'new Ireland'.[40]

The consideration of the nationalist notion of 'induced consent' raises an interesting issue: the compatibility of the traditional nationalist notion of 'induced consent' and the 'consent principle' in the 1998 *Belfast Agreement*. The *Belfast Agreement* 'recognises' that 'it is for the people of the island of Ireland alone ... to exercise their right of self-determination on the basis of consent ... to bring about a united Ireland ... accepting that this right must be achieved and exercised with and subject to the agreement and consent of a majority of the people of Northern Ireland'[41]. This is the consent principle in the *Belfast Agreement* which is obviously entirely compatible with the 'inducement' of unionist consent to the political unification of Ireland. The EU objective in the post 2016 Brexit negotiations was significantly directed to prevent a Brexit that would establish the precedent of a UK 'easy exit' perceived by the EU to be a threat to the progress and consolidation of the 'EU project' of European economic unification and political federation. But in the case of Ireland the 'old imperative' of Irish unity meant that the Irish (backed by the EU bureaucrats) demanded the 'backstop' that Northern Ireland remain within the EU single market/customs union post Brexit – that is, they demanded the economic breakup of the UK single market. The ideological calculation was that the economic breakup of the UK single market would in time effectively break the Union and consequently it is entirely rational to construe the negotiations on the 'backstop' (central to the negotiation of the 2019 Brexit withdrawal agreement) as an attempt on the part of the Irish leadership to use the context of Brexit to lay what they perceived would be the economic base for the subsequent induce-ment of unionist consent to Irish unity.

Accommodation of unionists in the 'new Ireland'

The stereotypical understanding of unionists and unionism demanded by the imperatives of Irish nationalism means that for Irish nationalists the accommodation of unionists within the political context of 'Irish unity' is not fundamentally problematic. Garrett Fitzgerald was a prominent example of this mode of nationalist understanding. Fitzgerald combined a rigid commitment to the 'one nation' claim central to Irish nationalism with a facile understanding of what would be required to accommodate unionists within his 'new Ireland'. The complete quotation from *Towards a New Ireland* stating Fitzgerald's 'one nation' claim is: 'history has created on the island of Ireland one nation with several different cultures'.[42] The import of this ideologically determined understanding is that unionism is reduced to nothing other than a cultural differentiation within the claimed 'one nation'. But this reductionist and apolitical understanding of the nature of unionism entails that unionists could be accommodated within Fitzgerald's envisaged 'New Ireland' with some unspecified adaptation to whatever (in his understanding) differentiated unionist 'culture' without threat to the fundamental 'one nation' base of Irish nationalist ideology.

Republicans and constitutional nationalists share an apolitical understanding of unionism as merely a cultural differentiation within the claimed Irish nation – 'a set of values comprising the Protestant ethos'.[43] For example, Adams suggested in *Pathway to Peace* that 'consti-tutional guarantees for those presently constituted as loyalists would be sufficient'.[44] Nothing more would be required other than a recognition of 'present day social reality' which would include 'provision for family planning and the right to civil divorce'.[45] The contemporary secularization of the Republic means that social policy has moved well beyond the provisions that Adams in 1988 suggested would be adequate to accommodate unionists in a politically united Ireland but without any negative impact on the unionist commitment to the Union. The 1984 *New Ireland Forum Report* claimed that in the context of a unitary Irish state a 'redefined relationship between Britain and Ireland would take account of the unionist sense of Britishness' and 'provide expression for the long established connection which unionists have with Britain'.[46] Adams' reference to 'those presently (meaning 'for the time being') constituted as loyalists' (here used as a pejorative term for 'unionists') and the *Forum Report* reduction of unionism to a 'sense of Britishness' (where the word 'sense' is used to connote a 'more or less indefinite or vague consciousness') both demonstrate a shallow reductionist and dismissive understanding of the nature of unionism and the commitment of unionists to the Union.

The ideological determination of the Irish nationalist understanding of unionism and what would be required to accommodate unionists in a 'united Ireland' is radically divorced from political reality. Irish nationalists have failed to grasp that the entire mode of nationalist argument lacks authority for unionists. Traditional Irish nationalism is a form of what is referred to in the literature on nationalism as 'ethnic nationalism' in which the 'Irish nation ' of nationalist political mythology is differentiated in terms of ethnicity with the stress on common descent (the Gael) and the myth of an historic cultural unity extending over many centuries before St Patrick to the time of Partition.[47] Ulster unionists do not perceive themselves to be some form of cultural differentiation within an Irish 'ethnic' nation and neither do they perceive themselves to be a distinct nation. Unionist self-perception is properly understood in terms of a political identity constituted by a shared allegiance to the Union. The self-identity of Ulster unionists was given concise expression in the 1912 *Ulster Covenant* in terms of a deep-rooted commitment to the 'cherished position of equal citizenship within the United Kingdom'. Unionist political identity is 'citizenship based' and the word 'cherished' displays the deep emotive roots of Ulster unionism which ground loyalty and patriotism (without which on the part of its citizens no state could long survive) and gives permanence to the unionist commitment to the Union.

The ideological blindness of Irish nationalists to the deep-rooted permanence of the unionist commitment to the Union means, as Terence Brown pointed out in *Ireland: A Social and Cultural History*, that from a nationalist perspective 'unionists can be accommodated in every way except one which essentially defines them'.[48] Clare O'Halloran in *Partition and the Limits of Irish Nationalism* made essentially the same point directed towards the *Forum Report* in which the 'characteristics of unionist "identity"' were defined as strictly cultural in the narrowest sense and excluded any right to choose to remain part of the United Kingdom'.[49] Nationalists fail to take account of the fact that 'the ending of the constitutional relationship between Northern Ireland and the rest of the United Kingdom would remove any substance from unionism as a political ideology'[50] – in short the political substance of unionism cannot in principle be accommodated within the nationalist imperative of 'Irish unity'.

Persuasion through the barrel of a gun

Unionist commitment to the Union is understood by nationalists as nothing more commendable than an 'intransigence' immune to rational persuasion and consequently the necessity of a coercive use of force against unionists is deeply ingrained in the nationalist political psyche. The option and practicality of the coercion of unionists is latent both in the *Forum Report's* characterization of British policy as 'backing down' in the face of unionist opposition to Irish home rule from 1912[51]and in Hume's sectarian recommendation to 'lance the Protestant boil' in response to unionist opposition to the Anglo-Irish Agreement.[52] The statement of the need to 'lance the Protestant boil' was not an isolated or uncharacteristic comment. Hume developed the linguistic façade of a 'post nationalist'[53] rhetoric which (*inter alia*) obscured a deep political (if not indeed personal) antipathy to unionists and unionism. In a *Crane Bag* interview (to cite but one example) Hume claimed that unionists are 'a petty people' possessed of a 'prejudice' equivalent to the 'whites' in 'Mississippi' and 'one of the most rightwing forces in Europe – nobody else would stand for them , anywhere' and responsible (not the IRA) for 'the present state of things in the North'.[54] Barry White records in *John Hume: Statesman of the Troubles* that Hume disagreed with Faulkner on the need to talk to the leaders of the May 1974 Ulster Workers strike. Hume's response to Faulkner's suggestion was 'I'll sit here until there is shit flowing up Royal Avenue … and then we will see who wins'.[55] These were not the words of a statesman open to the political accommodation of unionists – in addition to linguistic obscenity Hume was in effect demanding a coercive use of force against unionist opposition to the Sunningdale Agreement which is not at all surprising given Hume's derogatory understanding of unionism.

The ingrained notion of the legitimacy of a coercive use of force against unionists found extreme expression in the terrorism of the IRA from 1969-99 that resulted in the death of 3,352 people and the injury (in a great number of cases utterly horrific) of 48,029 people. The intensity of the killing can be displayed by a simple arithmetic calculation. Terrorism on the scale in which it occurred in Northern Ireland would have resulted in approximately 126,000 killed and 1.8 million injured in the UK and approximately 600,000 killed and 8.7 million injured in the US. But statistics cannot convey the full horror and the depth of moral barbarity of the terrorist onslaught against the citizens of Northern Ireland. The book, *Lost Lives*, contains the 'stories of the men, women and children who died as a result of the Northern Ireland troubles' to quote the sub-title of the book.[56] The book is not of course confined to the activity of the IRA but it contains a record of the literally horrific and calculated barbarity of IRA terrorism exemplified by the Bloody Friday bombing of Belfast on 21 July 1972[57] combined with the deep tragedy of the lost and broken lives of the murdered and injured and the pain and grief of those who loved them. The 'Claudy bomb' of 31 July 1972 killed nine people including two children – a sixteen year old boy and a nine year old girl. The bombing of Claudy displayed the calculated indifference of the IRA even to the death of a child. The nine year old girl was Kathryn Eakin who was cleaning the window of her parent's shop when the bomb went off. Her mother saw the bomber leave the car beside the shop:

> When he stepped out of that car he saw Kathryn standing at that window … He should have shouted at her. But he didn't, he just walked away.[58]

In 1990 the IRA developed a new tactic of terror – the use of the 'human bomb' deployed using a Londonderry Roman Catholic civilian, Patrick Gillespie to drive (under threat to his family) a primed bomb to a local Donegal border checkpoint where the IRA detonated the bomb killing Gillespie and five soldiers at the checkpoint. The Roman Catholic bishop Edward Daly, at Patrick Gillespie's funeral, described this IRA 'human bomb' tactic as crossing a 'new threshold of evil'.[59] The concrete detail of IRA terrorism in *Lost Lives* discloses the dimensions of evil that marked the IRA's three decades of terrorism in Northern Ireland.[60] The 'long war' of IRA terrorism displayed a mindset (matched by the so-called 'loyalist' terror gangs) virtually impossible for anyone possessed of a humane and moral sensibility to penetrate. The actions of the IRA present a challenge to our capacity to grasp the depth of the human potential for evil and in so doing present an instance of the 'enigma of evil'.

Context and ideology of IRA terrorism

The statistics of deaths due to terrorism in Northern Ireland from 1969-99 show that the republican terror groups (chiefly the IRA) associated with Irish nationalism were responsible for 2,139 deaths or approximately 60 per cent of the total. These statistics strongly indicate that terrorism in Northern Ireland after 1969 was driven by the Irish republican movement and in particular by the IRA.[61] That raises two crucial questions: (1) what was the context in which the IRA became operative in Northern Ireland from 1969 and (2) what 'ideological drive ' sustained the IRA terrorism for a period of three decades? The answer to the first question is that the Northern Ireland civil rights movement acted as a catalyst for unionist/nationalist polarization in Northern Ireland from the mid-1960s. Nationalists from the mid-1960s presented Northern Ireland as a 'pariah state' on a moral par with South Africa or Nazi Germany.[62] The language and imagery of the US civil rights movement was used by the civil rights agitators to give the appearance of substance to the entirely false claim of a 'nationalist nightmare' in Northern Ireland. The propaganda identification of Northern Ireland with oppression in the US and apartheid South Africa was directed to undermine the political and moral case for Partition[63] – hence the absurdity of the claim by the *Sunday Times* Insight team in *Ulster* that 'the new-look IRA [involved in the Northern Ireland civil rights movement] was prepared *de facto* to recognize Partition and the separate existence of Northern Ireland'.[64]

The ultimate *realpolitik* of nationalist involvement in the civil rights movement was perceptively grasped by Steve Bruce in *God Save Ulster*: 'a large part of the movement was always ultimately interested in dismantling Northern Ireland'.[65] This understanding was substantiated by Christopher Hewitt in his contribution to *The Northern Ireland Question: Myth and Reality*: nationalists involved in the civil rights movement 'were not implicitly accepting Partition by demanding civil rights but instead confident that this was the strategy which would end Partition'.[66] The core politics of the People's Democracy was that 'civil rights' could only be achieved within the context of an all-Ireland socialist republic and not without violence. Eamonn McCann in *War and an Irish Town* stated that the 'conscious if unspoken strategy' of radical civil rights activists in Londonderry was 'to provoke the police into over-reaction and thus spark off mass reaction against the authorities'.[67]

The strategy was more than successful – the civil rights movement was the catalyst for the emergence of the Provisional IRA but not without assistance from elements within the Lynch government in the Republic. Conor Cruise O'Brien set out the role of the Fianna Fail party in establishing the Provisional IRA in 1969 in his introduction to Martin Dillon's book, *The Dirty War*:

> The deal that launched the Provos was essentially this: certain members of the Lynch government approached those leading members of the IRA who were known to be disgusted with the Marxist leadership, on both nationalist and Catholic grounds, and also on operational grounds. These leaders – who were to become leaders of the Provisional IRA – were offered money, arms and general support if they would abjure operations outside Northern Ireland. The Provisional leaders to be agreed ... thus the Provos were born and the dirty war began.[68]

What was the 'ideological drive' that sustained IRA terrorism for three decades? The answer to that question goes to the heart of the ideology of Irish nationalism. The three decades of IRA terrorism was driven and ideologically sustained by a deep-rooted sense of 'historic grievance' and perceived injustice within the Irish nationalist psyche significantly nurtured by a self-segregated system of education in Northern Ireland.[69] This nationalist sense of grievance may be understood to be an expression of what Liam Kennedy in *Colonialism, Religion and Nationalism in Ireland* has described as a 'syndrome of attitudes that might be summed up in the acronym MOPE, that is, the most oppressed people ever'.[70] Kennedy's location of a MOPE syndrome at the heart of Irish nationalism is shared by a number of leading Irish historians – for example, the historian A.T.Q. Stewart in *The Narrow Ground* described the self-perception of northern nationalists as 'a picture of unrelieved blackness, of a people grievously oppressed and denied any means of redress'.[71] The contemporary Irish nationalist sense of 'historic grievance' is rooted in the political partition of Ireland in 1921 understood by nationalists as both itself a national injustice and the political 'frame' within which unionists inflicted on the nationalist population a 'nationalist nightmare' of discrimination and oppression. Joseph McCullough in his *Pocket History of Ireland* referred to 'the religious injustice inherent in the Northern Irish government' (that is, inherent in the Partition of Ireland) and 'the connection between the oppressed blacks in America and the Catholics of Northern Ireland'.[72] The Irish historian Liam de Paor wrote in *Divided Ulster* that in Northern Ireland 'Catholics are blacks who happen to have white skins'.[73] Michael Lillis (former Head of the Republic's Department of Foreign Affairs and Ambassador to the UN) in a letter to the *Irish Times* in 2012 claimed that in Northern Ireland post 1920:

> The fact is that the lives of hundreds of thousands of Northern Catholics were systematically thwarted during those sixty years. Daily life for many was a sustained and deliberate humiliation. Peter Barry's expression "the nationalist nightmare of the Northern Catholics" was no exaggeration.[74]

Politics of redemption and the mystique of the gunman

This deep-rooted sense of 'historic grievance' and the understanding of Partition as an injustice against the claimed Irish nation was reinforced as a driving force for nationalist resort to violence by a myth of national redemption central to the 'politics of redemption'[75] of Patrick Pearse.

The essence of Pearse's revolutionary nationalism was that the authentic 'self-determination' of the Irish nation required the 'blood sacrifice' of Irish patriots – particularly himself. This myth of national regeneration was forged by Pearse out of a combination of Gaelic mythology and the 'aggressively unorthodox' misappropriation of the soteriological themes of sacrificial death and resurrection that lie at the heart of the Christian tradition.[76] Pearse's political philosophy was that bloodshed and violence ('sacrificial death') were imperative for the regeneration of the Irish nation ('resurrection'). It is therefore no exaggeration to say that Pearse articulated an ethnic nationalism rooted in a 'cult of death'. This was classically expressed in Pearse's dictum in *The Coming Revolution* that 'bloodshed is a cleansing and sanctifying thing and a nation that regards it as the final horror has lost its manhood'[77]. Marianne Elliott in *The Catholics of Ulster* referred to Pearse as 'the dominant inspiration in militant Irish republicanism'.[78] Eamonn McCann in *War and an Irish Town* stated in an autobiographical recollection of childhood in Londonderry that:

> We came very early to our politics. One learned, quite literally at one's mother's knee, that Christ died for the human race and Patrick Pearse for the Irish section of it. The lessons were taught with dogmatic authority ... Pearse ranked high in the teeming pantheon of Irish martyrdom. There were others. They had all died in the fight to free Ireland from British rule, a fight which had paused in partial victory in 1922 ... It was our task to finish the job, to cleanse the remaining traces of foreign rule from the face of Ireland.[79]

Pearse's political legacy was identified by Conor Cruise O'Brien in *States of Ireland* as 'the mystique of the gunman as the predominant political theme in Irish politics'.[80] The 'mystique of the gunman' found expression in the terrorism of the IRA from 1969-99 as the membership of that terrorist organization responded to what O'Brien in *Ancestral Voices* referred to as the 'ghosts that call for blood':

> The reality is that the atavistic national-religious forces which moved Pearse and became articulate in him move the IRA, also. They have their mandate from the patriot dead. The IRA hear the ghosts that call for blood and they obey the call. That is their *raison d'etre* and their licence to kill.[81]

The 'mandate from the patriot dead' determines the nature of authentic patriotism for the so-called 'republican' tradition in Irish nationalism – for those committed to Pearse's demand for 'the shedding of blood' the true patriot must be willing to kill.

The 1977 IRA *Green Book* fully incorporates this understanding of authentic patriotism: the volunteer 'patriot' must have 'convictions which are strong enough to give him [or her] confidence to kill someone without hesitation and without regret'.[82] Resort to murder 'without hesitation and without regret' requires not merely absolutist 'convictions' supplied by the ideology of Irish nationalism reinforced by the nationalist 'MOPE mentality' but also the driving force of hatred – hatred destroys the sensibilities of compassion and sympathy that constrain human beings from violence and brutality. The chilling statement from the IRA *Green Book* expresses a morally disordered or distempered understanding of the imperatives of patriotism rooted in what Francis Shaw properly categorized as Pearse's 'gospel of hate'. The inculcation of the 'gospel of hate'[83] combined with the deep–rooted sense of 'historic grievance' within the Northern Ireland nationalist community issued in a 'killing rage' that was sustained for three decades in Northern Ireland after 1968 by individuals psychologically insensitive to human suffering and morally blind to the barbarity of their actions and therefore (apart from a few exceptions) entirely devoid of any feeling of guilt or genuine remorse for the murders they perpetrated.[84]

Perhaps the most powerful and compelling insight into the dimension of hatred involved in the IRA 'killing rage' was given in a letter by Judge Tom Travers published by the *Irish Times*, 8 April 1994. The letter records the murder of his twenty-two year old daughter Mary during an IRA attempt on his life and the life of his wife as the family walked home from Sunday Mass on 8 April 1984:

> At the time Mary lay dying on her mum's breast ... The murderer's gun which was pointed at my wife's head misfired twice. Another gunman shot me six times. As he prepared to fire the first shot I saw a look of hatred on his face, a face I will never forget ... The hatred on that face came from the depths of Hell itself ... Mary died, as she lived, gentle and full of grace, sweetness and love, and she is now with God.[85]

The IRA support base in Ireland

But in addition to the ideological sustaining factors of the 'historic grievance' and the 'Pearse legacy' the IRA was sustained by a nationalist support base in Northern Ireland without which the IRA could not have effectively operated. The electoral support base for Sinn Fein within the nationalist electorate pre-1998 when the Belfast Agreement was signed may be taken as an indicator of support for the IRA – Sinn Fein obtained an average of 35 per cent of the nationalist vote in Northern Ireland during the IRA terror campaign between 1982-96.[86] The nationalist vote for Sinn Fein represented a combination of unequivocal support for the IRA and what Conor Cruise O'Brien referred to as an 'historically rooted ambivalence'[87] towards the IRA. The nationalist support for the IRA derived from what Maurice Tugwell referred to as 'pre-propaganda' in his account of the mobilization strategies of the IRA:

> Northern Catholics educated in their own Catholic schools, joining only republican sporting and social clubs ... had from early youth received what Ellul calls pre-propaganda, the myths of ancient battles, of 1916 and the efficacy of violence ... It was towards this target audience that the Provisionals applied their mobilization strategy.[88]

The IRA support base within Northern Ireland was reinforced by the anti-RUC policy of the Social Democratic and Labour Party (SDLP). The 'Ulsterisation' of the security response to IRA terrorism[89] from the late 1970s put the RUC in the front line in the conflict with the IRA. The SDLP rejected a 'security response' directed to the defeat of IRA terrorism and conducted a sustained anti-RUC propaganda of which Seamus Mallon was a particularly vociferous exponent. For example, at the Brehon Law Society 'Irishman of the Year' award in Philadelphia on 24 April 1999, the then Deputy First Minister took the opportunity to inform his American audience that in 'the North of Ireland' the rule of law had been reduced by the RUC to 'little more than the rule of the jungle'. The sustained SDLP anti-RUC propaganda was directed at maximizing the 'alienation' of the nationalist community in Northern Ireland from the RUC with respect to both the counter–terrorist and civilian policing roles of the RUC.[90]

The SDLP rejection of security policy directed to the defeat of the IRA was based on the claim that the 'gun can only be taken out of Irish politics' by a political settlement. But the SDLP understanding of the nature of the required political settlement was directed by the political objective that the SDLP shared with IRA/Sinn Fein. That political objective was set out by Hume during the Hume/Adams 'talks' of 1988 in language devoid of ambiguity – the political objective articulated by Hume was to 'end the British presence in Ireland'.[91] This simply means that the *realpolitik* of the SDLP was that the way to end IRA terrorism was to concede the political objectives of the IRA which were also the political objectives of the SDLP. This tacit mutually beneficial relationship between the SDLP and Sinn Fein/IRA was expressed with characteristic perception by Arthur Aughey:

> An appropriate level of republican violence and an appropriate indication of nationalist alienation has always been functional to the party's [the reference is to the SDLP] strategy … The agenda of the SDLP is not now to destroy Sinn Fein or the IRA. It is to use them for increased leverage to shoehorn unionists out of the United Kingdom.[92]

IRA terrorism in Northern Ireland was also operationally sustained from the Republic by the refusal of the Republic to extradite IRA terrorists and to effectively co-operate with the United Kingdom on anti-terrorist security policy. Margaret Thatcher in *The Downing Street Years* set out her motivation for signing the Anglo-Irish Agreement of 1985 in terms of a 'hope' for a more co-operative attitude from the Irish government, security forces and courts. But there was, as Thatcher records, no reciprocation on those issues from the Republic:

> We knew that the terrorists went over the border to the Republic to plan their operations and to store their arms. We got no satisfactory intelligence on their movements. Once they crossed the border they were lost. Indeed, we received far better intelligence co-operation from virtually all other European countries than with the Republic.[93]

That raises a fundamental question: Why did the Republic of Ireland in effect significantly assist the terrorism of the IRA? That is a very difficult question. The Republic certainly shared the *realpolitik* of the SDLP – that is, to resist a security response to the IRA and in effect utilize the terrorism of the IRA to push for a 'political settlement' that would be credibly perceived to be at least transitional to the goal of a politically united Ireland.[94] The answer may also be located in a moral ambiguity that lies at the heart of contemporary Irish politics. The Republic of Ireland is a democratic state. But it is also a state that celebrates its origin in an undemocratic act of insurrection at Easter 1916 legitimized by a myth of patriotic 'blood sacrifice'. It may be that this moral ambiguity helped the political elite in the Republic to 'accommodate' IRA violence provided that it was confined to Northern Ireland perceived as a 'failed political entity'.[95] This accommodation was also assisted by the fact that IRA violence was perceived by significant members of the political elite in the Republic to be both: (1) caused (if not indeed justified) by what they regarded as the injustice of Partition and the claimed 'nationalist nightmare' of discrimination and (2) a legitimate continuation of Easter 1916. But whatever the reason it is beyond dispute that the 'accommodation' of IRA terrorism by the Republic significantly contributed to the long night of terrorism in Northern Ireland.[96]

The legitimization of IRA terrorism

The legitimization of IRA violence by the so-called 'republican movement' is embedded in a framework of belief which is a combination of historical and political fiction. This framework of belief is intended to establish 'just cause' and 'right authority' involving a tacit appeal (IRA/ Sinn Fein have not explicitly developed a 'just war' legitimization of the use of force) to the major *ad bellum* requirements of the just war tradition – that is, the just war requirements for a morally legitimate resort to the use of force. 'Just cause' and 'right authority' are the most significant of the just war *ad bellum* requirements. The fundamental premise of the IRA 'just cause' argument is common to all Irish nationalists – Partition is a denial of the right of self-determination and consequently an injustice against the 'Irish people'. But at this point the 'constitutional nationalists' and IRA/Sinn Fein diverge – the latter (but not the former) consider that the perceived injustice is sufficient to morally warrant resort to extreme violence to end Partition.

Resort to violence raises the issue of the just war *ad bellum* requirement of 'right or competent authority' to resort to the use of force. The
1977 IRA *Green Book* addresses the issue of 'right authority': 'The Irish
Republican Army is the direct representatives of the 1919 Dail Eireann
parliament and as such they are the legal and lawful government of the
Irish Republic'.[97] The *Green Book* makes the dual claim that the leadership of the IRA is: (1) 'the direct representative of the 1919 Dail Eireann
parliament' which for Irish republicans is the parliament of the Republic
proclaimed by Patrick Pearse outside the Dublin post office on Easter
1916 and (2) 'the lawful government of the Irish people' or the lawful
government of the claimed 'one nation' in Ireland.[98] The import of these
claims is that 'all operations and actions' directed by the IRA are 'the
lawful and legal actions of the government of all the Irish people' and
consequently are understood to be ultimately authorized by the 'Irish
people'. The IRA claim to 'right authority' is based on what are presented
in the *Green Book* as 'ethical facts' – that is, putative facts that have the
moral import (for the IRA) of legitimizing the post 1969 IRA/Sinn Fein
resort to terrorism to end Partition.[99]

There is an obvious problem of history with these claims – the claim
to 'right authority' is grounded on an historical fiction. The problem is
that the Republic to which IRA/Sinn Fein give their ultimate political
allegiance and from which they claim authority to resort to violence as
'representatives of all the Irish people' was refused recognition by the
Versailles peace conference (1918-19) and in fact never in any legal or
constitutional sense existed as a sovereign state:

> Because the Irish Republic proclaimed in 1916 was never a sovereign
> state and the self-styled all –Ireland parliaments of 1919-20 were never
> governments exercising control over the territory of Ireland, neither is
> capable of providing the IRA and its factions with a legitimate authority
> to wage war, either at that time or since.[100]

The legitimization of violence cannot be derived from a non-existent
state – in short the IRA/Sinn Fein claim of a 'right authority' to resort to
violence is entirely devoid of legitimizing foundation. Basically the same
position was substantively argued by Cardinal Daly in *The Price of Peace* in

which he concluded that 'the present self-styled "armed struggle" of para-military republicanism fails the test of "competent authority" to commit a country or a people to war'.[101] Further, the Sinn Fein/IRA appeal to 'just cause' as a legitimization of violence crucially depends on the existence of one nation on the island of Ireland without which Partition cannot be understood as an injustice. That raises a question which is absolutely fundamental for the logical and political coherence of Irish nationalism: is there a single nation on the island of Ireland?

The Irish nationalist 'one nation' claim

From the literature on national identity it is possible to abstract two approaches to the identification of nations. The objectivist approach focuses on criteria such as ethnicity, language and religion. The subjectivist approach stresses a shared national consciousness. Typically both approaches are combined in nationalist ideology and this is the case with Irish nationalism. But the problem for Irish nationalists is that their traditional objective criteria for national identity cannot establish the proposition that there is one nation on the island of Ireland. Traditionally Irish nationalist appealed to 'the three leaved shamrock'[102] of race and common descent, Catholicism and language as objective criteria. The problem with what was in the early twentieth century the traditionally dominant theme of the differentiation of the claimed Irish nation in terms of race or common descent is that the notion that the inhabitants of the island constitute a single race is impossible to sustain and pushes Irish nationalism in the direction of a form of racism. A.T.Q. Stewart argued in *The Narrow Ground* that in an 'island which was the terminus of so many westward moving waves of population throughout the ages the idea of an unmixed racial group ought to have been laughed out of court at the outset'.[103]

National identification in terms of Catholicism obviously cannot – given the Protestant population – establish the one nation claim. This religious identification had the unfortunate meaning for nationalists of making plain the religious exclusivism that was central to Irish nationalism for most of the twentieth century. But the identification of being authentically Irish with being Catholic is now anachronistic

– the Republic of Ireland is now one of the most secular countries in western Europe and is in the vanguard of liberal legislation repudiating traditional Catholic teaching on issues such as marriage and the sanctity of human life. Nevertheless the traditional nationalist identification of being authentically Irish with being Catholic may linger on in the Irish nationalist mind.[104] Appeal to language is particularly difficult for Irish nationalists. English is the common language of the inhabitants of the island of Ireland but for Irish nationalists English cannot express what they understand to be the Gaelic genius or prevailing character and spirit of the claimed Irish nation. The problem for Irish nationalists committed to the linguistic criterion is that the linguistic criterion would virtually reduce authentic membership of the Irish nation to the dwindling inhabitants of the *Gaeltacht* or Irish speaking regions in Ireland.[105]

The fundamental problem for Irish nationalists is that the one nation claim cannot be sustained by appeal to the traditional Irish nationalist 'three leaved shamrock' objective criteria of national identity. There is, in addition, no 'subjective' basis for the one nation claim. The French philosopher Ernest Renan (1823-92) in his essay, *What is a Nation?* argued that there are two things that constitute a nation which have come to be understood as the subjective criteria of national identity: 'One is the possession in common of a rich legacy of remembrances; the other is the actual consent, the desire to live together, the will to continue to value the heritage which all hold in common'.[106]Renan is here arguing that a nation is constituted by a shared collective memory involving a shared evaluation of the past and the will to value what is perceived by the members of the nation as a common cultural and political heritage.

But the simple fact of the matter is that there does not exist in Ireland a common political culture which subjectively differentiates an Irish nation inclusive of the unionist and nationalist inhabitants of the island. Unionist political self-identity and allegiance is defined in terms of citizenship of the United Kingdom and not in terms of identification with the ethnic nation and ideological imperatives of traditional Irish nationalist thought.[107] This situation is reinforced by the fact that, despite historical interaction within a small island over many centuries, the inhabitants of the island do not share a common evaluation of the past or collective memory which is the cement of national solidarity.[108] These considerations mean that the conditions for subjective national unity do not exist in Ireland. – to hold the contrary belief of Irish nationalists is to indulge in the 'inherent self-deception of nationalist thinking'.[109]

The logic of these considerations is that Irish nationalism is a self-refuting ideology. The objective and subjective criteria traditionally used by Irish nationalists to attempt to establish their core claim that there is a single nation on the island of Ireland actually establishes the opposite – these criteria indisputably show that that the inhabitants of Ireland do not constitute a single nation. This means that the traditional criteria cannot be employed to determine the identity of an Irish nation inclusive of unionists. Contemporary Irish nationalist leaders have resorted to simply asserting a common national identity in Ireland or trying to establish a common national identity by appeal to something like geographical determinism. Garrett Fitzgerald was typical of the 'asserters' with his historically refutable assertion that 'history has created on the island of Ireland one nation'.[110] The 'geographical determinism' view basically involves the claim that geographical location of birth determines the ethnic national identity required by Irish nationalism. For example, John Hume defined the 'Irish people' as 'the people who live on the island of Ireland'[111] which as a statement of geographical identity is trivially true. But Hume proceeded to endow the 'Irish people' geographically defined with a collective 'right of self-determination'[112] or self-government which involved attributing to the geographically identified 'Irish people' the political identity of a nation.

The problem for Hume (of which he was entirely unaware) is the movement/transition from an indisputable geographical identity to a disputable political identity – that is, being a single nation or 'people' with a collective right of self-determination. The mere fact of a population being contained within the geographical boundaries of an island has (contrary to the logic of Hume's position) no import or entailment for the political or national identity of the inhabitants in question – consequently the attribution by Hume of a collective 'right of self-determination' to the geographically defined 'Irish people' is without foundation and in effect denies 'the rights of unionists to that which defines them as unionists, their attachment to union with Britain'.[113] Hume's assertions amount to a textbook *non sequitur* which has the political significance of demonstrating the intellectual poverty and logical incoherence of Irish nationalist thought with respect to their 'one nation' claim – that would be of little significance were it not for the fact that the 'nationalist thought' that Hume and the self-designated 'constitutional nationalists' hold in common with IRA/Sinn Fein was the ideological driving force for three decades of IRA/Sinn Fein terrorism in Northern Ireland.

The import of the consideration of the Irish nationalist 'one nation' claim is that Irish nationalists both in the past and currently have failed to coherently establish the 'one nation' claim which is foundational for contemporary Irish nationalist thought and specifically for the understanding that Partition is an 'injustice' against the claimed Irish nation. This reality was stated by the Irish historian John A. Murphy with brutal clarity: reference to a single Irish nation is 'tired old 1918 nationalist prattle … there is no such political entity as the Irish people'.[114] The criteria of national identity traditionally employed by Irish nationalists cannot be coherently used to establish the claim that there is a single nation on the island of Ireland. There is a philosophical expression that can properly be applied to Irish nationalism – Irish nationalism is 'self-referentially incoherent'. The attempt to undermine the legitimacy of Partition and to legitimize the resort to extreme violence by Irish nationalists based on the 'one nation' political myth is a retreat from reality into a domain of political and historical fiction and logical self-contradiction which exemplifies the self-deception and logical incoherence characteristic of much Irish nationalist thought.[115] The moral import of this is that the IRA resort to violence is devoid of both 'just cause' and 'right authority' – the essential *ad bellum* requirements of the just war tradition. In addition the indiscriminate extremity of IRA violence is radically incompatible with the *in bello* requirements of the tradition or, as authoritatively stated by Cardinal Daly referring to the IRA campaign of terrorism: 'Every single condition for the just war or just revolution is violated in the Irish situation'.[116]

Conclusion

The IRA resort to violence in 1969 in pursuit of their stated aim of breaking the 'British connection' and the establishment of a 'democratic socialist republic'[117] was without: (1) legitimizing authority because of the non-existence of the 'proclaimed' 1916 Republic as an internationally recognized sovereign state and (2) devoid of 'just cause' because of the self-refuting logic of the 'one nation' claim. But the absence of 'right authority' and 'just cause' arguably mean that the three decades of terrorist conflict in Northern Ireland is inaccurately in a moral sense described as 'war' – the conflict is properly understood not as 'war' but as an armed insurrection against the state (the United Kingdom) by a criminal organization. The import of this is that 'IRA terrorism does not morally count as war but merely as murder and other violent crime'[118] – hence the entirely legal propriety of treating convicted IRA terrorists as criminals and murderers and the moral impropriety of releasing convicted IRA terrorists (and 'loyalist' terrorists) from prison under the terms of the 1998 Belfast Agreement.[119]

The rejection by the republican movement of the categorization of their actions as criminal is rooted in an ideology radically divorced from historical and political reality. But this divorce between the imperatives of nationalist ideology and the 'real world' combined with a deep-rooted sense of historic grievance produced in the leadership of IRA/Sinn Fein a 'fanaticism of the will' that issued in a literal 'killing rage' that resulted in the death and injury of thousands of innocent people in Northern Ireland over three decades.

A terrorist organization such as the IRA will attract adherents for a variety of reasons from psychopaths at one extreme to individuals motivated by a fanatical commitment to what they understand to be the imperatives of Irish nationalism. Leaving aside the psychopathic dimension the publicly known leadership and activists of the IRA were psychologically normal individuals but capable of something that most people would find impossible.[120] The known leaders and activists of the IRA combined the ordinary activities of everyday life (including in some cases devout religious observance) with the planning, authorization and carrying out of terrorist murder – sometimes indiscriminate car bombing of men, women and children and sometimes the deliberate targeting and murder of individuals often in their own homes and occasionally in front of their wives and children.[121] But this combination of ordinary everyday activity and murder on a daily basis disclosed what was morally exceptional about the individuals in question – the combination demonstrated a deep-rooted moral depravity.

The moral character of what was involved in IRA terrorism ought never be eclipsed. But that is precisely what occurred during the so-called 'peace process' that led to the 1998 Belfast Agreement – the erstwhile leadership and activists within the IRA were presented as committed to 'peace' and within the terms of the Belfast Agreement were elevated into government and released from prison. The leadership and 'fellow travellers' of the republican movement in the post-1998 period have devoted their efforts to an in effect re-writing of the history of the conflict with the dual objective of the moral exoneration of the IRA and the focusing of blame on the security forces and the 'British state'.[122] The re-writing of history aimed at the republican glorification of their violence and the shifting of blame is also intended to obscure the fact that with respect to the stated objective of IRA/Sinn Fein to secure an all-Ireland 'democratic and socialist republic' IRA terrorism was both a political and military failure – the IRA failed to secure its stated political objective of 'Irish unity' and it was in fact militarily defeated.[123] Rogelio Alonso in his insightful book, The *IRA and Armed Struggle* argued for the 'categorical delegitimization' of the IRA's 'armed struggle': 'The IRA's armed struggle has sent many people to their graves, but history must not allow its abject failure to be buried in oblivion as well'.[124] But in addition to the failure of the so-called 'armed struggle', the moral culpability of the leadership and activists of the IRA and the callous barbarity of their multiple crimes must not be permitted to be 'buried in oblivion' – to do so would amount to a factual and moral perversion of history and the effacing from history of the suffering of the innocent victims of republican terrorism.

Notes

[1]   The Brooke/Mayhew talks (April 1991-November 1992) were conducted by Peter Brooke (Secretary of State for Northern Ireland, 1989-92) and Sir Patrick Mayhew (Secretary of State for Northern Ireland , 1992-97). The talks were directed to the negotiation of a new and more broadly based 'three strand' agreement to replace the 1985 Anglo-Irish Agreement.

[2]   Sir Patrick Mayhew in a speech to the Irish Association on 12 May 1994 stated that' there are two traditions each of which , as it seems to me , is in every way as worthy

and legitimate as the other'. See also, Sir Patrick Mayhew , *Culture and Identity*, Centre for the Study of Conflict , University of Ulster, Coleraine 16 December 1993.

3   *Downing Street Declaration*, 15 December 1993.

4   *Towards a United Ireland: A Dual Strategy for Irish Unification*, Labour Party, 1988, Introduction, p. 2. The document was issued by the Labour Party's Front Bench Northern Ireland team which included Majorie Mowlan subsequently Secretary of State for Northern Ireland (1997-99)

5   On the economic feasibility of Irish unity see chapter 9.

6   Garrett Fitzgerald, *Towards a New Ireland* (London: Charles Knight and Co Ltd, 1972), p. 175. The distinction between 'constitutional nationalists' and 'republicans' is that the latter are committed to the use of force to remove what both believe to be the injustice of Partition.

7   Martin Mansergh (ed), *The Spirit of the Nation: Speeches of Charles J. Haughey* (Dublin: 1986), p. 689

8   Gerry Adams, *The Politics of Irish Freedom* (Dingle: Brandon Book Publishers, 1986), p. 88

9   Garrett Fitzgerald, op. cit., p.16

10   Clare O'Halloran, *Partition and the Limits of Irish Nationalism* (Dublin: Gill and Macmillan, 1987), p. 210

11   Martin Mansergh, op. cit., pp.737-38.

12   Dick Spring, Nationhood – a way to heal the ravages of nationalism, *Irish Times*, 17 March 1992.

13   Gerry Adams, op. cit., p.125; *A Pathway to Peace* (Cork: The Mercier Press, 1988), p.42.

14   Quoted in D. George Boyce, *Nationalism in Ireland* (London: Routledge, 1991), p. 407.

15   It's not just down to myself and John Hume, *Irish Times*, 17 March 1992.

16   The child-parent simile is deeply rooted in traditional nationalist thought and pre-dates both Adams and the Forum Report. See Clare O'Halloran, op. cit., p. 40.

17   Gerry Adams, *Pathway to Peace*, pp.42-43.

18   Clare O'Halloran, op. cit., p. 200.

19   Idem., p.201

20   D George Boyce, 'Southern Irish political parties and the Northern Ireland problem', in Patrick J. Roche and Brian Barton (eds), *The Northern Ireland Question: Myth and Reality* (Aldershot: Avebury, 1991), p. 176.

21   Joseph J Lee, *Ireland: Politics and Society:1912-85* (Cambridge: Cambridge University Press,1989), pp.14, 21, 59, 79, 596.. For critical comment on Lee's

understanding that 'racism is central to Ulster unionism' see Graham Walker, 'Old history: Protestant Ulster in Lee's Ireland', *The Irish Review*, Spring/Summer, 1992, pp. 65-71. See also Richard English, 'The Unionists', in John Wilson Foster (ed), *The Idea of the Union* (Vancouver: Belcouver Press, 1995), p.45.

22   Idem., p.3.

23   David Fitzpatrick, 'Ireland since 1870', in R.F. Foster (ed), *The Oxford History of Ireland* (Oxford: Oxford University Press,1989), p. 229.

24   T.O. Coogan, *Disillusioned Decades: Ireland 1966-87*, (Dublin: Gill and Macmillan, 1987), p. 195.

25   Idem., p.196

26   See, for example, Arthur Aughey, *Under Siege: Ulster Unionism and The Anglo-Irish Agreement* (Belfast: Blackstaff Press, 1989), p.10

27   D. George Boyce, *Nationalism in Ireland* (London: Routledge, 1982), p.400. Bryan A. Follis, *A State under Siege: The Establishment of Northern Ireland, 1920-25* (Oxford, Clarendon Press, 1995) is a notable exception.

28   Clare O'Halloran, op. cit., pp. 40-41, 56.

29   Patrick Buckland, *A History of Northern Ireland* (Dublin: Gill and Macmillan, 1981), p. 21.

30   Clare O'Halloran, op.cit., p.209

31   Quoted in Eric J. Hobsbawn, *Nations and Nationalism since 1780* (Cambridge: Cambridge University Press, 1991), p.12.

32   *New Ireland Forum Report*, par. 4.6,5.4

33   SDLP/Sinn Fein papers, *Irish Times*, 19 September 1988.

34   G. Adams, *A Pathway to Peace*, (Cork: The Mercier Press, 1988), p.11

35   Cahal Daly, Speech to British Catholic parliamentarians in House of Commons, *Irish Times*, 2 December 1993. For an assessment of Cardinal Daly's understanding of the IRA see Conor Cruise O'Brien, Cardinal error of judgment, *Sunday Independent*, 3 April 1994.

36   For the suggestion of significant change in republican thinking see Andy Pollock, 'How Sinn Fein found a new republican realism', *Irish Times*, 4 December 1993.

37   *Irish Times*, 28 February 1994

38   *Irish Times*, 29 November , 1993.

39   John Hume, 'The end of the unionist veto in Ulster', *London Review of Books*, 2 February 1989, p. 7. See also Northern Ireland – A Strategy for Peace, *SDLP policy document*, November 1980

40 Northern Ireland – A Strategy for Peace, *SDLP Policy Document 1980*. See Gerry Adams, op. cit., pp. 90, 91.

41 *Belfast Agreement*, 1998, p.2

42 Garrett Fitzgerald, op., cit., p. 175

43 *New Ireland Forum Report*, pars 5.1, 5.8, 6.1. See comment by Clare O'Halloran, op. cit., p. 199.

44 Gerry Adams, op. cit., p.88.

45 Ibid, p. 88

46 *New Ireland Forum Report*, 1984, Par. 6.6

47 See Martin Mansergh, op. cit.,, p. 450. For a critical evaluation of the understanding that the Irish nation can be differentiated in terms of a distinct and ancient culture see Arthur Green, 'The British Isles', in John Wilson Foster (ed), op., cit., pp. 20-26.

48 Terence Brown, *Ireland: A Social and Cultural History 1922-1985* (London: Fontana Press, 1985), p. 342.

49 Clare O'Halloran op., cit., p. 199. See also Cahal B. Daly, *The Price of Peace* (Belfast: The Blackstaff Press, 1991) for his politically insightful objection to the denial of the 'rights of unionists to that which defines them as unionists, their attachment to the union with Britain' (pp.12, 55-56).

50 Terence Brown, op. cit., p.342.

51 *New Ireland Forum Report*, 1984, par. 3.6

52 *Observer*, 27 April 1986.

53 For characteristically perceptive analysis of Hume's politics see Arthur Aughey, 'Hume and Unionists', in Sean Farran and Denis Haughey, (eds), *Hume: Irish Peacemaker* (Dublin: Four Courts PressLtd, 2015). See also, Patrick J. Roche, 'John Hume', *Ulster Review*, Issue No. 22, Spring 1997 and 'The SDLP mask is beginning to slip', *News Letter*, 27 February 1989.

54 Interview with John Hume, *Crane Bag*, Vol. 4, No. 2,1981, pp.41-42.

55 Barry White, *John Hume: Statesman of the Troubles* (Belfast: The Blackstaff Press, 1985), p. 170.

56 David McKittrick, Seamus Kelters, Brian Feeney and Chris Thornton, *Lost Lives*, (Edinburgh and London: Mainstream Publishing Company, 1999)

57 Ibid. 487, pp. 229-31

58 'The victims of the Claudy bombing', *BBC News*, 24 August 2010

59 David McKittrick et al., op.cit., p. 1215.

[60] See also David Patterson, *A Legacy of Tears*, SAVERNAVER, 2006. This book conveys in the words of the innocent victims the initial trauma and permanent grief of those who lost husbands and fathers and brothers and, in one account, a mother in the 'killing fields' of South and North Armagh. The book was serialized in the *Belfast Telegraph*, 4-8 July 2006.

[61] David McKittrick et al, op. cit., Table 3, p.1476.

[62] Patrick J. Roche, 'Fr Reid's Nazi claim is divorced from reality', *Belfast Telegraph*, 15 October 2005. See *Irish Examiner*, 28 January 2005 for the comment by President McAleese in which she claimed on the sixtieth anniversary of the liberation of Auschwitz that 'the Nazis gave their children an irrational hatred of Jews in the same way that people in Northern Ireland transmitted to their children an irrational hatred of Catholics'.

[63] Patrick J. Roche, 'Unionists must challenge this "most oppressed people ever" mentality', *News Letter*, 18 April 2018.

[64] Sunday Times Insight Team, *Ulster*, (Harmondsworth, Penguin Books, 1972), p.49.

[65] Steve Bruce, *God Save Ulster: The Religion and Politics of Paisleyism*, (Oxford: Oxford University Press, 1986), p.266.

[66] Christopher Hewitt, 'The roots of violence: Catholic grievances and Irish nationalism during the civil rights period', in Patrick J. Roche and Brian Barton (eds), *The Northern Ireland Question: Myth and Reality* (Aldershot, Avebury, 1991), p.28.

[67] Eamonn McCann, *War in an Irish Town* (Chicago: Haymarket Books, 2018) p. 62. See Christopher Hewitt, op. cit., pp.37-38. See also Simon Prince, *Northern Ireland's '68: Civil Rights, Global Revolt and the Origins of the Troubles* (Dublin: Irish Academic Press, 2007), pp. 124-125. For the origins of the civil rights movement see chapter 4.

[68] Martin Dillon, *The Dirty War* (London: Hutchinson, 1991), pp. xiv-xv. See also Conor Cruise O'Brien, Ancestral Voices; Religion and Nationalism in Ireland (Dublin, Poolbeg Press Ltd, 1994) p.158. See also Conor Cruise O'Brien, States of Ireland (London: Hutchinson & Co, 1972), pp. 208-216.

[69] Christopher Hewitt, op. cit., p.34 for Hewitt's consideration of the socializing influences particularly of home and education and his argument that 'most Irish nationalists are Irish nationalists for the same reason that are Roman Catholics – because they were taught to be so'.

[70] Liam Kennedy, *Colonialism, Religion and Nationalism in Ireland* (Belfast: Institute of Irish Studies, 1996), pp. 217-223

[71] A.T.Q. Stewart , *The Narrow Ground :Patterns of Ulster History* (London: Faber and Faber, 1977), p.177.

[72]   Joseph McCullough, *A Pocket History of Ireland* (Dublin: Gill & Macmillan, 2010), p.235.

[73]   Liam de Paor, *Divided Ulster* (London: Pelican Books, 1970), p.13.

[74]   Martin Lillis, *Irish Times*, 19 September 2012. *The New Ireland Forum Report*, pars 3.3, 3.9, provide a highly accentuated expression of the MOPE syndrome. For an assessment of the extent of discrimination in Northern Ireland post 1920 see chapter 5.

[75]   See Sean Farrell Moran, *Patrick Pearse and the Politics of Redemption* (Washington: The Catholic University of America Press, 1994).

[76]   For a critique of Pearse's political philosophy as 'aggressively unorthodox' and a 'gospel of hate' see Francis Shaw, 'The Canon of Irish History: A Challenge', *Studies*, Vol. LXI, Spring 1972.

[77]   Patrick Pearse, *Political Writings and Speeches* (Dublin: The Talbot Press, 1952), p.99.

[78]   Marianne Elliott, *The Catholics of Ulster: A History* (London: Penguin Books, 2001), p.443.

[79]   Eamonn McCann, *War in an Irish Town* (Chicago: Haymarket Books, 2018), p.35.

[80]   Conor Cruise O'Brien, *States of Ireland*, p. 309.

[81]   Conor Cruise O'Brien, *Ancestral*, p.159.

[82]   Brendon O'Brien, *The Long War: The IRA and Sinn Fein 1985 to Today* (Dublin: The O'Brien Press, 1993), Appendix 1, p.290.

[83]   Francis Shaw, op. cit., p. 126.

[84]   For a broader evaluative perspective on the activists within the IRA see Rogelio Alonso, *The IRA and Armed Struggle* (London: Routledge, 2007). Arguably the most perceptive book written on the IRA.

[85]   *Irish Times*, 8 April 1994.

[86]   Sydney Elliott and W. D. Flackes, *Conflict in Northern Ireland: An Encyclopedia* (Santa Barbara: ABC-CLIO, 1999), pp. 553-589.

[87]   Conor Cruise O'Brien, 'Terrorism under democratic conditions: the case of the IRA', in M. Crenshaw (ed), *Terrorism: Legitimacy and Power* (1981), p.84

[88]   M. Tugwell, 'Politics and Propaganda of the Provisional IRA', in P. Wilkinson (ed), *British Perspectives on Terrorism* (London: Routledge, 1981), p.20.

[89]   Sydney Elliott and W. D. Flackes, op. cit., pp. 638-689.

[90]   See Margaret Thatcher, *The Downing Street Years* (London: Harper Collins Publishers, 1993), p.404 where Thatcher records a discussion with John Hume on 27 February 1986 during which she 'urged that the SDLP should give more open support to the security forces but to no avail'.

91   'SF proposals and SDLP's detailed response', *Irish Times*, 19 September 1988

92   Arthur Aughey, *Under Siege: Ulster Unionism and the Anglo-Irish Agreement*, p.175. See also Conor Cruise O'Brien, 'Hollow critics of the IRA', *Times*, 24 March 1989 which records a comment by Danny Morrison that 'the SDLP's political influence rides on the back of the IRA'. The *realpolitik* of the SDLP was obscured by the 'post nationalist' and 'peace' rhetoric of Hume. For an assessment of Hume's 'new rhetoric' of Irish nationalism see Patrick J. Roche, 'John Hume', *Ulster Review*, Spring 1997, pp 9-11, See also Patrick J. Roche, 'The SDLP mask is beginning to slip', *News Letter*, 27 February 1989. For a highly perceptive insight into Hume's *realpolitik* see Arthur Aughey, 'Hume and Unionists', in Sean Farren and Denis Haughey (eds), *Hume: Irish Peacemaker* (Dublin: Four Courts Press, 2015).

93   Margaret Thatcher, op. cit., pp. 409-410. See also p.384.

94   Margaret Thatcher op. cit., pp. 393-415 for insight into the *realpolitik* of both Charles Haughey and Garret Fitzgerald

95   An expression coined and repeated *ad nauseam* by Charles Haughey

96   See Gearoid O Faolean, *A Broad Church: The Provisional IRA in the Republic of Ireland 1969-1980* which is a substantiation of the thesis that longevity of the 'Troubles' was very significantly due to the 'toleration and support for militant republicanism that existed among all layers of Irish society, and all professions' particularly in the Republic. (p.107). See also Conor Cruise O'Brien's reference to a 'rhetorical and sentimental tradition (in the Republic) and a blurring of realities, which helped to maintain for the IRA ... the status of a half-acknowledged though submerged institution, still trailing clouds of romantic legitimacy' in *Herod: Reflections on Political Violence* (London: Hutchinson, 1978), p.135.

97   Brendan O'Brien, *The Long War: The IRA and Sinn Fein 1985 to Today* (Dublin: The O'Brien Press, 1993), p.289

98   Brendan O'Brien, op. cit., p. 289

99   Brendan O'Brien, op., cit., p. 289

100 David A. George, 'The Ethics of IRA terrorism', in Andrew Vals (ed), *Ethics in International Affairs* (Oxford: Rowman and Littlefield,2000), p.86.

101 Cahal B. Daly, *The Price of Peace* (Belfast: The Blackstaff Press, 1991), p.64.

102 J.J. Lee, op. cit., p.658

103 A.T.Q Stewart, op. cit., p.27

104 See Robin Bury's treatment of the issue of being authentically Irish with being Catholic in chapter 10.

105 See Patrick J. Roche, 'Irish nationalism', *Salisbury Review*, Winter 1996, pp.24-25

106 Ernest Renan, 'Qu'est-ce qu'une nation?', in John Hutchinson and Anthony D. Smith, (eds), *Nationalism*, (Oxford: Oxford University Press, 1994), p.17.

107 Arthur Aughey, *Under Seige: Ulster Unionism and the Anglo-Irish Agreement*, p.19 . See also 'Unionism and Self-Determination', in Patrick J. Roche and Brian Barton (eds) , *The Northern Ireland Question: Myth and Reality*.

108 Patrick J. Roche, op. cit, p.25

109 Clare O'Halloran, op., cit., p.209

110 Garret FitzGerald, op. cit., p. 175

111 Hume interview, *Irish Times* , 13 January 1989. See also, 'Campaign in conflict with Tone's vision,' *Irish Times*, 19 September 1988.

112 Ibid

113 Cahal B. Daly, op., cit., pp. 12-13 where Cardinal Daly with characteristic acumen philosophically critiques the logic of the nationalist (he refers specifically to 'republican' but his argument equally applies to Hume) identification of geographically determined 'Irish people' with the 'republican/ nationalist people' – that is, with the Irish nation as understood within Irish nationalist thought.

114 John A. Murphy, *Sunday Independent*, 31 October 1993.

115 A dominant theme in Clare O'Halloran, *Partition and the Limits of Irish Nationalism*.

116 Cahal B. Daly, op. cit., p.62.

117 Brendan O'Brien, op. cit., p.291.

118 David A. George, op. cit., p.97.

119 See Neil Southern, *Policing and Combatting Terrorism in Northern Ireland* (London: Palgrave Macmillan, 2018).

120 See H. Lyons and H. Harbison,' Comparison of political and non-political murderers in Northern Ireland, 1974-84', *Medicine, Science and Law*, Vol. 26(3), 1986, pp.193-198.

121 See Cahal B. Daly, op. cit., p.55

122 See contribution by Cillian McGrattan in chapter 7.

123 See contribution by William Matchett in chapter 6.

124 Rogelio Alonso *The IRA and Armed Struggle* (London: Routledge, 2007), p. 198.

4

Irish republicans and the civil rights movement

Andrew Charles and Patrick J. Roche

Naivety and ignorance

This chapter explores the genesis and legacy of the civil rights movement in Northern Ireland and focuses on a key question: was the civil
rights movement a genuine attempt to secure legitimate rights or was it
a nationalist front for raising the issue of Partition aimed at securing the
nationalist imperative of Irish unity? The dominant understanding of the
civil rights movement is that it was a response by the Catholic nationalist
minority to perceived unionist misrule and systematic discrimination
in Northern Ireland post 1920 divorced from the traditional nationalist
objective of Irish unity. The demand for reform within Northern Ireland
was understood from this perspective to involve an at least tacit acceptance of the constitutional *status quo* and the republican involvement in
the civil rights movement was understood as a movement away from what
had been the central Irish nationalist demand to end Partition.

This understanding was reinforced by the claim that in Northern
Ireland in the 1960s there was a movement away from Irish nationalism
among the Catholic population. The *Economist* of 23 August 1969 stated
that John Hume was 'more concerned with social justice than old nationalism' and able 'to carry with him a younger generation which wanted to
change the living conditions of Catholic Ulster without worrying too
much about a united Ireland'.[1] The influential 1969 report of the Cameron
Commission put forward the view that the commitment to nationalism
and the ending of Partition was in decline among Catholics in Northern
Ireland:

These traditional patterns of antagonism [the reference was mainly to the 'religious division'] have at last begun to erode in recent years ... This trend has coincided with a decline in preoccupation with the border as an immediate political issue among, and in the appeal of nationalism to, the Catholic population.[2]

The *Cameron Report* was correct in recognising a decline in Protestant/ Catholic religious antagonism and a more ecumenical disposition in Northern Ireland in the 1960s but certainly incorrect in considering that this 'trend coincided with a decline in preoccupation with the border' among the Catholic population. Christopher Hewitt in a contribution to *The Northern Ireland Question: Myth and Reality* effectively argued that: 'In part these evaluations are a result of naivety and ignorance of northern Irish history and politics' and that 'no evidence exists to support these assumptions'.[3] Hewitt correctly argued that voting for parties committed to Irish unity is an obvious indicator of nationalist sentiment. But data on the nationalist vote as a percentage of the total vote in Stormont elections, Westminster elections and Belfast council elections showed that in 1965 'immediately prior to the Northern Ireland Civil Rights Movement (NICRA) agitation, nationalist sentiment was at a peak comparable to what it was just before the IRA campaign started in 1956'[4] – the reference is to the IRA border campaign 1956-62. Hewitt used the 1968 Loyalty Survey conducted by Richard Rose for his 1971 book *Governing Without Consensus: An Irish Perspective* to cross tabulate approval/disapproval/ don't know responses to two questions: (1) approve/disapprove/don't know if 'Catholics began protesting very strongly against cases of religious discrimination', and (2) approve/disapprove/ don't know if 'nationalists agreed to stop debating partition and accepted the present border as final'.

Table 4.1 Association between support for civil rights protests and attitudes to Partition

	Approve civil rights protest	Don't know	Disapprove civil rights protest
Don't accept border	57	24	39
Don't know	16	49	23
Accept border	27	27	38
	100% (n=.293)	100% (n=.98)	100% (n=.143)

Source: Christopher Hewitt, op. cit., p.52.

The results of the cross tabulation were contrary to the dominant under-standing that the objectives of the civil rights movement were divorced from the traditional concerns of Irish nationalists:

> The results are striking and contrary to the traditional view. Civil rights supporters were significantly more intransigent over the border and less likely to accept the existing position of Northern Ireland.[5]

The alternative and diametrically opposed understanding of the civil rights movement is that it was the initiative of republicans committed to the orthodox nationalist view that Northern Ireland is an 'artificial entity' that required anti-Catholic/nationalist systematic discrimi-nation to survive with the import for nationalists that the ending of discrimination would end Partition. Gerry Adams in *The Politics of Irish Freedom* categorically claimed that 'republicans were actually central to the formation of the NICRA' and that the civil rights movement was the 'creation of the republican leadership' – the reference being to the Cathal Goulding leadership of the 1960s IRA after the failed IRA 1956-62 border campaign.[6] The Adams claim was not merely a verbal tactic on the part of Adams to centrally identify the IRA with the formation of the civil rights movement. The claim was a statement of fact. Purdie (one of the most authoritative historians of the civil rights movement) in a 1988 contribution to *Irish Political Studies* concluded that 'the involvement of republicans in the setting up of the NICRA cannot be denied'.[7]

Claims about unionist systematic discrimination in Northern Ireland were accentuated by analogies with apartheid South Africa and segre-gation in the United States. The objective was to sensationalise and legitimise the civil rights movement in Ulster as part of a wider interna-tional protest movement taking place in western Europe and the United States and South Africa in the 1960s and by this means to reintroduce the 'Irish question' into British politics. The ending of Partition was in fact at the heart of the Northern Ireland civil rights movement. For example, Purdie in *Politics in the Streets: The Origins of the Civil Rights Movement in Northern Ireland* stated:

They [nationalists] had often made the propaganda point that Catholics in Northern Ireland were denied equal rights as citizens of the United Kingdom , but this had never been more than a means of exposing the unionists in front of British public opinion; the solution was seen as a united Ireland.[8]

The early ideologues

The thinking that informed the 1960s republican formation of the civil rights movement pre-dated the 1960s and derived from a number of intellectuals associated with the Connolly Association and the Wolfe Tone Societies. The Wolfe Tone Societies were established in 1964. The Societies were established following the events organised to mark the bi-centenary in 1963 of the birth of Wolfe Tone – the objective was to maintain the momentum of republican support gained from the bi-centenary celebrations. The purpose of the Wolfe Tone Societies was to advance the nationalist objective of a united Ireland: 'the primary objective was a united, independent and democratic Irish Republic in accordance with the principles of the 1916 Proclamation and the Democratic Programme of the First Dail'.[9] This was also the objective of the Connolly Association. The Connolly Association was established in 1938 and was based on the UK mainland and linked to the Communist Party of Great Britain (CPGB). The objectives of the Association set out in its 1955 constitution were: (1) to win support in Britain for a united Ireland, and (2) to effectively demand 'equal treatment' of the Irish in Britain.[10] Both organisations connected the pursuit of 'civil rights' (conceived as the dismantling of a unionist apparatus of alleged discrimination and oppression) in Northern Ireland with the ending of Partition.

The historian Charles Desmond Greaves (1913-88) was a key driver of this strategy within the Connolly Association extending back to the 1950s – Greaves was a republican and a communist and a member of the CPGB and editor of the *Irish Democrat*, the magazine of the Connolly Association. But to effectively connect the issues of 'civil rights' relating to Northern Ireland with the ending of Partition Greaves considered that it was necessary to break the 'wall of silence' at Westminster relating to the powers devolved to Stormont under the terms of the 1920

Government of Ireland Act. Greaves focused on two provisions of the 1920 Act: (1) Section 75 which stated that the 'supreme authority' of the Westminster parliament 'shall remain unaffected and undiminished over all persons, matters and things in Northern Ireland' and (2) the stated intention of the 1920 Act to provide for the 'better government' of Northern Ireland.[11] The Greaves position was that Section 75 did not preclude Westminster intervention in the devolved affairs of Northern Ireland despite a convention of non-interference and that the maladministration of Northern Ireland actually required Westminster intervention in the interest of 'better government' in the 'north of Ireland'.[12] The objective of securing Westminster intervention was to bring into question the 1920 Government of Ireland Act. This was explicitly set out by Greaves in his pamphlet *The Irish Question and the British People* published in 1963:

> The most important thing required in Britain is to place a question mark over the Government of Ireland Act once more. Evidence has been advanced for the view that it may already have been subjected to scrutiny behind closed doors. But this is not satisfactory. If Britain's Irish policy is being reconsidered, the British people are entitled to know with what in mind. The examination must be conducted in the full light of day. The only way to ensure this is an open public enquiry into the functioning of the Government of Ireland Act in all its aspects. To press for this is one of the first duties of those who want a democratic settlement of the Irish question.[13]

The Greaves strategy was not to raise issues of claimed maladministration in Northern Ireland merely to have these remedied by Westminster – it was not a 'reformist' strategy. The ultimate objective was to discredit the operation of devolved government in Northern Ireland as the basis for the nationalist demand for the repeal of the 1920 Act and the replacement of the Act by a 'democratic settlement' which is 'nationalist-speak' for the ending of Partition. Greaves was, therefore, committed to the view that 'campaigning against the abuses of civil rights in the north of Ireland' was the means of achieving the overarching nationalist objective of Irish unity.[14]

Basically a similar strategic perspective informed the thinking of the Wolfe Tone Societies of which the Marxist / republican intellectuals

Anthony Coughlin and Roy Johnston were 'the intellectual leaders'. [15] Coughlin was born in Cork and did postgraduate study at the University of London in social policy before returning to Ireland in 1961 to lecture at Trinity College – while in London he was a member of the Connolly Association and a friend of Greaves and on returning to Ireland joined the Dublin Wolfe Tone Society in 1963 acting as its secretary. Coughlin was a contributor to many Irish nationalist publications including the *The United Irishmen* and *Tuairisc* which was the paper of the Wolfe Tone Societies. Johnston was a theoretical physicist resident (1960-63) in London where he was a member of the Connolly Association and the CPGB and like Coughlin a friend of Greaves and a Marxist.

Republican strategic thinking in the 1960s

The key strategic thinking of Coughlin and Johnston in relation to the pursuit of Irish unity was set out by Purdie in his account of the origins of the civil rights movement:

> Johnston and Coughlin … argued for a strategy of building republican support through involvement in agitation on social and economic grievances as well as by a principled stand for a united and independent Ireland.[16]

This type of strategic thinking was apparent in the 1966 June edition of Wolfe Tone Societies' journal *Tuairisc*. The editorial posed two questions. The first was: 'How do the practical problems encountered by the common people of Ireland derive from the connection with Britain?'[17] The unstated import of the question is essentially nationalist; the 'practical problems' do in fact derive from the 'connection with Britain'. The second question was directly related to the objectives and organisation of the civil rights movement under consideration by republicans in 1966:

> How can these practical problems be tackled by mobilising the demands of large numbers of ordinary people towards simple and realisable objectives, the achievement of which will (a) prove to them the power of their numbers and organisation and (b) whet their appetite for further advances that will ultimately be such as to enable the existing structure [Stormont]

to be toppled and a new thirty two county structure to be instituted, based firmly on the democratic organisation of the common people? [18]

The distinction between 'strategy' and 'tactic' is implicit in the question. The strategy envisaged the pursuit of immediate 'simple and realisable' demands (easily categorised as 'civil rights') to achieve the ultimate objective of Irish unity ('thirty two county structure'). The tactic explicit in the question was 'mobilisation' involving politicisation and empowerment of the 'common people'. The editorial recommended that the organisation required to effect the 'mobilisation' must avoid a dual illusion: (1) the illusion that 'parliamentary action alone is sufficient to make any significant change in the social structure' and (2) the illusion that 'a simple-minded armed struggle against the British occupation is alone sufficient to generate sufficient popular support to complete the national revolution'.[19] The reference to 'completing the national revolution' is a reference to the achievement of Irish unity. The thinking that informed the *Tuairisc* editorial represented a dimension of Marxist thought that was a distinctive feature of Irish republicanism during the 1960s Cathal Goulding leadership of the IRA. The dimension of Marxist thought was significantly due to the influence of Johnston (who was a member of the IRA) and Coughlin within the republican movement and specifically within the Dublin Wolfe Tone Society.

Cathal Goulding took over the leadership of the IRA as Chief of Staff in 1962 after the failed 1956-62 IRA border campaign – the failure of which was for the new 1960s thinking within the republican movement a paradigm case of a 'simple-minded' resort to 'armed struggle'. Documents seized in 1966 from the prominent republican and IRA member Sean Garland (subsequently leader of the Workers Party) by the Irish police suggested that: 'Republicans were still a secret military organisation and were arming and training, but there had been a substantial shift in emphasis from militarism to open political agitation'.[20] Goulding was the key to this 'substantial shift' in the strategic thinking of the IRA. Goulding as IRA Chief of Staff maintained that the IRA should remain a military force but argued that the movement had to change its strategy in pursuit of its objective of Irish unity. The crucial issue for Goulding after the failure of the IRA 1956-62 border campaign (set out in a retrospective 1970 contribution to the *New Left Review*) was the question of the 'form' of the next IRA campaign:

When the campaign in the Six Counties ended in 1962, the leadership of the movement was faced with the question: what form will our next campaign take? We had to ask this question of ourselves, because we knew that if we were to retain the leadership of the movement, and maintain the movement itself as a revolutionary organisation, we would need to have a policy for the next phase of the fight against British imperialism in Ireland.[21]

This displays a traditional Irish nationalist mind-set involving an unremitting commitment to the ending of 'British imperialism' in Ireland where the use of the expression 'British imperialism' displays a traditional nationalist understanding of Partition. But Goulding in his 1970 contribution to the *New Left Review* outlined a dimension of the strategic thinking of the IRA that had been absent during the failed IRA 1956-62 border campaign – the need to mobilise popular support which coincided with the strategic thinking of Johnston and Coughlin.

The 1956-62 border campaign failed due significantly to a lack of support within the nationalist community in Northern Ireland or indeed in Ireland. This lack of support was understood by Goulding to be due to the fact (for him) that 'the people had no real knowledge of our objectives' and consequently were not effectively mobilised to support the 'fight against British imperialism in Ireland'.[22] The import of this thinking was that the key issue for the successful outcome of the 'struggle' was to effectively mobilise popular support. Goulding's core position was that the ending of Partition required the IRA to adopt 'policies' which connected the 'struggle' to the 'everyday problems of the people' both in the Republic and in Northern Ireland. Goulding in the *New Left Review* contribution explained that the republican movements first objective must be:

> To involve themselves in the everyday problems of people; to organise them to demand better houses, better working conditions, better jobs, better pay, better education- to develop agitationary activities along these lines. By doing this we felt that we could involve the people, not so much in supporting the republican movement for our political ends, but in supporting agitation so that they themselves would be part of a revolutionary force demanding what the present system just couldn't produce … So, we believed that

political power must be our objective, whether we got it through physical force or through the ballot box or by agitation. The means are immaterial. Of course we believed, as a revolutionary organisation, that the people can't get real power by simply having representatives elected.[23]

The import of Goulding's thinking which informed his leadership of the IRA in the 1960s and reflected the intellectual influence of republican ideologues such as Johnston and Coughlin was that the effective mobilisation of support for the pursuit of Irish unity must be embedded in a socialist transformation of Ireland required for the successful implementation of 'policies' to alleviate the 'everyday problems' (in for example the domains of employment, housing, education) of the 'people'. The thinking was both revolutionary 'demanding what the present system just couldn't produce', and anti-democratic: 'the people can't get real power by simply having representatives elected'. The import here is that the path to 'real power' may lie not through the ballot box but through extra-parliamentary political agitation and ultimately if necessary through the barrel of a gun. The significance of the republican strategy of mobilisation against alleged systematic unionist discrimination in Northern Ireland was that the republicans believed that the 'unionist regime' could not survive the destruction of what they perceived to be a unionist structure of systematic discrimination and oppression directed against the nationalist minority in Northern Ireland. The strategic implication for republicans and the radical left involved in the Northern Ireland civil rights movement was that the effective mobilisation of the nationalist population in Northern Ireland against 'discrimination' would result in the end of the 'unionist regime' and with that the end of Partition.

The republican input into the civil rights movement

The Marxist orientated strategic thinking within the 1960s IRA under Goulding's leadership and the intellectual leadership of Johnston and Coughlin within the Wolfe Tone Societies was underpinned by a deep-rooted nationalist anti-Partition objective. English in *Armed Struggle* noted that: 'Republican input into the civil rights movement, and the deeply anti-Partitionist ambition behind that input are frequently ignored or downplayed in readings of the North's descent into violence'.[24] English's

comments provide a significant corrective to the 'downplayed' contribution of the republican movement to the setting up of the Northern
Ireland Civil Right's Association (NICRA). Bob Purdie in his history of
the NICRA categorically attributed the setting up of the NICRA specifically to Johnston, Coughlin and the Dublin Wolfe Tone Society:

> The initiative in setting up the NICRA was very much that of Johnston,
> Coughlin and the Dublin Wolfe Tone Society ... It was the Dublin Wolfe
> Tone Society which suggested a civil rights campaign and republicans
> and communists were centrally involved in the creation of the civil rights
> movement and that involvement of republicans in the setting up of the
> NICRA cannot be denied.[25]

The NICRA was formed in Belfast on 9 April 1967 and 'the NICRA's
effective officers belonged to either the Communist Party of Northern
Ireland or the Belfast Wolfe Tone Society'.[26] The NICRA was the creation of
the 1960s republican leadership but the NICRA was not in the strict sense
a republican front – that is a movement under the direct control of republicans. The NICRA was not intended by republicans to be strictly a republican
front. Adams in the *Politics of Irish Freedom* states that: 'Republicans were
actually central to the formation of the NICRA and far from using it as a
front organisation those of us who attended the inaugural meeting were
directed to elect only two of our membership to the executive.'[27]

But if not strictly controlled by the 1960s republican leadership the
'the republicans were active in influencing the direction taken by the
NICRA.'[28] which was the development of broadly based political agitation (incorporating a range of organisations under the umbrella of the
NICRA) focused in Northern Ireland on the issue of 'discrimination'[29]
with the ultimate objective of 'dismantling Northern Ireland'.[30]

The early civil rights marches

The NICRA authorised the first civil rights march from Coalisland to
Dungannon which took place on 24 August 1968. The march was organised
by Austin Currie (the local nationalist MP) assisted by two nationalist councillors and three republicans.[31] Currie and the then Republican

Labour MP Gerry Fitt led the marchers with stewards provided by the local IRA.[32] The march was peaceful but not inaccurately described by Prince in *Northern Ireland's '68* as an 'Irish nationalist parade'.[33] The march, contrary to the judgment of the Cameron Report[34] provided a visible link between the civil rights movement and Irish republicanism:

> The very first civil rights march from Coalisland to Dungannon displayed its nationalist, and even IRA sympathies in a blatant fashion. The bands played 'who fears to speak of '98' an anti- British ballad commemorating the United Irishmen uprising in 1798, and 'faith of our father', a Catholic hymn … frequently played at nationalist gatherings.[35]

The march ended in Dungannon where Fitt and Currie delivered speeches in which analogies were drawn between the Soviet suppression in Eastern Europe (the Soviet Union had invaded Czechoslovakia on 21 August 1968 a few days prior to the march) and the Stormont 'regime' in Northern Ireland. Currie referred to the membership of the unionist government at Stormont as 'Orange bigots' and Fitt branded the two senior RUC officers policing the march as 'a pair of black bastards' (the *Cameron Report* referred to the 'regrettable and irresponsible abuse of the police by Mr Fitt')[36] and he assured the crowd that 'the lights would not go out until they had achieved civil rights and a thirty-two county republic.'[37]

The first civil rights march reinforced for unionists their perception of the civil rights movement as the 'old nationalist enemy in new clothes' – that is, the perception that behind the civil rights movement there was a Marxist orientated Irish republicanism committed to the ultimate nationalist goal of the destruction of Northern Ireland.[38] Fitt and Currie's rhetoric of nationalist insult was not directed to inciting violence and in fact 'republican marshals repeatedly stopped marchers from attacking the police in Dungannon.'[39] This meant that the march, despite its displays of overt nationalist sentiment, offered no real challenge to the authority of the Stormont government and made little (if any) contribution to the type of crisis that would have pressurised Westminster to intervene in the affairs of Northern Ireland.[40]

The second civil rights march took place in Londonderry on 5 October 1968 and was authorised by the NICRA but organised by the

Derry Housing Action Committee (DHAC) controlled by Londonderry-based left-wing radicals within the republican movement and the NICRA. Eamonn McCann in *War and an Irish Town* recorded that the NICRA sponsorship of the march was 'nominal'. The NICRA was regarded by the DHAC as a 'liberal body with no pretensions to revolutionary politics' to which the DHAC paid 'little attention' [41] – the organisation of the march was effectively under the direction of the DHAC. The 'game plan' of the march organisers was to put into effect a tactic of deliberate provocation.[42] The *Cameron Report* concluded that:

> We have good reason to believe that during the six weeks since the Coalisland to Dungannon march certain left wing activists had decided that their campaign would benefit from violent conflict with the authorities.[43]

There had been in Northern Ireland at the very least a tacit understanding that certain marching/parade routes were 'off limits' for non-unionists and other routes 'off-limits' for unionists. The DHAC organisers of the 5 October march deliberately selected a route in Londonderry to break that convention with the objective of having the march banned as a threat to civil order. The game plan was that the banning of the march would give rise to a context for confrontation with the police. The route selected by the DHAC was informed by the calculation that: 'The one certain way to ensure a head-on clash with the authorities was to organise a non-Unionist march through the city centre'.[44]

The march was banned by the government on 4 October. The response by the DHAC was to tour the nationalist areas of Londonderry to appeal to 'people to come out tomorrow and show your contempt for the law'.[45] The DHAC calculation was that 'a ban would encourage thousands of outraged citizens who would not otherwise have marched to come out and demonstrate their disgust'.[46] In the event the march was attended by about four hundred participants which included local nationalist politicians and three Westminster MPs. The expected confrontation occurred ('we had indeed set out to make the police over-react'[47]) and was initiated by the radical element at the head of the march[48] and probably encouraged by speeches that at least tacitly encouraged 'the use of violence to break the police line'.[49] The *Cameron Report* was particularly critical of the nationalist Westminster MP, Gerry Fitt:

Mr Fitt sought publicity for himself and his political views, and must clearly have envisaged the possibility of a violent clash with the police as providing the publicity he so ardently sought. His conduct in our judgment was reckless and wholly irresponsible in a person occupying his public position.[50]

The over-reaction by the police in breaking up the demonstration was the focus of the media coverage that the DHAC had anticipated:

By the next morning, after the television newsreels and the newspaper pictures, a howl of elemental rage was unleashed across Northern Ireland, and it was clear that things were never going to be the same again ... At a stroke we had shaken the (Stormont) government ... and made Derry world news.[51]

The nationalist 'howl of elemental rage' in Northern Ireland and the worldwide publicity given to the 5 October march initiated a new trajectory of violent confrontation and mass protest (a march in Londonderry on 16 November 1968 attracted a crowd of 15,000) that increasingly marked subsequent civil rights marches. The events of 5 October transformed the NICRA (initially 'a self-selected group of activists'[52]) into a Northern Ireland wide civil rights movement which 'transformed the political situation in Northern Ireland, producing sectarian tensions, instability and violence'.[53]

The People's Democracy and the descent into violence

The student based People's Democracy established on 9 October was a significant catalyst for the descent into instability and violence in 1969. The activism of the People's Democracy directed by a combination of Irish republicanism and radical socialism reflected the 1960s milieu of student protest in western Europe and the United States. The most significant activity of the People's Democracy was a four-day 'long march' from Belfast to Londonderry on 1 January 1969 – the marchers claimed as their model the 1965 Martin Luther King Selma to Montgomery marches. Following Prime Minister Terence O'Neill's conciliatory speech on 9 December 1968 the NICRA agreed a moratorium on marches 'but on 20 December the People's Democracy defied the government, liberal public opinion and the mainstream of the civil rights movement'[54]by announcing their determination to march from Belfast to Londonderry. The route of the march was deliberately chosen by the leadership of the People's Democracy to provoke violence:

> A violent confrontation, however, was exactly what Farrell wanted [Michael Farrell was one of prominent leaders of People's Democracy] to provoke. 'I believed', he told an interviewer , 'that if you attacked on a number of fronts the whole thing would collapse ... the state might dissolve – and then the demands you'd been making could be achieved ... Either the government would face up to the extreme right ... and protect the march ... or it would be exposed as impotent in the face of sectarian thuggery and Westminster would be forced to intervene.[55]

These comments more than suggest that the leadership of the People's Democracy utilised civil rights marches as a tactic for violent confrontation to bring about the ultimate republican goal of the collapse of the 1920 Stormont settlement which was precisely the view expressed by the *Cameron Report*:

> While the 'manifesto' of the People's Democracy largely echoes and endorses the objectives of the Civil Rights Association, it is plain from the evidence frankly given to us that the real objects and purposes of the more effective leaders of the movement are much more radical, the achievement of which would almost necessarily involve the submergence of existing political boundaries and (as an inevitable consequence) the break up of the present political and constitutional links between Northern Ireland and Great Britain.[56]

The marchers were indeed (as anticipated) met with hostility as they passed through unionist areas and at Burntollet (near Londonderry) they were met with a violent response from loyalists despite what the *Cameron Report* referred to as a 'serious effort to protect the marchers'[57] by the police who accompanied the marchers and the ambush was strongly condemned by unionist MPs.[58]

The fact that members of the People's Democracy and in particular the leadership saw (as claimed by Paul Arthur in the *People's Democracy 1968-73*) their task as 'the destruction of the state no matter what the consequences'[59]does not mean that this radical motivation was shared by all the participants. But to understand their participation in terms of an extreme form of political innocence is simply absurd. The 'innocence thesis' was put forward by the nationalist politician Eddie McAteer and Frank Gogarty, chairman of the NICRA. McAteer referred to the marchers as 'dewy eyed innocents' and Gogarty referred to them as 'innocents, the wee folk out to slay the dragon'.[60] Paul (now Lord) Bew provided a more sophisticated version of the innocent 'wee folk' thesis:

> If one had been more attuned to the society itself one would have said, 'Well can one march between here and Derry 70 miles in these little Protestant villages, is this a wise thing to do?' In fact what we said was, 'We are socialists. We are progressive. Trying to stop us marching through your villages is ridiculous because we are carrying a banner of enlightenment.[61]

The import of Lord Bew's characterisation of the marchers who did not necessarily share the strategic objectives of the organisers is that they were blinded to political reality by a heightened sense of their own 'enlightenment' to the extent that they were incapable of discerning the difference between political wisdom and political folly.

But whatever the motivation of the marchers the outcome of the 'long march' was an intensification of political instability and violence in Northern Ireland. The apex of violent confrontation was reached in Londonderry on 12 August 1969 in the wake of the traditional Apprentice Boy's parade commemorating the 'relief of Derry' in 1689. Republicans formed the Derry Citizens Defence Association (DCDA) in anticipation of an attack on the Bogside (a nationalist area of Londonderry) by the Apprentice Boys despite the fact that no such attack had occurred in the past. It was nationalist youths from the Bogside who attacked the Apprentice Boys parade. Professor Brian M. Walker has provided an eyewitness account of what happened:

> During the last stages of the Apprentice Boys parade.. stones were thrown at the marchers and the police ... by young people from the Bogside ... Then a torrent of stones and eventually petrol bombs were directed at the police , until after two hours the first baton charge took place and from there the fight escalated.[62]

133

The confrontation moved to the Bogside where the police were met by a well organised and obviously pre-planned response described by McCann in *War and an Irish Town*:

> Barricades went up all around the area, open-air petrol bomb factories were established, dumpers hijacked from a building site were used to carry stones to the front. Teenagers went on the roof of the block of High Flats which dominates Rossville Street and began lobbing petrol bombs at the police below.[63]

The conflict (subsequently referred to as the 'Battle of the Bogside') was certainly not spontaneous and lasted for forty eight hours. The leaders in the Bogside called for assistance and the diverting of police resources away from Londonderry by organised street protest in other places. The NICRA on 13 August urged widespread demonstrations (outside Belfast) to protest about the situation in Londonderry and wherever they occurred they ended in violence:

> We are satisfied that the spread of the disturbances owed much to a deliberate decision by some minority groups to relieve police pressure on rioters in Londonderry. Amongst these groups must be included NICRA, whose executive decided to organise demonstrations in the Province so as to prevent reinforcement of the police in Londonderry. We were told that they intended to exclude Belfast from their plans; but we have no doubt that some activists, so far from accepting the decision, did co-operate with some in Londonderry to call for demonstrations in Belfast. [64]

Republican activists organised marches in west Belfast contrary to the directions of the NICRA which simply means that by this stage the NICRA had decisively lost control of what was happening. The republican demonstrations in west Belfast resulted in extreme and almost certainly pre-planned violence directed against the police:

> Two RUC stations were attacked by rioters with missiles and petrol bombs. A battering ram was used to attempt to smash the door of Hastings Street station. Commercial properties were torched and barricades were erected.

Assaults on the police included a hand grenade attack and small firearms fire. One police officer and two civilians received gunshot wounds. The police now believed, incorrectly, but understandably, that they faced a major insurrection.[65]

The belief that Northern Ireland faced a major insurrection was, not without justification, widespread among the unionist population. This was reinforced on 13 August 1969 by Taoiseach Jack Lynch's 'the Irish government can no longer stand by' speech. Lynch's position was that 'the present situation is the inevitable outcome of the policies pursued for decades by successive Stormont governments' and that the eventual solution was the 'restoration of the historic unity of our country' and in the meantime he called for 'the British government to apply immediately to the United Nations for the urgent dispatch of a peace-keeping force to the six counties of Northern Ireland' which was in effect a call for a British withdrawal.[66]

This widespread violence in turn led to a loyalist backlash on 14-15 August in Belfast involving large crowds of nationalists and loyalists in which seven people were killed and thousands lost their homes the majority of which were Catholic.

Conclusion

The 1969 descent into violence in Northern Ireland was not unrelated to the combination of Marxism and traditional Irish nationalism that constituted the 'ideology' that informed the 1960s republican thinking that directed the formation of the civil rights movement. Discrimination was the focal point for both strands. Irish nationalism is characterised by an essentially superficial understanding of unionism. This superficial understanding has been expressed by nationalists in a multiplicity of ways but in the context of the 'civil rights' era it took the form of the understanding that Partition could not survive without discrimination and that once unionists ceased to be the beneficiaries of discrimination their unionism would simply erode.[67] This nationalist thesis was reinforced by the Marxist component that the 'benefits' of discrimination blinded unionists (or the unionist 'working class') to their true class solidarity with nationalists with the import that the ending of discrimination would give rise to a class solidarity between nationalists and erstwhile unionists thus creating the class basis for an all-Ireland socialist republic.

The republican and radical left thinking that was dominant within the civil rights movement discounted the long-term effects of the violent confrontation that they increasingly deliberately provoked. The understanding was that the ending of discrimination (and the ending of Partition) would liberate unionists from the political blindness that prevented them from seeing unionism as 'the charlatanry and humbug that it is'.[68]

The exact opposite occurred. The roots of unionist commitment to the Union are deeper than nationalists had the capacity to perceive and the notion of 'class solidarity' is a core component of a now defunct Marxism. The 'ideology' of the dominant players within the civil rights movement was in fact divorced from political reality. The result was that contrary to the thinking of the republican and radical left civil rights activists the confrontational tactics of the civil rights mass protests polarised unionists and nationalists and this led to the context of violence that reached a peak in August 1969. The violence of August 1969 could not be contained by a stretched and exhausted RUC. The British army was deployed on the streets of Belfast and Londonderry on 14 August 1969 and on 11 January 1970 the IRA split and the Provisional IRA (PIRA) came into existence. The era of mass civil rights protest was effectively over and the decades of IRA terrorism were about to begin.

Notes

[1]   Economist 23 August 1969.

[2]   Lord Cameron DSC, *Disturbances in Northern Ireland: Report of the Commission appointed by the Governor of Northern Ireland (The Cameron Report)*, (Belfast: HMSO, 1969), Par. 11.

[3]   Christopher Hewitt, 'The roots of violence: Catholic grievance and Irish nationalism during the civil rights period', in Patrick J. Roche and Brian Barton (eds), *The Northern Ireland Question: Myth and Reality* (Tonbridge: WordZworth Publishing, 2013), p.53.

[4]   Ibid., p.51.

[5]   Christopher Hewitt, op. cit., p.52.

[6]   Gerry Adams, *The Politics of Irish Freedom* (Dingle: Brandon Book Publishers Ltd, 1986), p.12, 17.

[7]   Bob Purdie, 'Was the Civil Rights Movement a Republican/Communist Conspiracy?', *Irish Political Studies*, Vol. 3, 1988, pp.33,34,36.

[8]   Bob Purdie, *Politics in the Streets: The origins of the civil rights movement in Northern Ireland* (Belfast: The Blackstaff Press, 1990), p

[9]   Ibid., p.123.

[10] Sean Redmond, *Desmond Greaves and the Origins of the Civil Rights Movement in Northern Ireland*, p.5. Available at www.connollyassociation.org.uk/desmond-greaves/origins-civil-rights.

[11] Ibid., pp.5-6.

[12] Ibid., p.6

[13] Ibid. ,p.3

[14] Sean Redmond, op. cit., p.2.

[15] Bob Purdie, op.cit., p.123.

[16] Bob Purdie, op.cit., p.124

[17] Tuairisco, June 1966, p.1.

[18] Ibid., p.1.

[19] Ibid., p.1

[20] Bob Purdie, 'Was the Civil Rights movement a Republican/Communist conspiracy?', *Irish Political Studies*, Vol.3, 1988, p.37.

[21] Cathal Goulding, 'The New Strategy of the IRA', *New Left Review*, Vol.2, 1970.p.51.

[22] Ibid., p.52.

23   Ibid., p.52

24   Richard English, *Armed Struggle: A History of the IRA* (Basingstoke and Oxford: Macmillan, 2003), p. 90.

25   Bob Purdie, op. cit., p.33,34, 36. See Richard English, op. cit., p. 91.

26   Bob Purdie, *Politics in the Streets*, p.115

27   Gerry Adams, op. cit., p.12.

28   Bob Purdie, op. cit., p.174.

29   Ibid. p.127.

30   Ibid. p.157.Purdie refers to Steve Bruce, *God Save Ulster: Religion and the Politics of Paisleyism* (Oxford: Clarendon Press, 1986), p.266 where Bruce argues that 'a large part of the movement was always ultimately interested in dismantling Northern Ireland'.

31   Christopher Hewitt, op. cit., p.55.

32   Christopher Hewitt, op. cit., p.29.

33   Simon Prince, *Northern Ireland's '68: Civil Rights, Global Revolt and the Origins of the Troubles,* (Dublin: Irish Academic Press, 2007),

34   *The Cameron Report,* Pars, 34-35.

35   Simon Prince, op. cit., p.121 and Christopher Hewitt, op. cit., pp. 29-30.

36   Ibid. p.122 and the *Cameron Report,* Par. 34. But post-1969, Fitt was implacably opposed to republican (republicans destroyed his Belfast home in 1983) and 'loyalist' violence and in a House of Lords speech on 8 November 2000 Lord Fitt spoke in opposition to the implementation of the Patten report stating that ' if it had not been for the RUC, Northern Ireland would have sunk into a pit of anarchy'. See Chris Ryder, *Fighting Fitt* (Belfast: Brehon Press, 2006), p.378.

37   Bob Purdie, op. cit., pp. 136-137.

38   Ibid., p. 123. See also Richard English, op. cit., p. 96 and Christopher Hewitt, op. cit., p.52.

39   Simon Prince, op. cit., p.124.

40   Ibid., p.124

41   Eamonn McCann, *War and an Irish Town* (Chicago: Haymarket Books, 2018), p.66.

42   Ibid., p.62. See also Simon Prince, op. cit., p. 156.

43   *Cameron Report,* Par 44

44   Eamonn McCann, op. cit., p.62

45   Ibid., p.67.

46 Ibid., p.67.

47 Ibid., p.69

48 *Cameron Report,* Par. 46, Par. 51.

49 Ibid., Par 50.

50 Ibid. ,Par. 46.

51 Eamonn McCann, op. cit., pp.69-70

52 Bob Purdie, op. cit., p.155.

53 Ibid. p.156.

54 Ibid. p.213.

55 Simon Prince, op. cit., p.205, p. 206.

56 *Cameron Report,* Pars. 100, 195.

57 Ibid., Par. 101. See also Simon Prince, op. cit., p. 208.

58 See *Belfast Telegraph*, 3 January 1969 and *Belfast Telegraph*, 6 January 1969.

59 Paul Arthur, *The People's Democracy 1968-73* (Belfast: Blackstaff Press, 1974), p.41

60 Bob Purdie, op.cit., p.216.

61 Simon Prince, op. cit., p.207.

62 Brian M. Walker, 'Eyewitness to history', *Belfast Telegraph*, 4 September 2019.

63 Eamonn McCann, op. cit., pp.85-86.

64 *Violence and Civil Disturbances in Northern Ireland in 1969* (*Scarman* Report) (Belfast: HMSO, 1972), Par 1.22.

65 Brian M.Walker, op. cit.

66 *Jack Lynch*, Wikipedia.

67 Sean Redmond, op. cit., p.19.

68 Simon Prince, op. cit., p.99.

5

Discrimination in housing and employment in Northern Ireland[1]

Graham Gudgin

Introduction

Accusations of discrimination against Catholics by unionist governments in Northern Ireland from 1921-72 played an important role in the politics of the time. This was particularly true in the years leading up to the outbreak of the Troubles in 1968 and it remained true of the subsequent period under direct rule up to the 1998 Good Friday Agreement. After the Good Friday Agreement the issue of discrimination largely disappeared from active politics even though the objective conditions in housing and employment changed little for several decades.

Once nationalists were in a power-sharing government from 1998 there was little political mileage from campaigning on discrimination. In part nationalists may have trusted their politicians to deal with the issue, but since little actually changed on the ground its disappearance indicated that it had been used largely for political purposes. The underlying issue in the politics of Northern Ireland was of course Irish unity and even minor issues of discrimination could be, and were, used to further the cause and to argue that Northern Ireland was a failed, and even an irreformable state.

Accusations of discrimination, and more general abuse of civil rights, formed the backbone of sympathy for the nationalist cause among neutral observers, and of antagonism to the unionist case. Even though unionists had had minimal power in Northern Ireland for a quarter of a century up to 1998, the accusations were regularly repeated and renewed. There were essentially four charges. These were discrimination in housing and

THE NORTHERN IRELAND QUESTION

employment, gerrymandering and abuse of civil power. Only the first two are addressed here.

This chapter deals with allegations of discrimination in housing and employment since the focus here is on how power was used rather than on how power was achieved. Related issues including gerrymandering of electoral boundaries, abuses of civil power, in the use of legislation (for example, the Special Powers Act of 1922) are not considered here. Allegations of abuse of civil power can be seen as much as a consequence of the rejection of the Stormont government by nationalists as a cause of that rejection. Since it is the latter which is of concern here, neither this nor gerrymandering to maintain dominance in face of nationalist intentions to dismantle the state, are the subject here.

The burden of this chapter is that discrimination was never as important in social and economic terms as it was made out to be. It was however enormously important in political terms because nationalists persuaded the world that they were hugely disadvantaged. Unionists remained strangely inert in face of accusations they should have known were greatly exaggerated. Part of the political problem was the anti-intellectual nature of political unionism, with little effort put into gathering and analysing data or arguing their case. Famously, the Ulster Unionist Party (UUP) failed to make any submission to the 1968 Cameron Commission on the causes of the disturbances in Northern Ireland.

Fifty years later the surviving politicians from that time remain unable to explain this lapse. Perhaps typical of unionist feebleness in this respect was the view of the UUP Westminster MP Martin Smyth in 1981 that Protestants were constrained from responding to republican allegations in the media of unionist discrimination by 'decent Ulster decency'. Unionist 'did not go to the media because they did not have the whole story'.[2] It does not seem to have occurred to Smyth and other unionists to get the whole story.

Paul Bew in *Ireland: The Politics of Enmity 1789-2006* considered that once protests began in 1968:

> Cocooned in their devolutionist shell the unionists found it particularly difficult to defend the peculiarities of their system to outsiders. They found it particularly difficult to explain themselves to the London political elite.[3]

Public opinion, in Great Britain and elsewhere, was easily convinced that discrimination was the cause of political discontent and violence in Northern Ireland. Constitutional stability in Great Britain for decades or even centuries up to the 1960s meant that there was little understanding of, or feeling for, nationalistic territorial disputes. It was easier to view Northern Ireland through the lens of sectarianism manifested through discrimination. The historical interpretation may change in future as Brexit educates British public opinion in the importance of national identity. The way in which Irish nationalists have linked Brexit to Irish unity is also making it clear to British opinion that Irish nationalists will turn almost any issue into a case for Irish unity. The rise of the SNP playing a similar role in Scotland also educates English public opinion on how nationalists play politics to support independence.

The importance of the allegations of discrimination lay in the fact that it could be argued that Northern Ireland Protestants are not trusted to form a government even in circumstances in which they gained a clear majority of votes in democratic elections. This lack of trust underpinned all constitutional talks up the Good Friday Agreement and resulted not only in a power-sharing government in the new Northern Ireland assembly, but also in a strong form of power-sharing which ensured that former terrorists would form part of the executive as well as the parliament. One of the important but unremarked aspects of the 1998 Agreement has been the justification it provides for the view that all previous forms of regional government in Northern Ireland were unacceptable.

A belief in the importance of past discrimination is not the only factor underpinning the inevitability of power-sharing government. The need to accommodate a large permanent minority and to bring an end to the violence has led to a search for unconventional political arrangements, but the form of these arrangements was heavily coloured by an ethos of victims and oppressors. Without this ethos the outcome might have been different, and we might note that situations in which violence is difficult to eradicate did not lead the Spanish authorities to adopt the power-sharing 'solution' of Northern Ireland.

In aggregate little changed in the two decades after the suspension of the unionist-dominated parliament in March 1972. Even the overt use of housing location for electoral advantage in a few local authorities had already been dealt with. While protesters were correct to complain about the abuses which did occur prior to 1972 the civil rights movement (which did not raise the cases of discrimination against Protestants in nationalist controlled councils) was quickly taken up as a stick with which to beat unionism.

Historians Treatment of Discrimination

In any other society the reaction to localised problems of discrimination would plausibly have been to reform housing allocation in the small number of offending councils. In Northern Ireland the issue helped to initiate thirty years of violent conflict. This over-reaction to a serious but limited problem has been legitimised by its treatment in academic and journalistic accounts of the period. Michael Farrell's self-consciously partisan account, for instance, highlights only one area (Fermanagh), confuses general housing shortage with misallocation and fails to mention any instance of nationalist discrimination against Protestants.[4]

All of the many histories of the Stormont period 1921-72 tell the sequential story of the civil rights protests against discrimination and the subsequent descent into violence from which Northern Ireland is yet to fully recover. The sequence of events and its frequent repetition has led the causes of the Troubles to become closely linked in many people's minds with discrimination. This is almost axiomatic among the nationalist community in Ireland and their supporters elsewhere, and the violence of the last thirty years is widely interpreted as having at least some justification in the behaviour of the unionist people and government of the 'failed political entity' of Northern Ireland. It is also increasingly common in middle and professional class circles within the unionist community where a sense of guilt or at least embarrassment is an important element underlying political development.

One result of years of largely undefended allegations is that Northern Ireland Protestants are frequently described in terms usually reserved for the world's least savoury political cultures. Consider the following from Bowyer Bell, professor of history at Columbia University and author of several major books on Northern Ireland

Many Protestants, who were mostly plain, often poor children of their own history, were also prejudiced practically from birth, decent folk but fearful of the alien. The system began by teaching toddlers differences, superiority and privilege. Thus, most were bigots, some simple and gentle, others nasty and if need be brutal.[5]

To the celebrated Irish historian, Professor Joe Lee of University College Cork, the northern Protestants have a 'herrenvolk' mentality.[6] Political scientists Brendan O'Leary and John McGarry take a similar view in stating that, 'the UUP could rely on ingrained ethnic prejudices to sustain discrimination'.[7] More political writers have been even less restrained. For instance, Michael Farrell (1976) and Eamonn McCann (1974), the latter later a columnist for the *Belfast Telegraph*, depicted discrimination as being so pervasive as to be the foundation of the state.[8] Paul Foot, *Daily Mirror* columnist and nephew of a former British Labour Party leader, wrote, 'nowhere in the world was bigotry taken to such extravagant lengths as it was in Northern Ireland'.[9] Perhaps most influential was the report of the New Ireland Forum, established by the government of the Republic of Ireland, in 1983, that northern Catholics were 'deprived of the means of social and economic development'.[10]

Perhaps not many would follow Foot in assessing discrimination in Northern Ireland as being worse than in apartheid South Africa or in the pre-integration southern states of the USA, but the tide of rhetoric on this issue has been so strong that many people are willing to view the Stormont regime as having strong similarities with these odious regimes. This is the case despite a growing tendency for histories of Northern Ireland written in the 1990s to take a more objective or even overtly pro-unionist view.[11]

Some of the most prominent Northern Ireland historians from a unionist background have tended to write rather little about discrimination. Patterson and Kaufman have only seven glancing references to discrimination in their exhaustive examination of *Unionism and Orangeism in Northern Ireland since 1945*. Patterson's *Ireland Since 1939* does not include the word discrimination in its index but the text does have some limited discussion of discrimination in housing, partly based on Gudgin[12] and hence not new to readers of this chapter.

Paul Bew's Oxford history of Ireland also has no references to discrimination in its index although the word does appear in the text.[13] Both Bew and Patterson focus on the politics and the politicians rather than underlying social or economic influences on the politics. Bew does refer to discrimination in housing. He points out that Catholics were over-represented in local authority housing but adds, 'this reality co-existed with another, in the town of Dungannon the council was gerrymandered and not one new Catholic family had been offered a house in twenty-four years'.[14] The aim here seems to have been to show that discrimination did occur (in at least one case). There is no attempt to assess the scale of the problem across Northern Ireland. Since the 1971 census does not provide housing data by religion for local authorities, it is not possible to check whether Catholics in Dungannon were being allocated social housing from the Northern Ireland Housing Executive instead, but this seems likely. If so, Bew's reference to Dungannon gives an incomplete picture.

On employment Bew relies on a study by Edwin A. Aunger[15] which shows that in 1971 Catholics were significantly disadvantaged. They had a larger tendency to work in occupations which were less skilled, less well paid and with less prestige. The differences were not large but were substantial for males, more of whom were in unskilled occupations. There is no suggestion in the Aunger study that these differences were due to discrimination, but as Bew observes: 'in a context of inflamed sectional passions this sector [that is, unskilled Catholic workers] constituted an immense reservoir of opposition to unionism and indifference to moderation'.[16]

Anthony Alcock's rather brisk history *Understanding Ulster* is generally favourable to the unionist cause but provides limited assistance in understanding or evaluating the scale of discrimination either in housing or employment. On housing he wrote erroneously that: 'Housing was still [implicitly in 1968] controlled by local government and allocated on the basis of allegiance rather than need'.[17] This may have been intended to refer to perception rather than fact but is left unclear. Three pages later he quotes Professor Rose's 1971 study as making 'it clear that there was no systematic overall discrimination against Roman Catholics in public housing or jobs'. [18]

On employment he stated that 'Catholics were still drastically under-represented in jobs in unionist controlled local councils, the judiciary and public corporations'. As for the private sector high Roman Catholic unemployment was seen (Alcock does not say by whom) as being due to Protestant owners of firms 'giving preference to members of their own community'. No evidence is presented for these assertions which again he says later are refuted by Rose's study. He also asserts that the unionist government had a deliberate policy of fostering economic development to favour Protestant areas including the location of a university campus in (mainly Protestant) Coleraine.[19] This assertion had already been countered by a study by three Queen's University Belfast academics.[20]

An exception is Jonathan Bardon's 900-page magisterial *History of Ulster*. Bardon devotes three chapters to the period since 1945 and has many useful anecdotes about discrimination even if, once again, the word does not appear in the index. As with the other historians, there is no attempt to provide a comprehensive assessment of discrimination in either housing or employment. Individual cases focus heavily on Dungannon urban district council a small town with a population of 7,000, including the Caledon case, but give an impression that these are examples of a much wider malaise. Bardon is heavily influenced by McCluskey's dossier for the Campaign for Social Justice (see below) which he says: 'shows that housing discrimination was widespread in Northern Ireland particularly west of the Bann.'[21] As argued below the dossier does not do this, and Bardon fails to examine McCluskey's figures rigorously. Bardon does quote Professor Richard Rose's conclusion that 'the proportion of Catholics in subsidised housing is slightly higher than that of Protestants' but adds that 'this was more than offset if family size was taken into account'.[22] The latter wording does not appear in Rose and Bardon uses a secondary source rather than Rose's own book.

There is thus a tendency in Bardon to overstate and over-generalise the problem. This stems no doubt from a general frustration with the unionist regime of 1921-72 and its failures to attempt to bring Catholics into its party or government even when conditions were favourable as in the early 1960s. Effective one-party states are not uncommon across Europe and Japan, and it is perhaps with hindsight that the unionist regime's failures in this respect seem so stark but all agree that more could have done. This is however different from discrimination in jobs and housing where much was done to try to achieve fairness. Perhaps less than other historians Bardon tends to report allegations. The case of Sir John Lockwood's report on the siting of the new university is an example. Bardon reports nationalist outrage at Londonderry not being chosen but fails to mention Lockwood's reasoning for choosing Coleraine (the nearby availability of seaside accommodation suitable for students out of season).[23] More generally Bardon is somewhat naïve about industrial location. He suggests that a reason for the great success in attracting artificial fibres plants to Northern Ireland was the availability of water (admittedly plentiful in Northern Ireland). The real reason was the payment of capital grants in this most capital intensive of industries. These were available in assisted areas across the UK but were more generous in Northern Ireland which as a result managed to attract the majority of this sector to the Province.

In the criticisms of local authority reluctance to provide houses for new Catholic tenants (as opposed to the many being rehoused from slum conditions) Bardon gives no figures for the social housing provided by the state-funded and scrupulously fair Housing Trust. An earlier reference to the Housing Trust[24] states that Housing Trust rents were initially (that is, in 1945) set too high to help the poorest tenants. Nothing more is said about the Trust, and as Rose showed, Catholic families were over-represented in social housing at virtually all income levels. Bardon concludes that 'most of the new [social] dwellings were provided by local authorities and no steps were taken to ensure the even-handed allocation of houses'.[25]

Bob Purdie of Ruskin College Oxford provided a detailed examination of discrimination and is the only book to clarify the housing situation in Dungannon urban council[26]. Even he does not provide a complete context based on census figures but his treatment of the most politicised of the housing disputes, as in Dungannon is more comprehensive than can be obtained from any other account.

The best-known evaluation of the extent of discrimination under the Stormont regime was undertaken by the late Professor John H. Whyte.[27] There are three reasons why this issue was revisited in the original version of this chapter and why an attempt was made to add to Whyte's scholarly assessment. Firstly, Whyte's article was largely a literature review, albeit the most wide-ranging available, making limited use of comprehensive census material to give an overview. Since the available literature inevitably focuses on problems rather than normality, attempts to provide a complete census-based picture are important.

Secondly, recent research, especially in the area of labour economics, was unavailable to Whyte and this affected what was perhaps the weakest part of his review, namely job discrimination within the private sector. Finally, it is clear from living in Northern Ireland that Whyte's balanced assessment has had a limited impact on public perceptions, even among the most highly educated.

Discrimination in housing

Accusations of discrimination in housing were among the most important criticisms of the Stormont regime. This is not only because of the intrinsic importance of housing — a roof over one's head is after all among the most basic of necessities — but because the civil rights movement and hence the Troubles themselves began around the issues of housing allocation.

However, there has been much exaggeration. Professor Tom Wilson stated in *Ulster: Conflict and Consent*:

> The charge of discrimination directed against unionist policy has been repeated so often and with such total assurance that its validity now appears to be widely accepted without evidence, as though it had been fully substantiated as to have made any further presentation of the evidence no longer necessary.[28]

Allegations of discrimination in housing have a long history in Northern Ireland but they first came to more than local prominence in the civil rights campaign in the 1960s. The civil rights movement began with a campaign against the mis- allocation of housing by Dungannon rural district council — an area of 25,000 people. The campaign had begun with a campaign led by Conn McCluskey and his wife, two local doctors who formed the Campaign for Social Justice in 1964 in the Wellington Park Hotel in Belfast.

The campaign was later advanced by Austin Currie and others (Currie later became an Irish TD and government minister). These organised the squatting in two council houses in Caledon, county Tyrone, by two Catholic families waiting to be re-housed. One family, the McKenna's, was evicted and the house allocated to Miss Emily Beattie, a single Protestant, 19 years old, and secretary to the local unionist councillor who was also a unionist parliamentary candidate.

As Austin Currie said, 'if we had waited a thousand years, we would not have got a better example', hence indicating that it was an unusually stark case. In fact, Miss Beattie was engaged to be married, and married a few weeks later. Her future husband was from Monaghan and hence ineligible to register for the house in his own name. She came from an over-crowded home and her brother, an RUC officer involved in the eviction, came to live with her and her husband. However, as Lord Cameron said in his 1968 report of the Cameron Commission, 'by no stretch of the imagination could Miss Beattie be regarded as a priority tenant.'[29]

This incident was widely reported internationally and came to symbolise the abuse of civil rights by unionist authorities in Northern Ireland. Of course, the incident could not have attracted so much sympathy, were it not for accusations of discrimination in housing over a number of years.

The accusations largely concerned a number of small local authority districts west of the Bann, especially Dungannon and in Fermanagh. Figures from the McCluskey's and from similar reports in Fermanagh are repeated in all histories of the Troubles. These instances are usually taken uncritically as examples of discrimination in Northern Ireland as a whole, although the figures for the rest of Northern Ireland are never included in these accounts. In particular, Belfast is almost never mentioned.

The strength of the accusations has, if anything, grown over the years, and become all embracing: Let us return again to Bowyer Bell writing in 1993:

> The construction of small council houses for the poor caused most resentment. The state-controlled houses for the poor. And houses, like all else, went to unionists. Many Catholics felt that if houses did not go to Protestants they simply would not be built. Without a house the Catholics would go away. With a house the Catholics would stay and put the gerrymandered districts to threat. So there were few houses for Catholics.[30]

The picture painted here is clear, and is widely believed, including by a significant number of Protestants. It is, however, untrue, as can be clearly seen in the 1971 census of population taken in the dying months of the 50-year unionist rule from Stormont.

In that year there were 148,000 local authority dwellings in Northern Ireland, of which between 45,000 and 55,000 were occupied by Catholic families (depending on what is assumed about the religion of those who declined to answer the religion' question in the population census of that year). We can see immediately that the idea that there were few houses for Catholics is completely wrong. In fact, Catholics had a disproportionately large share of local authority housing. Catholics comprised 26.1% of households but occupied 30.7% of local authority households (see Table 5.1). Forty percent of Catholic families were in local authority houses compared with just over 30% of Protestants.

We might ask how it can be that it is widely believed that the unionist authorities built few houses for Catholics, when in fact the statistics show that they provided proportionately more for Catholics than for Protestants. The first thing to say is that even with the figures in Table 5.1, it may have been that unionist authorities were still not responding fully and fairly to the need of Catholics. There are three obvious ways to measure needs: firstly, relative to income; secondly, relative to family size; and thirdly in light of the existing housing conditions.

By luck there is some good quality evidence on these issues. A major survey was undertaken in 1968 by an American professor based in Glasgow, Richard Rose. This was published in his authoritative book on Northern Ireland, *Governing Without Consensus*. The survey covered

Table 5.1 Distribution of local authority housing by religion in Northern Ireland in 1971

	Percentage of households	
	All households	Households in local authority dwellings
Catholic	26.1	30.7
Other Denominations	65.2	60.8
Not Known	8.7	8.5
Total	100.0	100.0

Source: Northern Ireland Census of Population, 1971

a very wide range of political and social issues and provides an invaluable benchmark of conditions and attitudes in the last years of the Stormont regime and immediately prior to the Troubles.

The survey included a section on housing conditions, and Professor Rose discovered what was later confirmed by the 1971 census, that is, that Catholics had a disproportionately large share of local authority houses. The advantage to Catholics was very marked in Belfast, which had a unionist council (19% of Catholics were in local authority houses compared with 9% of Protestants), and in areas with nationalist councils (39% of Catholics compared with 15% of Protestants). Elsewhere, Catholics and Protestants got an equal share of local authority houses. Professor Rose's conclusion was that there was:

> ... no evidence of systematic discrimination against Catholics. The greatest bias appears to favour Catholics in areas controlled by Catholic councillors.[31]

Professor Rose controlled for the possibility of differing needs for local authority housing, firstly, by taking into account the incomes of families. He examined the allocation of local authority houses between Catholics and Protestants within six separate income groups. In five out of the six income categories the proportion of Catholics in local authority housing was higher than for Protestants. In other words, Catholics did not get more local authority houses only because they were poorer. At any given level of income Catholics fared distinctly better than Protestants.

The reason for this advantage is likely to be the larger family size of Catholics — in most housing allocation systems in the UK larger families receive priority — a practice formalised within the Northern Ireland Housing Executive from its inception in 1971. Prior to the establishment of the Housing Executive it is possible that large Catholic families did not receive as much priority as the (much less common) large Protestant families. For families with six plus children (78% of which were Roman Catholic) Rose reported that there were 12% more Protestants than Catholics in local authority housing. Rose does not provide figures for other family sizes.

The end of fifty years of housing policy in Northern Ireland, largely under unionist control, left Protestants over-represented in privately rented housing — usually thought of as poorer in quality to either local authority or owner-occupied housing, although much owner-occupied property in rural areas may have been of very low quality.

By 1971, the census of population showed that 30% of homes in Northern Ireland still lacked exclusive use of basic amenities including hot water, a fixed bath and indoor toilet. The figures for homes lacking amenities also show that Catholics were worse off than Protestants, although poor housing conditions were widespread in both communities. Thirty-six per cent of Catholic homes lacked these basic amenities, compared with 31% for Church of Ireland members and 27% for Presbyterians. The reasons for these differences are unclear and may reflect a range of influences including patterns of urban and rural home ownership.

All denominations clearly suffered poverty and poor housing, and differences between religions were not huge. Slum conditions were well known to both communities. A Building Design Partnership study of Belfast in 1969 found 'gross deficient' standards in most houses in both Catholic Cromac Street and Protestant Sandy Row. The unionist regime may be criticised for not raising standards for all. However, its resources were limited through much of its history. A significant housing problem had built up during the financially difficult inter-war years when only 50,000 new houses were built, a level only proportionately half as large as that in the rest of the UK.[32] In the post-war years up to 1970 a total of 178,000 houses were built, of which 120,000 were built by the public sector, a major achievement. However, it was not until 1985 when a further 150,000 houses had been built that the housing shortage can be said to have finally disappeared.

The thorny issue of differences between Catholics and Protestants in family size is important in understanding the housing issue.

This issue here, which is almost never raised in discussions on the allocation of housing in conditions of shortage (or indeed in respect of unemployment or public spending), is how can housing be allocated on a fair basis when one community has consistently higher birth rates than the other as was the case in Northern Ireland where church religious teaching led many Catholics to avoid birth control and consequently to have larger families.

In fact, one recent book does describe the difficulties in an open way. This is the autobiography of Maurice Hayes, formerly town clerk in Downpatrick and later permanent secretary in the Department of Health and Social Services and ombudsman for Northern Ireland. Hayes' account of the difficulties faced by the nationalist council in Downpatrick are worth repeating.

Down council attempted a fair allocation of local authority housing in the 1960s and was in Hayes' view one of the first councils to introduce a points system. This system favoured larger families and hence Catholics received most houses. To avoid this over-representation the council subsequently introduced two separate lists, one for Catholics and one for Protestants. This in turn had the undesirable consequence that single Protestants were allocated houses while large Catholic families remained on the waiting list. This in turn was viewed as unacceptable and the council reverted to its earlier points system.[33] Similar problems may have been responsible for a large disproportion in the allocation of council houses in Newry in 1963 where all but twenty-two of the 765 houses were allocated to Catholics.[34]

Here we have a conundrum. When a unionist council in Dungannon gave a house to a single Protestant in preference to a Catholic family, the result was the civil rights movement leading to international condemnation and eventually onto the Troubles. When a nationalist council did exactly the same, for the best of motives, it attracted no national or international attention whatsoever either then or since. Despite the fact that Catholics did best in local authority housing, unionist councils as a whole became tarred with the brush of discrimination. Despite Rose's view that the clearest evidence was of nationalist councils discriminating against Protestants, nationalists attracted little opprobrium.

One point to make is that much of the argument on housing took place between 1964 and 1969 when the Northern Ireland Housing Executive was announced (although it was not set up until 1971). Few systematic figures on the allocation of housing between Roman Catholics and Protestants were available until Professor Rose's book *Governing Without Consensus* was published in 1971 and until the religion tables of the 1971 census were published in 1975. By then the civil rights argument on housing had been won by nationalists.

Even so, we might reasonably ask why the facts have not subsequently been corrected or at least acknowledged by historians and other analysts of the Northern Ireland problem? One answer is that, in general, historians are ill-equipped to answer such questions, too rarely examining statistical sources. To be fair to them they usually see their task as reporting significant events (such as the origins of the civil rights movement in Northern Ireland), and repeat what contemporary activists said or thought about the events. Because the accusations of discrimination in housing were not countered at the time, some historians were content to report contemporary opinion. Historians might also argue that what people thought at the time was a more important influence on events than what was true.

Some historians have however gone further and give the clear impression that the allegations of discrimination were true. In this respect, they go beyond their competence in an un-self-critical way. Some might also be accused of, at best, a lack of professionalism. Professor Bowyer Bell, for instance, refers in his forward to his 'friend' Professor Rose. He has, however, ignored his friend's evidence on the allocation of housing. Professor Bell is one particularly stark example. Other historians appear to follow each other. Dungannon and the McCluskey's appear again and again, but the census figures quoted above are almost wholly absent.

The McCluskey evidence appears to be widely regarded. Bardon for instance calls it 'an impressive dossier'.[35] Although its contemporary political importance cannot be doubted, as a survey of discrimination and especially of housing conditions it leaves much to be desired. The authors confuse disadvantage with discrimination and make sweeping assertions where the evidence is purely circumstantial. The main section on housing consists of five short paragraphs and is largely concerned not with housing conditions but with the location of housing for purposes of gerrymandering. The housing figures for Dungannon are incomplete and difficult to assess. The only complete figures are for Omagh and Armagh. In both of these cases the allocation of houses between Catholics and Protestants is close to their respective shares in the local population. What the McCluskey pamphlet does show for Dungannon, Omagh and Armagh (but nowhere else) is that the local unionist councils built few houses for Catholics. Instead houses for Catholics in these areas were mostly built by the Northern Ireland Housing Trust (a public authority founded in 1945), which controlled around 40% of state-owned housing in Northern Ireland. As we argue below no assessment of housing standards in Northern Ireland can be made without taking into account the role of the Housing Trust.

Among the historians, only Purdie provides any clear detail for housing in Dungannon.[36] He states that in 1963 the Dungannon council owned 411 houses and the Housing Trust was reported as owning 392. Catholics occupied 343 of this total of 803 social houses (43%). The 1971 census puts the proportion of self-described Catholics in the new (wider) Dungannon council area of 42,000 people at 42%. Of the population stating a religion, Catholics were 47%. Since the Catholic proportion of Dungannon population was rising quite rapidly (it reached 55% by 1991) the safest thing to say might be that the Catholic share of social housing in Dungannon in 1963 was close to their population share. Catholics may however have been under-represented in Dungannon taking into account their incomes and especially their larger family size.

It may thus be correct that some Catholic families in Dungannon were not able to get social housing to the extent that would have been the case under an objective points system giving priority to low incomes and especially to family size. However, this is a long way from the impression given by most historians that it was difficult for any Catholics in Dungannon to gain access to social housing. Criticism of the Dungannon council also fails to take account of the difficulties described above for Downpatrick. The McCluskey's were pressing for better housing conditions but were not fully aware of the context and when this later became strongly political, they backed out of protesting.

What happened in housing more generally is relatively clear at least for the 1960s. A number of small local authorities in Fermanagh and Tyrone built very few houses for Catholics either within their boundaries or in areas where doing so would upset the electoral balance. This was made clear at the time in a series of exhaustive articles on Fermanagh by the then young *Belfast Telegraph* reporter Dennis Kennedy, later to become deputy editor of the *Irish Times* and EC representative in Belfast.

Kennedy's articles showed clearly that the unionist council in Enniskillen built houses for Catholics only in the one ward which returned a nationalist electoral majority. This was an open practice. No one attempted to deny it. The councillors were acutely concerned about where these would be built. In the Enniskillen case, many of the houses for Catholics were built not by the council itself, but by the Northern Ireland Housing Trust operating with a subsidy from Enniskillen council. Other houses for Catholics were built just outside the town boundary in anticipation of future boundary changes.

All of this is very unsatisfactory. It certainly amounts to malpractice to maintain unionist control. It does not however amount to an attempt to deprive Catholics of housing equal in standard to that allocated to Protestants. What these councils established was not necessarily a discriminatory regime in the availability of housing, but certainly a segregated housing pattern.[37] Whether this made much difference in practice is harder to say. Maurice Hayes describes ruefully how his attempts to integrate local authority housing in Downpatrick failed due to the location of churches and schools (in some cases due to the absence of co-operation from education authorities).

Perhaps the best summary of the housing issue was made by Charles Brett, the first chairman of the Northern Ireland Housing Executive:

> It is my view that the majority of councils did not consciously or deliberately engage in any kind of discrimination; but a minority did so and thereby discredited the whole.[38]

Many councils, notably including Belfast, had in John A. Oliver's view a blameless record in housing and most 'struggled manfully to maintain standards and to do the right thing'.[39] Even the Cameron Commission in commenting on the four councils most affected by disturbances concluded that houses were allocated in rough proportion to numbers of Catholics and Protestants. Cameron's criticism in these areas was again one of using housing to maintain electoral control.[40] It should also be noted that no legal challenge was ever mounted to the many Northern Ireland housing acts, all of which required and got royal assent. Moreover, when a British based ombudsman and commissioner for complaints were installed in 1968 they received few complaints, and in his first report in 1971 the ombudsman praised the quality of administration in Northern Ireland ministries.[41]

Almost all allegations of discrimination in housing ceased when the Northern Ireland Housing Executive was set up in 1972 to take responsibility from both the local authorities and the Housing Trust. It should be said immediately that the Stormont regime's delay in responding to the indefensible behaviour in a few councils west of the Bann was not excusable and played no small part in its downfall. With sixty-eight local authorities for a population of only 1.5 million, many were tiny. The pool of talent among elected officials must have been greatly stretched, and the temptation to misallocate housing in councils which built only a handful of units each year would always have been considerable. Local control of housing is always open to abuse in one party administrations and it is only the unusual circumstances of Northern Ireland west of the Bann which made the problem so much worse than in similar one-party situations in Scotland, south Wales or north east England. It was however typical of unionist politics to ignore the need for institutional change. Whereas Ulster conservatism contributes much to aspects of social stability in Northern Ireland, unionist conservatism in delaying the reform of badly performing institutions was the Achilles heel of a government faced with, admittedly daunting problems. Oliver, a permanent secretary during this period, takes the view that behaviour of the small local authorities close to the border was wrong, but understandable in the context of continuous and often violent opposition to the state. He says, 'our failure to deal with those attitudes and practices was one of our most serious failures overall, for while the practical effect was limited, their psychological and political effect was great'.[42]

Table 5.2 Distribution of local authority housing by religion in Northern Ireland in 1991

	Percentage of households	
	All households	Households in local authority dwellings
Catholics	32.8	38.3
Other Denominations	60.1	54.5
Religion Not Known	7.1	7.2
Total	100.0	100.0

Source: Northern Ireland Census of Population, 1991

More than a quarter century after the formation of the Housing Executive little however had changed in the distribution of houses between Catholics and Protestants. Table 5.2 shows that in 1991 Catholics were over-represented relative to their numbers by almost exactly the same amount as they were at the end of the Stormont years. Moreover, the degree of physical segregation, about which the McCluskeys complained most bitterly remained worse after thirty years of terrorist violence.

More has changed since the 1991 census including since the Good Friday Agreement. The proportion of households living in social housing had fallen to 15% by 2011 from a figure of 35% at the end of the old Stormont regime in 1971 and 31% in 1991. Owner-occupation has risen and there has been a small fall in private renting despite the increase in demand from the larger number of young people in higher education. By 2011 almost 20% of the population said they had no religion or refused to answer the religion question in the census. Even so, 37% of all households remained self-described as Catholic and these were still slightly over-represented in the remaining social housing (Table 5.3). The convergence of family sizes is likely to have meant that Catholics now have only a slight advantage over Protestants in eligibility for social tenancies.

By 2011 the proportion of Catholics and Protestants who were in social housing was fairly similar (Table 5.4). Protestants were somewhat more likely to own their homes and a higher proportion of Catholics were in (generally inferior) private rented accommodation. These differences are not however a matter of political contention.

Table 5.3 Distribution of Households by Religion in Northern Ireland in 2011 (percent)

	All Households	Households in Social Housing
Catholics	37.4	38.2
Protestants	44.5	43.0
No Religion	10.9	8.7
Not Stated	7.2	10.1
Total	100.0	100.0

Source: Northern Ireland Census of Population, 2011

Table 5.4 Households by tenure 2011 (percent of households in each religion)

	Households in Social Housing	Owner Occupied	Private Rented	Other & NS
Catholics	15.2	65.3	16.6	2.9
Protestants	14.4	70.9	11.4	3.4
No Religion	11.9	62.1	23.7	2.3
Not Stated	20.9	56.9	18.4	3.8
Total	14.9	66.9	15.1	3.1

Source: Northern Ireland Census of Population, 2011

Table 5.5 Households Self-Describing as Catholic

	% of All Householes	% of Households in Social Housing
1971	26.1	30.8
1981	32.8	38.3
1991	37.4	38.2

Sources: Census Religion Tables 1971,1991,2011

The main change in Catholic representation in social housing over the four decades since the abolition of the Stormont parliament has been initially to perpetuate the over-representation of Catholic households and more recently to diminish it. In each case it is likely that changes in birth-rates and hence family size are the main reasons just as was the case before 1971.

The fact that Catholic family sizes have always been larger than those of Protestants is obvious from Table 5.6. However, there has been a degree as convergence since average household size has declined faster in the case of Catholics. Average Catholic households were 31% larger than Protestant households in 1971. In 1991 the gap had declined only a little by 2011 it was much smaller at 14%.

Table 5.6 Average Household Size by Religion (number of people)

	Catholic	Protestant	Other
1971	4.15	3.18	3.30
1991	3.40	2.66	2.79
2011	2.76	2.42	2.40

Sources: Census Religion Tables 1971,1991,2011

Our conclusion is that Catholics were over-represented, not under-represented, in social housing at the end of the unionist regime in 1971 and the degree of over-representation has diminished especially over recent decades. The evidence is that this over-representation reflected more than income differences which in any case were not large. Because Catholics had larger families, they got more social houses. As the difference in family size has declined over the years the degree of Catholic over-representation has diminished. The degree of international opprobrium heaped on the unionist regime was largely unwarranted. That a small number of individually small local authorities tried to house Catholic tenants where unionist electoral advantage was served was wrong, but it did not lead to Catholics receiving fewer houses. Nor as far as we know was the quality lower.

The lesson for unionists was that they already had a reputation for discrimination which they had done little to dispel and when accusations were made of discrimination in housing, outsiders found them easy to believe. The evidence of Professor Rose was ignored and later in 1975 when census information for 1971 became available few seemed interested to analyse the data. Nationalists had won their political battle on housing discrimination and as usual unionists made no effort to counter the accusations. The UK government was more interested in introducing institutional reforms for perceived problems in order to counter national disaffection and republican violence. Whether the problems were real appeared to be a secondary concern. This was a pattern which was to be more obvious in the area of allegations of discrimination in employment where a series of fair employment acts were introduced, and a Fair Employment Agency FEA) set up in 1976 to deal with a problem of unemployment differentials that never seemed to go away. The FEA became the Fair Employment Commission (FEC) in 1989.

Discrimination in employment

Allegations of discrimination in employment, like those in housing go back to the first days of the Stormont regime and before. Catholic workers had been violently expelled from the Belfast shipyards several times during the nineteenth century. Catholics had obtained jobs in engineering while Protestants were fighting in the 1914-18 war, and were expelled from the Harland and Wolff shipyard and other large engineering firms during the 1920 sectarian unrest which preceded partition.[43] Although there were clear examples of segregation and discrimination in employment in the Stormont years these did not play a large role in the civil rights movement despite featuring strongly in the McCluskey's memorandum. Unlike housing the issue of job discrimination remained alive up to the Good Friday Agreement[44] and frequently featured in Sinn Fein criticisms of the administration of Northern Ireland. Despite the passing of two fair employment acts, in 1976 and 1990, and the setting up of the FEA (later the FEC),) and the Standing Advisory Commission on Human Rights (SACHR), belief in job discrimination appeared almost as strong in the lead-up to the Good Friday Agreement as it was thirty years earlier. In 1998 further strengthening of the fair employment act was undertaken.

Central government

Throughout the Stormont period there appears to have been some bias towards employing Protestants in the civil service. Catholics were certainly greatly under-represented at senior levels within the civil service. The Campaign For Social Justice recorded that between the rank of deputy principal and permanent secretary in the civil service Catholics occupied only 7.4% of posts. On the other hand, autobiographical accounts now exist from at least four former civil servants who reached the highest rank of permanent secretary, two of whom are Catholic and two Protestant.[45] All of these paint a convincing picture of a fair and efficient civil service.

Both Shea, a Catholic, and Oliver, a Protestant, refer directly to the issue of under-representation of Catholics among the most senior jobs, around fifty in all, which needed the approval of cabinet ministers who were of course almost invariably unionist. Shea records that he had good reason to believe that his promotion to the second highest grade (assistant secretary) was delayed for perhaps a decade, although he makes no comparison of qualifications and experience and makes too little of the fact that as a non-graduate he faced tough competition from the stream of Oxbridge graduates entering the Northern Ireland civil service through national UK competitions. Bloomfield, who eventually became head of the civil service in the 1980s, asserts that he never encountered religion or politics in almost forty years of experience on selection and promotion committees. It does however seem likely that some of the partition generation of unionist politicians were unwilling to promote Catholics to the top policy making positions, although Bonaparte Wyse, a Dublin Catholic, was permanent secretary in education from 1927-39. Once the next generation of unionists gained power in the person of Terence O'Neill there was a relaxation and this may be associated with the fact that Shea was promoted to assistant secretary. At the end of the Stormont period Shea eventually got the top job of permanent secretary in the department of education, despite not being a graduate. Indeed until 1992 he was the only holder of this post not to have been at either Trinity College Dublin or at Oxbridge. We might note as a curiosity that from partition until 1998 no Ulster Protestant ever rose to the rank of permanent secretary in the department of education.[46]

None of this should suggest that there was an ethos of personal hostility to Catholics. Shea comments:

> The cabinet ministers with whom I came into contact were, almost without exception, kind to me, conscientious in their attitude to the public services, anxious to manage their departments efficiently. In private conversation many of them showed a liberality of mind pleasantly at variance with the accepted image of unionist politicians.[47]

The unionist ministers preferred senior civil servants who were in their eyes 'loyal' and saw little purpose in employing in senior positions those who were or might be dedicated to the overthrow of the state. It is possible to have some understanding with this view and many of those who easily decry this behaviour come from jurisdictions were the problem does not arise. Oliver for instance defends the principle that ministers should have in their small private offices those they prefer to work with.[48] The real charges against unionist ministers were that they indiscriminately treated all Catholics as *ipso facto* disloyal, including cases like Shea's where there was no evidence of disloyalty. They also carried these attitudes on for too long after partition. As Shea says: 'a little magnanimity would have gone a long way'.[49]

Finally, ministers, in Shea's view, far too often appeared to bend to the wishes of the Orange Order against their own better judgement.

At the same time there were too few Catholic applicants to challenge these prejudices. Shea suggests that too many Catholics preferred second class citizenship to working for the government. Even in the 1970s as permanent secretary in the department of education Shea, as someone who had 'gone over to the other side', was rarely invited to Catholic schools in Belfast. Oliver adds that Catholic hostility in the 1920s and 1930s towards working for the Northern Ireland state inevitably meant that 'there could be few rising to the highest ranks in the 1940s, 1950s and 1960s'.[50] Entrance to the Northern Ireland civil service was open to high fliers to apply through the London first division competition from 1929 onwards, but it was not until the mid-1960s that the first Catholic succeeded in entering through this path despite the complete absence of any taint of discrimination or influence from unionists.

Whether or not this made much difference to all but those few like Shea who were directly affected is difficult to say. Of the eight permanent secretaries in the 1960s, three were from the British mainland recruited through national competitions. A pro-rata share for Northern Ireland Catholics at this rank might have thus been two if suitable candidates had been available. There may have been some justification in unionist ministers preferring officials with a reasonably similar outlook, as is normal in the USA. However, in the circumstances of Northern Ireland it was surely important to publicly demonstrate that Catholics could and should rise to the highest administrative positions and indeed were willing to do so. Once again unionists acted unintelligently either because of their own predilections or due to pressure from their supporters. In the latter case the lack of an active intellectual strand among unionist politicians meant that these pressures were too rarely questioned or countered.

Whether unionist administrations had a deliberate policy of job discrimination 'with a view to maintaining the population balance between the two communities', as suggested by Boyle and Haddon[51] and O'Malley[52] is open to much more doubt. Neither Boyle and Haddon nor O'Malley provide evidence for this strong proposition, the former instead referring readers to the 1987 Standing Advisory Commission on Human Rights (SACHR) report 'for a general review of issues and statistics on discrimination in employment', and the latter referring to studies of Catholic disadvantage rather than discrimination.

Local authorities

Perhaps the clearest examples of job discrimination came among the non-manual employees of local authorities. By 1971 total employment in local authorities had grown to 5,700 of which an estimated 1,600 or 28% were Catholic.[53] Hence the under- representation of Catholics in the overall employment of local authorities was slight, a matter of perhaps 300 jobs in total.

There was though a strong tendency in smaller, rural and western areas for councils, both unionist and nationalist to discriminate in favour of their own supporters. Local imbalances were often large even if the aggregate employment balance was more reasonable. The local imbalances in gerrymandered areas of Fermanagh, Dungannon, Omagh and Armagh caused particular resentment since few Catholics were employed, especially in the better paid non-manual posts, despite local Catholic majorities among the population at large.[54]

Equally large imbalances within nationalist controlled councils, for instance Newry urban district council where only three out of 161 employees were Protestant, attracted little if any public attention.[55] Cameron for instance appeared to excuse officials in Newry on the grounds that 'in Newry there are relatively few Protestants', that Protestant unemployment was low and that in recent years Newry council had introduced a competitive examination system in local authority appointments.[56] In fact Protestants comprised 25% of the population of Newry and its immediate environs, and were thus heavily under-represented. Cameron's reference to unemployment betrays a lawyer's limited understanding of how labour markets work. It seems likely that the refusal of many unionists to co-operate with the Cameron Commission led their case to be understated.

These imbalances (but not those in favour of Catholics in national-ist controlled councils) were highlighted by the McCluskeys and before them by Frank Gallagher in his book *The Indivisible Island*.[57] Gallagher pointed out that in 1951 while Catholics comprised 31.5% of local authority employees (slightly more than their share of the population of working age), they held only 12% of the 1095 non-manual jobs in Northern Ireland's local authorities. Some of the latter imbalance may have reflected differences in educational attainment, but many may have been due to discrimination, at a direct cost of around 200 jobs to the Catholic community. Bardon argues that favouritism and patronage in appointments had long been endemic throughout Ireland and were entrenched by the 1898 local government act.[58] Once again the unionist government's failure to modernise and reform practices which were no longer widely accepted, except under severe pressure, was both inexcus-able and ultimately self-defeating.

Although the instances of discrimination against Catholics in the public sector were of both political and individual importance the num-bers involved were very small, amounting to less than 400 jobs foregone by a Catholic population of economically active adults of around 250,000. To assess the claim of the Irish government's *New Ireland Forum Report* in 1984 that northern Catholics were 'deprived of the means of social and economic development' we must turn to the private sector which, during the Stormont years, employed three out every four of those working in Northern Ireland.

Private sector employment

There are two ways in which Catholics have claimed to be discrim-inated against in the Northern Ireland private sector. One is in the location of workplaces, the other is through an employer's preference for Protestants in recruitment, retention or promotion. In the former case nationalists claimed that inward investment projects coming into Northern Ireland were steered to the east and away from the more predominantly Catholic areas west of the Bann. There is no evidence to support Catholic suspicions that unionists attempted to influence incoming firms to locate in predominantly Protestant areas and these were described by Oliver as 'nonsense'.[59] Oliver lists an impressive range of multinational companies who were induced to locate in the west, along with the major infrastructural developments undertaken to assist large international chemical companies such as Du Pont to locate in county Londonderry. One personal experience comes from the head of the British Enkalon artificial fibres company, which moved to Antrim in 1957 to eventually to employ 3,000 people, who attests that his firm, one of the single largest inward investors, was left completely free to locate where-ever best suited the company.[60] The normal higher rate of grant was available to locate west of the Bann, but the company's best interests were served by a location closer to the east coast ports and the airport, and thus it chose Antrim fifteen miles west of Belfast and drew employees from much of the west.

Bradley, Hewitt and Jefferson in a 1986 study for the Fair Employment Commission found that jobs in in-moving firms were distributed across Northern Ireland in approximate proportion to the population of working age.[61] This was particularly the case after 1963 when UK regional policy was stepped up following Labour's accession to power in Great Britain. Incoming firms did not however choose locations fully in proportion to the distribution of the unemployed who were proportionately most numerous in western areas despite higher rates of grant.

Since high unemployment was the main criterion for giving assistance to incoming firms within Great Britain this might be viewed as evidence of failure by the Stormont government to steer jobs to areas of highest unemployment. Similar difficulties were experiences in Great Britain where locational controls (Industrial Development Certificates) were used to force manufacturing firms to move north and west. It is possible that similar controls in Northern Ireland may have risked deterring firms from moving to Northern Ireland at all. In any case unemployment was high by Great Britain standards throughout Northern Ireland. Locational controls were dropped in Great Britain when unemployment similarly became a national rather than regional problem in the late 1970s.

Accusations of bias by the Stormont government were a normal attempt by nationalist politicians to make gains for their areas in the west. The higher rate of grant to attract firms to locate west of the Bann were also a normal policy response to higher unemployment, in line with regional policy norms throughout the UK. Since grant levels for firms locating in the west were high and any attempt to widen the difference between east and west in the value of grants is likely to have involved lower grant levels in the east. This could have deterred some firms like British Enkalon which although locating in the east attracted recruits from all parts of Northern Ireland. We might also note that during the same period most firms moving into the Republic of Ireland chose east coast locations. In both north and south this was to prove a disadvantage for these eastern areas in the economically difficult 1970s and 1980s when many companies closed their Irish branches.

The main allegations of discrimination within the private sector were focused on the hiring practices of major engineering companies in Belfast. These companies, the Harland and Wolff shipyard, the Shorts aircraft factories, and Mackies textile machinery works employed relatively few Catholics despite the proximity of Catholic residential areas. Although more than one thousand Catholics worked in these companies at the end of the Stormont period there can be little doubt that Catholics had, and continued to have, strong difficulties in getting and keeping jobs in these firms.

Paddy Devlin, in his autobiography *Straight Left*, describes how as a young man in the 1930s he obtained a job at Mackies where his fellow workers threw nuts and bolts as well as abuse at him, and he left after a few days and there is little reason to think that these conditions had fully disappeared by the 1960s.[62] Protestant workers had similar experiences in Catholic dominated firms and a pattern of job segregation was also common in many areas.

Robert G. Cooper, later to become chairman of the FEC, worked in management in the engineering industry in the 1960s and asserted that Catholic job applicants were weeded out at an early stage of recruitment processes. Much of the problem seems to have stemmed from shop-floor antagonisms between Catholic and Protestant manual workers. These antagonisms have a long history, including sporadic outbreaks of violence, which were soon to erupt again in the post 1969 Troubles. The exclusion of many Catholics from these firms can be seen as an aspect of the perennial constitutional dispute and as a kind of cold war. Both management and government made little concerted effort to change this state of affairs and can be blamed in this respect although the difficulties they faced must not be under-estimated. When changes in the balance of advantage between the Catholic and Protestant working classes began to occur in the late 1960s the cold war in the work-places quickly turned hot on the streets.

The pattern of job segregation in parts of the private sector was well established by the 1960s but it played little part in the civil rights movement or in the report of the Cameron Commission. This may have been because it was an accepted part of life for many, or because a rapid flow of new firms was coming into Northern Ireland with unbiased hiring policies. The problem of job discrimination may also not have been as widespread as is often assumed. The entire mechanical and transport engineering sector in Northern Ireland employed under 5% of all those at work in 1971. Nor should it be assumed that active discrimination accounted for all, or even most, of the under-representation of Catholics in these firms. Over a quarter of a century later, following two fair employment acts and many reforms in personnel practice, the Catholic share of jobs within these engineering companies remains under 11%. Active discrimination is no longer an issue, but these firms nevertheless retain a predominantly Protestant workforce for a range of other reasons. Much former recruitment was on a father and son basis, but this was prevented by fair employment legislation. However since in these were mostly industries with declining employment there was in any case relatively little new recruitment. An industry that had earlier employed over 40,000 men declined rapidly and now employs a declining 4,000 mainly in the Bombardier (formerly Shorts) aircraft company. Working in this industry had been of decreasing value for many decades. Despite an affirmative action programme at Shorts involving objective recruitment procedures, contacts with Catholic schools and setting up a new plant in Catholic west Belfast, 82 % of Short's 5000 jobs in the late 1980s were Protestants.[63]

The pattern of under and over representation across all sectors at the end of the Stormont period is shown in Table 5.7.

Table 5.7 Percentage of under/over representation in employment

	1971	1991	2011
Private Sectors			
Agriculture	-2.8	-4.4	-8.9
Mining & Quarrying	2.3	-6.7	3.8
Manufacturing	-11.3	-9.1	-2.6
of which transport engineering	-26.2	-27.4	na
Construction	9.3	8.2	7.8
Gas, Electricity, Water	-15.1	-16.4	-9.6
Transport & Communications	-1.8	-1.8	-2.7
Distribution	-4.2	-7	-2.9
Financial & Business Services	-12.3	-7.8	-2.1
Legal Services	0	na	na
Other Professional Services	-7.7	na	-2.3
Hotels, Pubs, CLubs etc.	29.4	8.9	1.4
Public Sector			
Education	-0.9	3.8	2.3
Medical	-6.7	2.`	1.3
Government, Administration	-6.7	2.`	-7.6
RUC, Army, Fire	-18.6	-29.5	na
All Sectors	**-2.7**	**-4.4**	**-1.1**

The figures represent the percentage excess or deficit of Catholic employment in each sector, relative to the percentage of Catholics among the economically active population in each year. The greatest degree of over- representation in 1971 among the sectors separately identified in Table 5.7 occurred in the hotel, pubs and clubs industry. In this sector the percentage of Catholics employed was 29% higher than the percentage of Catholics among the economically active in 1971 (34%). This degree of over-representation of Catholics was even greater than their under-representation in the shipbuilding aircraft and textile machinery engineering sectors or the security services. Catholics were also considerably over-represented in construction. Catholic under-representation was greatest in shipbuilding and aircraft engineering, the security services, public utilities and in financial and business services. The reasons differed in each sector.

The fact that Catholic over-representation in some sectors never became a major political issue may reflect the small-scale organisation of the drink and construction industries which were dominated by small family businesses usually with lower pay levels than in engineering. It is sometimes argued that the drink and construction industries, which included a number of lower paid jobs, acted as a kind of sink for Catholics excluded from other sectors. Although a common argument, it is almost never thought through and is more complex that it looks. It underestimates the value of such jobs and ignores the large numbers of Protestants who were in low paid occupations or who were unemployed. We might also note that the Irish in England were also at that time concentrated in construction without any suggestion of discrimination. It is true that even within each sector Catholics tended to be in less well-paid occupations.[43] However this again does not prove discrimination and could have been due to social class, educational attainment or other factors. Catholics in Northern Ireland were for instance much better off in this respect than the children of manual workers in Britain where there was also no issue of discrimination for the British case.[64]

What is striking about the overall level of Catholic under- representation is that it got worse, not better, over the two decades following the fall of the unionist government in 1972. Almost twenty years after the end of the period in which unionists had minimal political influence, much of industry came under state or external control, the public sector doubled in size, and two fair employment acts were passed, the level of Catholic under-representation had grown from 2.7% in 1971 to 4.4% in 1991. There was also little change in the level of over- or under-representation in several of the most imbalanced sectors. In manufacturing, construction and the public utilities the percentages in 1991 remained much as they had been twenty years earlier. The same is true of ship-building and aircraft engineering where Catholic under-representation increased from 23% in 1971 to 27 % in 1991. Although the share of jobs in this sector going to Catholics increased over the period, the rate of increase was less than that in the wider economically active Catholic population.

What this tells us is that patterns of under-representation in employment are complex and cannot be simply equated with discrimination as has so often been done in Northern Ireland. Employment practices today are tightly controlled and widely viewed as fair and yet imbalances increased in the two decades since the last days of unionist government. What many observers fail to take into account is that labour forces are continually in flux. In the context of a persistent oversupply of labour in Northern Ireland migration was traditionally an important labour market response. If Catholic migration were to diminish in an expectation of greater job opportunity a consequence is an increase the number of economically active Catholics relative to what would otherwise have been the case.[65] If the number of Catholic job-seekers rises faster than the actual availability of jobs the level of imbalance remains the same or even grows.

Eventually, however the religious composition of employment has come to more closely reflect the supply of labour and skills irrespective of religion. The overall degree of under-representation of Catholics had declined to only 1.1% by 2011. In some of the most unbalanced sectors in Table 5.7 the degree of convergence was dramatic. In some cases, it was because major sectors had greatly declined or even disappeared. This was the case in shipbuilding where little was left of Harland and Wolff by 2011 (and in 2019 it has finally closed later to re-open with a minimal workforce). It was also a factor in construction which lost 38% of its jobs following the banking crisis of 2008. Catholic over-representation remained much the same, but the sector became smaller. The high levels of take-up of some social security benefits (including sickness benefits), irrespective of local unemployment levels, in Catholic areas suggests a greater propensity to live on benefits. This tendency will make it difficult to achieve a fully balanced representation of Catholics.

Taking this into account there may be little remaining imbalance in employment. Remaining sectoral imbalances are likely to reflect structural factors. These include the decline of farm employee jobs in agriculture leaving (predominantly Protestant) proprietors running farms. The growing number of East European workers in less-skilled jobs in agriculture and in the hospitality industry also leads to a replacement of indigenous (and most often Catholic employees).

Unemployment

The same issues affect the interpretation of differences between Catholics and Protestants in rates of unemployment. The fact that Catholic unemployment was twice as high as Protestant unemployment stimulated many in the past to conclude that the reason must be discrimination.[66] Under the Stormont regime the reports by Isles and Cuthbert and by Sir Robert Hall had both pointed to the difficulties in reducing unemployment when job creation could never keep pace with the rapid rate of natural increase of population[67]. However, once the Troubles came to dominate direct rule thinking on Northern Ireland such insights were dropped. Instead, ministers tended to focus on fair employment as something that might meet nationalist concerns and help to end the violence.

The major study commissioned from the Policy Studies Institute (PSI) in 1989 by (SACHR) suggested that around half of the unemployment differential must be due to discrimination because all other influences had been eliminated[68].

President Clinton writing in 1992 similarly assumed that high Catholic unemployment must reflect discrimination in writing that, 'the British government must do more to oppose the job discrimination that has created unemployment rates two and half times higher for Catholic workers than Protestant workers'.[69]

In fact, the PSI deduction was insupportable, as Wilson and others have observed.[70] The PSI study followed a standard approach in taking a wide (but hardly exhaustive) set of personal characteristics for both Catholics and Protestants at a single point in time. These characteristics

Table 5.8 Ratio of Catholic to Protestant Unemployment

	Male	Female	All
1971	2.6	1.9	2.4
1991	2.2	1.7	2.0
2011	1.6	1.4	1.5

Sources: Censuses of Population 1971, 1991, 2011

Note: Unemployment rate is defined as number of unemployed divided by the population of working age.

included such things as age, location and educational qualifications. Having accounted for the potential impact of such factors on Catholic and Protestant unemployment, the study implies that any remaining differences are likely to be due to discrimination. However, this approach by its very nature was unable to take any account of important factors which unfold over time (rather than being personal characteristics at any one point in time). These include the faster rate of population growth among Catholics and differences between Catholics and Protestants in the response of migration to levels of unemployment.

It is possible to combine these 'dynamic' factors with the personal characteristics included in the PSI study and in similar analyses. Gudgin and Breen[71] did this using a simple simulation model and claim to show these dynamic factors can interact with the personal characteristics to produce a Catholic unemployment rate double that of Protestants without any need to invoke discrimination.

This report provoked strong opposition mainly over technical issues connected with such things as the modelling of migration behaviour.[72] What these criticisms overlook however is that it is only necessary to demonstrate a single plausible mechanism by which unemployment rates can diverge considerably between Catholics and Protestants to show that such divergence need not necessarily imply the presence of discriminatory behaviour. Gudgin and Breen pointed out that this does not of course disprove the existence of discrimination, either now or in the past, but it does invalidate the tendency for people to argue that high Catholic unemployment must indicate discrimination both today and *a fortiori* in previous years. Those who believe that discrimination is or was an issue can no longer rely on the circumstantial evidence of unemployment but must find more direct evidence.

There are in essence two competing hypotheses to explain the large gap between Catholic and Protestant unemployment. One view is that discrimination is responsible. The other view is that the more rapid growth of population in Northern Ireland than in Great Britain, particularly in the Catholic community, caused a chronic oversupply of labour in a situation in which employment in Northern Ireland grew at a rate close to the UK average. Since firms in Northern Ireland faced the same growth of demand as well as the same exchange rate, interest rate and employment law as in Great Britain, they found it difficult to grow much faster than in Great Britain. Lower wages and the availability of grants helped a little, but the net result was that for most of the past, population growth in Northern Ireland outstripped the expansion of jobs.

Over the period 1970-96 for instance there was a cumulative shortfall of 185,000 jobs for males[73]. The consequence was a high rate of out-migration accounting for 58% of this shortfall.[74] A rise in economic inactivity (including higher rates of staying on in education and early retirement) accounted for 15%. Only 25% contributed to higher unemployment. In a context of persistent job shortage, the level of unemployment depends on the responsiveness of migration to the shortage of jobs. If fewer people move elsewhere for jobs, unemployment will rise. The importance of this insight is that any difference in the responsiveness between Catholics and Protestants will result in an unemployment differential.

Gudgin and Breen argued that, although the rate of migration has been higher for Catholics than for Protestants, if Catholic migration had been less responsive to high unemployment than has been the case for Protestants then this could generate an unemployment differential. As a result, Catholic unemployment rates would rise above those of Protestants, not only at a province-wide scale, but also in areas where there are Catholic majorities despite the generally superior record of job creation in these areas. It is a little-known fact that across local authority areas in Northern Ireland there was almost no correlation between job growth and unemployment. Having more jobs in an area had almost no impact on unemployment. Instead, unemployment was almost always higher in areas with Catholic majorities irrespective of employment growth. These areas have higher growth in population and hence in the supply of labour.

To avoid high unemployment, these areas needed higher levels of out-migration or at least high levels of commuting out to other parts of Northern Ireland. Lower rates of out-movement than were needed to equalise unemployment rates may have occurred in predominantly Catholic areas due to a cultural attachment to Irish institutions including the GAA, the Catholic church as well as Irish language, music and culture, which were less easily reproduced in Great Britain and elsewhere than would be the case for Protestant culture which is more British. These factors were not proven by Gudgin and Breen, but they remain possibilities providing an explanation for higher Catholic unemployment which does not rely on discrimination.

Gudgin and Murphy predicted in 1992 that such factors would make high Catholic unemployment only very slowly responsive to fair employment legislation since its fair employment institutions did not address the issues of job shortages and the responsiveness of migration.[75] Instead the prediction was that unemployment differentials would only slowly subside even if hiring and firing in every sector were strictly proportional to the size of the two communities. Moreover convergence of unemployment differentials would decelerate as the jobs gap became smaller.

As birth-rates in Northern Ireland slowly converged with those in Great Britain, and as high Catholic birth-rates converged with those of Protestants, the overall shortage of jobs in Northern Ireland has diminished and unemployment rates have slowly converged as predicted. As we saw in Table 5.6 religious differences in family sizes have diminished. Birth rates are now closer to those in Great Britain and at the same time there has been a remarkable improvement in job creation across the UK (albeit at the cost of languishing productivity and hence wages). This was reversed for a time by the collapse in construction jobs in Northern Ireland after 2008 but even so employment rose by 20% over two decades to 2017. As a result, the previously endemic job shortfall has disappeared and the responsiveness of migration to unemployment is no longer an important issue. Indeed, migration flows have changed. For the first time in perhaps a century there have been more people moving into Northern Ireland as moving out over the last two decades.

As predicted the unemployment differential has slowly diminished. It remained high for several decades after the fair employment acts were introduced but is finally reaching a low level (Charts 5.1 and 5.2). Even as late as 2005 Catholic unemployment remained double that of Protestants even though there had been no real question of discrimination for decades. In the latest figures (for 2016) Catholic unemployment remains 40% higher than for Protestants. As the studies quoted above had predicted, the unemployment differential has subsided only slowly even in the absence of discrimination.

Chart 5.1 Unemployment rate Catholic:Protestant Ratio

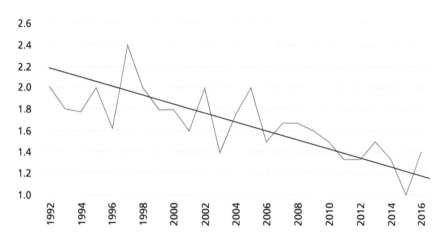

Source: NISRA Northern Ireland Religion Report

Chart 5.2 Unemployment Differential (C-P ratio)

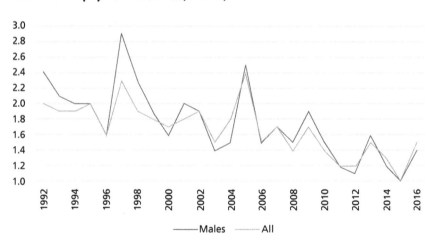

Source: NISRA Northern Ireland Religion Report

At the level of individual organisations similar factors were at work. The Fair Employment Commission's (FEC) first major investigation was into Belfast City Council. The draft report concluded that an under-representation of Catholics reflected unfair practices. When the Council asked the Northern Ireland Economic Research Centre (NIERC) to investigate whether this was a reasonable conclusion, NIERC found that the median employee had been in post at the council for twenty years and that recruitment had fairly reflected the proportion of Catholics in the Belfast labour force at the time of recruitment. The FEC accepted this analysis but in a display of bureaucratic inertia were reluctant to change their conclusions.

The unemployment differential is however coming down. It could eventually disappear but equally may stabilise at say 25% above the Protestant rate as long as general unemployment remains low.

A recent study attempts to explain why the decline from the mid-1980s up to the present day in the Catholic/ Protestant unemployment differential has been so slow. It considers the ending of the Troubles, the Good Friday Agreement, fair employment legislation, alongside hidden unemployment, and major structural changes as contributions of these changes. Despite an extensive statistical analysis, the conclusions are banal and suggest more than the analysis actually indicates. For instance:

> It is difficult to draw any firm conclusions about [whether the contribution of discrimination has diminished over time] or about whether religious discrimination is a salient characteristic of the contemporary Northern Ireland labour market. Nevertheless, if the decrease in the unexplained (religion) component of the unemployment gap captures changes at least in part associated with discrimination, then many of the factors discussed above (structural change, equality legislation, wider social and political change) may have contributed, either via a reduction in the effects of discrimination, or a reduction in the extent of religious prejudice within Northern Ireland, or both.

As so often in research on unemployment differentials in Northern Ireland there is a tendency to assume that higher Catholic unemployment is likely to reflect discrimination even though no direct evidence for this proposition is presented. Even though the authors are aware of the hypothesis that higher Catholic unemployment may be due to higher Catholic birth-rates combined with differences in propensity to migrate in the face of job shortages, the report fails to take this seriously and makes no mention of convergence in birth-rates over the study period. The study instead concludes that:

> Relative changes in observable productive characteristics between Catholics and Protestants, employment growth in industries not disproportionately employing Protestants, increasing education levels among the Northern Ireland workforce, and successive rounds of equality legislation are all likely to have played a role.[76]

None of this is proven and remains unconvincing. The analysis is static depending on characteristics at single points in time. Without a dynamic framework indicating how individuals react to changes in employment opportunities, including via migration, it is not possible to assess how any of the factors listed above might affect unemployment. Falling birth-rates, combined with a dramatic acceleration in UK job creation, have removed the persistent job shortages in Northern Ireland which underlay Ulster's previously high unemployment. Without this vital context it is difficult to say much of value about declining unemployment differentials. It should be unacceptable that research studies fail to build on previous research or least explain why they do not do so.

There is other evidence to show that unemployment rates do differ in circumstances where discrimination is not an issue. Unemployment rates for Church of Ireland Protestants were for instance 45% higher than for Presbyterians in Northern Ireland in 1971, and differences in personal characteristics are unable to account for all of this gap, yet no-one has suggested that discrimination occurs between Protestant denominations. Similarly, unemployment rates for the Catholic majority in the Republic of Ireland are 70% higher than for the Protestant minority in the Republic.[77] The unemployment gap between Catholics and Protestants living in the southern border counties is larger than in the adjoining counties in Northern Ireland. Again, personal differences between Catholics and Protestants cannot account for all of the gap in unemployment rates.

Because religion tables from Northern Ireland censuses were not published until 1975, the size of the unemployment gap between Catholics and Protestants in Northern Ireland was not recognised until after the fall of the Stormont government. As a result, unemployment differences did not play an explicit role in the civil rights protests. Instead the later discovery that Catholic unemployment rates in 1971 were double those of Protestants has been subsequently used to reinforce the presumption of widespread discrimination. The persistence of the unemployment gap has led many, including Mo Mowlem, the Secretary of State for Northern Ireland (1997-1999), to conclude that discrimination still remained a problem, thus reinforcing the presumption that it was likely also to have been a problem in the past.

As with housing our conclusion is that despite the fall of the Stormont regime and many subsequent reforms, remarkably little changed in the religious balance of employment and unemployment for twenty years after the end of unionist rule. The Catholic share of jobs and population continued to grow but by 1991 Catholics remained more under-represented in employment than in 1971 and the unemployment gap was as large as ever. If the degree of imbalance in 1991 was not regarded as indicative of discrimination, at least by most practitioners in the field of fair employment, then it would be illogical to regard a similar degree of imbalance thirty years ago as likely in itself to indicate discrimination. This is not to deny the existence of some discrimination as recorded by Devlin, Cooper and others, nor to diminish the impact of discrimination on those individuals who were directly affected. It would however undermine the unsubstantiated judgement made by the 1986 New Ireland Forum that Catholics were deprived of the means of economic development.

This subject remains controversial and more research would be valuable. The working of labour markets containing two communities with different birth-rates remains poorly understood. In Northern Ireland further understanding has too often been resisted with many preferring to fall back on the simple deduction that higher Catholic than Protestant unemployment must in part at least reflect both ongoing and past discrimination. One of the ironies of Northern Ireland is that high Catholic birth rates displaced Protestants from jobs that they would have otherwise been likely to gain until the last two decades when employment growth has been fast enough to absorb an expanding labour force

Table 5.9 Change in Employment Numbers

	Total	Catholics	Catholic share %
1971-91	23268	37605	162
1991-2011	220,313	123,171	58
1971-2011	243581	165776	68

Source: Censuses of Population Northern Ireland

growth. It is a little-known fact that all of the net increase in jobs between the 1971 and 1991 censuses went to Roman Catholics while the number of Protestants in jobs declined. Since 1991 the favourable job-creation record of the UK, including Northern Ireland, has allowed employment to rise in both communities. Most jobs have gone to Catholics since their labour force is still growing fastest reflecting the higher birth-rates of earlier decades.

Conclusion

Having undertaken this review of the evidence it is difficult to disagree with the conclusion of Oliver:

> Those of us who served in the [Stormont] administration are convinced both from our own experiences and from those totally impartial judgements, [i.e. the ombudsman, commissioner for complaints, and the royal commission on the constitution, 1973] that the so-called grievances and complaints that have been publicised all over the world have been hugely exaggerated.[78]

Oliver notes that the grievances began before the Stormont regime had made any decisions and have continued long after its demise. In his view the faults, mistakes and shortcomings of the regime were used by nationalists to denigrate the state and to try to pull it down.

In addition, the reasons for religious imbalances were, and indeed still are, poorly understood. Differences between Catholic and Protestant birth rates, and hence rates of population growth, impinged on both housing and employment. On housing 'fair' allocation systems usually prioritise children and hence larger families. In Northern Ireland this meant giving priority to Catholic families. Under conditions of general housing shortages which in Northern Ireland essentially lasted from WW1 to 1985, this meant keeping many Protestant families at the back of the queue. This chapter has shown that preference was indeed given to Catholic families in allocating social housing. It also described the way in which the nationalist Downpatrick urban council wrestled with the issue of differing family size.

In employment the issue was that, until recent decades, the labour force in Northern Ireland expanded faster than its economy, constrained by membership of the UK economic union, could grow. Unemployment differences then depended on the degree of migration, or mobility more generally, adjusted to the shortages. The likelihood is that Catholics were slower to move away in the face of any given level of job shortage, since there was less 'cultural distance' for Protestants in moving to Great Britain.

This is not to deny the clear abuse of local powers by a limited number of local authorities mainly in border areas, for electoral advantage or the atmosphere of communal hostility with which some private employers had to contend. Lord Cameron, writing in the report of the Cameron Commission, had some sympathy for the position in which unionists found themselves particularly in western local authorities

> It is in a sense understandable that, given the political history of Northern Ireland, in certain areas in particular, local unionist groups should seek to preserve themselves in power by ensuring that local authority housing is developed and allocated in ways which will not disturb their electoral supremacy.[79]

In reference to the disturbances which we now know led on to thirty years of violence he added, 'It is however natural that most Catholics should feel that the basis of administration in such areas is radically unfair'

With the considerable benefit of hindsight it seems likely that although Lord Cameron was well aware of the political dimension to the protests again discrimination, and had information on IRA influence at protest rallies, he underestimated the extent to which civil rights protests would mutate into more direct nationalist ambitions. His hope that the reforms announced by the government in response to the civil rights movement would constitute an important step towards 'eliminating causes of division and sectarian strife ... helping to unite the people of Northern Ireland' looks naive in retrospect.[80.] Thirty years of violence followed his report but in the end the lack of dispute on the allocation of housing or jobs must have contributed to the Belfast Agreement (even though neither Sinn Fein nor the DUP actually signed it). Even if somewhat naïve, Cameron did at least recognise that the nationalists territorial claim over Northern Ireland was part of the context. The unionist response was gerrymandering of some electoral boundaries in the west of the province but only for local elections and not for provincial or national elections. Nationalists did, and still do, under-estimate the consequences of their continual political pressure to achieve Irish unity and hence take Protestants mostly unwillingly into a country they do not wish to join.

It is possible to agree with Oliver that nationalists made a blunder in not throwing in their lot with the state before 1945 as they have under different circumstances in 1998. Their decision not to put their aspiration for Irish unity 'on ice', until too late, led inevitably to a culture of grievance which at the very least made the emergence of the Troubles more likely. We might note that Irish nationalism has never pressed for a more practical solution to the problem of identity such as a repartition taking majority Catholic border areas into the Republic for instance. The pressure has always been for a full territorial transfer including all areas in which Protestants were (and still are) in a majority.

At the same time Oliver is surely correct in his assessment that the unionists political short-fall was if anything greater, since they failed to take what opportunities they had to bring the nationalists into the political system to offer them a greater stake in the future of the province and to reform the outmoded system of local elections. The history of the 1950s and 1960s contains many examples of a hard line when greater generosity would surely have paid dividends.[81] Both unionists and nationalists were in some senses trapped by a turbulent history and an intricate geography and crippled by an unnecessary constitutional uncertainty (all of which remain with us) but the quality of their struggle against these difficulties prior to 1972 left much to be desired.

Finally, writing the first version of this article in the week of the tragic Omagh bombing causing the death of twenty nine people, including many women and children, it was poignant but easy to agree with Patrick Shea's conclusion after a lifetime as a Catholic in the Northern Ireland civil service:

> I am totally convinced that whatever may be said about the righting of past wrongs or the maintenance of inherited power and privilege, there has been no moral justification for violence or threat of violence for political ends in Ireland at any time in the present century.[82]

Notes

[1]   This is an updated and revised version of an earlier chapter, 'Discrimination in housing and employment under the Stormont administration', which first appeared in Patrick J. Roche and Brian Barton (eds), *The Northern Ireland Question: Nationalism, Unionism and Partition* (Aldershot: Ashgate Publishing Ltd, 1999).

[2]   Quoted in Henry Patterson and Eric P. Kaufman, *Unionism and Orangeism in Northern Ireland since 1945* (Manchester: Manchester University Press, 2007), p. 209

[3]   Paul Bew, *Ireland: The Politics of Enmity 1789-2006* (Oxford: Oxford University Press, 2007), p. 488.

[4]   Michael Farrell, *Northern Ireland: The Orange State* (London: Pluto Press, 1976)

[5]   J. Bowyer Bell, *The Irish Troubles: A Generation of Violence 1967-1992* (Dublin: Gill and Macmillan, 1993), p.10.

[6]   Joseph J.Lee, *Ireland 1912-1985: Politics and Society* (Cambridge: Cambridge University Press, 1989), pp. 79, 421, 596.

[7]   Brendan O'Leary and John McGarry, *The Politics of Antagonism: Understanding Northern Ireland* (London: Bloomsbury, 2016), p.129.

[8]   See Michael Farrell op. cit., and Eamon McCann, *War and an Irish Town* (Harmondsworth: Penguin Books, 1974). This was Whyte's summary of Farrell and McCann's views in J. Whyte. 'How much discrimination was there under the unionist regime', in T. Gallagher and J. O'Connell (eds), *Contemporary Irish Studies* (Manchester: Manchester University Press, 1983), p. 29.

[9]   Paul Foot, *Ireland: Why Britain Must Get Out* (London: Chatto, 1989), p.3.

[10] *New Ireland Forum Report*, Dublin, 1984, Pars3.3, 3.9.

[11]   See Anthony Alcock, *Understanding Ulster* (Belfast: Ulster Society, 1994); Jonathan Bardon, *A History of Ulster* (Belfast: Blackstaff Press, 1992); Thomas. Hennessey, *A History of Northern Ireland, 1920-96* (Dublin: Gill and Macmillan, 1997); Christopher. Hewitt, 'The roots of violence: Catholic grievances and Irish nationalism during the civil rights period', in P.J. Roche and B. Barton (eds.), *The Northern Ireland Question: Myth and Reality* (Aldershot: Avebury, 1991) and Christopher Hewitt, 'Catholic grievances, Catholic nationalism and violence in Northern Ireland', *British Journal of Sociology*, vol. 34, no.3, 1981; J. Oliver, 'The Stormont administration' in P. J. Roche and B. Barton op. cit.

[12]   Graham Gudgin, 'Discrimination in housing and employment under the Stormont administration', in Patrick J. Roche and Brian Barton (eds), *The Northern Ireland Question: Perspectives and Policies* (Aldershot: Ashgate Publishing Ltd, 1999).

[13]   Paul Bew, *Ireland: The Politics of Enmity 1789-2006* (Oxford: Oxford University Press, 2007).

[14]   Paul Bew, op. cit., p.488 quoted from Henry Patterson, *Ireland since 1939: The Persistence of Conflict* (Dublin: Penguin Ireland, 2006), p.202. Note that Patterson says 34 years not 24.

[15]   E.A. Aunger, Occupation and Social Class in Northern Ireland', *Economic and Social Review*, Vol. 7 (1), 1975, pp. 1-18.

[16]   This may be true, but no evidence is presented by Bew for the importance of the unskilled in republicanism. Not all of the IRA were from such backgrounds and the IRA leaders, Adams and McGuiness, had grammar and technical school backgrounds respectively.

[17]   Anthony Alcock, *Understanding Ulster* (Belfast: Ulster Society, 1994), p.56.

[18]   Idem., p.59.

[19]   Idem., p.56.

[20]   J. Bradley, V.Hewitt and C. Jefferson, *Industrial Location Policy and Equality of Opportunity in Northern Ireland*, Research Paper No. 10, Fair Employment Agency, Belfast 1986.

[21]   Jonathan Bardon, *A History of Ulster* (Belfast: Blackstaff Press , 1992), p.638.

[22]   Idem., p.642.

[23]   Jonathan Bardon, op. cit., p. 625.

[24]   Idem., p. 592

[25]   Idem., p.593.

[26]   Bob Purdie, *The Origins of the Civil Rights Movement in Northern Ireland* (Belfast: Blackstaff Press, 1990).

27 John H. Whyte, op. cit.

28 Tom Wilson, *Ulster: Conflict and Consent*, (Oxford: Blackwell, 1989), p. 124

29 *Disturbances in Northern Ireland*, Report of the Cameron Commission appointed by the Governor of Northern Ireland, Cmnd 532, HMSO, London, 1969, p.21.

30 J. Bowyer Bell, op. cit., p.49

31 Richard Rose, *Governing without Consensus: An Irish Perspective* (London: Faber and Faber, 1971), p.293.

32 Tom Wilson, op. cit., p.125.

33 See Maurice Hayes, *Minority Verdict: Experiences of a Catholic Public Servant* (Belfast: Blackstaff Press, 1995).

34 See P. Barritt and C.F.Carter, *The Northern Ireland Problem: A Study in Group Relations* (Oxford: Oxford University Press, 1962).

35 Jonathan . Bardon, op. cit., p.638.

36 Bob Purdie, op. cit., chapter 3.

37 Dennis Kennedy, *Belfast Telegraph*, 1968

38 C.E.B. Brett, *Housing in a Divided Community*, Dublin and Belfast, 1986

39 John A. Oliver, op. cit., p.92.

40 *Disturbances in Northern Ireland*, op. cit., Par. 140.

41 *Report of the Northern Ireland Parliamentary Commission for Administration*, 1971, p.4.

42 John A. Oliver, 'The Stormont administration', in Patrick J. Roche and Brian Barton, *The Northern Ireland Question: Myth and Reality* (Aldershot: Avebury,1991), p.92.

43 Jonathan Bardon, op. cit.

44 Fionnuala O'Connor, *In Search of a State: Catholics in Northern Ireland* (Belfast: Blackstaff Press, 1993), p.182.

45 See Patrick Shea, *Voices and the Sound of Drums: An Irish Autobiography* (Belfast: Blackstaff Press, 1981); Maurice. Hayes, op. cit; Kenneth Bloomfield, *Stormont in Crisis: A Memoir* (Belfast: Blackstaff Press,1994); John A. Oliver, 'The Stormont administration', in P. J. Roche and B. Barton (eds.), op. cit.

46 I am grateful to Arthur Green, formerly under-secretary in the department of education for this point.

47 Patrick Shea, op cit., p.196

48 John A. Oliver, op. cit., p.90..

49 Patrick Shea, op. cit., p.196

[50] John A. Oliver, op. cit., p.89

[51] K. Boyle and Tom Hadden, *Northern Ireland: The Choice* (London: Penguin, 1994), p. 45.

[52] Padraig O'Malley, *The Uncivil Wars: Ireland Today* (Belfast: Blackstaff Press, 1983), p.149

[53] Census of Population, 1971.

[54] *Cameron Report: Disturbances in Northern Ireland*, Report of the commission appointed by the Governor of Northern Ireland, Cnmd 532, HMSO, Belfast, 1969, Para. 138

[55] Thomas Hennessey, op. cit., p.113.

[56] *Cameron Report*, op. cit., Para. 138.

[57] Frank Gallagher, *The Indivisible Island; The Story of the Partition of Ireland* (London: Gollancz, 1957).

[58] Jonathan Bardon, op. cit., p. 639.

[59] John A. Oliver, op. cit., p. 84.

[60] Personal statement from Dr Roelof Schierbeek, MD of British Enkelon and later Chairman of NI Electricity, the NI Economic Research Centre and Castleward Opera. Dr Schierbeek had been taken by the Nazis as a slave labourer when a student in the Netherlands during WW2. He returned to complete his degree after the war and later went to Harvard Business School and subsequently joined the German Dutch Akzo chemical company. He set up the huge British Enkalon nylon spinning plant in Antrim in 1963. When the plant closed in 1982 he and his family remained in Antrim and Dr Schierbeek became a strong supported of economic and cultural development in Northern Ireland.

[61] J. Bradley, V. Hewitt and C. Jefferson, *Industrial Location Policy and Equality of Opportunity in Northern Ireland*, Research Paper No. 10, Fair Employment Agency, Belfast, 1986.

[62] Paddy Devlin, *Straight Left: An Autobiography* (Belfast, Blackstaff Press, 1993).

[63] E. A. Aunger, 'Religion and class: an analysis of 1971 data', in R.J. Cormack and R.D. Osborne (eds), *Religion, Education and Employment: Aspects of Equal Opportunity in Northern Ireland* (Belfast: Appletree Press, 1986).

[64] H. Goldthorpe, *Social Mobility and Class Structure in Modern Britain* (Oxford: Clarendon Press, 1980), Table 2.2.

[65] Increase in the number of economically active people can occur because out-migration is reduced, in-migration rises or the number of people seeking work expands.

[66] Brendan O'Leary and John McGarry, op. cit., pp. 129-30.

[67] K. S. Isles and N. Cuthbert, *An Economic Survey of Northern Ireland*, Belfast, 1957.

[68] D. J. Smith, *Equality and Inequality in Northern Ireland. Part 1 Employment and Unemployment* (London: Policy Studies Institute, 1987).

[69] C. O'Cleary, *The Greening of the White House* (Dublin: Gill and Macmillan, 1996), p.22.

[70] Tom Wilson, op. cit.

[71] Graham Gudgin and R. Breen, 'Evaluation of the ratio of unemployed rates as an indicator of fair employment', *Central Community Relations Unit*, Belfast 1996.

[72] A. Murphy, 'Comments', in Graham Gudgin and R. Breen, op. cit. and V.K. Borooah, 'Is there a penalty to being a Catholic in Northern Ireland', forthcoming in *The European Journal of Political Economy*.

[73] Graham Gudgin, 'The Northern Ireland labour market', in Anthony F. Heath (ed), Ireland North and South: Social and Political Issues, British Academy, 1998.

[74] A rise in economic inactivity (including higher rates of staying on in education and early retirement) accounted for 15% and an increase in unemployment for 25%. Across Great Britain unemployment generally accounted for only 10% of any shortfall, see Graham Gudgin, 'The Northern Ireland Labour Market', in Anthony F. Heath (ed), *Ireland North and South, Social and Political Issues*, British Academy, 1998.

[75] Graham Gudgin, and A. Murphy, 'The labour market context and potential effectiveness of Fair Employment legislation in Northern Ireland', *International Journal of Manpower*, 13(6), 1992, pp. 41-51.

[76] N. Rowland, D. McVicar, I. Shuttleworth 'The Evolution of Catholic-Protestant Labour Market Inequality in Northern Ireland, 1983-2014', IZA Institute of Labour Economics Discussion Paper No. 11633, June 2018

[77] Graham Gudgin, 'Catholic and Protestant Unemployment in Ireland, North and South', *Northern Ireland Economic Research Centre Working Paper*, No. 10, Belfast 1994.

[78] John A. Oliver, op. cit., p.96.

[79] Cameron Report, op. cit., Para. 141.

[80] Ibid., Para. 131.

[81] See for instance Henry Patterson, 'Party versus Order: Ulster Unionism and the Flags and Emblems Act', *Contemporary British History*, Vol 13 (4), 1999.

[82] Patrick Shea, op. cit., p.201.

6

When winning is losing

William Matchett

Introduction

Any study of the Troubles is contentious. Even the timeline. In this examination December 1969 is regarded as the start and the 1998 Belfast Agreement the end. Northern Ireland's Troubles was an 'irregular war' – that is, a conflict involving insurgency and counter-insurgency common throughout the world today. The Provisional Irish Republican Army (PIRA) came into existence in 1969. PIRA was the insurgent backed by its propaganda partner Sinn Fein collectively called the 'Provisionals' or 'Provos'. Sinn Fein propagated the 'lies and slander' required to sustain a campaign of mayhem and murder. Sinn Fein was the Orwellian 'voice' of the IRA that categorized murder victims as 'legitimate targets'; denied the IRA 'disappeared' victims such as Jean McConville; excused the torture and execution of 'informers' when they were not informers; blamed police and soldiers for the death and injury of civilians caught in 'no warning bombs' to hide inadequate warnings; described the shooting of teenagers that left them crippled for life as 'punishment beatings' and pervasively referred to the police as 'sectarian thugs'. Sinn Fein propaganda was significantly effective in engendering and maintaining localized support for the IRA in Northern Ireland and the Republic and in the promotion of sympathy for the IRA at an international level and particularly in the United States.

The PIRA resort to 'bomb and bullet' from 1969 was directed at the destruction of Northern Ireland and the realization of the nationalist goal of a politically united Ireland. Margaret Thatcher was elected Prime

Minister in 1979 and it was only then (after ten years of deadly chaos) that there was at the level of government a commitment to a strategy robust enough to defeat violent insurgency. The security dimension of the strategy was based on intelligence dominating the security response of police and soldiers. The objective was to deprive the PIRA of the capacity to effectively pursue the insurgency. There was also a political dimension aimed at bringing political closure that would break the wheel of republican violence by demanding from the PIRA leadership a public recognition of the wrongness and futility of their insurgency as a precondition to any peace. The significance of closure based on a recognition of wrongness and futility was that it would have meant no post conflict portrayal of terrorist as victims.

Thatcher was forced to resign in 1990 by which time the strategy of 'intelligence dominating the security response' had virtually broken the IRA. But in the post Thatcher era of Major and Blair the demand for political closure based on a clear recognition of wrongness and futility on the part of the PIRA was abandoned. The terms of the 1998 Belfast Agreement permitted unrepentant ex- PIRA leaders, rebranded 'peacemakers' by political chicanery, to enter the government of Northern Ireland. One major outcome was the establishment of a divisive and powerful 'legacy set up' to deal with the past that has disproportionally focused on former police and soldiers giving rise to a portrayal of the Troubles that is partial in suppressing the exigencies of security policy and skewed in favour of the PIRA 'rebrand' of the conflict. The result has been a limited and distorted understanding of the phenomenon of the 'irregular war' that occurred in Northern Ireland post 1969. The distortion involves the movement of culpability in the direction of the security forces and away from the insurgent PIRA. The first 'steps' of this distortion were in fact contained within the terms of the Belfast Agreement in the provision for the release of terrorist prisoners and the terms of reference of the Patten report that destroyed the RUC – the law enforcement agency that by the early 1990s had the 'number' of the PIRA.

The chapter outlines the 'threat' dimension of IRA insurgency followed by a consideration of various phases of the security response classified as reaction (1969-75); adjustment (1976-82) and maturity (1982-98). The chapter also deals with a post-Troubles (1998-?) 'scapegoat' dimension involving 'dirty war' accusations against the intelligence led response to the IRA insurgency. This is a practitioner's perspective. Any bias is in that direction. The PIRA feature heavily in the explanation of security policy. This is not an intention to ignore loyalist terrorism or its significance. Rather, the focus on the PIRA is a recognition that the main threat prolonging the Troubles came from violent PIRA insurgency and that the loyalist violence was reactionary which of course is not to suggest that the loyalist response was not extreme. The chapter loosely charts the internal security solution and its arrest-centric criminalization policy fronted by the Royal Ulster Constabulary (RUC) most effective under Special Branch – the nemesis of violent insurgency in Ireland and what the Provos feared most. The conclusion provides a focused challenge to any understanding of how the Troubles ended that marginalizes the security response or characterizes the response as 'dirty war'.

The main threat: insurgency professionalized for the modern era

David Galula in *Counterinsurgency Warfare* distinguishes 'conventional warfare' from 'irregular war': 'In conventional war, either side can initiate the conflict, only one- the insurgent- can initiate a revolutionary war, for counterinsurgency is only an effect of insurgency'.[1] The Provos were the insurgents in the 'irregular war' in Northern Ireland euphemistically referred to as the 'Troubles' – in 1969 the PIRA started the Troubles. Insurgents employ both widespread and selective terrorism. Steven Metz in his contribution to the *Routledge Handbook of Insurgency* notes that insurgents heavily employ terrorism at the start to 'awaken' supporters and attract them to the cause.[2] The initial phase of the PIRA insurgency was intense during the period 1971-76 when PIRA was responsible for 817 murders or 38 per cent of the total of republican killing during the Troubles. Widespread indiscriminate terrorism exemplified by the PIRA 'weapon of choice' (the car bomb) was directed to the literal terrorizing of a community into surrender to the demands of the terrorist – terrorism is bullying on the grandest scale.

The terrorism may also be selective – directed against a target group but indiscriminate with respect to the members of the group. The object is to involve a support base community in the struggle and to obtain as a minimum its passive complicity in order to lay the basis for an extended conflict.[3] This minimal requirement of passive support was crucial for the Provos because , unlike Mao's peasant uprising, the Provos lacked widespread active support from nationalists in Northern Ireland.[4] Passive support compensated. The Provos used the selective tactic of sectarian killing. Michael Burleigh in *Blood and Rage* accurately described the PIRA's first chief of staff, Sean MacStiofain, as indulging in 'indiscriminate sectarian murder'.[5] The PIRA killing of Protestants was a deliberate tactic to provoke Protestants into killing Catholics. This tactic was directed to a twofold effect The first was the consolidation of active support within the ghettoized Catholic areas where the Provos imposed their 'rule' and declared themselves 'defenders' in the face of potential Protestant sectarian attacks on Catholics. Deeping the sectarian divide in Northern Ireland allowed the PIRA to profit from the ghettoization of Catholic areas where they imposed their ideology and declared themselves 'defenders'. This became their base controlled through counter-societies that legalized lawlessness and erected a wall of silence in an update of IRA/Sinn Fein tactics from the Anglo-Irish conflict. Loyalist terrorists copied the template.[6] For violence to continue the Provos had to stop police officers having normal interactions with Catholics. Most of all, they needed the state to make mistakes – to implement repressive measures and to try untested solutions so that the PIRA could exploit the resentment of the ghettoized Catholic areas against the 'British'.

The second use of the tactic of sectarian killing was the consolidation of a sympathetic passive support (as a reaction to the Protestant retaliatory murder of Catholics) within the nationalist community in Northern Ireland in addition to the active support within the ghettoized areas of west Belfast, the 'Bogside' in Londonderry and parts of the border counties. But passive support was not confined to Northern Ireland. Gearoid O Faolean in *A Broad Church; The Provisional IRA in the Republic of Ireland* documents the extent of the support for the IRA in the Republic during the 1970s: 'The scale and longevity of the Provisional IRA's campaign emphasizes that there was a sizeable though ultimately immeasurable body of tolerance if not support for militant republicanism at all levels of the population throughout the Republic of Ireland'.[7] This support extended across the main political parties in the Republic – Fianna Fail,

Fine Gael and Labour. Constitutional nationalist leaders on the occasion of terrorist outrage invariably asserted disgust of violent insurgency but their refusal to acknowledge their contribution to such objectively facilitated the continuation of the very insurgency they ostensibly condemned.

The Republic of Ireland was in effect a 'safe haven' for IRA terrorists. The Republic tended to view PIRA killing as a political act – of the 113 extradition requests by the United Kingdom during the Troubles eight were successful and it was fifteen years into the Troubles (in 1984) before a Dublin court extradited a terrorist suspect to the United Kingdom. [8] The moral and political hypocrisy of the political and judicial establishment in the Republic was fully exposed by Judge Tom Travers (whose twenty two year old daughter Mary was shot dead by the IRA in an attempt on the life of the Judge and his wife on 8 April 1984) in a letter to the Irish Times in 1994. The letter was a response to the Dublin High Court refusal to permit the extradition of an alleged republican to Britain suspected of the murder of a soldier on the grounds that killings carried out by republicans were political acts, committed under the guise of upholding the Republic's constitutional territorial claim to Northern Ireland. Judge Travers wrote:

> In 1979 I went to Drogheda with my wife and two daughters to see the Holy Father. There we heard him say, "Murder is murder and never let it be called by any other name". We took comfort from his words. The great and the good of the church, politics and the law murmured their approval. In this some were hypocritical because, as future events were to show, they must, when they heard the Holy Father's words, have had mental reservations. These people suffering with an obsession with the "constitutional imperative of reintegration of the national territory", must in reality have believed that murder could be called by another name. [9]

James J. F Forest in *The Terrorist Lectures* argued that 'ethno-nationalist' terrorist groups like PIRA tend to 'draw their support from those who share their ethnic/racial background even if they live elsewhere' (p. 12) as in the case of Irish-American support for the Provisionals. [10] The phenomenon of both active and passive support was reinforced by the potency of what Conor Cruise O'Brien referred to as the 'ancestral voices' of Pearse and the 'Easter patriots' and an atavistic hatred of Britain deeply rooted in the Irish republican tradition.[11] O Faolean considered that the fact that 'a considerable proportion of the state's [Republic] population possessed irredentist tendencies goes some way to explaining this phenomenon'.[12] Passive support was not unique to the Troubles – it is a major factor in nearly every contemporary theatre of 'irregular warfare' and trans- national threats such as al-Qaeda and Isis.

The moral problem with passive support for the PIRA is that terrorism presents a binary moral choice in which terrorism is intrinsically evil by the very nature of the terrorist act – indiscriminate killing directed towards the literal terrorizing of a target population. There is such a thing as an 'accidental guerilla'.[13] But most PIRA activists preferred violence to democratic remedies and some such as the 'Surgeon' credited with seventy murders were homicidal maniacs.[14] Official PIRA policy had PIRA execute, usually after torture, every soldier and police officer taken prisoner and some eighty civilians, mostly Catholics, for 'collaborating' with the state , including women and children with learning difficulties.[15] An ex-IRA chief 'strips it back' in his perception that his former colleagues 'had lost any sense of the wider perspective and were just obsessively absorbed by the details of the next killing'.[16] In insurgency terrorism is rationalized by ideology that instills belief in a cause and distorts basic moral values by justifying murder, soothing the conscience of those fighting for the cause and supporters of it. The SDLP and Dublin were on the wrong moral side in providing passive support (and in the case of members of Fianna Fail active support in the late 1960s) for the PIRA in both Northern Ireland and the Republic. The same moral logic extends to Libya's largesse under Gaddafi with the supply of weapons and Semtex explosives and to the millions of dollars raised in the United States to finance the PIRA insurgency.[17]

The media was also used to strengthen the PIRA support base both in Ireland and internationally particularly in the United States. Communication is the insurgent's greatest weapon. Insurgents skillfully manipulate the media to cover stories they choose that tarnish the state. Modern theorists such as Daniel Betz in his contribution to the *Routledge Handbook of Insurgency and Counterinsurgency* stress the importance of irregular war being 'mediatized', arguing that the perception constructed by the media rather than the material actuality is half the battle. PIRA was no exception.[18] Provo public relations chief Danny Morrison admitted that Sinn Fein 'wanted to control everything' and rewarded journalists uncritical of Sinn Fein and the PIRA.[19] Terrorist insurgency is a monster that lies as it breathes.

React phase (1969-1975): tumult and confusion.

Michael Collins regarded the Royal Irish Constabulary (RIC) as the 'cement that held the British presence in Ireland together'.[20] The RUC was based on the RIC police model. London had arguably the finest counter-insurgency force at its disposal. Described as the 'British Gendarmerie', the RUC was sturdier than the Westminster 'British Bobby' police model. The RUC was able to perform normal policing but could also step up to counter armed insurrection due to the 'secret intelligence' role of Special Branch at the heart of the RUC. The Irish police model migrated with great success throughout the Commonwealth and continues to operate effectively in places such as India, Jordon and Singapore.[21]

But in August 1969 the Wilson Labour government 'displaced' the RUC and put the army in charge of law and order – something that nationalist politicians had pushed for.[22] This occurred against the context of widespread civil disorder in 1968-69 occasioned by civil rights marches throughout Northern Ireland but particularly in Londonderry and Belfast in August 1969. In 1968 the RUC was a force of 3,000 officers but Stormont ignored appeals that the force was 'numerically inadequate for the violent challenges facing it'.[23] During the period of widespread civil disorder in 1968-69 a third of RUC officers suffered injury – a fact that was 'very little acknowledged by the press'.[24] The injuries reflected the reality that the RUC had inadequate riot kit and were only minimally protected from stones and petrol bombs. Constant riots overwhelmed the civil power and exposed police deficiencies[25] and the policing response alienated a large number of Catholics.[26] But while accepting that the RUC had made mistakes in responding to the 1968-69 descent into civil disorder the *Scarman Report* rejected 'the general case of a partisan force co-operating with Protestant mobs to attack Catholic people'.[27] The Social Democrat and Labour Party (SDLP) perception of the RUC, a predominantly Protestant force, was that it was biased against Catholics.[28] But Ronald Weitzer in *Policing under Fire* rated the RUC a highly professional organization.[29] Much of the nationalist criticism of the RUC correlated low Catholic recruitment to sectarianism, omitting or downplaying other significant factors such as the SDLP policy of not supporting the RUC and the PIRA threat to Catholics joining it. Nationalists complaints of a pro-British RUC were a 'copy' of the republican slander of the RIC (approximately 70 per cent Catholic) during the Anglo-Irish conflict (1919-21).[30]

The *Hunt Report* of January 1970 was a further political concession to nationalists.[31] The *Hunt Report* recommended the disarming of the RUC which occurred on 26 March 1970 under the Police (Northern Ireland) Act. The Act meant that in effect Westminster tried to turn Ulster constables into 'British Bobbies'. This followed the emergence of PIRA in December 1969. The implementation of the *Hunt Report* exposed the unarmed RUC to the initial phase of the PIRA terrorist onslaught. In the first two years of the Troubles, sixteen unarmed RUC police officers were murdered and four seriously injured in ten separate PIRA attacks. The officers were serving Catholic citizens in Catholic neighbourhoods. That was a problem for the Provos. These were not defensive actions by PIRA and most preceded internment in August 1971.[32] Between the formation of the Provos in December 1969 and the introduction of internment in August 1971, insurgents committed 95 per cent of the killings.[33] Yet most nationalists still saw them as defenders.[34] Increased violence (and its sectarian nature) dominated Belfast and Londonderry. This, and likely loyalist reaction if it continued, concerned Northern Ireland Prime Minister Brian Faulkner:

> All of this was happening in a small province with only 1.5 million people. Perhaps it can be better grasped by translating it into proportionate figures for the whole of the United Kingdom. Thus, it would have meant over 2,000 dead, and in seven months 11,000 bombings, 11,600 shootings and 22,000 people injured. In view of later reaction to the Birmingham bombings in Britain it is worth bearing these figures in mind when assessing the reaction of the Ulster government in 1971 and the extent of the restraint of ordinary people in the face of a ruthless onslaught on their society.[35]

WHEN WINNING IS LOSING

Faulkner's response was detention without trial which was put into effect under Operation Demetrius on 9-10 August 1971 with the agreement of Westminster. Dublin had introduced internment during the IRA border campaign (1956-62) at the same time that it was introduced in Northern Ireland. Despite the effectiveness of the joint Northern Ireland/Republic use of internment during 1956-62, Dublin did not introduce internment in 1971. Taoiseach Jack Lynch was concerned that violence might spill over into the Republic.[36] Lynch's worst fears proved false and because PIRA policy did not threaten Dublin the Republic became a 'safe haven' for the PIRA and the border a strategic asset.[37] Politics was Dublin's big concern – not security. The fact of the Republic being a 'safe haven' for the PIRA was clearly manifested by the Dublin response to a request for extradition in 1973. Four off-duty soldiers were lured by several females into a PIRA 'honey trap' in a flat in Belfast in 1973. IRA gunmen burst in. The soldiers were searched, taken prisoner and then shot in the head. Miraculously one survived but Richard Muldoon (25), Barrington Foster (28) and Thomas Penrose (28) did not.[38] The investigating detective had evidence connecting one of the women, who fled to the Republic, to the murders. A Dublin court subsequently ruled the offences political (not criminal acts) in refusing an application for extradition.

Internment was intensely unpopular with nationalists and because it was based on intelligence Special Branch took most of the blame for what Ellison and Smyth, Taylor, and Coogan have projected as internment's worst features – sectarian policing, poor intelligence and maltreatment of prisoners.[39] In some respects the claims have merit:

> Army primacy had created a confused chain of command. The Ministry of Defence and Home Office blamed each other for the introduction of harsh interrogations. The techniques followed a government study by Bowen (1966) into RAF air crews subjected to mock captures by the enemy. They were held for several days and put through stress situations (that the study did not consider torture) to see if they would break. At the start of internment the same techniques were piloted on fourteen detainees … Special Branch detectives due to their local knowledge conducted the interrogations under the Army's supervision. This contravened Special Branch's knowledge and empathy approach. It was a bad professional

misjudgment and Special Branch's lowest moment of the conflict ... Championing nationalist torture claims, the Republic brought the UK to the European Court of Human Rights in Strasburg in 1978. The Court ruled against torture but found the techniques inhuman and degrading.[40]

Despite Amnesty International continuing to claim from 1971 a persistent maltreatment of terrorist suspects on the part of the security forces it also recognized that the harshest aspects were discontinued.[41] The European Commission on Human Rights found, with respect to allegations of internment being sectarian, that no sectarian discrimination had taken place in applying the powers of detention[42] and on the issue of 'intelligence' internment was not 'based on poor intelligence; it is closer to the truth to say it had been based on limited intelligence'.[43] But despite these considerations Sinn Fein propagandists succeeded in sparking liberal outrage against internment which occasioned the Gardiner Report of January 1975 that ended internment on 5 December 1975.

Internment triggered a dramatic increase of insurgent violence that brought loyalists into the mix. Loyalist terrorism split security resources and made an effective response to terrorism doubly difficult for the security forces. But notwithstanding internment's drawbacks, had it run for another six months it might well have defeated the PIRA and ended the Troubles:

> The great irony with internment is, for sure it was badly implemented and fuelled further violence, but as time went on security successes increased. Even though Special Branch was against internment, and notwithstanding the stain of harsh interrogations, they made the most of it. Accurate intelligence increased monthly. Internment was not the unmitigated disaster republican mythmakers portrayed ... By 1974 half the IRA were in custody and its leadership refuged in the Republic. IRA buoyancy had been deflated. Most arrests were made outside of internment, terrorists processed through the normal criminal justice system. Despite its hamfisted introduction, had internment lasted for another six months the IRA was finished. Internment brought the IRA to the brink of defeat.[44]

The *Gardiner Report* (1975) ended internment.[45] Internment without trial was replaced by the employment of Diplock non-jury courts introduced under the Northern Ireland (Emergency Provisions) Act 1973 in response to the escalation of terrorist activity post 1969 and the intimidation of witnesses and jurors by terrorist organisations. The December 1972 *Diplock Report* recognized that 'intimidation by terrorist organizations' was 'the main obstacle to dealing effectively with terrorist crime in the regular courts of justice'. The fundamental principle of the report was that the 'problem of intimidation cannot be overcome by any changes in the conduct of the trial, the rules of evidence or the onus of proof, which we would regard as appropriate to trial by judicial process in a court of law'.[46] The exceptional feature of the Diplock courts in context of insurgency ('small war') was not the absence of jurors but rather in prosecuting terrorist suspects (individuals charged with 'scheduled offences') the police were required to present evidence in a criminal court to prove guilt beyond reasonable doubt to the standard of 'due process' expected of a liberal democracy. The replacement of internment with Diplock courts ended the 'special category status' given to both republican and loyalist prisoners which permitted certain 'privileges' such as not having to wear prison uniform or do prison work. This had amounted to a de facto 'prisoner of war' status (the illusion that a terrorist was a 'prisoner of war' equal in moral and legal status to police officers and soldiers) which Secretary of State William Whitelaw granted in 1972 to prisoners convicted of 'scheduled offences'.

In Londonderry on 30 January 1972 on 'Bloody Sunday' soldiers shot dead fourteen innocent Catholic civilians at a Northern Ireland Civil Rights Association anti-internment protest parade in a city pregnant with menace where two police officers murdered by the IRA had been buried twenty four hours earlier.[47] Long before the event of 'Bloody Sunday' nationalist euphoria that had initially in 1969 greeted troops had evaporated. Soldiers were now seen in the same anti-Catholic light as police officers. The army bore the brunt of the punishment in the early years after 1969 losing 286 soldiers or almost 60 per cent of total army losses during the Troubles with 1972 being the bloodiest year.[48] As this was happening the RUC was reforming – getting fit for purpose. This high PIRA attrition directed against the army together with the crucial political development of the collapse of the Sunningdale power-sharing Assembly and Executive in the face of the Ulster Workers Council strike in May 1974 was the context within which the Secretary of State Merlyn Rees announced in March 1976 a policy of 'police primacy' (or 'Ulsterization'). This coincided with the ending of 'special category' prisoners and consequently marked the treatment of insurgency violence as criminal rather than political and a matter primarily for the police rather than the army with Special Branch central to the post 1975 'police primacy' strategy.[49]

The *Morton Report* (1974) was a landmark in preparing Special Branch for its central role in the 'Ulsterization' strategy. The *Morton Report* separated Special Branch from the Criminal Investigation Department (CID) and the uniformed or ordinary police (Uniform).[50] The separation of Special Branch from CID and Uniform better protected secret sources and methodologies. But Special Branch remained strategically integrated throughout the RUC organizational structure and daily briefed CID and Uniform. Special Branch officers were now under the command of Regional Heads of Special Branch who linked into the central RUC chain of command under the Chief Constable. Despite tension between Military Intelligence and Special Branch, relationships were good as was the relationship between Special Branch and the larger CID. The *Morton Report* also recognized that Special Branch needed its own surveillance arm in addition to its handling of informers. Special Branch officers in frontline stations recruited and ran sources, guided local police and military, did surveillance and armed response. But multiple roles by one officer was ineffective against new terrorist tactics.[51] Non-Special Branch personnel were recruited which weakened the 'need to know' ethos undoubtedly at the cost of some sources and sensitive methodologies.[52] This bottom-up tactically driven structure was the 'evidence based understanding of what is happening on the ground' recommended for 'irregular war' by counter-insurgency experts such as David Kilcullen in his contribution to the 2012 *Routledge Handbook of Insurgency and Counter Insurgency*.[53] But a rapidly changing insurgency environment that rendered most operation procedures redundant was a constant difficulty. There was no play-book for a threat that no one had seen before.

WHEN WINNING IS LOSING

Adjust phase (1976-82): investigation-led policing poleaxed by propaganda

Sean O'Callaghan provided a former senior PIRA commander's perspective on the restoration police primacy as a strategy to confront the PIRA insurgency:

> A force that had been utterly demoralized by the events of 1969 took years to recover some sense of mission and purpose. It wasn't until police primacy in 1976 that a revamped and reinvigorated RUC took on the slow and deadly task of taking back control of IRA-controlled areas in Belfast and Derry. [54]

The Northern Ireland Secretary of State, Roy Mason, commissioned the 1978 *Hannigan Report*. The report recommended what is referred to as a 'whole of government strategy' the central aim of which was to increase stability by making the police more acceptable to nationalists by having normal policing take over from security policing wherever possible thereby steadily taking soldiers off the streets – a policy that Hannigan recognized the PIRA would oppose because it directly threatened their control over republican enclaves specifically in Belfast and Londonderry.[55] This strategy of restoring 'normality' and attracting Catholic support for the rule of law loosely mirrored traditional counter insurgency thinking as set out for example by David Galula in *Counterinsurgency Warfare* and Robert Thompson in *Defeating Communist Insurgency*.[56] The 'whole of government' policy was a strategy in which politics partnered security. But the restoration of 'police primacy' was the last thing that the Provos wanted. They wanted generals back in charge. So did the army.[57] To this end the PIRA murdered eighteen soldiers at Warrenpoint and Lord Mountbatten in Sligo on the same day on 27 August 1979[58] but Prime Minister Margaret Thatcher was not for turning.

Crime Squads (seasoned detectives who had devastated organized crime in London's East end) was a concept imported from England. Detectives interviewed terrorist suspects and proved adept at extracting admission statements.[59] Maltreatment of prisoners to force confessions was alleged from 1976, almost as soon as Crime Squads started. The use of Crime Squads and the successful extraction of admission statements

201

outraged groups such as Amnesty International that Mason referred to as a 'second front'.[60] Loyalist terrorist organization were 'complicit allies' with PIRA in the public relations campaign against Crime Squads:

> Complicit allies in the PSF's anti-Crime Squads PR campaign were loyalist terrorist organisations. The Hannigan Report highlights that the Ulster Defence Association (UDA) , Red Hand Commandos (RHC) and Ulster Volunteer Force (UVF) were suffering low morale and factionalism because of security successes ... The UDA in particular know that thay cannot go too far in this direction (anti-RUC propaganda campaign) in case they alienate the Loyalist population.. In their statements in public they have shown a certain circumspection by stating that they ` are not anti-RUC in general but just opposed to an 'elitist' hard core of Special Branch detectives.[61]

What Mason called the 'second front' in the propaganda war with Amnesty International and suchlike organisations got too much for liberal sensitivities and government failed to counter anti-RUC propaganda and did little to project 'their side of the case'.[62] The *Bennett Report* (1979) ended Crime Squads despite no officer being prosecuted and the report's recommendation that the system for investigating complaints against the police should remain. Had weight been given to the accusations, the complaints system that exonerated Crime Squad detectives would have been replaced.

The Chief Constable's 1997 *Annual Report* recorded 1,276 persons charged with terrorist and serious public order offences in 1976 when Crime Squads started in contrast to 550 in 1980, the first year after the initiative ended. In the 1997 Report 17,799 persons were charged with similar offences between 1972 and 1997 which works out at approximately 19,000 charged with terrorist and serious public order offences during the Troubles (December 1969 to April 1998) and some 13,000 prosecuted.[63] The number charged with terrorist and serious public order offences in 1976 (1,276 when Crime Squad was at its height) was over three times the charge rate for the lowest year thereafter – 380 in 1990 prior to the first ceasefire in 1994. These statistics show why Provos and loyalists wanted the use of Crime Squads stopped The use of Crime

Squads was replaced in 1981 by the introduction of the 'super-grass system' which had been used successful in England against organized crime and in Italy against the terrorist Red Brigades.[64] Between 1981 and 1983, 405 terrorists suspects were charged.[65] As with Crime Squads there was often no corroborating evidence and courts questioned the reliability of the super-grass as a witness and the initiative collapsed by 1985.[66] The Provos once again secretly conspired with the loyalists on the public relations front to end the super-grass initiative.[67] The 1981 Hunger Strike and the 'armalite and ballot paper' strategy were the specific Provo response to investigation-led initiatives that treated the PIRA as a criminal organization.[68] The effect of ten republican prisoner deaths on support for the PIRA offset security setbacks to PIRA inflicted by Crime Squads and the super-grass initiative.

Nevertheless Roy Mason had in fact come close to defeating the IRA and ending the Troubles during the early stages of police primacy and the use of Crime Squads up to 1979. The focus of the PIRA shifted from Belfast and Londonderry to cross-border PIRA brigades.[69] On the security front by the late 1970s security policy was more sophisticated than at the start of the Troubles. Provos based in Belfast and Londonderry were within easy reach of the long arm of the law but for PIRA cross-border brigades that was not the case. Here the problem was the lack of security co-operation from the Republic despite the 1985 Anglo-Irish Agreement which Margaret Thatcher signed in anticipation of greater security co-op-eration from the Republic.[70] The Republic's response to the murder of twenty one year old Constable Tracy Ellen Doak– one of four officers delivering 'normal' policing killed by a 1,000lb bomb outside Newry on 20 May 1985 – exemplified the refusal of the Republic to admit the 'safe haven' status of the Republic for 'cross-border' terrorists. Chief Constable Sir John Hermon visited the scene and saw the 'dismembered bodies and mangled remains of the police car scattered over a wide area'. Hermon subsequently issued statements based on fact (tachograph data of the bomb vehicle) to show that the device had been made in and detonated from the Republic only for Dublin and the SDLP to sharply deny the factual claims made by Hermon.

Clearly, both Dublin and the SDLP were sensitive to the suggestion of nationalist empathy for the PIRA and antipathy to the RUC. After the Newry attack, Northern Ireland Secretary of State Tom King found that in talks with Dublin, although they condemned the incident, the main worry of the Irish 'seemed to be RUC decisions on the rerouting of Orange marches'.[71] Murdered RUC officers were not a major concern of nationalist leaders. Garrett Fitzgerald discounted the cross-border dimension. Fitzgerald in his autobiography *All My Life* estimated that the cross-border element accounted for 3 per cent of insurgent incidents in Northern Ireland.[72] The SDLP leader John Hume shared Fitzgerald's view.[73] Nationalist politicians Paddy Devlin and Gerry Fitt believed that Hume's antipathy to the RUC meant that the RUC did not get the SDLP endorsement that they believed it deserved.[74] But contrary to the Fitzgerald estimation, Funston in a contribution to *Legacy* estimated for the latter half of the Troubles that 73 per cent of all insurgent killings had a cross-border dimension. This was most obvious in Fermanagh where the PIRA were responsible for 104 murders with a 5 per cent clearance rate – a clearance rate that reflected the 'safe haven' status of the Republic.[75] But despite these considerations RUC efforts did not go unnoticed by nationalists. In a 1985 opinion poll 47 per cent of Catholics supported the RUC – more than the SDLP publicly acknowledged which is why stability did not fully translate into increased nationalist confidence in the RUC.[76]

Mature phase (1982-98): intelligence-led policing dominates

The termination of the use of Crime Squads in 1979 and the collapse of the super-grass initiative in the early 1980s was followed by intelligence-led policing. Investigation-led policing deals with events that have happened. Intelligence led policing deals with events yet to take place. Intelligence is not evidence. Rather, it can lead to evidence, like the 'red-handed' apprehension of suspects with weapons. But with intelligence-led policing not every evidential opportunity can be acted on otherwise intelligence sources would dry up. During the late 1970s Special Branch was being developed to undertake intelligence-led counter-terrorist policing in preparation for the contingency of the collapse of investigative-led policing. Special Branch was subject to reviews by senior MI5 officers at regular intervals from 1974. For example, the 1979 *Parker Report* commended Special Branch systems, record keeping and intelligence sharing and stressed that Special Branch occupied 'the fundamental position in intelligence attacks on terrorist organisations'.[77] The *Parker Report* also stressed the role of Special Branch in the crucial co-ordination and flow of intelligence: 'Special Branch is a highly professional agent handling organisation which has consistently over the years produced most of the intelligence on which the SF (security forces) operate'.[78] By the late 1970s the traditional intelligence arm of Special Branch had, under the tactical control of Special Branch chiefs, its own highly trained SWAT and surveillance teams, along with Special Forces surveillance units and the SAS for armed response in the highest risk scenarios.[79]

Most intelligence-led policing translated into routine briefings to inform and guide the front line of uniform officers, detectives and soldiers on suspects, tactics and threat.[80] But in 1982 SWAT teams in three separate incidents shot dead six suspect insurgents. The local MP told the Commons that those killed along with their associates had been responsible for 222 murders.[81] In 1987 the SAS wiped out a marauding cross-border PIRA brigade at Loughgall.[82] Covert operations of this kind have been popularly labeled 'shoot-to-kill' or characterized as 'the anatomy of police failure'. They were in fact the exception: 'Arrests were always the explicit aim and occurred 96 per cent of the time in a covert context and 99.5 per cent of the time when including the overt context via disruptive/pre-emptive arrests/searches etc usually at local level'. [83] The SAS shot dead three IRA activists in Gibraltar on 6 March 1988. A subsequent inquest in Gibraltar in September 1988 returned a verdict of 'lawful killing'.[84] The decision was appealed to the Strasburg European Court of Human Rights and it ruled in 1995 that the SAS operation had been in violation of Article 2 the European Convention on Human Rights. The technical and controversial decision of the Strasburg court constituted Gibraltar as the only instance of unlawful killing by the security forces in a covert operation relating to Northern Ireland.

In response to 'outrage from the usual quarters' London in 1984 appointed John Stalker, the Manchester deputy chief constable, to investigate the SWAT team shootings of 1982. Stalker in his 1988 book, *John Stalker: Ireland, 'Shoot to Kill' and the 'Affair'* in effect rejected intelligence-led policing in favour of investigation-led policing as the proper response to the insurgency situation facing the RUC in Northern Ireland. Stalker assimilated the insurgency challenge confronting the RUC in Ulster to the criminal exigencies facing 'normal policing' in Salford. Charles McLachlan in the 1987 review by Her Majesty's Inspectorate of Constabulary effectively invalidated Stalker's findings. McLachlan's findings were summarized for Parliament by Tom King in 1988 when he stressed that 'intelligence is the lifeblood' of counter-insurgency:

> Fighting a vicious and ruthless terrorist enemy, intelligence is the lifeblood of that fight. Without it the security forces are seriously handicapped. It is vital that this is protected. Moreover, knowledge of even the procedures of Special Branch and other RUC officers will not only make their task still more difficult, but it will put lives at even greater risk.

In the same parliamentary session Ken Maginnis added that Stalker had:

> Communicated both his position and his prejudices on the issue on an almost daily basis to Michael Unger, the editor of the *Manchester Evening Standard*. Is it not a fact that he has, since then, turned the enquiry into a drama, an entertainment or even a farce, where fact cannot be differentiated from fiction?[85]

After Stalker more of the same with the three enquiries conducted by the then Cambridge deputy chief constable John Stevens (later Sir John and then Lord Stevens) that extended over a fourteen year period from September 1989 until April 2003 with the third enquiry specifically focused on the killing of the solicitor Pat Finucane on 12 February 1989. The issue common to the three enquiries was 'collusion'. The problem here is that 'collusion' despite its 'legalistic tone' has no specific legal meaning in criminal law:

> 'In relation to collusion it should be noted that whilst there is or may be conduct which may be characterized as collusion, there is no offence of collusion known to the criminal law of Northern Ireland'[86]

Stevens operated with his own definition of 'collusion':

> Collusion is evidenced in many ways. This ranges from the willful failure to keep records, the absence of accountability, the withholding of intelligence and evidence, through to the extreme of agents being involved in murder[87]

The Stevens enquiries produced in excess of one million pages of documentation at a cost of £millions on the basis of which Stevens claimed that there had been security force 'collusion' in the murder of Patrick Finucane and 'the circumstances surrounding it'.[88] But on 25 June 2007 the Director of Public Prosecutions produced a public statement to the effect that in the entire corpus of the Stevens material there was insufficient evidence to meet the Test for Prosecution for anything that could be construed as state collusion specifically in the murder of Patrick Finucane. The judgment outraged the Finucane family, Amnesty International and the Northern Ireland Human Rights Commission.[89]

High grade intelligence is axiomatically crucial to intelligence-led counter insurgency. But within both the Stalker and the Stevens reports there was the absence of an appreciation of the exceptional legal (and indeed moral) complexities peculiar to the sustained operation of an informer placed deep within a terrorist organization such as the PIRA. The 2012 De Silva *Report of the Patrick Finucane Review* showed some appreciation of this issue with its recognition that:

> Intelligence gained from human agents is clearly a potent weapon for the State in countering terrorism of the kind that prevailed during the Troubles … An agent could only provide the most valuable, and potentially life-saving intelligence if they were infiltrated into the heart of a terrorist group. It followed that agents who were so infiltrated would, in order to maintain their cover, be required of necessity to engage in criminal conspiracies with their terrorist associates whilst in theory seeking to help the security forces to frustrate the realization of these plans.[90]

De Silva stressed on the basis of this consideration that: 'Nowhere was the need for a proper legal framework for agent-handling thrown into sharper focus than in Northern Ireland'.[91] De Silva concluded that 'there was a willful and abject failure by successive governments to provide the clear policy and legal framework necessary for agent-handling operations to take place effectively and within the law'.[92] This 'willful and abject failure' on the part of government was inexcusable for at least two reasons: (1) 'successive governments knew that agents were being run by the intelligence agencies in Northern Ireland without recourse to any effective guidance or a proper legal framework' [93]and (2) senior RUC and other security personnel had made 'repeated attempts' to 'raise this very issue with Government Ministers at Cabinet level' and it was 'not until 1993 that some Cabinet Ministers came belatedly to support the creation of a legislative framework'.[94] De Silva recognized the significant practical implications of this 'willful and abject failure ' on the part of successive governments: 'It meant that agent-handlers and their superiors were expected to gather intelligence without clear guidance as to the extent to which their agents could become involved in criminal activity in order to achieve this objective'.[95] This meant that the three agencies running agents (the RUCSB, Army's Force Research Unit (FRU) and the Security Service) had 'to operate under their own separate regimes'[96] which of necessity had to derogate from guidelines for what De Silva referred to as 'ordinary decent crime'. These considerations mean that security force derogation, necessary for a sustained informer penetration of the PIRA and the loyalist terror gangs, had more than the tacit approval of government and was not based on some autonomous decision on the part of the security forces unknown to successive governments.

But it is crucially important to bear in mind that, despite the necessary derogation from guidelines for the handling of non-insurgent criminality, the fourteen year Stevens investigation failed to produce sufficient evidence of actual security force (specifically RUC Special Branch) 'collusion' involving murder to pass even the Test of Prosecution never mind conviction in a court of law. Stalker and Stevens did prove popular with nationalists but for the first time the propaganda wing of the republican insurgency failed to dislodge a security effort that threatened its armed wing. Normal policing gained traction in republican areas reducing the profile of the army. In annual *Community Surveys* carried out in the 1990s 'around 80 per cent of Protestants and 76 per cent of Catholics found them (RUC police officers) to be helpful'. The PIRA insurgency was constricting, not spreading. Internally and externally the Provos were under pressure to give up violence. From a Special Branch perspective intelligence-led policing prevented 80 per cent of all terrorist attacks[97] and an insurgent perspective puts the prevention rate at 90 per cent.[98] The murder clearance rate between 1973 and 1977 was 34 per cent but from 1977 to the first PIRA ceasefire in 1994 the clearance rate was 54 per cent.[99] In contrast the clearance rate for 1998-2019 was below 2 per cent for terrorist murders by residual republican insurgents and loyalist gangsters.[100]

The 1981 *Richards Report* correctly anticipated just over a decade prior to the political endgame how intelligence-led counter insurgency could over time confront the PIRA with the imminence of defeat. Richards refers to the RUC perfecting over time in collaboration with the Army 'a sophisticated method of operation based on good intelligence and surveillance leading to the red-handed capture of active terrorists'. Special Branch was 'the key-stone of offensive counter-terrorist operations'. Timely intelligence allowed policing into areas where this was previously not possible, along with covert successes by SWAT teams reacting to Special Branch or Special Forces surveillance units and occasional flexes of ferocious power by the SAS.

Such was the range, relentlessness and precision of the intelligence attack on both shades of extremists that Provo leaders realized that 'armed struggle' would soon face humiliating defeat that even the most accomplished propagandist could not hide. The former PIRA commander Sean O'Callaghan in his review of *Secret Victory: The Intelligence War that Beat the IRA* stressed that the restoration of police primacy in law enforcement and intelligence gathering from 1976 allowed the security forces to eventually take back control of the IRA controlled areas of Belfast and Derry accompanied by a slow and sure assertion of the rule of law: 'The centre of IRA activity began to retreat more and more to the rural heartlands bordering the Irish Republic'.[101] At the endgame in the early 1990s: 'Armed struggle was on its knees, its last redoubt in South Armagh's killing fields on the verge of collapse'.[102]

The former PIRA hunger striker Gerard Hodgins in a *Guardian* newspaper interview on 28 January 2014 clearly set out the extent of the Special Branch intelligence-led penetration of the PIRA:

The infiltration was undoubtedly colossal and fatal. The British were regularly one step ahead of us on the ground ... Squads were being captured, dumps compromised, (IRA) volunteers executed; even the Eksund (an IRA arms smuggling ship intercepted in the 1980s) was never intended to make it to Ireland. The British penetrated the Provos at every level and put their agents and spies in place to ruin us from within and to deliver us precisely to where the British state wanted us. Add to this the success of the British in pioneering agent recruitment and handling, where they delivered one of the most resilient guerrilla armies, the IRA, to just where they wanted us.[103]

In the few years prior to 1993, when the PIRA/Sinn Fein leadership asked the British Minister for help to end the 'armed struggle' security was at its strongest.[104] RUC primacy and intelligence-led policing had by the late 1980s delivered an historic opportunity to defeat the IRA. This was anticipated by the Conservative MP Airey Neave (who was Margaret Thatcher's mentor) even prior to his murder by republican extremists in 1979. Neave understood from his wartime experience and his service with the post 1945 Nuremberg War Crimes Tribunals what it takes to eradicate evil ideology – his security strategy was to 'bring in more SAS and take the war to the enemy'.[105] The murder of Airy Neave in March 1979 stiffened Thatcher's resolve: 'No amount of terror can succeed in its aim if even a few outspoken men and women of integrity and courage dare to call terrorism murder and any compromise with it treachery'.[106] But when Thatcher left office in 1990 the same forces that moved her and Neave did not move Prime Ministers Major and Blair. The 1998 Belfast Agreement conceded the main PIRA demand for the release of all PIRA prisoners. The major demand of the leadership of the SDLP and Republic's political parties was to get rid of the RUC and create a police ombudsman with powers to retrospectively investigate the RUC. It was a deal that proved politically convenient for all sides and laid the basis for the 'scapegoat phase'.

Scapegoat phase (1998-?):
squalid deals, lawfare and re-write

After the1919-21 Anglo-Irish conflict IRA/Sinn Fein influenced the southern press into printing inaccurate stories directed to tarnish the Royal Irish Constabulary (RIC). These reports were intended to disclose a set of 'symptoms' indicative of an unlawful 'disorder' at the heart of the RIC or what was termed a 'dirty war syndrome'.[107] The same tactic has been deployed post 1998 against the security forces and in particular the RUC. There are two sides to the tactic. The insurgents (PIRA/ Sinn Fein) are presented as 'peace-makers'. The other side of the tactic involves the attempt to attribute the ultimate blame for the violence of the Troubles to the security forces and to legally and morally exonerate the actual insurgents. This is a tactic of 'demonisation' directed significantly against the RUC and deeply embedded in the 1999 *Patten Report* and the terms of reference for the Patten Commission set out in the 1998 Belfast Agreement.

The *Patten Report* incorporated the letter and spirit of the section on policing in the Belfast Agreement. The Report presented the RUC as at the 'heart of ... the problems that politicians have been unable to resolve in Northern Ireland.[108] The effective destruction of the RUC was the core of a process that the Report claimed was required to restore the 'values of liberty, the rule of law and mutual respect'[109] and to 'reorient policing in Northern Ireland onto an approach based on upholding human rights and respecting human dignity'.[110] The authors of the Patten Report obviously considered that these values were absent from policing in Northern Ireland and that their restoration and maintenance was incompatible with the continued existence of the RUC. The Report explicitly stated that 'by means of a fresh start for policing, our aim is to help ensure that past tragedies are not repeated in the future'.[111] This was a gross and offensive insult to the memory of the RUC/RUCR officers who were murdered (302) and maimed and injured (nearly 10,000) by the PIRA in the defense of liberty and the rule of law in Northern Ireland against the onslaught of thirty years of PIRA/Sinn Fein terrorism and lies.

The tactic of attributing a 'dirty war syndrome' to the security forces in general and the RUC in particular was directed to the moral and legal exoneration of the PIRA/Sinn Fein insurgents actually responsible for the terrorism of the Troubles. This is an inversion of historical reality reliant on a radical re-write of the past. The *Irish Independent* columnist Eoghan Harris wrote in 2012 of a Sinn Fein cult that peddles the big lie that the Provos made peace which has 'recruited much of the media and a large section of the Irish intelligentsia to help them revise their history'.[112] This drive to re-write the history of the Troubles is reinforced by what is accurately characterised as republican 'lawfare'. The Irish historian Ruth Dudley Edwards warned in 2019 of a destructive 'lawfare' directed against the security forces, especially the RUC, conducted by the PIRA 'hardmen' still in charge of Sinn Fein behind the scenes using the resources of the law and the expertise of lawyers to silence critics and in effect to render the security forces legally and morally blameworthy for the Troubles.[113]

The type of thinking that informs the re-write of history and the 'lawfare' directed against the RUC was exemplified by the eulogy given by the ex-Provo leader and Sinn Fein TD Gerry Adams at the funeral of the longest serving PIRA chief of staff Kevin Mckenna in July 2019. Adams asserted that PIRA men like McKenna ' never went to war, the war came to us'.[114] The implementation of the requirements of the 1999 Patten Commission (the destruction of the RUC) was in effect a capitulation by the Blair government to the PIRA/Sinn Fein inversion of moral and legal reality. The destruction of the RUC marked the Blair capitulation to the SDLP and PIRA/Sinn Fein claim of a 'dirty war' syndrome at the heart of the security response involving a claimed 'collusion' between the security forces and loyalist paramilitaries. Collusion is seeded in Provo propaganda.

The collusion allegation seems to have been first used in 1973 when Sinn Fein vilified SDLP leader Gerry Fitt for saying that responsibility for sectarian killings lay with the PIRA. PIRA/Sinn Fein blamed the 'professional killers in the British Army and Special Branch' and accused Fitt of 'collusion with the British in the same breath as security forces were blamed for collusion with loyalists'.[115] Collusion is the crack cocaine of legacy and arguably the world's longest running fake news story. Many local academics place a 'health warning' on Special Branch and its officers. Powerful pressure groups traditionally hostile to security policy like Relatives for Justice and law firms specializing in legacy have rowed in behind. This has opened the door for a monumental blame game orchestrated by PIRA/Sinn Fein and the so-called constitutional nationalist parties directed against the security forces and security policy.[116]

The ongoing re-write of the past has given rise to a deep sense of injustice within the unionist community and specifically among former members of the security forces. The sense of injustice stretches back to the early release of prisoners within the terms of the Belfast Agreement and to secret 'comfort letters' to high profile 'on-the-run' terrorists and to the destruction of the RUC and to the principles of a legacy structure that in effect equates police officers to terrorists. Neil Southern in *Policing and Combatting Terrorism in Northern Ireland* showed that the RUC and their families have been 'alienated in post-Agreement Northern Ireland'.[117] The sense of injustice drove retired RUC officers to take legal action in 2016 against the investigation by the Police Ombudsman into allegations of security force collusion with loyalist terrorists who murdered six innocent Catholic men in Loughinisland in 1994. Mr Justice McCloskey ruled that the Police Ombudsman had deprived the investigated retired officers of basic legal rights and essential elements of justice:

> The Police Ombudsman's unhesitating and unambiguous determination that RUC officers were guilty of collusion with UVF terrorists in the execution of the Heights Bar murders in substance differs little, if at all, from a verdict of guilty beyond reasonable doubt.

Indeed the "no hesitation" and 'unambiguously" ingredients in the Police Ombudsman's determination to this effect could be said to be expressed more forcefully than such a verdict.
But:

> The unhesitating and unambiguous determination that RUC officers had colluded with UVF terrorists in the commission of the Heights Bar murders and other offences was not the product of a criminal trial or a disciplinary process.

Mr Justice McCloskey ruled that the Police Ombudsman had reached a verdict against RUC officers that 'in substance differs little, if at all, from a verdict of guilty beyond reasonable doubt' without the RUC officers being provided the protection of 'due process':

> The effect of this is that none of the police officers to whom these destructive and withering comments apply had the protection of due process. They were, in effect, accused, tried and convicted without notice and in their absence. None of the essential elements of the criminal or disciplinary process existed. In particular, and in very brief summary, there was no accusation, no presumption of innocence, no legal representation and no right of disclosure, one of the key features of the modern criminal process.[118]

The Police Federation on Northern Ireland (PFNI), responded in September 2018 to a legacy consultation relating to the draft Northern Ireland (Stormont House Agreement) Bill proposed by the Northern Ireland Office (NIO). The PFNI expressed concern at political deals that 'discriminate against one group of local people, police officers' which is sure to be exploited under the terms of the 2018 proposed draft legislation if the draft bill becomes law. The PFNI in its September 2018 submission to the Northern Ireland Office stated that:

> 2. Legacy has been a travesty for the rule of law, criminal justice, equality, and basic human rights. Its institutions have marginalized the police family, damaged the reputation of officers and the police organization, mostly with an ambiguous word 'collusion' that sits outside the law. The draft bill fixes this; 'non-criminal police conduct' is the new collusion as set in legislation, and even though the draft bill cannot define it , a HIU (Historical Investigation Unit) Director will. It is certain to incite complaints against the police and flood the courts with civil claims by making officers (serving, retired and dead) retrospectively liable.

> 4. Equating terrorists to police officers is morally wrong. Yet this has been a major feature of the current legacy mechanism and this is set to continue throughout the proposed structures.[119]

Sinn Fein propaganda of a 'dirty war syndrome' at the heart of the security response to the PIRA terrorist insurgency has imposed on the political mainstream a Sinn Fein communication strategy directed to the legitimization of a PIRA terrorist insurgency that is intended to mask its devastating effects.[120] But this republican propaganda is vulnerable to the facts. If the RUC was anti-Catholic, how come the murder clearance rate for Catholics killed was almost double that for Protestants?[121] If security was brutal how does this explain a 99 per cent arrest rate of terrorists or three times more security forces killed than insurgents?[122] Or a Catholic population in the Troubles that increased from 35 per cent to 43.5 per cent?[123] And if the internal security solution and its normalization character was not restrained or human rights compliant enough for nationalists leaders and so-called human rights groups what 'human rights' compliant security solution have they in mind consistent with the necessity of an effective counter-insurgency? If insurgents were defenders, why did they commit the majority of the killings, execute defenceless prisoners and kill twice as many Catholics as the security forces?[124] And if the PIRA were 'peace-makers' and all it took to end the Troubles was to talk to them, why did that not happen in 1972 when they talked to William Whitelaw or in 1974/75 with Merlyn Rees and why the long war strategy?[125] The Ulster Unionist Party MLA, Doug Beattie, has forcefully derided successive weak governments and the NIO for facilitating republicans to use a legacy regime to re-write history as:

> bordering on the delusional when some commentators seriously question why so few police and troops served jail time when thousands of republicans did. This totally misses the fact that the equivalent to those terrorists held in the republican wings in the Maze, were those terrorists held in the loyalist wings.[126]

Conclusion

Nowhere in this chapter should it be misread that the security forces or security policy was perfect. Or that loyalist terrorists were not as depraved as republicans. Neither should it be taken that Special Branch deserves all credit, it would be remiss not to praise resources inside and outside terrorist organisations who courageously reported terrorist crimes to the authorities. Or indeed that politics was not crucial in bringing peace. Whilst covert operations occupied most headlines and incidents like Loughgall landmarked the start of the PIRA's demise, it was a brave and professional frontline of uniform police, CID detectives and soldiers that won the hard yards. Policing a community under the control of a violent insurgent organization like the PIRA and as a result withholds support for the police is remarkably different and far more difficult to policing a community that supports police. Normalisation for Catholics living under the Provo jackboot was meeting constables like Tracy Doak against a backdrop of violent republican and loyalist extremists going to prison. Intelligence-led policing in an irregular war is an invisible partnership with communities under siege. Intelligence owns all the risks.

Splitting the Troubles into three phases timelines how security and politics behaved in distinct periods in response to evolving insurgency. The 'scapegoat phase' explains the political imperative for nationalists to avoid painting the Provos the aggressor and to avoid associated negative connotations for nationalism. 'Dirty war' is its consolable parable. Thatcher, Special Branch and SAS, is Irish nationalism's triumvirate of British villainy. To see them as anything else is unthinkable, unspeakable, and unbearable. The political and legacy process put in motion by the Belfast Agreement conferred virtue on the PIRA for ending the Troubles and shame on the security forces for prolonging the Troubles. That is a morally repugnant trade-off for all except those for whom the definition of murder magically changed in 1998 and fits into Tammy Bruce's, *The Death of Right and Wrong* where murderers and innocent victims are the same.[127]

Former PIRA leader, Sean O'Callaghan, lamented the 'vitriol and lies, sometimes spurned on by unthinkable ignorance', that Special Branch officers alive and dead have been subjected to by the terrorists' fellow-travellers in the media and human rights industry. He regarded British and Irish and US governments as 'mealy-mouthed, at best, in the face of an orchestrated campaign of lies and slander – led by Sinn Fein'. O'Callaghan castigated those who may 'deride or ignore' security's contribution:

choosing instead to believe that whatever fragile peace Northern Ireland enjoys today is bestowed by Tony Blair, Gerry Adams and Bill Clinton and an assortment of peaceniks, chancers and conflict resolution groupies. Many such people have lined their own pockets by grossly inflating their influence in the 'peace process' and exporting their inanities to gullible audiences worldwide. In reality they reaped the peace that others had sown in a long intelligence war.[128]

This chapter questions the legitimacy of any account of how the Troubles ended that suppresses security or characterizes it 'dirty war'. And if one accepts this viewpoint, one cannot but marvel at the Orwellian world that makes it controversial.

Notes

[1] David Galula, *Counterinsurgency Warfare Theory and Practice* (London: Praegar Security International, 2006), p.1..

[2] Steven Metz, 'Rethinking Insurgency', in Paul B. Rich and Isabella Duyvestetn (eds), *The Routledge Handbook of Insurgency and Counterinsurgency* (New York: Routledge, 2012), p.38.

[3] David Galula, op. cit., p. 40. See also Mao Tse-Tung, *On Guerrila Warfare*, translated by Samuel B. Griffith (USA: Praegar, 2007) pp.430-44 where Mao argues that guerilla warfare cannot succeed without the support of the masses.

[4] Robin Evelegh, *Peacekeeping in a Democratic Society* (London: C. Hurst & *Company Publishers*, 1978, p.108. See also David Petraeus et al., *The US Army and Marine Corps Counterinsurgency Field Manuel* (Chicago: Chicago University Press, 2007), p. 10 where it shows PIRA/SF similar to jihadist insurgent networks in Iraq 'had little or no popular support'.

[5] Michael Burleigh, *Blood and Rage: A Cultural History of Terrorism* (London: Harper Press, 2008), p. 298.

[6] Francis Costello, The Irish Revolution and its Aftermath 1916-1923: Years of Revolt (Dublin: Irish Academic Press, 2003). See also Chris Ryder, The RUC: A Force Under Fire, (London: Mandarin House, 1990), pp. 211-213.

[7] Gearoid O Faolean, *A Broad Church: The Provisional IRA in the Republic of Ireland 1969-1980*, (Newbridge: Merrion Press, 2019), p. 171.

8   Stephen Dempster, 'What about Dublin?', *BBC Spotlight* documentary aired on BBC1, 7 February 2012. The INLA leader Dominic McGlinchey was the first insurgent that the Republic agreed to extradite. See Henry McDonald and Jack Holland, *INLA: Deadly Divisions* (Dublin: Poolbeg Books Ltd, 2010), pp. 277-278. Ironically McGlinchey had to be extradited back to the Republic because the non-jury Diplock Court was not satisfied that the evidence against him was beyond reasonable doubt.

9   David McKittrick et. al., *Lost Lives: The Stories of the Men, Women and Children Who Died as a Result of the Northern Ireland Trouble* (Edinburgh: Mainstream Publishing, 2616), p. 981.

10 James J. F Forest, *The Terrorism Lectures: A Comprehensive Collection for Students of Terrorism, Counterterrorism and National Security* (Santa Ana: Nortia Press, 2012) p. 12.

11 Conor Cruise O'Brien, *Ancestral Voices: Religion and Nationalism in Ireland* (Chicago: University Chicago Press, 1995). See also Robert Kee, *The Green Flag: A History of Irish Nationalism* (London: Penguin Press, 2001).

12 Gearoid O Faolean, op. cit., p. 171.

13 David Kilcullan, *The Accidental Guerilla: Fighting Small Wars in the Midst of a Big On* (London: Hurst and Company Publishers, 2009), p.128

14 Toby Harnden, *Bandit Country: The IRA and South Armagh* (London: Hodder and Stoughton, 1999), p.221.

15 William Matchett, 'The RUC Special Branch: How effective was it at defeating an insurgency', University of Ulster, EThOS (PhD thesis) , British Library, 2014, pp.80-81 and Appendix D.

16 Eamon Collins, *Killing Rage* (London: Granta Books, 1997), p.77.

17 A. R. Oppenheimer, *IRA Bombs and Bullets: A History of Deadly Ingenuity* (Dublin: Irish Academic Press, 2009).

18 Daniel J. Betz, Cyberspace and Insurgency', in Paul B. Rich and Isabelle Duyvesteyn, op. cit., pp. 56-58.

19 Rogelio Alonso, 'Terrorist skin, peace-party mask: the political communications strategy of Sinn Fein and the PIRA', *Terrorism and Political Violence*, Vol. 28 (3), pp. 520-540.

20 Chris Ryder, op. cit., p.26.

21 William Matchett, *Secret Victory: The Intelligence War that Beat the IRA,* (UK 2016), pp.87-88.

22 Chris Ryder, op. cit., p.115.

23 Sir John Hermon, *Holding the Line,* (Dublin: Gill and Macmillan, 1997), p.76.

24 David R. Orr, *RUC Spearhead: The Royal Ulster Constabulary Reserve Force 1950-1970,* (Newtownards: Readcoat Publishing, 2013), p.302.

25 David R. Orr, op. cit., p.304.

26 Nicholas van der Bilj, *Operation Banner*, (Barnsley: Pen and Sword Books Ltd, 2009), 19 and Chris Ryder, op. cit., p.115.

27 Sydney Elliott and W. D. Flackes, *Conflict in Northern Ireland,* (Santa Barbara: ABC-CLIO, 1999), p.641.

28 Paul Routledge, *John Hume*, (London: Harper Collins, 1997).

29 Ronald Weitzer, *Policing Under Fire: Ethnic Conflict and Police-Community Relations* (Albany: State University of New York Press, 1995).

30 Ernest McCall, *The Auxiliaries: Tutor Toughs* (Newtownards: Redcoat Publishing, 2011), pp. 17-18. McCall points out that throughout its history the RIC was approximately 70 per cent Catholic. See also Arthur Hezlett, *The 'B' Specials: A History of the Ulster Special Constabulary*,(Belfast: The Mourne River Press, 1997). Hezlett in a footnote (pp.24-25) wrote that 'it has been difficult to find the exact percentages' (of the RIC). Lloyd George in a Memorandum in 1922 claimed that the RIC was 82 per cent Catholic.

31 *The Report of the Advisory Committee on Policing in Northern Ireland* better known by the name of the chairman of the Committee Baron John Hunt CBE DSO as the *Hunt Report*. The *Hunt Report* resulted from an earlier *Cameron Report* which dealt with the causes and nature of the disturbances in 1969 surrounding the policing of civil rights protests.

32 For details see Sam Trotter, *Constabulary Heroes 1869-2009: Incorporating the RUC GC/PSNI and their Forebears including the USC* (Coleraine: Imprint Printing, 2009), pp. 70-84.

33 William Matchett, op. cit., p.126.

34 M.L.R Smith, *Fighting for Ireland: The Military Strategy of the Irish Republican Movement* (London: Routledge, 1996), p.93

35 Brian Faulkner, *Memoires of Statesman* (London: Weidenfeld and Nicholson, 1978), p.115.

36 Thomas Hennessey, *The Evolution of the Troubles 1970-72* (Dublin: Irish Academic Press, 2007), p.45.

37 Ed Maloney, *A Secret History of the IRA* (New York: W.Norton and Co, 2002). See also Henry Patterson, *Ireland's Violent Frontier: The Border and Anglo-Irish Relations During the Troubles* (Basingstoke: Palgrave Macmillan, 2013).

38 David McKittrick, et al, pp. 343-344.

39 Graham Ellison and Jim Smyth, *The Crowned Harp; Policing a Divided Society* (London: Oxford University Press, 1991). Peter Taylor, *Beating the Terrorists? Interrogation in Omagh, Gough and Castlereagh* (Harmondsworth: Penguin Books, 1980). Tim Pat Coogan, *The Troubles: Ireland's Ordeal 1966-96* (London: Hutchinson, 1995).

40 William Matchett, op. cit., p.129.

41 Amnesty International, *A Report on Allegations of Ill-Treatment made by Persons Arrested under the Special Powers Act after 8 August 1971*, and Report of an Amnesty International Mission to Northern Ireland 28 November- 6 December 1977 (London: International Secretariat, 1977)

42 Merlyn Rees, *Northern Ireland: A Personal Perspective* (London: Methuen, 1985), pp. 308-309.

43 Martin J. McCleery, op. cit., p.428.

44 William Matchett, op.cit., p.133-134.

45 Lord Gardiner, *Report of a Committee to Consider in the Context of* Civil *Liberties and Human Rights , Measures to Deal with Terrorism in Northern Ireland* (London HMSO, 1975).

46 Lord Diplock, *Report of the Commission to Consider Legal Procedures to Deal with Terrorist Activities in Northern Ireland* (London: HMSO, 1972), Chapter 2, Par 7.

47 David McKittrick et al., pp.143-149

48 Ibid, p.1473

49 Sydney Elliott and W. D. Flackes, op. cit., pp. 650-651.

50 William Matchett, *The RUC Special Branch: How Effective was it at Defeating* an *Insurgency?* (EThOS, PhD Thesis, British Library, 2014), p.239.

51 William Matchett, *Secret Victory*, pp. 159-171.

52 Idem, pp. 159-171.

53 David Kilcullen, 'The state of a controversial art', in Paul B. Rich and Isabelle Duyvesteyn, op.cit., pp. 142-143.

54 Sean O'Callaghan, 'Heroes of a dirty war', *Quadrant*, April 2017, pp.71-73.

55 William Matchett, op. cit., , p.242.

56 Robert Thompson, *Defeating Communist Insurgency: The Lessons of Malaya* and *Vietnam* (New York: Praeger, 1996), pp. 111-114 and David Galula, op. cit., p. 49.

57 Chris Ryder, op. cit., p.222.

58 David McKittrick et al., pp. 793-799.

59 Chris Ryder, op. cit., p.191.

60 Roy Mason, *Paying the Price* (London: Robert Hale, 1999), p.213.

61 William Matchett, *The RUC Special Branch*, p.122.

62 Robin Evelegh, *Peacekeeping in a Democratic Society* (London: C. Hurst and Company Publishers, 1978), p. 43.

63 A pamphlet by the RUCGC Foundation estimates that 'between 1972 and 20-01,10,957 republicans and 8,099 loyalists were charged with terrorist/serious public order offences'. The total broadly mirrors that of Chief Constable's Annual Reports. If one considers just over half of those prosecuted pleaded guilty and around 50% who fought the charges were prosecuted, we arrive at approximately 13,000 persons convicted for terrorist/serious public order crimes. The Transitional Justice Institute (TJI) of Queen's University Belfast (QUB) and Committee on the Administration of Justice (CAJ) , however, who formed the Model Bill, on the 4 September 2019 briefed the Northern Ireland Affairs Committee (NIAC) that 30,000 to 40,000were convicted for Troubles related offences. The higher data range seems to include crimes outside those annually published and tracked in official RUC reports and extends to jurisdictions outside of Northern Ireland.

64 Tony Gifford, *Supergrasses: The Use of Accomplice Evidence in Northern Ireland* (London: The Cobden Trust, 1984), pp. 4-9.

65 Ibid., p.10.

66 Ibid.

67 Eamon Collins, *Killing Rage* (London: Granta Books, 1997), p.313

68 M.L.R. Smith, op. cit., chapter 6. For the Hunger Strikes see Richard O'Rawe, *Blanketmen: An Untold Story of the H-Block Hunger Strike* (Dublin: New Island, 2005).

69 Sean O'Callaghan, 'Heroes of a Dirty War, p.71.

70 Margaret Thatcher, *Margaret Thatcher: The Downing Street Years* (London: HarperColins, 1993), pp.410-415.

71 Henry Patterson, *Ireland's Violent Frontier: The Border and Anglo-Irish Relations During the Troubles* (Basingstoke: Palgrave Macmillan, 2013), pp. 187-189. See Sam Trotter, op. cit., pp. 368-370.

72 Garret Fitzgerald, *All in a Life: Garret Fitzgerald, An Autobiography* (Dublin: Gill and Macmillan, 1991), pp. 572-575.

73 Paul Routledge, op. cit., p.204.

74 Chris Ryder, *Fighting Fitt* (Belfast: Brehon Press, 2006) and Paddy Devlin, *Straight Left* (Belfast: Blackstaff Press 1993).

75 See Ken Funston contribution to Jeffrey Dudgeon (ed) , *Legacy: What to do about the Past in Northern Ireland* (Belfast: Belfast Press, 2018).

76 Ronald Weitzer, *Transforming Settler States: Communal Conflict and Internal Security in Northern Ireland and Zimbabwe* (Berkeley: University of California Press, 1990), p.213.

77 William Matchett, op. cit., p. 169.

78 Ibid., p. 137

79 Ibid., pp. 141-153.

80 Ibid., p.

81 Hansard, Commons Sitting, HC 17 February 1988 Vol. 127, cc 977-996.

82 For Loughgall see Mark Urban, *Big Boys' Rule* (London: Faber and Faber, 1993).

83 William Matchett, op. cit., p.200. But the public focus tended to be on the 4 per cent so-called 'shoot-to- kill' covert operations with writers like Fionnula Ni Aolain in *The Politics of Force: Conflict Management and State Violence in Northern Ireland* (Belfast: Blackstaff Press, 2000) labeling intelligence-led policing 'the anatomy of police failure' (p.55 and p.59).

84 Fionnula Ni Aolain, *op. cit.,* p.266.

85 Hansard Commons Sitting, HC 17 February 1988 Vol. 127cc 977-996.

86 Statement by the Director of Public Prosecutions for Northern Ireland in Relation to Decisions as to Prosecution Arising out of Stevens 111, Par. 9, Belfast Chambers 25 June 2007. The statement can be found at the PPS website, www.ppsni.gov.uk

87 Stevens Enquiry: Overview and Recommendations, 17 April 2003, Par 4.7. *http:// cain.ulst.ac.uk/issues/collusion/stevens3/stevens3summary.htm* (assessed 1 June 2019).

88 Ibid. Par 4.6-4.7.

89 Statement by the family of Pat Finucane, Amnesty International and the NI Human Rights Commission, 25 June 2007. *http://cain.ulst.ac.uk/victims/docs/group/pat finucane_finucane_centre/pfc_finucane_250607.pdf* (accessed 2 July 2019).

90 The Rt Hon Sir Desmond de Silva QC, *The Report of the Patrick Finucane Review,* (London: The Stationary Office, 12 December 2012), Vol. 1, Par. 21-22, p.6.

91 Ibid., Par. 21, p.6.

92 Ibid., Par. 26, p.7.

93 Ibid., Par. 24, p.7

94 Ibid., Par. 24, p.7.

95 Ibid., Par. 25, p.7.

96 Ibid., Par. 23, p. 6.

97 Jack Holland and Susan Phoenix, *Phoenix: Policing the Shadows- the Secret* War *Against Terrorism in Northern Ireland* (Edinburgh: Hodder and Stoughton, 1999), p.266.

98 Brian Feeney, *Insider: Gerry Bradley's Life in the IRA* (Dublin: O'Brien Press, 2009), p.234.

99 Michael Addison, *Violent Politics: Strategies of Internal Conflict* (Oxford: Palgrave, 2002), p.119.

100 Paul Nolan, 'The cruel peace: killings in Northern Ireland since the Good Friday Agreement', 23 April 2018. *http://www.thedetail.tv/articles/the-cruel-peace--killings-in-northern-ireland-since-the-good-friday-agreement* (accessed 1 June 2019).

101 Sean O'Callaghan, op. cit., p.71.

102 Ibid., p.71.

103 Henry McDonald, 'Irish dissident groups thwarted by surveillance technology', *The Guardian* , 28 January 2014.

104 John Major, *John Major: An Autobiography* (London: HarperCollins, 1999), 431.

105 Henry McDonald and Jack Holland, *INLA: Deadly Divisions* (Dublin: Poolbeg, 2010), pp. 166-167.

106 Margaret Thatcher, *Margaret Thatcher: The Downing Street Years* (London: HarperCollins1993), p. 414.

107 Charles Townsend, *Britain's Civil Wars: Counterinsurgency in the Twentieth Century* (London: Faber and Faber, 1986), p. 67.

108 *A New Beginning: Policing in Northern Ireland* (Norwich: HMSO, 1999), Par. 1.2, p.2.

109 Ibid., Par. 1.7, p.4.

110 Ibid., Par. 2.5, p.11

111 Ibid., Par. 1.7, p.4.

112 Eoghan Harris, 'Sinn Fein's Scientology is the cult of "moving on"', *Irish Independent*, 8 July 2012.

113 Ruth Dudley Edwards, 'IRA hardmen are still in charge and are waging war through lawyers', *Irish Independent,* 10 March 2019.

114 'IRA right to fight says Gerry Adams at Kevin McKenna's funeral', *Belfast Telegraph*, 27 June 2019.

115 William Matchett, *The RUC Special Branch*, p.82.

116 Mary O'Rawe, 'Accountable intelligence and intelligence accountability: rogue elements in Northern Ireland or classic failures in modern global systems of governance', *Selected Works of Mary O'Rawe,* bepress.com, April 2008. Chris Thornton, 'Cold case team "must change" says academic', *Belfast Telegraph,* 17 September 2008. The Thornton reference was to Professor Patricia Lundy of the University of Ulster. See also, Vincent Kearney, 'Independence of HET comes under criticism', *BBC News Northern Ireland,* 3 April 2012 and Prerequisites for Progress in Northern Ireland: Written Evidence of Dr Patricia Lundy ... to the Commission of Security and Co-operation in Europe, US Helsinki Commission, 21 March 2012.

[117]   Neil Southern, *Policing and Combatting Terrorism in Northern Ireland: The Royal Ulster Constabulary GC* (Switzerland: Palgrave Macmillan, 2018), p.263.

[118]   Judgment in the High Court of Justice in Northern Ireland Queen's Bench Division(Judicial Review) in the matter of an application by Thomas Ronald Hawthorne and Raymond White for Judicial Review-v-Police Ombudsman for Northern Ireland, Ref McCosh10504, JR 16/68976/01, delivered by McCloskey J, 19 January 2018. Par 73-77, pp41-42.

[119]   Police Federation of Northern Ireland, *On 'Addressing the Legacy of Northern Ireland's Past', Submission to the Northern Ireland Office*, September 2018, Par. 3-4, p.3.

[120]   Rogelio Alonso, 'Terrorist skin, peace-party mask: the political communications strategy of Sinn Fein and the PIRA', *Terrorism and Political Violence*, 28:3, 2016, pp. 520-540.

[121]   'This Brave and Resolute Force' by the RUC GC, 2014 has 50 per cent murder clearance rate for Catholic victims and a 30 per cent for Protestants.

[122]   See for relevant statistics, David McKittrick et al., Table 1, pp. 1473-1474.

[123]   See *http://www.4ni.co.uk/northern_ireland_news.asp?id=6135* (accessed 9 June 2019) and the CAIN website at *http://cain.ulst.ac.uk/ni/popul.htm* (accessed 9 June 2019).

[124]   Henry Patterson, *The Politics of Illusion: Political History of the IRA* (London: Serif, 1997), p.10.

[125]   William Whitelaw, *The Whitelaw Memoirs* (London: Arum Press, 1989), p.149. See also David Fairhall's obituary of Sir Frank Cooper in *The Guardian*, 31 January 2002 where Fairhall states that Cooper 'working for Conservative Northern Ireland Secretary, William Whitelaw was among the first to try talking to the Provisional IRA in the search for a political solution'.

[126]   Doug Beattie, 'Meek government and NIO let republicans write history', *NewsLetter*, 11 July 2019. Doug Beattie is a former and distinguished officer in the Royal Irish Regiment awarded the Military Cross in Afghanistan (2003) and Ulster Unionist Party Member of the Legislative Assembly (2016-)

[127]   Tammy Bruce, *The Death of Right and Wrong* (New York: Three Rivers Press, 2003), p. 165.

[128]   Sean O'Callaghan, *Heroes of a Dirty War*, p.71.

7

Nationalism and dealing with the past in Northern Ireland, 1998-2018: the disarticulation of unionist memory

Cillian McGrattan

David Park's acclaimed novel, *The Truth Commissioner*, works as a kind of counter-factual history of the peace process. Specifically, it revolves around the question of what would a truth and reconciliation commission have looked like in Northern Ireland? James Fenton, one of the central characters – a former Royal Ulster Constabulary intelligence officer, pensioned-off when the force was re-instituted as the Police Service of Northern Ireland – is to be called to appear before the truth commission. He is informed of this when climbing Slieve Donard with his successor, Alec who also warns him not to mention the name of a republican 'Minister for Children' in relation to a case where an adolescent was disappeared and murdered. Agitated, Fenton opines, 'They' – the political classes – 'took the badge, they took the name, any kind of respect that was owed, and now they want to take the truth and twist it into whatever shape they think suits them best.[1]

The novel is worth revisiting in the light of what has actually occurred in the area of dealing with the past in Northern Ireland over the past two decades. This chapter suggests that some of the more troubling aspects of Park's 'What if … ?' have in effect come to pass: political exigency characterizes and has become constitutive of what passes for political decision-making and the past has been airbrushed to such an extent that it sometimes truly resembles the 'foreign country' of L.P. Hartley. The chapter advances two arguments by way of explanation: Firstly, the cynicism of

Park's Fenton is well-placed: 'truth' and 'reconciliation' ought to be read as synonyms for 'peace'; or, more exactly, proxies for what Mick Fealty of the Slugger O'Toole blog capitalizes as The Peace Process TM[2] – the highly expedient and *ad hoc* way in which peaceful, democratic politics in Northern Ireland have been calibrated towards the perceived necessity of bringing violent republicans into the political process.[3] This predisposition has geared political developments towards nationalism in general and republicanism in particular and, in terms of the latter, was based on the facilitating Sinn Féin's passage into routine, institutional politics. The preferential option has allowed nationalism to turn what ought to have been remarkably difficult historical territory into nutritious soils.

Secondly, the more specific area within the peace process of legacy issues or dealing with the past has been structured with an implicit *ideological bias* in which the noun '*a* transition' has become replaceable with its verb form – '*to* transition'. This has facilitated the representation of 'legacy issues' as primarily transitional to an end state as distinct from them being about culpability for the injustices and violence of the past. The ideological bias, then, to be clear, is that that understanding lends itself to nationalist understandings that the Northern state is illegitimate and must be transcended.

Dealing with the past as a 'narrative'

The former deputy First Minister and SDLP leader Seamus Mallon complained in 2015 that it had been a 'mistake' to allow Sinn Féin into government outwith decommissioning of PIRA weaponry after the 1998 Belfast/Good Friday Agreement (B/GFA). Mallon blamed the then Taoiseach and Prime Minister Bertie Ahern and Tony Blair for pursuing their chance to get into the 'history books'. It was, he asserted,' bad tactical politics and devalued and tarnished the agreement and the currency of politics':

> Some people don't realise that two and a bit years before Good Friday, the Provos [Provisional IRA] had already done their negotiations with London and Dublin and with America [...] They had been talking to the British, they had been talking to [John] Hume and had been talking to Dublin and they had been talking to America.[4]

Appealing to a counterfactual, Mallon suggested that things 'could and should have been done differently'. And, he concluded, the 'total fundamental weak part of it was that the governments allowed them [Sinn Féin] to set the agenda'. The SDLP were, however, instrumental in these developments. As Eamonn O'Kane points out in his history of Anglo-Irish relations: Once the two governments had asked the PIRA to move – in decommissioning weapons – and they replied negatively, there was only one other position that could move: Unionism.[5] Mallon's position in 1999 was ostensibly quite different: Although the New Labour government had refused to stick with its demand of decommissioning, Mallon laid the blame at the lack of political progress squarely at the feet of his erstwhile allies in government, the Ulster Unionists: 'What they are doing is worse than failing to operate an inclusive Executive. They are actually preventing its creation. They are dishonouring the Agreement, they are insulting its principles'.[6]

How to explain such a discrepancy? Vivian Lowndes and Mark Roberts suggest that a common, normative understanding attaches to any institution. They argue that a 'story' is told about institutions that exists separate to the functional understandings or legal remits. The stories that institutions 'tell' about themselves are found in press briefings or on institutional websites; but they are also inherent in the ways that people associated with the institutions understand them to work. As Lowndes and Roberts explain: narratives 'provide an account not just of *how* we do things around here, but also *why* we do things the way we do'.[7] One example of this in practice, they suggest, is how the NHS is framed within political debates: even in the midst of arguments about the need to reduce debt by cutting government spending, politicians are often careful to reassure voters that the NHS will be protected. This, in turn, works to constrain persistent governmental attempts to reform the NHS through marketization. What Mallon characterizes as a 'mistake' points to a failure of political imagination and leadership on his part – a failure of imagination that would have allowed him to appreciate the difficulties involved for unionists to countenance Sinn Fein's participation in government; but also a failure of leadership to tackle the difficulties that excluding Sinn Fein would have created for the SDLP with nationalist voters at the time.

Mallon's framing of the decision to go into government without PIRA decommissioning as a 'mistake' speaks to an ideological understanding and a specific narrative about these early years of the devolved institutions. That 'story' is ideological and self-serving, premised, as it seemingly is, on the idea that it was primarily the responsibility of unionists to make politics work. We can, thus, see how easily storytelling, as a means of conveying understandings, is one of the ways in which ideologies them-selves become operationalized. Indeed, in the work of one of the most important contemporary scholars on ideology, Michael Freeden, stories are almost synonymous with ideologies. In Freeden's view an 'ideology' is often a pejorative term – it is something political opponents do and it can be something to do with lying or propaganda or spin. But addressed in an analytical fashion, he suggests ideology can be seen as doing three things: It describes or diagnoses a point of view – namely a 'problem'. It defines it: namely, it attributes a 'cause' or a diagnosis'. Secondly, it offers a prescription, a remedy or a solution. The third thing an ideology does is, in Freeden's terminology, it *decontests* meaning.[8] Thus, the stories that conservatives might tell about the concept 'poverty' will allow commu-nication based on shared meaning – that it is a ubiquitous issue, perhaps, or an inevitable result of social hierarchies. These stories may differ from those told by socialists about the same concept – that it is a problem arising from capitalism, perhaps. For Seamus Mallon, then, 'decommissioning' was and perhaps remains indicative of an approach to politics that negates cross-community compromise. In other words, the shared meaning behind the idea of decommissioning within the nationalist imagination – as artic-ulated by the positions held by Mallon – is that it was something to do with obduracy: firstly, on the part of the unionists led by David Trimble and then (later in 2015) on the part of republicans. The alternative that might have seen Mallon back Trimble's stance to a greater degree than he did around the turn of the millennium does not feature in the ideological equation: recognition of that gap or lacuna would call into question the notion that the issue was someone else's problem. I wish to suggest that a similar process of ideological construction has taken place in relation to the subsequent peace process and that that the area of dealing with the past crystallises and encapsulates much of the nationalist confluence or decontestation about contemporary politics in Northern Ireland.

Dealing with the past, 1998-2019

Of the over-3,600 conflict-related murders, republican paramilitaries were responsible for just under 60 per cent of the total Troubles-related deaths – the Provisional Irish Republican Army (PIRA) alone killed 1,771 people. This compared with loyalist paramilitaries being responsible for around 30 per cent and the remaining 10 per cent being attributable to state forces, most of which were carried out in defence of the law. The PIRA sustained 293 deaths compared to the Royal Ulster Constabulary's (RUC) 303.[9] Various institutional mechanisms have been introduced since the late-1990s to deal with the legacies of the conflict. Invariably, they become subject to the same historical dynamics that perpetuated political conflict and entrenchment for so long. The first attempt to deal with the legacies of the Troubles was the appointment of Sir Kenneth Bloomfield as Victims' Commissioner in October 1997. This move was itself seen as a response to the grow-ing unionist perception that republicans 'owned' the peace process. Although Bloomfield's report recommended a series of measures for dealing with victims' issues – including greater compensation to victims and their support groups; asking the government to give greater priority to trauma and pain treatment; improved employment opportunities for victims; and a series of symbolic ideas for a memorial day and an archive for victims' stories – it was roundly condemned by nationalists who felt that it ignored the victims of state-sponsored violence.[10] In June 1998, the first Minister for Victims, Adam Ingram, established the Victims Liaison Unit within the NIO to implement Bloomfield's proposals concerning financial assistance. The announcement by the British government in January 1998 of an inquiry into Bloody Sunday served to placate nationalists.

Northern Ireland's bloody past was an intrinsic part of the politics of the Belfast /Good Friday Agreement, which was signed in April of 1998. The way that the Agreement dealt with the past was, however, Janus-faced: the Agreement looked to the past to justify moving on and drawing a line in the sand. Thus, the second paragraph of the 'Declaration of Support', which prefaced the Agreement stated that:

The tragedies of the past have left a deep and profoundly regrettable legacy of suffering. We must never forget those who have died or been injured, and their families. But we can best honour them through a fresh start, in which we firmly dedicate ourselves to the achievement of reconciliation, tolerance, and mutual trust, and to the protection and vindication of the human rights of all.[11]

The Agreement provided for no overarching truth and reconciliation or truth recovery mechanism. In fact, victims merited three paragraphs on the eighteenth page of the 30-page document, while a key provision was the 'accelerated release of prisoners' within a two-year time frame. The failure to link prisoner releases to decommissioning and the demonstrable gulf in the treatment of convicted terrorists and their victims angered many people within constitutional nationalist and unionist communities. For unionists, in particular, it gave rise to the perception that the Belfast /Good Friday Agreement was about the valorisation of the republican explanatory narrative and the simultaneous obliteration of their experiences of the conflict out of history.[12]

The reform of the police was intrinsic to this growing disillusionment. Although the police ombudsman – which was established under the reforms – was instrumental in securing additional funding for injured RUC officers and their widows, it is undeniable that much of the ombudsman's work has been perceived by unionists as perpetuating republican ideas about the corruption of the police and the irreformability of the Northern state. This perception is heightened due to the lack of reciprocation or serious engagement from republicans on the question of their actions – that is, beyond the recourse-to-history, 'if-you-had-been-there-you would-have-done-the-same' argument. For example, Martin McGuinness infamously resisted giving information to the Saville Inquiry, citing an oath of allegiance to his (former) colleagues; the Smithwick Tribunal into collusion between the PIRA and An Garda Síochána (the Irish police) expressed 'disappointment' that the PIRA only cooperated by supplying written evidence and would not assent to being 'tested under cross-examination'[13]

The British government has continued to argue against the idea of policing the past through official inquiries. For example, the then Secretary of State, Peter Hain, commented in 2007 that:

> Huge amounts of money are involved which cannot be spent on meeting the concerns of today. Recent political progress in Northern Ireland should make us pause and ask whether re-living or even re-fighting the Troubles in the courtroom or the public inquiry or through police investigation is really a healthy way forward.[14]

Hain was speaking at the launch of the Consultative Group on the Past in Northern Ireland (CGPNI), which has, arguably, remained the most significant attempt to deal with the past institutionally. Certainly, the CGPNI was instrumental – the basic parameters it envisaged (a branch-like structure of distinct areas – policing; information recovery; oral history) have persisted within governmental thinking. One reason for this might be that, in fact, the Group was charged with a particularly instrumental approach to dealing with the legacies the conflict – its dual task was to find the best way in which Northern Ireland should 'deal with the past' and to make 'recommendations ... on any steps that might be taken to support Northern Ireland society in building a shared future'.[15] That the Group accurately understood its task of making the past subservient to the needs of the present was reflected in its choice of an epigraph: 'To look backward for a while is to refresh the eye, to restore it, and to render it more fit for its prime function of looking forward'.[16] The public relations shambles of the launch of the Group's Report in 2009 also suggested to some more sceptical observers that it in fact recognised its task only too well: the proposed £12,000 award to all victims regardless of whether or not their relatives had been killed on active terrorist duty, served to distract attention from its other recommendations and essentially ended any chances that they would be taken seriously by government.

Despite that, the CGPNI's proposals formed the basis of subsequent attempts to deal with what became known as 'legacy issues': namely, the Stormont House Agreement of 2014 and the legacy white paper and consultation process, which was published in 2018 and is continuing at the time of writing. The consultation paper proposes to establish two main bodies for working through the unsolved murders (just under 2,000) from the Troubles – other associated features of the terror campaigns including injuries, intimidation, punishment beatings (frequently of minors) and various other forms of violence including the seemingly widespread cover-up of sexual abuse of children by republicans will presumably be considered as part of the adjunct oral history centre, depending on how its (presently nebulous) remit is decided. Those two bodies are a forensic, investigatory force, supplementary to the PSNI and an information retrieval unit in which information can be deposited that will not be admissible in any future court case.

Truth recovery, reconciliation and the disarticulation of Ulster unionism

Although, seemingly, history is never far from political discourse in Northern Ireland, the very idea of truth recovery has reinvigorated debates over the past. As the political discourse of Provisional republicanism and constitutional nationalism demonstrates, truth recovery is filtered through and back into and, in the process, serves to transform ideas about identity, justice, reconciliation, and history. The use of ideas about the past is yet another way of the Provisional project securing its position within mainstream northern Catholic politics. In addition, due to its essential 'revisionist' approach to questions of historical accuracy or responsibility, Provisional republicanism's utilisation of the past is, in important ways, a re-writing. In this regard the party's juxtaposition of its commitment to truth recovery and what it sees as the British state's allegiance to 'truth suppression'[17] is a false one; for truth recovery in the Provisional republican mode ought to be understood as truth creation. The idea of 'wiping the slate clean' then becomes a literal description of a political project: as R.F Foster has pointed out, the fact that the Provisional IRA campaign entrenched partition more than any governmental initiative and the fact that Sinn Féin now administer British rule in Northern Ireland is perhaps pragmatic, but 'should the bad old days return, there will be little evidence that [Adams and Sinn Féin] ever adapted [their] analysis'.[18]

The establishment and constant maintenance of that analysis through an intensive commemoration industry, then, has as its main audience the Catholic community – but in order for that maintenance to make sense the 'British state' acts as a proxy for Ulster unionists. In other words, the republican and nationalist approach to the past has as one of its key goals the creation of an oblivion – a gap or a hole – relating to the Protestant experience of the conflict. This occurs by directly effacing unionism and replacing it with the 'British' and by disarticulating the core historical beliefs and memories of unionists – suggesting, for instance, that 'collusion' of state forces with loyalist paramilitaries was systemic and 'repression' of Catholic communities a direct result of a resilient neo-imperialist impulse within Westminster and the government's security apparatus. These ideas stand in contrast to unionist ideas that the conflict was an unjustified attack on a reforming state, or that that terror campaign was sectarian and involved the deliberate targeting of Protestants, tantamount to ethnic cleansing, often occurring around the border leading to massive depopulation of local Protestant families.

The transitional politics of republicanism

While Sinn Féin remains haunted by the past,[19] for the most part, it has tried to evade unwelcome spectres. Indeed, a critical feature of the contemporary Sinn Féin project is the attempt to circumvent troublesome legacy questions, such as the 'disappeared' or its own compromise on its stated goals of a 'thirty-two county socialist republic';[20] and does so by creating a narrative based on the culpability of the British state for the conflict. This idea underpins the policy position that 'independence and credibility' are 'critical issues' for dealing with the past and that truth recovery therefore necessitates 'maximum involvement from the United Nations or a similar reputable organisation in the process [of truth recovery]'.[21] In Sinn Féin's view 'The British state was the major protagonist in the conflict'. This conclusion arises from its narrative understanding of Irish history, which proceeds from the idea that 'British policy in Ireland is at the root of cyclical conflict here'.[22] The party's recommendations reflect this viewpoint, but also incorporate insights from the broader truth recovery paradigm:

THE NORTHERN IRELAND QUESTION

> What is needed is a truth-recovery mechanism which will help: [t]o make
> known the truth about the conflict; [t]o take seriously the needs of all
> victims; [t]o build in society the capacity to distinguish the truth from the
> myths; [t]o learn lessons about the past in order to guard against future
> conflict; [t]o broaden ownership of and responsibility for the process of
> conflict transformation; [and t]o explore conditions under which political
> actors can nurture greater trust, confidence, and generosity towards each
> other.[23]

The idea that Irish history is cyclical and determined by the injustice
perpetuated by British state involvement is, of course, not restricted to
Sinn Féin.[24] To take forward Freeden's notions about what an ideology
does: the diagnostic, structural understanding that the Troubles were the
fault of 'the British' gives way to a prognosis that the British state cannot
be trusted to be transparent. The agreement on this structural approach
works to decontest or efface awkward questions such as those relating to
unionists who also consider themselves British.

Republicans have been instrumental in utilising the law to promote
a state-centric, structuralist understanding. Thus, the idea of human
rights and international inquiries based on the European Human Rights
Convention sometimes comes to fill the absence of a truth and reconciliation commission; alternatively, republicans have also been supportive
of local oral history initiatives – (ostensible) state crime and collusion are
often a marked feature of both of these pincer-like fronts. Both types of
approach transpose the *noun* transition into its *verb* to transition. Whereas
the noun is objectifiable, measurable and it logically implies an end, the
latter posits an end-state but, by definition, does not need a conclusion.
Proceeding along that understanding, nationalists and republicans con-
flate rights issues with truth recovery to give the latter a progressivist
force.

Decontestation occurs at that point: transition or progress becomes the
yardstick for measuring objectivity and validity and dissenting opinions
or alternative framings of victims' rights can (or ought to) be discarded.
A case in point is the interview that Norman Tebbit gave on BBC One on
the twenty-fifth anniversary of the Brighton bomb in which a PIRA attack

on the hotel in which the Conservative Party's annual conference was being held resulted in five fatalities and injuries to many others – including Tebbit's wife who was left permanently disabled. During the interview, Tebbit drew a distinction between the politically motivated 'terrorists' of the PIRA and Islamic fundamental 'psychopaths' and claimed that 'To forgive people who have no contrition, no repentance, is to make a mockery of forgiveness. It is simply wrong. It also runs the risk of ... raising a flag that says "We are easy meat".'[25] The then spokesperson for Relatives for Justice – a victims' group which focuses on state crimes[26] – Clara Reilly, took exception to Tebbit's sentiments and claimed that:

> Obviously Mr Tebit [sic] is a deeply hurt individual who has difficulty in reconciling his victim-hood and experience to the progress of the peace process more generally ... It is a great pity that he cannot make any positive or meaningful contribution like that of many others[27]

In other words, opinions and testimony are measured against a predefined yardstick of political 'progress'; those sentiments that measure-up are represented as somehow 'valid' or 'meaningful' and are therefore held to be important enough to be listened to. Furthermore, within this logic, the truth recovery paradigm turns full circle and the claim is made that this sort of 'understanding' about the events and trajectory of the conflict is not only socially edifying but it can 'contribute towards personal healing and reconciliation'.[28] Despite Tebbit's idea that the PIRA and Sinn Féin should be granted greater indulgence than Al Qaida, it is, perhaps, unsurprising that his views provoked an intemperate response from Relatives for Justice. Not only was Lord Tebbit a leading member of Thatcher's Conservative administration, which was the target of particularly vicious resentment among republicans owing to Thatcher's hard-line stance during the hunger strikes (1980-81), but Tebbit was articulating a discourse that offers a radically different alternative to that of the transitional paradigm. This discourse is based on the idea that perpetrators should be held to account for their crimes and that while forgiveness and reconciliation are difficult, they are at least possible as long as the perpetrator repents or forsakes his or her criminal past.[29] Since Sinn Féin continue to hold the view that the armed struggle was entirely justified, Tebbit is logically correct in dismissing the issue of forgiveness as (presently) meaningless.

The Provisional republican approach to truth recovery draws suste-
nance and inspiration from research into the Northern Irish transition
from violence to peace. In particular, it coincides with the dominant ways
in which transitional justice is framed in Northern Ireland.[30] Often, this is
a result of academics directly advising community groups based in republican areas. For example, the transitional justice scholar Brandon Hamber
of the University of Ulster 'facilitated' the local community group Eolas on
publishing a 'Consultative Paper',[31] while two other University of Ulster
sociologists, Bill Rolston and Patricia Lundy, were also involved in the
project.[32] This community and academic work tends to promote the idea
that truth recovery is necessary to build peace and achieve reconciliation:
'For advocates of truth recovery, dealing with the past and uncovering
the truth is regarded as a key cornerstone and basis upon which trust can
begin to be built and society can move forward'.[33] Reasonable and laudable as the ideals of building trust and moving forward are, they are also
nevertheless ideologically biased.[34] This is revealed in their intensely political framing of the debate in Northern Ireland in which concern for due
process and the punishment of terrorist and state crimes or ideas about
historical accuracy, are downplayed or ignored in favour of an over-the-
orised dichotomy between 'restorative' and 'retributive conception[s]
of justice'.[35] While Lundy and McGovern attempt to engage unionism
in debate,[36] this perceived broadening simply ignores the possibility that
unionism does not necessarily wish to engage in and on the terms of the
transitional and progressivist paradigm. For example, the most comprehensive account of unionist politics since the 1998 Agreement and – in
particular – unionists' attitudes towards the post-conflict situation points
out that 'unionists *want to tell their stories*, but fear that in [so] doing they
will subject those stories to critical scrutiny, and that they will potentially
become inadvertent participants in truth projects' that are aimed at transitional or progressivist ends.[37]

The progressivist commitment to a 'holistic, community-oriented
approach' misses the point: it is wishful thinking to suppose that such an
approach may 'open up' 'spaces of controversy' and 'allow testimony to be
translated into an exchange of trust'[38] when the overriding fear of unionists

is that 'imposed, manufactured history by Irish republicans (with assistance from the British and/or Irish governments) would elide individual and collective 'biographies of suffering'.[39] Furthermore, the structural bias of the progressivist approach recurs in the complaint that '[s]ome of the strongest opposition to truth recovery has come from within unionism and loyalism'.[40] Loyalist terrorist spokespersons have also adopted the same self-serving, self-exculpatory approach of Provisional republicans[41] Lundy and McGovern's obliviousness to this dynamic reveals not only the limitations of the progressivist paradigm but also its potential for coinciding with ethnicised viewpoints. For example, the implications of the 'holistic, community-oriented approach' are similar to those that emanate from the loyalist compliant about being ostracised from mainstream unionism as a result of violence:[42] both approaches elide the plurality of communities in Northern Ireland and end in valorising those communal, ethnic chauvinist experiences and beliefs that were the principal drivers in perpetuating the killing and mayhem for so long.

Ethics and truth: The SDLP's Ideologisation of the past

The mixing of more overt claims to ethics than republicanism together with historical storytelling characterises the SDLP's understanding of the Northern Irish conflict. At times this appears as abstract, wishful thinking: For instance, ignoring the need for a dis/incentive structure, it has argued that 'Truth, healing, justice and dealing with the past will be stalled if those who know the most and did the worst over the years of conflict in state organisations and illegal groups fail to step forward in openness and honesty'.[43] The party has advocated 'an ethical approach to the past.[44] While it suggests that '[c]onsensual agreement is the ideal', the document also points out that any proposals concerning the legacies of the past 'should be assessed on ethical standards not on the aspiration for consensus'.[45] This aspiration forms the basis of British government policymaking on the question,[46] however, the SDLP argue that it deliberately sets too high a 'threshold' for taking action.[47]

As with Sinn Féin, the SDLP's attitude to dealing with the past stems from its own understanding of the history of the conflict and its own place within that history. Indeed, the idea of 'an ethical approach to the past' is intimately linked to the party's narrative understanding of its own past. Thus, the 'ethical approach' means that

> [T]here is a need to acknowledge that there were many people, who by their actions and attitudes cannot be held culpable for the wrongs of others. People across the community held to democratic practice, a sense of justice … and acceptance of difference. This was the majority of people.[48]

The SDLP's 'truth' and its articulation of its own history originates from the participation of its first generation of leaders in the Northern Irish civil rights movement of the late-1960s. The perception that this movement was usurped by a cabal within the republican movement who saw an opportunity to take a war to the British Army, remains a central trope in contemporary SDLP self-understandings. Whereas Sinn Féin's narrative explicitly blames 'the Brits' for starting and perpetuating the conflict, the SDLP's narrative stresses the corruption of the Northern state prior to the civil rights movement.

The personal histories of some senior SDLP members, who suffered intimidation and physical violence at the hands of republicans, serve to establish a problematic dynamic for the SDLP itself. In other words, SDLP representatives face the problem of finding a position between differentiating themselves from Sinn Féin and the need to maintain or represent nationalist unity. In contrast to the ethical dimensions attached to the idea of an 'inherited' identity, the *ethnic* logic inherent in this problem relates more specifically to issues of intra-bloc contestation. For example, the SDLP explain that the party has lost electoral ground to Sinn Fein because the latter has simply appropriated the SDLP's strategic vision and many of its policies.[49] As such, the SDLP attempts to appropriate a kind of moral high ground above electoral politics. Thus, the SDLP's attempt to differentiate between what might be called an SDLP moral vision and that of Sinn Féin is limited (politically) by what is acceptable to its supporters. In other words, in the Northern Irish context, truth recovery is not only filtered through a political, ethnic and/or ideological prism, its reach is limited by what is acceptable to ethno-nationalist communities.

The SDLP's response to the Consultative Group on the Past in Northern Ireland cited the notion that all parties to the conflict were equally culpable, which it viewed was a 'central flaw' and a 'failure to challenge those who did the worst and know the most about the past to acknowledge and account for their actions'.[50] Indeed, in this legalistic view, the political dilemma of criticising Sinn Féin and the PIRA does not exist – or rather, it is resolved in ethical terms. For the SDLP, accountability and truth recovery are also linked to what it calls the 'experience of democratic nationalism'. However, that experience is being systematically undermined by the party's effective promotion of a structuralist understanding of the conflict that chimes with that of Provisional republicanism.

Arguably, a more fundamental question – certainly in terms of policy direction and the discursive framework of post-Belfast/Good Friday Agreement-Northern Ireland – relates to whether the SDLP's public and long-standing commitment to 'reconciliation' contributes to the marginalisation of victims' voices and the amplification of the Provisional narrative. This is perhaps inevitable given the internalisation by many nationalists of what might be termed a 'soft-focussed view' on the Provisional campaign – a 'sneaking regard' to use a colloquialism. In this regard, the SDLP may not simply be caught between a rock and a hard place as trapped within a nationalist schizophrenia in which, despite their surface-level ethical aversion to Sinn Féin's historical record, Catholic voters nevertheless feel 'guilty' by not voting for them and instead voting SDLP – not because they perceive themselves to 'be letting their side down', but because the Sinn Féin's historical narrative continues to resonate with ideological tropes and taboos that the SDLP pander to but are unable – or unwilling – to disabuse. The point recurs when the SDLP comes to consider unionist voices which it continues to frame in regard to a progressivist or transitional yardstick: 'as the discussion around the past evolves, some elements in unionism are participating, though some contributions clearly do not endorse a comprehensive truth process'. The unionist problematic for the SDLP is that unionists have a problem. Of course, that is not expressed in so many words, but it is latent within what the SDLP perceive to be a unionist fixation on the role of the Irish government in perpetuating the Troubles – through ideological and material support and by acts of omission in failing to provide adequate security on the border:

> The unionist leadership needs to acknowledge that to embed reconciliation and the healing that can further transform our society requires an ethical approach to the past. This needs to be comprehensive, so that a full and balanced account is developed. In calling on a government to acknowledge an alleged role or one person to admit membership of an organisation is not going to address as fully as we need to, the past that we share or the future that we can build.[51]

Ethics seem to lie in the eye of the beholder – it is difficult to discern, for instance, an ethical approach in the backing of SDLP councillors to the naming of a playpark in Newry after a PIRA hunger striker who had been convicted of attempted murder.[52] Although the current SDLP leader, Colum Eastwood, defended his decision to carry the coffin of another republican terrorist, it seems that ethics in that instance ended at personal loyalty – the deceased was, Eastwood claimed, a childhood friend.[53]

Collusion and amnesia

The umbrella organization, Justice for Innocent Victims of Terror (JIVT), which represents over twenty victims' and survivors' groups has rejected the government's 2018 proposals on a number of grounds including the principled objection that it elides the distinction between paramilitaries killed while on 'active service' – for instance, the PIRA 'volunteer' shot by the British army during a mission – and those on whom terrorists' actions were visited. The group's repudiation of the proposals goes further, however, and touches upon a distinction on how 'the past' is framed and understood.

> It has been increasingly plain over recent years that terrorist apologists have been at the heart of legacy planning. The government has been hopeless in defending the UK's own record. They might say they left it to local politicians to decide, but they should have helped those who want to defend a state that prevented civil war against liars and propagandists.[54]

The added emphases point to an incommensurability between the views that the conflict was part of a structural or historical struggle between two different sets of identities – Irish/nationalist versus British/unionist – and those that consider the campaign of violence to be an unjustified attack on law and democracy. JIVT is correct in its assertion that the current drift of policy and planning in this area seems to be towards the structuralist explanations and away from the law and democracy ones. Two key pieces of legislation are instrumental in that regard. Firstly, the Belfast Agreement provided an effective amnesty – paramilitary prisoners were granted early release, which would apply to any subsequent prosecutions relating to events that occurred before the signing of the Agreement. Secondly, the legal definition of victims and survivors was set down in 2006 and was so broad to ensure that that distinction that JIVT make between perpetrators and innocent victims was effaced. According to the Victims and Survivors (Northern Ireland) Order, 2006, definition of a victim or survivor is:

(a) someone who is or has been physically or psychologically injured as a result of or in consequence of a conflict-related incident;

(b) someone who provides a substantial amount of care on a regular basis for an individual [qualifying in the above clause]; or

(c) someone who has been bereaved as a result of or in consequence of a conflict-related incident.[55]

The promotion of amnesty within the judicial process has not stopped with the 1998 Agreement. Although the inadmissibility of evidence that features in the 2018 proposals is but one further outworking of the idea, it has been controversial both within victims' groups but also among Sinn Fein, which has seen it as a way of protecting British service personnel from prosecution. Despite those reservations, Sinn Fein was instrumental in obtaining a clandestine amnesty measure for what were known as 'On-the-Runs' (OTRs): PIRA members who had evaded justice in the UK by absconding to different jurisdictions – mainly, the Republic of Ireland – and who, thus, fell outwith the provisions of the Belfast Agreement. The then prime minister, Tony Blair, decoupled immunity for all conflict-related offences from amnesty for the OTRs in correspondence with Sinn Fein leader, Gerry Adams, in 2006. In 2007, the government sent letters to around 200 individuals stating: 'There are no warrants in existence, nor are you wanted in Northern Ireland for arrest, questioning or charging by police. The Police Service of Northern Ireland are not aware of any interest in you by any other police force'. These letters only came to light in 2014 when a case against John Downey, who had been accused of the Hyde Park bombing of 1982 in which four soldiers were killed, collapsed. On receipt of the letter, the judge had decided that Downey should not be prosecuted because he had been given a guarantee that he would not face trial.[56]

In a 2009 book on unionist memory politics, Kirk Simpson concluded that 'many unionists now increasingly define themselves as oppositional or peripheral'. He stated that unionists tend to fear that their social memory of the conflict is being manipulated and distorted by their ideological opponents. As such, the reluctance of many within the unionist community to engage in public policy initiatives on dealing with the past or truth recovery is a product of their 'trepidation about the potential elision of their biographies of suffering'. 'They want their stories to be told', argued Simpson, 'but fear that trying to make their voices count politically could be a futile and enervating process. This is because they believe that historically there has been "no audience" for their remembrance, even when they were the innocent victims of abhorrent terrorist crimes'.[57] A decade on from Simpson's devastatingly bleak ethnographic findings, this chapter has argued that the situation is even more desperate: that nationalism has disarticulated unionist memory of the conflict in a systemic fashion within ideological and policy spheres. I have argued that, in part, this is an almost inevitable product of the verbizing of 'transition'.

The process of disarticulation is complete once unionists accept the memory politics of nationalism. In this regard, the emerging debate over 'collusion' is suggestive of the shape of things to come. One of the most recent books on the issue, *Counterinsurgency and Collusion in Northern Ireland*, by Mark McGovern, which was launched at the Catholic teacher training college, St Mary's, on the Falls Road, by the journalist John Ware and Geraldine Finucane, who has campaigned on the issue following the killing of her husband by loyalists in 1989. Finucane's son John, a Dublin-based lawyer was at one point positioned as a Sinn Fein presidential candidate in the Republic, while his brother Michael has recently been elected a Sinn Fein councillor in Belfast.[58] The launch was organized by

Relatives for Justice, who have publicized the work as 'seminal'.[59] Gerry Adams claimed that the book 'adds significantly to our knowledge of how this British military and political policy worked'. In addition, he goes on to state that, it 'gives an important insight into why successive British governments have constantly blocked progress on legacy issues'.[60]

Adams' review touches upon the two key aspects of 'collusion' that can be weaponized in the service of memory politics. Firstly, it entails the imputing that British government policy in Northern Ireland was premised on the deliberate suspension of law and order. As Fionnuala ni Aolain contends, 'lethal force ... is not an isolated aspect of state practice ... It is an integral part of the state's evolving policy of conflict management".[61] The lesson that is drawn is that Britain could not and cannot be trusted. Correlation does not equal causation, however, and collusion experts shift easily from claims about systemic practices to more qualified assertions.[62] Outwith a robust and empirically verifiable definition, the tendency seems to be to fall back on notions of context. As McGovern explains: 'it is important that collusion should not simply be attributed to, or examined in terms of, individual actions or attitudes. Collusion has been ideologically and historically framed and shaped by the structures of a prevailing social order and a specific complex of power relations'.[63] Of course, the same might be said for claims of collusion that are made without clear lines of cause and effect, planning or culpability. But it is the hazy, smoke-and-mirrors methodology of the collusion claim that lends it a conspiracy-theorist impression. The creation of uncertainty and the denial of unverifiability – after all, it is the nature of collusion that it would be covered up, hence the lack of evidence of systemic abuse is merely evidence of its existence [64]– is politically advantageous because it works to undermine the unionist or law-and-order narrative about the past. In other words, once we take collusion into account then we cannot be certain that republicans were even responsible for the majority of the killings. This is the second way in which collusion can be weaponized. As Kieran McEvoy explained the Defence Committee of the House of Commons,

> the normal figure that is used relating to state killings is approximately 10% of the conflict as a whole but, ... in cases where there is an allegation of state collusion ... it is possible that other state actors could be subject

to prosecution. In other words, the prosecution net could spread more widely in the context of allegations of collusion if state actors had been involved in murders that were committed directly by the paramilitaries.[65]

McEvoy's assertion was made in response to a question by the DUP's Gavin Robinson. Hansard records no follow-up question. However, Robinson was apparently impressed enough to commend McEvoy's evidence to the House of Commons during a debate the following year.[66]

Conclusion

Robinson may, of course, have been misremembering – alternatively, he may not have thought of asking a follow-up question along the lines of how such an assertion could be verified. Both scenarios are troubling; the first, perhaps more so than the second because it speaks to an inability to grasp fundamental facts about the past resulting in a kind of amnesiac blindness – which could, in turn, be a perquisite to the kind of critical thinking needed to question the methodological rigour behind claims about historical responsibility. The link between forgetting and responsibility, or, more explicitly, amnesty and amnesia, has been highlighted by Paul Ricoeur. Drawing attention to the 'semantic kinship' between the terms (in French and in English), Ricoeur asserted that amnesty was essentially nothing more than 'organized forgetting':

> The institutions of amnesty are not all the institutions of forgiveness. They constitute a forgiveness that is public, commanded, and that has therefore nothing to do with … a personal act of compassion. In my opinion, amnesty does wrong at once to truth, thereby repressed and as if forbidden, and to justice, [as] it is due to the victims.[67]

Towards the end of Park's novel Fenton reflects on his interrogation before the Truth Commission – his past had been directed down the path of lawyers' questions and nothing of the reality, as he remembered it, had been given recognition: 'Everything [had been] falling apart, breaking up in front of their eyes, and they [the police] were supposed to work some miracle, to hold it all together when it was hard to hold yourself together. It couldn't be done, things got broken and damaged'.[68] The damage caused by

Fenton's use of a child informant had instead been the focus of the questioning. Fenton's memories of a record of distinguished service had counted for little he is left to conclude: 'He's been used and spat out, pensioned off with every other inconvenient legacy of the past'.[69] I have tried to suggest that for the purposes of political expediency the past is, like Fenton's memories, being parcelled out and boxed away. The ideological implication of this is an effacing of unionist memory of the conflict. Fenton's story does not really end in Park's novel, though he remains on the brink of accepting the 'truth' imposed by politicians and lawyers. This chapter has pointed out that the disarticulation of memory resides in the final instance in the giving away of it by its holders – I have posited that that process has begun.

Notes

[1] David Park, *The Truth Commissioner* (London: Bloomsbury, 2008) p. 134.

[2] Mick Fealty, 'McKee murder reveals that our Peace Process™ has been sustaining a Cold War by stealth', Slugger O'Toole, 23 April 2019. Available at *https://sluggerotoole.com/2019/04/23/mckee-murder-reveals-that-our-peace-process-has-been-sustaining-a-cold-war-by-stealth/*; accessed on 8 May 2019.

[3] Cillian McGrattan, 'Order Out of Chaos": The Politics of Transitional Justice', *Politics*, 29 (3) (2009) 164-72.

[4] BBC, 'Seamus Mallon: "Mistake" to allow Sinn Fein into government without decommissioning', 1 October 2015. Available at *https://www.bbc.co.uk/news/uk-northern-ireland-34406343*; accessed on 9 May 2019.

[5] Eamonn O'Kane, *Britain, Ireland, and Northern Ireland since 1980: The Totality of Relationships* (Abingdon: Routledge, 2008) p.163.

[6] *The Guardian*, 'Assembly farce as deputy first minster Mallon resigns', 15 July 1999. Available at *https://www.theguardian.com/uk/1999/jul/15/northernireland*; accessed on 8 May 2019.

[7] Vivian Lowndes and Mark Roberts, *Why Institutions Matter: The New Institutionalism in Political Science* (Basingstoke: Palgrave Macmillan, 2013), p.64.

[8] Michael Freeden, *Ideology: A Very Short Introduction* (Oxford: Oxford University Press, 2003).

[9] David McKittrick, Seamus Kelters, Brian Feeney and Chris Thornton, *Lost Lives: The Stories of the Men, Women, and Children Who Died as a Result of the Northern Ireland Troubles* (Edinburgh: Mainstream, 1999).

[10] *We Will Remember Them: Report of the Northern Ireland Victims' Commissioner, Sir Kenneth Bloomfield KCB* (Belfast: NIO, 1998).

[11] The text of the Agreement is available at *https://assets.publishing.service.gov.uk/government/uploads/system/uploads/attachment_data/file/136652/agreement.pdf*; accessed on 15 May 2019.

[12] Kirk Simpson, 'Untold Stories: Unionist Remembrance of Political Violence and Suffering in Northern Ireland', *British Politics*, 2008 3(4): 465-89.

[13] 'Report of the Tribunal of Inquiry into Suggestions that Members of An Garda Síochána or Other Employees of the State Colluded in the Fatal Shootings of RUC Chief Superintendent Harry Breen and RUC Superintendent Robert Buchanan on the 20th March 1989', pp.412-13. Available at *http://opac.oireachtas.ie/AWData/Library3/smithwickFinal03122013_171046.pdf*, accessed on 28 May 2019.

[14] *Belfast Telegraph*, 22 June 2007.

[15] 'Hain announces group to look at the past', Northern Ireland Office, press release, 22 June 2007. Available at *https://cain.ulster.ac.uk/victims/docs/british_gov/nio/hain_220607.pdf*; accessed on 28 May 2019.

[16] Report of the Consultative Group on the Past, available at *https://cain.ulster.ac.uk/victims/docs/consultative_group/cgp_230109_report.pdf*; accessed on 14 May 2019.

[17] Sinn Féin, 'Truth Recovery', 2009. Author copy, p. 11.

[18] R.F. Foster, *The Irish Story: Telling Tales and Making it Up in Ireland*, (London: Allen Lane, 2001), p. 184.

[19] Rebecca Graff-McRae, Popular Memory in Northern Ireland', in *War, Memory and Popular Culture: Lessons on Modes of Remembrance and Commemoration*, edited by Michael Keren and Holger H. Herwig (Jefferson: McFarlane & Co, 2009), pp. 41–56.

[20] Gerard Murray and Jonathan Tonge, *Sinn Fein and the SDLP: From Alienation to Participation* (London: C Hurst and Co Publishers, 2005),

[21] Sinn Féin, 'Truth recovery', p. 8.

[22] Ibid.,, p. 12.

[23] Ibid., p. 28.

[24] See, for example, the key SDLP position paper, which formed the basis of the party's approach to the peace negotiations of the 1990s, "SDLP analysis of the nature of the problem: submission to Brooke Talks, June 1991", Linenhall Library, Northern Ireland Political Collection, P9283.

[25] BBC, *The Politics Show*, 11 October, 2009. Available from: *http://news.bbc.co.uk/1/hi/programmes/politics_show/8301332.stm*; accessed on 6 March 2010.

26   At the time of writing, a cursory glance at the Relatives for Justice website reveals four top stories: 'Gerard Gibson: Murdered by the British army, 11 July 1972'; 'Paul Topper Thompson Remembered [on the 25th anniversary of his killing by loyalists]'; a report on the non-accessibility of files at the National Archives in Kew on the killing of two children by plastic bullet tives for Justice, 'Norman Tebit [sic] Comments on BBC, *Politics Show*', October 2009. Available from: *www.relativesfor-justice.com/norman-tebit-comments-bbc-politics-show.htm*; accessed 6 March 2010.

28   Ibid.

29   Patrick Roche, 'Why Should We Shake the Hands of Reconciliation?', *Belfast Telegraph*, 25 January. 2010. Available from: *www.belfasttelegraph.co.uk*; accessed 26 January 2010.

30   Cillian McGrattan op. cit.

31   Kieran McEvoy records that Mark Thompson, latterly of Relatives for Justice, was instrumental in the work of Eolas and that the group also included republican former prisoners. See 'Healing Through Remembering: Making Peace with the Past: Options for Truth Recover Regarding the Conflict In and About Northern Ireland', Kieran McEvoy, 2006. Available at *https://pure.qub.ac.uk/ws/files/6412571/Making_Peace_with_the_Past.pdf*; accessed on 28 May 2019.

32   See *http://www.brandonhamber.com/clients.htm*, accessed, 6 March 2010; see also Eolas, 'Consultation', p. 2.

33   Patricia Lundy and Mark McGovern, 'Attitudes towards a Truth Commission for Northern Ireland in Relation to Party Political Affiliation', *Irish Political Studies*, 22 (3), (2007), p. 323.

34   Henry Patterson, 'Truth and Reconciliation in Northern Ireland? Not Much Hope of Either', *Parliamentary Brief*, February, 2009

35   Patricia Lundy and Mark McGovern, op. cit., pp. 321-22.

36   Patricia Lundy and Mark McGovern, 'A Trojan Horse'. A Trojan Horse? Unionism, Trust and Truth-Telling in Northern Ireland, *International Journal of Transitional Justice*, 2 (2008), pp.42-62.

37   Kirk Simpson, *Unionist Voices and the Politics of Remembering the Past in Northern Ireland* (Basingstoke: Palgrave Macmillan, 2009), p. 122; original emphasis.

38   Lundy and McGovern, 'A Trojan Horse', p. 62.

39   Kirk Simpson, *op. cit.*, p. 115.

40   Lundy and McGovern, 'Attitudes', p. 323.

41   Cillian McGrattan, op. cit.

42   EPIC *Truth Recovery: A Contribution from Loyalism* (Belfast: EPIC, 2004).

43 SDLP 'Victims and the Past' (N.D.). Available at *www.sdlp.ie/index.php/the_issues/victims_and_the_past/*; accessed 7 March 2010.

44 The section in question comprises two pages of a seventeen-page paper; SDLP, 'SDLP Response, pp.3-4.

45 Ibid. p. 6.

46 Northern Ireland Affairs Committee, *House of Commons, Northern Ireland Affairs Committee: The Report of the Consultative Group on the Past in Northern Ireland* (London: The Stationery Office, 2009).

47 SDLP, 'SDLP Response', p. 7.

48 Ibid, p. 4.

49 Gerard Murray and Jonathan Tonge, op. cit.

50 SDLP, 'SDLP Response, p. 8.

51 SDLP, 'Addressing the Past: "A Comprehensive Truth Process and The Ethical Way Forward', November 2012; author copy.

52 BBC, 'SDLP "broke promise over IRA play park" 14 December 2017. Available at *https://www.bbc.co.uk/news/uk-northern-ireland-42349506*; accessed on 28 May 2019.

53 Liam Clarke, 'Colum Eastwood: Why I carried INLA man's coffin', *Belfast Telegraph*, 29 September 2015. Available at *https://www.belfasttelegraph.co.uk/news/north-ern-ireland/colum-eastwood-why-i-carried-inla-mans-coffin-31566062.html*; accessed on 28 May 2019.

54 *Belfast Newsletter*, editorial, 'Victims cannot stop the legacy process but they can give lie to the notion it is victim-centred', 13 May 2019. Available at *https://www.newsletter.co.uk/news/opinion/victims-cannot-stop-the-legacy-process-but-they-can-give-the-lie-to-the-notion-it-is-victim-centred-1-8924680*; accessed on 20 May 2019.

55 The Victims and Survivors (Northern Ireland) Order 2006; available at *https://www.legislation.gov.uk/nisi/2006/2953/article/3*; accessed on 20 May 2019.

56 Greg McKevitt, BBC, 'On the Runs – key questions and inquiry findings', 24 March 2015. Available at *https://www.bbc.co.uk/news/uk-northern-ireland-26359906*; accessed on 21 May 2019.

57 Simpson, *Unionist Voices*, p.115.

58 Shona Murray, 'Son of murdered solicitor emerges as latest possible presidential candidate', *Irish Independent*, 16 July 2018. Available at *https://www.independent.ie/irish-news/son-of-murdered-solicitor-emerges-as-latest-possible-presidential-candidate-37123071.html*; accessed on 21 May 2019.

59   Relatives for Justice, 'Counterinsurgency and collusion United States book tour'. Available at *https://www.relativesforjustice.com/counterinsurgency-and-collusion-united-state-book-tour/*; accessed on 21 May 2019.

60   Gerry Adams, 'Counterinsurgency and collusion – Britain's dirty war in Ireland', Leargas blog, 17 May 2019. Available at *http://leargas.blogspot.com/2019/05/counterinsurgency-and-collusion.html*; accessed 21 May 2019.

61   Fionnuala Ni Aolain, *The Politics of Force: Conflict Management and State Violence in Northern Ireland* (Belfast: Blackstaff, 2000), back cover.

62   Although Anne Cadwallader's, *Lethal Allies*, asserts that not 'every RUC officer or UDR soldier was collusive, or every loyalist was manipulated, or every judge or British cabinet minister mendacious' (p.16), she nevertheless concludes that 'systemic collusion' existed (p.368). Anne Cadwallader, *Lethal Allies: British Collusion in Ireland*. (Cork: Mercier Press, 2013).

63   McGovern, *Counterinsurgency*, p.4.

64   Anne Cadwallader, op. cit., p.369.

65   House of Commons, Defence Committee, Oral Evidence: Investigation into Fatalities Involving British Military Personnel, 7 March 2017. Available at *http://data.parliament.uk/writtenevidence/committeeevidence.svc/evidencedocument/defence-committee/investigations-into-fatalities-in-northern-ireland-involving-british-military-personnel/oral/48520.html*; accessed on 21 May 2019.

66   See, House of Commons, Hansard, 'Northern Ireland Budget (No.2) Bill, 9 July 2018. Available at *https://hansard.parliament.uk/commons/2018-07-09/debates/5ED51B28-46BC-4AA0-BDCD-EF66925D0854/NorthernIrelandBudget(No2)Bill*; accessed on 21 May 2019.

67   'Memory, history, forgiveness: A dialogue between Paul Ricoeur and Sorin Antohi', 10 March 2003. Available at *http://www.janushead.org/8-1/Ricoeur.pdf*; accessed on 21 May 2019.

68   Park *Truth Commissioner*, p.357.

69   Ibid, p.356.

8

Nationalism, unionism and the three syndromes of Brexit

Arthur Aughey

Introduction

Observing the course of the Brexit debate since June 2016 has been a paradoxical experience. On the one hand, to adapt the title of Marshall Berman's 1982 book, all that one thought solid about British party politics and constitutional practice seems to have melted into air[1]. Much of what one took for granted has been confounded, from cabinet responsibility to the executive's control of the House of Commons. From the referendum result of 2016, the general election of 2017 to the votes on the Withdrawal Agreement, the predictions of most experts have been often seriously awry. On the other hand, the public rapidly sensed that Brexit had become the equivalent of Groundhog Day, especially when the Conservative government was forced to concede its series of 'meaningful' and 'indicative' votes in Parliament. Brexit had become a long-running show, more Mousetrap than Backstop, but a long-running show without a finale, one with which the public was losing patience. Simultaneously, the predictable had become unpredictable and the unpredictable, predictable. The English language is not very good at expressing paradoxical complexity like this though in Northern Ireland during the peace process we got used to employing the term 'constructive ambiguity'.

A recommended idle pleasure for those perplexed, bemused or simply maddened by the course of politics since 2016 is to consult entries in the online *Dictionary of Obscure Sorrows*, a dictionary that tries to capture complex realities for which we do not have words in English[2]. Some of its entries appear aptly descriptive of the Brexit paradoxes. On the one hand, the word *adomania* attempts to convey the sense people have of a future that is arriving ahead of schedule. To adapt that definition, dates – like those changing dates of the end, 29 March, 12 April, 30 June, 31 October 2019 – break from the realm of the hypothetical into the present. In the dictionary's own terminology, these dates buck 'the grip of your expectations while you lean and slip in your saddle, one hand reaching for reins, the other waving up high like a schoolkid who finally knows the answer to the question'. Some might think the answer is failure, others betrayal, others still hard reality. On the other hand, *altschmerz* conveys that sense of weariness with the same old issues, the same boring flaws and anxieties going on for years, leaving you with nothing interesting to hope for any longer. For Leavers, that may be a good definition of their experience of Theresa May's premiership and its effect on Brexit. For Remainers, it would be a fair assessment of the poverty of thought in arguments for Brexit. Perhaps *nodus tollens* can sum up (politically) for many the experience since 2016: the feeling that the plot does not make sense to you anymore. According to the dictionary, it is that condition in which, 'although you thought you were following the arc of the story, you keep finding yourself immersed in passages you don't understand'. To put that more colloquially, there developed a pervasive mood across the UK that politicians had 'lost the plot', leaving people uncertain about the future, frustrated with the same old issues and confused about the arc of the country's story.

Political argument, whether defined as ideology, belief or disposition, always involves some attempt at persuasion. Its art of persuasion intends to convince whatever audience that its 'narrative' (to use the currently popular academic term) is credible. It is concerned to 'abate mystery', as Michael Oakeshott suggested, and to simplify complexity in a way that satisfies the expectations of supporters, addresses their anxieties and professes a purpose. In sum, political activity claims to understand and deal with those same old issues, has a plot that makes sense of the past and present and knows the answer to the question of what the future will (or should) bring. The subject of this chapter is concerned mainly with the Brexit effect on unionist and nationalist expectations and anxieties, especially their respective 'plots' about 'where things are going'. I identify three distinct but related 'syndromes' of Brexit. The first is the (Humphrey) Lyttleton syndrome, sceptical about either predictable directions or certainties in politics and history yet not necessarily ruling out the possibility of a new reality. The second is the (Tom) Nairn syndrome, confident that moments in history have a necessary and a predictable course that political analysis can specify clearly. The third is the (Michael) Fish syndrome, assuming that everything is calm and will carry on as normal, only to be surprised by unexpected events. The chapter discusses the character of these syndromes, relates them to unionism and nationalism and makes some short concluding remarks about the Brexit effect on Northern Ireland.

Three syndromes

Who knows for certain where things are going? The most apt sceptical response to questions about the future course of events was given not by a philosopher but by a musician and broadcaster. Humphrey Lyttleton once responded to a question by a journalist about where he thought jazz was going by saying 'if we knew where it was going it would be there already.' That response is many things. It is funny, it avoids a definitive answer but it also expresses a truth. If Lyttleton had been a Hegelian he might have been tempted to say that the owl of Minerva only spreads its wings at the falling of dusk – but he had a sound English compass when it came to sounding either pompous or ridiculous. Of course, some *do* think they know where things are going, a confidence which is informed by a secularised faith in the providential course of history, a faith rarely dented by the evidence of the failings of that secular god[3]. The belief that one has definitive insight into 'where things are going' is, as John Gray puts it, the belief that there is a 'common historical destination'. As he admits, this is not 'the result of any process of rational inquiry but an expression of faith', be that faith liberalism, socialism or nationalism[4].

All the noise and hysteria that has followed the result of the EU referendum may lead one to the conclusion that the novelty of the present crisis is on a scale never experienced before, especially if one goes by the journalism of the 24-hour news cycle. Journalists have an interest in the drama of the moment and may be excused their reluctance to take the longer view. Many of the issues currently shaping the Brexit crisis were discussed half a century ago when intellectuals wrote of the 'suicide of the nation' and engaged with questions of trust and confidence. The 'suicide' then concerned the (apparent) inefficiency of the political system and the (apparent) failure of the country to adjust to modern economic and scientific change. Scholars observed a generational crisis of belief (and self-belief) in the political elite. What scholars note today is also a generational crisis of belief (and self-belief) in the political elite and the loss of faith in traditional institutions like Parliament.[5] To both of those things one should add now the (apparent) disintegration of the UK as a state.

Therefore, it is not surprising that the 'where are we going' question has become more insistent in politics since 2016. Two broad answers have been given to that question. On the one hand, Brexiteers argue there is the 'soaring dove' answer: that only when it is finally un-caged from the constraints of European Union membership, will the United Kingdom soar free into the blue skies of economic empowerment and political renewal. On the other hand, critics of Brexit visualise a 'Kant's dove' (from his *Critique of Pure Reason*) answer: 'The light dove, cleaving the air in her free flight, and feeling its resistance, might imagine that its flight would be still easier in empty space'. The so-called pre-referendum 'Project Fear' was nothing if not a relentlessly graphic tracking of the plummeting Brexit dove in the empty space of EU exit and it has continued relentlessly in subsequent argument. What both the soaring dove and plunging dove both share is a lack of scepticism and little sense of the Lyttleton syndrome.

While both positions very broadly demarcate different and opposing partisan positions, there is an interesting political intersection – or opportunism – where versions of these two positions, suitable re-expressed, have become actually complementary. That intersection can be found in nationalist advocacy mainly, though not exclusively, in Northern Ireland. In short, there is now the argument that the Brexit effect will mean the 'Kant's dove' crashing of the UK's politics and economy such that it will promote its constitutional fracturing. One consequence will be the soaring dove of freedom as people find the key to unlock the UK prison house of the nations (and this sort of thinking is evident amongst different factions of English nationalism as well). In particular, it is most dramatically at the Irish border that the flightpath of Kant's dove (the crash of the UK post-Brexit) intersects with the soaring dove of Irish nationalist expectation (unity is just a border poll away).

Certainly, in a period of political confusion like the present, it is difficult to feel that any constitutional ground is secure. That confusion leads to all sorts of speculation that is based as much on wishful thinking as it is on hard evidence (as the Lyttleton syndrome would recognise). Nationalist argument that not only do they know where the Union is going but that, to some extent, it is there already may very well be true. However, it is at times like this that a historical perspective comes in handy, if only because the immediacy of today's news cycle, as well as the relentless urgency of social media, often mean that such perspective can be lost. A historical perspective helps, at least, to detect patterns of reasonably consistent political argument. The point is not that history will always repeat itself. Rather, it is that one should not necessarily overemphasise either the novelty of the present or the changes currently taking place. The word 'necessarily' is added in order to qualify an equal and opposite wishful thinking that 'nothing much changes' and to concede that things could well be very different when (or if) Brexit ever happens. With all those caveats acknowledged, a historical perspective identifies the sceptical truth in the Lyttleton syndrome. Take just two examples from recent history that may encourage interpretative caution.

First, one only has to think back to the 1970s. It was a decade of intense constitutional speculation about the future of the UK. There was the violent threat to Northern Ireland's place within the Union. There was deep division over joining the (then) EEC in 1973 and the subsequent referendum on continued British membership in 1975. There was the challenge of nationalism, not only in Scotland but also in Wales along with related debates about the possible impact on the Union of any devolutionary arrangement. There was widespread concern – and serious academic debate, much like today – about the possibility of the UK becoming ungovernable. Moreover, the text that seemed to prophesy the calamity (if one was a unionist) or deliverance (if one was a nationalist) or the beginning of the revolution (if one was a Marxist) was Tom Nairn's *The Break-Up of Britain: Crisis and Neo-Nationalism*[6]. The second syndrome of this chapter, the Nairn syndrome, takes its name from his work. It is hard to underestimate the influence of his thinking on political commentary. His originality lay in being an inventive melodist of destiny, in particular marrying the 'historical law' of Marxism to the romance of national emancipation. In sum, he brilliantly conscripted historical logic and political identity into the service of a narrative according to process that may be called 'endism' (of capitalism, the Union, the old order, and so on), a narrative repeated *ad nauseam* by Nairn's less gifted acolytes. The relationship is contextual – the historical *contingency* of the Union fits neatly with the *inevitable* historical process of the Union's demise. Hence the attractively (self-serving) political claim: the uncertainty of the Union's present confirms the certainty of our historical logic. It is a narrative existing independently of historical events, even if it is not divorced from them, though the wished-for outcome is always parent to the interpretation of events.

Interestingly, the publication of Nairn's influential *The Break-Up of Britain* was in 1977, the year of the Queen's Silver Jubilee. In her Address to Parliament in Westminster Hall, the Queen had inserted a personal and controversially anxious passage. In an echo of present-day concerns about the 'left behind' influence on the Leave vote of 2016, she observed that the complexities of modern administration prompted the feeling that central government – the term she used was 'Metropolitan Government' – was too remote from the lives of ordinary people. That sense of remoteness, the Queen observed, had revived 'an awareness of historic national identities in these islands'[7]. In 1977, the Queen's fervent wish had been that the Silver Jubilee would remind people of the benefits which the Union had conferred on everyone in all parts of her realm, once more anticipating eerily the words of Theresa May when promoting the virtues of her Withdrawal Agreement in 2018. One is reluctant to make the Queen into the voice of anti-Nairn in that Address, but her celebration of the 'many advantages' of the Union was a useful (and so far, enduring) corrective.

Reflecting on that period a few years later – he called it a period of 'flux' – the political scientist Richard Rose commented that too many books and articles had been written, explaining events that had *not* happened[8]. Irish unity had not happened. The UK had *not* voted to leave the EEC. The UK had *not* broken up. The country had remained relatively stable and there had *not* been a socialist revolution as Tony Benn, the Corbyn of his day, had advocated. In other words, Rose proposed that there was something deeper to the Union than its many critics (not only nationalists) were prepared to admit. He accepted that the future of the Union was uncertain and he was not suggesting that it could never break up. His point was a simple one and appropriate for speculative reasoning today. It was that it is intellectually superficial to read into each, and every, political crisis the never-ending story of imminent constitutional collapse, even in the case of Northern Ireland (with which Rose was more familiar at the time than most other commentators)[9].

Second, one can also recall the late 1990s and the constitutional reforms of the first New Labour government. Reflecting one mood of those times, Norman Davies's popular bestseller *The Isles: A History* (1999) accounted for 'the rise and fall of Britishness'[10]. The political point of his massive study was that the UK would break-up and that it would happen soon. Indeed, Davies thought the UK would be lucky to last beyond 2007, the three hundredth anniversary of the Anglo-Scottish Union. Later he amended the date to 2014, mainly because he expected that the Scots would vote for independence. Tom Nairn – who had never really gone away – also orchestrated that mood to a receptive audience of nationalists and radicals. In his polemical book *After Britain*, he wrote of the Union's 'transition from the management of decline into the management of disintegration, leading eventually to a suitable testament and funeral arrangements'.[11] Here was a variation on a popular 1994 film but in this case, it was not *Four Weddings and a Funeral* but four nations and a (British) break-up. To put that otherwise – nationalists felt they no longer needed to delegitimise the Union because history had already done that job. Robert Hazell was the new millennium's Richard Rose to these speculations. Considering this regenerated narrative of disintegration, Hazell formulated what he called the five 'Cs' of UK politics – consent, custodianship, constitutionality, consistency and confidence[12]. Like Rose twenty five years earlier, he argued that that the Union rested on much broader and firmer foundations than critics realised and for whom the ideological wish is always father to the historical argument.

However, one also needs to be careful about interpretative complacency. The experience of politics after the 2016 referendum has certainly raised public doubts about consent, custodianship, constitutionality, consistency and confidence in British politics along with doubts about the institutional stability that Hazell believed these terms reflected (and in 1977, the Queen believed were a source of national 'joy'). In other words, for those who comfort themselves with the thought that nothing much is going to change and that history is more about long continuities than it is about radical change, one needs to factor in the third syndrome of this chapter, the (Michael) Fish syndrome (that unfortunate scapegoat of complacent weather forecasting in 1987). Ignoring the warnings of change may mean wondering subsequently how it all went wrong. As an illustration of that particular syndrome, it is worth taking some intellectual detours and discuss one attempt to manage a condition of 'expectations of the end' with which I am personally familiar.

In the middle years of the 2000s, I participated in an academic project organised by the Constitution Unit at UCL and directed by Robert Hazell. It tried to minimise the intellectual temptation of either the Nairn syndrome ('the Union is inevitably doomed by the logic of history') or the Fish syndrome ('Keep calm and carry on'). It attempted as well to temper the scepticism of the Lyttleton syndrome ('the course of history cannot be sensibly predicted') by a systematic attempt to apply 'futures' methodology to possible constitutional trends in the UK. That project tried to adapt the scenario modelling of business management and financial consultancy to the known knowns and known unknowns of politics (to use Donald Rumsfeld's celebrated terminology). The book that emerged from this systematic application of speculative modelling was *Constitutional Futures Revisited: Britain's Constitutional Futures to 2020* appeared in 2008[13]. As that book's opening chapter admitted, future studies is 'inextricably linked to uncertainty' and the compilation of essays tried to factor uncertainty into possible constitutional developments. It did this by employing a two-step mapping process[14].

The first step involved 'clustering' responses to two questions: What *is* happening that might matter? What *could* happen that might matter? This required identifying those drivers of, or constraints on, change that push policy in one direction or another. The second step involved 'prospection', formulating a limited number of plausible future scenarios, each involving equally feasible explanatory narratives. This approach is formulaic but it has the virtue of transparency. Most of the chapters in *Constitutional Futures Revisited* remain worthy and relevant today, but there are two important caveats. First, it failed to anticipate the financial crash that happened only a year later, with all its consequences for contemporary political programmes based on the end of 'boom and bust' or on the 'Celtic Tiger'. Second, no one in all of the detailed sessions attending the planning of that book considered that the UK's membership of the EU was worthy of a dedicated chapter. It had been categorised as peripheral to the big constitutional questions of the coming decade. In both cases one can point to the blind spots of the historical moment, even when those in that moment were trying to formulate thoughts about 'where things are going'. To be fair, very few anticipated the financial crash and the outcome of the EU referendum – and that is the point. The lesson for this chapter is this: when thinking through what one expects (a more honest version of the Nairn syndrome) one needs to leave room for 'I wasn't expecting that' (the Fish syndrome), an admission that one can never be too sure about any prediction (the truth of the Lyttleton syndrome). This is especially the case in Northern Ireland.

Northern Ireland futures

In 2012, four years after the publication of *Constitutional Futures Revisited*, I spoke at a conference in Belfast that was concerned with identifying possible trends in Northern Ireland over twenty years. To avoid the pitfalls of the Nairn and Fish syndromes and to provide a structure for participants, I returned to the system of that book (now chastened by experience) and tried to apply the model it had used. At least four inter-connected 'issue clusters' suggest themselves then. These were (and remain) Northern Ireland's internal political balance; the constitutional shape of the UK; the position of the UK and Ireland in relation to the EU; and Northern Ireland's relationship with the Irish state. I suggested that the key drivers and constraints in each case appeared to be self-evident. The politics of Northern Ireland would be driven by generational changes in communal demography; the constitutional shape of the UK would be influenced by nationalist demands in England as well as in Scotland and Wales and that these would affect political debate in Northern Ireland. At the time, it was uncertain if a referendum on UK membership of the EU would take place (few expected that Cameron's Conservative Party would win an overall majority in 2015 and so confront the promise to hold one). Even so there was little doubt that there would have to be a serious debate about what sort of long-term relationship the UK should have with the EU. I certainly did not envisage Brexit (it seemed inconceivable in 2012). Finally, I suggested that how the Irish state and Irish public opinion engaged with and responded to changes within Northern Ireland, the UK and the EU would also define the politics of the island.

Those detours indicate that the present debate about 'where things are going in Northern Ireland' has roots much deeper than the 'moment' of the EU referendum result. First, one can find the Nairn syndrome already deeply ingrained in nationalist narrative (as it has always been). Drawing on well-established discourse, the narrative stressed the value of national identity in the contemporary world especially within the EU. Nairn had argued in 2008 that the UK was now one of the 'old lags' of the 'bigger-and-better epoch' of twentieth century statehood, a member of the 'great-at-all-costs' club. If the old question used to be survival and development in an industrial world of big states, the question now had changed: 'Are you small and smart enough to survive, and claim a positive place in the common global culture'? This, for Nairn, was not old-style nationalism but the chance for 'nations of a new and deeply different age' to participate as equal voices – in this case, in the European and not British Union[15].

The reading across to Northern Ireland was as follows. It assumed that there was a profound divide in the UK about national identity and attitudes to European integration – in particular, that English nationalism was profoundly Eurosceptic. The intersection of these and other political divisions, it was argued, would generate a crisis of allegiance and make break-up more likely. The background in the first part of this decade was the prospect of Scottish independence. If Scottish independence were to happen, the prospect of Northern Ireland remaining part of an English-dominated 'rest of the UK', perhaps outside the EU, could prove unattractive not only to unionists but also to the English. This train of events would compel unionists to look more favourably on a closer relationship with Dublin and possibly unity. That scenario explained the anticipatory republican strategy of putting Irish unity back on the agenda and Sinn Fein's advocacy of a border poll. Then, it had little to do with the state of public opinion in either part of Ireland but in the hope that external crises would force the pace. It was a statement of articles of faith – the end of the UK is inexorable and the process towards unity in Ireland is already under way. That the Scots did *not* vote for independence in 2014 was only a temporary disappointment for the rise of the Scottish National Party kept that soaring dove of expectation in the air. The vote in the EU referendum gave that dove Irish wings.

Second, the Fish syndrome was also lurking in unionist discourse. Here was a narrative of continuity taking its cue from Rose's venerable point: too much is said and written in politics about things that do not happen. For unionists, the expectation is that the constraint on radical change is stronger than the push to radical change. The Scots would not support independence and the least likely path for the future of the UK is a disintegrative one. The 'fact' of the Union, especially in the material or instrumental terms of public spending and services, would remain solid. In short, reports of the death of the UK are still much exaggerated and the corresponding assumption is that the UK's integrity remains certain well beyond the next twenty years. Unionists could point to the polling evidence appearing to show that support for Irish unity was low in order to confirm the view that there was no perfect storm out there to disturb present circumstances. Even if a referendum on the EU did take place, the narrative exuded a complacent character. It assumed that the prospect of life even outside the EU would have few consequences either for the stability of the UK or for Northern Ireland's place within the Union. The problem here was not that unionists – particularly the Democratic Unionist Party (DUP) – did not factor in possible 'unknown unknowns'. They could not, if only because they are unknown. The problem was that they did not anticipate the consequences of a vote to leave the EU and were equally guilty of not being sceptical enough of their own assumptions about where things were likely to go if there was a Leave victory.

Northern Ireland, though, has a known unknown and it is a question of whether it can secure a balance between stability and instability. To put that otherwise, as *Constitutional Futures Revisited* admitted generally, the future of Northern Ireland is 'inextricably linked to uncertainty' and a vote to leave the EU was likely to increase that uncertainty. Who would have thought a few years ago (even if they may have feared or welcomed it) that once again the Irish border would be at the heart of UK and European politics like a re-run of the Third Home Rule crisis? Who would have imagined that the issue of the Irish border would re-emerge, like Churchill's dreary steeples of Fermanagh and Tyrone, to drain the life out of yet another British government? Who would have thought that, as Seamus Heaney prophetically suggested, after the terrorist attacks of 9/11 be the world would become 'a big Ulster'? Since the beginning of the negotiations for the UK's withdrawal, it has appeared, over the details of Brexit, that UK-EU relations have become 'a big Ulster'. How has the debate about Brexit informed the expectations and anxieties of nationalism and unionism in Northern Ireland?

2007-16 a golden age?

David Mitchell speculated recently 'that history may record the decade 2007-2017 as a golden age' for 'Northern Ireland in the UK'[16]. That 'age' begins with the restoration of devolution at Stormont following the agreement of the (by then) two major parties, DUP and Sinn Fein, to share power. The 'age' ends with Sinn Fein collapsing the Executive and Assembly following the EU referendum which it justified by claims of DUP maladministration. On the significance of the first date, Mitchell cited Frank Millar's observation that 'the parties made history yesterday, but they didn't end it'. The uncertainty of the Lyttleton syndrome was evaded in this 'golden era' on the assumption that we do know where things are going because they *are* here already. Rather like Hegel's philosophy of history, 'the good is already fulfilled just in virtue of the fact that it is in the process of being fulfilled'. In short, things 'are as they ought to be because they are on the way to being what they ought to be'[17]. Nationalists (in particular, republicans) could believe the Agreement really was as it ought to be because it was on the way to becoming what it ought to be – Irish unity. The DUP's own trajectory implied that the Agreement was in the process of becoming what it ought to be through their amendment of it and yet already was what it ought to be, because its leadership had signalled willingness to accept it.

The 1998 Agreement which established the basis for the 2007 compromise can be described as, to adapt a phrase of Michael Oakeshott's, a 'modification of Irish circumstances', those modified circumstances embodying still, and unresolved, the old antagonisms of the past[18]. The Agreement was a grand political wager that the practical benefits of new institutional arrangements would manage communal anxieties and expectations such that a common sense of benefit would emerge, outweighing a sense of particular loss. In short, it was hoped that the DUP and Sinn Fein would become joint 'stakeholders' with a joint interest in both 'making Northern Ireland work' and in fostering good relations between north and south. As Mitchell suggested, a tentative consensus emerged amongst students of Northern Ireland politics that the 1998 Agreement did mark (at least) the end of a particular era of destabilisation that had begun with the civil rights campaign in the 1960s. There was reluctance to go further and to conclude that what the expression 'the Troubles' designated – widespread political violence – could not be rejuvenated.

Nevertheless, J. C. Beckett's observation on the end of the earlier Troubles in the 1920s seemed apt for the post 1998 era, bringing the necessary historical perspective to bear. 'Though the settlement left a legacy of bitterness, issuing occasionally in local and sporadic disturbances, it inaugurated for Ireland a longer period of general tranquillity than she had known since the first half of the eighteenth century'[19]. In very different circumstances, and for very different reasons, the 1998 Agreement created the possibility for greater tranquillity in the new millennium. This was no 'end of Irish history' as institutional dysfunction and the divisions over marches, symbols, Irish language and flags revealed. Yet it was possible to indicate one area of political contention that appeared no longer a matter of active contention. Remarkably – given its symbolic and constitutional significance in Irish politics – that area of contention was the border. The radical journalist Eamonn McCann observed, if the 1998 Agreement meant that nationalists had accepted the fact of Northern Ireland (at least for now) it did not mean that they had accepted 'symbolic representations of it'[20]. To put that otherwise, the communal hostility, previously defined by arguments about the border, was defined now by arguments about communal precedence. Despite the efforts of Sinn Fein to argue otherwise, opinion polls suggested that neither northern nor southern nationalists accorded unity any immediate significance – which did not mean that unity was without significance. There was a dual benefit effect.

For unionists, the 1998 Agreement took the border out of politics. There had been a deep concern about North/South institutional arrangements as a transition to Irish unity. In fact, the practical outworking of Strand II of the Agreement meant that the issue for most unionist voters, and certainly for party leaders, fell off the political radar. The operation of the North South Implementation Bodies and the functioning of the North South Ministerial Council filtered rarely into partisan politics, especially when the DUP committed, under the St Andrews Agreement of 2006, to work arrangements in good faith and in a spirit of genuine partnership. For nationalists, the Agreement helped to take the border out of the island allowing them to feel more comfortable in a Northern Ireland that remained part of the UK. Of course it is true that European matters were peripheral to the negotiation of the Agreement and its subsequent revisions. Yet the European 'context' (both the UK and Republic of Ireland being members of the EU) helped to frame the identities of being either British or Irish, or both, in Northern Ireland (as the Agreement specified). This context was certainly more important for nationalists than it was for unionists but it was not without meaning for both.

Nationalist anxiety and expectation

Therefore, there is a paradoxical character to the nationalist response to the result of the 2016 EU referendum. On the one hand, one notes the Fish syndrome. There was a collective response to that vote north and south expressing outrage at the betrayal of expectations. The result was a psychological blow and raised fundamental questions not only about the principle of consent nationalists derived from the 1998 Agreement but also about expectations derived from the changing balance of relations between communities within Northern Ireland. There was also a disordering of expectations about the emerging balance of political influence on the island. The shock of the result revealed just how vulnerable were their assumptions about 'where things are going'. On the other hand, one also notes the Nairn syndrome. The referendum result generated renewed expectation about the inevitability of Irish unity. Here a traditional view was given an accelerated push. Ideologically, the inevitable end-point of Irish unity usually was pitched a generation away, usually (another) 'twenty years' hence. Following the EU referendum result, there have been breathless announcements of the march of history resuming and Brexit bringing about the end of the Union within a few years. Of course, these two sides of the paradox connect to an inverted form of the Lyttleton syndrome – if only because nationalists think they know where things are going because they *are* here already. All that is required is a recognition of reality. Let us consider further the first part of the paradox, the Fish syndrome.

In a House of Lords debate on Brexit and Northern Ireland, Lord Bew supplied a very persuasive explanation for this part of the nationalist response. He accepted that the 'impact on the psychology of north-ern nationalists' of the referendum result had been harmful. The 1998 Agreement allowed them 'to consider themselves citizens of Europe—possibly evolving towards Irish unity, possibly not—and continuing to enjoy the National Health Service and their pension from London as before'. In short, 'it allowed a very happy set of slightly conflicting assump-tions in people's minds'. The prospect of Brexit involved, he argued, 'a certain type of assertion of the United Kingdom as a separate state, which is a problem'. It is a 'problem' because it disorders a deep-seated expec-tation about where things are going. To illustrate his point, Bew referred to secret negotiations that took place between the government of John Major and the IRA in 1993. The British representative had declared: 'The final solution is union. It is going to happen anyway. The historical train—Europe—determines that. We are committed to Europe. Unionists will have to change … The island will be as one'. Bew's conclusion was that if the UK government carried through the democratic obligation to leave the EU, 'the truth of the matter is that we are now not committed to Europe. The message is extinct. It is dead. It is an ex-message. That is the reality of where we are now, and life has changed for a lot of nationalists in Northern Ireland who would like to believe that something like that message represents the truth of things'[21].

Bew's understanding seems a fair representation of what one could call a nationalist mood, if not a movement. The mood involved a comforting assumption of movement in the direction of unity (which would arrive at some point, that old article of faith) without the immediate disruption to lives and prospects (having to pay for it with jobs and taxes in the here and now). Polling evidence suggested a limited public appetite for pushing the goal of Irish unity. However, Bew was also correct to point to the problem for nationalists (north and south) of a 'certain type of assertion of the United Kingdom as a separate state'. It is a problem not only because it appears to reverse the expected trend of history but also because it raises the anxiety, however unfounded, of a return to unionist 'domination'. In December 2017, Leo Varadkar expressed the traditional core of this anxiety when he announced that 'no Irish government will ever again leave Northern nationalists and Northern Ireland behind'[22]. That use of language conjured up nationalist myths and fears of sectarian domination and powers, myths and fears that went deep in the nationalist psyche. The writer Malachi O'Doherty put the point very succinctly. He predicted that pragmatic nationalists (like himself, happy to share the mood but not to be part of the movement) would have to re-evaluate their position. Now they confronted the prospect of living in Northern Ireland as part of the UK 'without the protections that come from Europe – and the underpinning of a common identity with the Irish that also comes from Europe'[23]. The re-assessment that O'Doherty predicted has been under way for three years and the proposition that northern nationalists are victims (again) of British policy has released deep-seated historical tropes.

The second part of the paradox, the Nairn syndrome, translates the anxiety of this new mood into the expectation that an irresistible movement towards Irish unity (and the end of Northern Ireland) is now inevitable. The march of history has resumed and the end is now in sight. For example, Siobhan Fenton announced that 'for the first time in my life, the prospect of a united Ireland is not only credible but inevitable'[24]. Kevin Meagher – a former special adviser to Shaun Woodward, Secretary of State for Northern Ireland from 2007 to 2010 – argued that Irish unity is the modernising position. In language that could have been taken directly from Nairn, he claimed that defence of the Union is the last redoubt of nostalgic romantics (like those who supported Brexit) and the long-term interest of the north requires participation in the dynamic all-island, globalised, economy secure within the EU. Returning to the familiar notion of the early peace process, it is in the long-term interest of the UK to persuade Ulster unionists to accept that inevitable destiny (or face the consequences of demographic change anyway). This is especially the case, so the logic goes, when some unionists can now recognise the greater importance of EU citizenship rather than UK citizenship[25].

The Sinn Fein leadership illustrates the Nairn syndrome in action. The party's Northern Ireland leader, Michelle O'Neill, was confident that not only are those previously apathetic about a united Ireland re-engaged but also those who would have been opposed to Irish unity are now reconsidering their position: 'There is no doubt that Brexit has been a catalyst for mainstreaming the debate now underway, where people of all shades of opinion are considering the benefits of remaining within the United Kingdom against the merits of staying within the European Union through a unified Ireland'. Her message was that whatever the outcome of the relationship between the UK and the EU, things had changed irrevocably, that Irish unity is 'no longer a long-term aim' and that a border poll will inevitably deliver that result.[26]

That dynamic concurrence of the Fish and Nairn syndromes, however, demonstrates its own paradox. That paradox returns us to the Lyttleton syndrome. The nationalist argument proposes that Irish unity is inevitable (the course of history is certain) but it is based on historical contingency (few expected the 2016 result and the course of politics subsequently appears to show that nothing is certain in politics any longer). Both parts of the paradox sit uneasily together and are connected only by ideological anxiety and expectation. Moreover, the proposition is that Brexit will be an act of (short-term) economic self-harm brought about by romantic Ulster unionists in league with equally romantic English nationalists who have put the illusion of state sovereignty before rational self-interest. Yet Irish unity is also an act of (short-term) economic self-harm. Nationalists demand continuing British subsidy to mitigate its effect and as Bew intimates, the most likely to be affected disproportionately is the nationalist middle class in the public sector. However, this self-harm is justified by the cause of state sovereignty and the romantic destiny of Ireland. Ideology, of course, is not concerned with logic but with winning, and as the former

THE NORTHERN IRELAND QUESTION

leader of the Ulster Unionist Party, Mike Nesbitt, feared Brexit could be a decisive unionist 'own goal' that gifts victory[27]. How do we understand unionist expectation and anxiety?

Unionism: expectation and anxiety

It may appear counterintuitive to begin this section with unionist 'expectation' or to discuss its own distinctive version of the Nairn syndrome, at least in the same terms as nationalism. After all, commentary on unionism has usually argued that it is defined collectively by political pessimism or, as Steve Bruce once described it, that it shares a 'dismal vision'[28]. Dismal vision in this sense has a double meaning. It can mean either an active preference for projects which are ultimately self-defeating. Or it can mean passivity sceptical of all schemes for political improvement or compromise. In both cases there is little room for optimism and, following Schopenhauer, the noun 'optimism' is usually qualified by the adjective 'unscrupulous'. Why get involved in schemes for one's own undoing? Why move when movement can only be in a hostile direction? Things are unlikely to change for the better, only for the worse, an attitude that can marry pessimism (the world is going to the dogs) with complete defiance (no surrender). Ironically – and this often missed – it is a condition of certainty and simplicity that can bring its own comforts. Certainty, even the certainty of betrayal, orders the world and arranges its political materials, providing a defensive barrier against subversion. Positively, it can encourage strength of purpose based on the consolation of survival. This is a very austere form of strength indeed but, even so, being able to survive in a hostile world can also help to secure some of one's interests, to profit from circumstance and to make the best possible fist of the hand which fate has dealt you.

If nationalism is prone to understand itself to be *en marche*, then unionism tends to understand itself to be on the defensive. As Bew put it in his history of *Ideology and the Irish Question*, the end that unionists seek is not a future goal but a present release. He noted how a *Ballymoney Free Press* editorial of May 1912, at the height of the Irish Home Rule crisis, made the declaration: 'The statement of Unionist Ulster is that it merely wants to be let alone'. Unfortunately, 'since Satan entered the

Garden of Eden good people will not be let alone'[29]. Unionists have always sought to be 'left alone' and for the troubling of unionist Ulster to end. Yet as the *Ballymoney Free Press* wisely acknowledged, in that political contest between political right and political wrong, the threat of subversion would never go away. If nationalists hope that an expected ending (the Union) means the future belongs to them, unionists also fear that they may well be right. This may be an exaggeration of a complex disposition but it intimates a truth. It is that unionism has a conservative character, if only because its ideological vocation is to maintain Northern Ireland's position within the Union.

Therefore the Nairn syndrome, conservative-style, does not involve unionist faith in the movement towards an (inevitable) end. Rather it involves hope in the effectiveness of resistance. Like the Prince of Salinas in Lampedusa's novel *The Leopard*, a suitable unionist motto would be: 'Delay is life'. This notion of delay is freighted with the possibility that major change – like the nationalist expectation of Irish unity – can be avoided altogether or that the impact of change can be sufficiently tamed in order to render it either acceptable or manageable[30]. In is possible to argue that by 2016 the DUP was sufficiently confident of the stability of Northern Ireland (in that supposed 'golden age' after 2007) to feel secure enough to support Leave in the EU referendum without worrying about the consequences. That was especially the case if one considers also the widespread anticipation by most commentators that Leave was going to lose (and that nothing would change). Like nationalism, this conservative version of the Nairn syndrome, involved its own paradox. On the one hand, the DUP proposed a double dismissal. Specifically, it dismissed concerns about the 'where' of the border and dismissal of concerns about the 'what' of the border for Northern Ireland. Hard border or soft border, north/south or east/west, nothing would change. On the other hand, and integrally involved in the Leave campaign nationally, the DUP also proposed that Brexit would change everything in the UK's relations with the EU and with the rest of the world. Like a soaring dove, the UK as a whole would be free from being 'shackled to the corpse' of the EU and free to make its way as a sovereign state in global markets. To put that in the terms of this chapter's framing, the hope of the Nairn syndrome was almost indistinguishable from the complacency of the Fish syndrome.

For example, if one followed closely the House of Commons Northern Ireland Affairs Committee inquiries before the EU referendum, the consistent line taken by DUP MPs was to reject concerns that Brexit would upset unionist (or nationalist) expectations about the stability and continuity of relationships north/south and east/west. For example, Gavin Robinson did not foresee any change to the Irish border because the 'UK and the Republic of Ireland already have border arrangements of co-operation' such that 'we both look after one another and co-operate quite closely outside of what is a unified European Union border process'[31]. Ian Paisley Junior provided an alternative to the concerns about hard and soft borders. He claimed that the 'current Northern Ireland border is an electronic border. Every single vehicular movement on the border and every single person movement on the border is electronically recorded'. Like Robinson, his conclusion was that if the current border was already secure, with people and vehicles managed electronically, there should be no change if Britain exited the EU[32]. After 2016, Paisley's view was the one that the Irish government and the EU negotiators dismissed in turn as 'magical thinking'. The views of Robinson and Paisley were not, of course, a universally held view within unionism and many were worried about the complacency it revealed. The UUP took the decision to support Remain on the basis that Brexit had the potential to disrupt the fragile *modus vivendi* on the island. The major 'existential' threat to Northern Ireland's place in the UK that concerned the UUP leader, Mike Nesbitt, was precisely the 'where' of the border if the UK were to leave the EU. He feared that any Brexit negotiations could lead to a point where a choice was forced on the UK government between Union and Brexit. That was a question he thought all unionists – and not just those in Northern Ireland- should consider very seriously before voting Leave[33].

Of course, the distinctive conservative/radical, no-change/all change paradox was not just confined to the DUP. The former UUP leader, David (now Lord) Trimble, avoided Nesbitt's worries and was confident that the problem of the border was entirely manageable. Historically, he argued, Northern Ireland had experience for fifty years of the situation that would exist, post-Brexit. 'I mean, from 1920 until we joined the European Union there was a border where there were [trade] tariffs there and people moved back [and forth] and there was never any serious problem'. Moreover, 'there was a long time in which we were not in the European Union and there were different tariffs – in fact, largely imposed by Dublin – and that didn't cause any problems'[34]. That reasoning – that we have been here in the past and that nothing was going to change in the future – glossed over the diplomatic and practical complexities of the negotiations between the UK and the EU. It also ignored any strategy that the Irish government might adopt to secure its interests (backed up as part of the twenty seven member states of the EU) as well as the corresponding 'existential' impact a Leave vote would have on nationalists in Northern Ireland. If unionism was divided on the merits of Brexit, nationalism certainly was not divided on its threat and it is no surprise that the vote in 2016 was taken as a victory for one community at the expense of the other. As the deputy editor of the *Newsletter* warned before the vote, unionists have a poor record of strategic thinking and they should be mindful that nationalist acceptance of Northern Ireland remained contingent and that things could unravel quickly. Sovereignty (at least as the Leave campaign presented it) was not a positive message for nationalists who rejected what was implied in 'taking back control'[35]. Therefore, already qualifying the hubris and complacency of the unionist Nairn and Fish syndromes was a dangerous prospect: be careful what you hope for and take for granted because there are storms out there that you are not expecting. In other words, Brexit could mean an inversion of unionist expectations: things changing significantly between Northern Ireland and the UK while, on the island of Ireland, nothing (EU-related) would change at all. That possibility emerged in December 2017 in the form of the so-called 'backstop' and became a diplomatic fact in the Draft Withdrawal Agreement of November 2018. Since then the intimate connection between expectation and anxiety in unionist thinking about the direction of UK/EU relations has become central to its politics. It is a question of national belonging and the question has very strong echoes of traditional fears of betrayal.

The common unionist position after the referendum can be described as an integrative one. It is that the vote was by the UK as a whole (as a member state of the EU) and that in constitutional law the vote of Northern Ireland has as little distinctive salience as the vote of either Yorkshire or Lancashire (and there is no requirement to accord either of those historic counties 'special status'). It is not the majority in Northern Ireland (who voted Remain) that counts. It is the majority in the whole of the UK (who voted Leave) that counts. Constitutionally, it is a view upheld by the UK Supreme Court. While that argument has its novel characteristics in the conditions of Brexit, it actually replays an older thesis that Rose advanced four decades earlier. It is that Northern Ireland is a test case for the UK as a state. Almost four decades earlier, reflecting what the experience of Northern Ireland revealed about the UK 'as a state', Rose proposed that 'the United Kingdom might be said to exist for some purposes, but not for others, that is, the United Kingdom may be only partially or intermittently a state'. Rose assumed that 'integrity is essential for a modern state' (and, one may argue, the rallying slogan of Leave in 2016 – 'take back control' – made that assumption central to its campaign success). However, even though Westminster carries out a variety of administrative tasks within Northern Ireland, he did not think this was not proof that the UK is a state there. 'For this to be the case, Westminster must assert an effective monopoly of organised force, and protect the territorial boundaries of the United Kingdom. It must also maintain the integrity of the United Kingdom, and not treat Northern Ireland as if it were an alien land or a colony'. On all three of these criteria, Rose argued in 1983, 'Westminster fails'. He concluded that: 'In effect, Westminster handles the problem of Northern Ireland by denying the integrity of the United Kingdom'[36].

That was a provocative – and contested – academic view in 1983 but it has returned to define the deep concern of unionists about the Withdrawal Agreement and its controversially integral requirement, the backstop. Is it not self-pitying and insensitive for unionists in Northern Ireland to feel treated as if they are not fully part of the UK state? Has not Prime Minister May made no secret of her dedication to the 'precious, precious Union'? Has not the whole negotiating strategy of the UK government been to defend the integrity of the UK in its withdrawal from the EU? Is not the 'backstop' ironic evidence of the outcome of that strategy, potentially keeping the whole of the UK within the EU Customs Union in order to protect the integrity of that 'precious, precious' Union? It has not appeared that way to unionists, not only in Northern Ireland but also in Great Britain. As one anonymous author put it in an article for *Briefings for Brexit*: 'It should be fairly obvious that Northern Ireland will be under the guardianship of the Irish government in matters where the EU holds power'. The conclusion s/he came to was that 'the Backstop casts the Irish government in the role of Northern Ireland's government, even if the UK will provide the staff, infrastructure and funds to serve the EU on Backstop issues. The UK government will be reduced to a foreign government making diplomatic representations in respect to what the EU does on what is supposed to be UK territory. Yet the EU insists, and the Irish government insist that nothing undermines UK sovereignty, and nothing promotes Irish unification'.[37] This is an echo of that vintage Rose argument. Daniel Moylan, a former adviser to Boris Johnson, made the case even more forcefully. It is hard to see, he observed, why any Northern Ireland unionist would accept a situation 'in which the province became a sacrifice Britain needed to make in order to break free of the EU'. Unionists cannot 'really be sure that, if forced to choose at some future date between the benefits of global free trade and retaining Northern Ireland, sentiment in Britain might not see merit in letting the province go.'[38] That such speculation is not entirely misplaced has been underlined by well-informed journalism. As Benn observed 'economic rules do matter. Where trade and customs arrangements are made, and how they get political legitimacy, really are consequential. The backstop could well accelerate centrifugal forces that are already pulling the Union at the seams'.[39]

Conclusion

When writing this chapter, I was struck by another of the words invented by the *Dictionary of Obscure Emotions* – *anecdoche,* a state in which everyone is talking but nobody is listening and like Scrabble everyone is concerned only to increase their advantage until everyone runs out of things to say. The politics of Brexit, in their immediacy and in their rhetorical dramatization, make difficult any coherent interpretation of longer term effect. Rather than attempt a single narrative, this chapter assessed the aftermath of the 2016 referendum in terms of three syndromes. In reverse order from the introduction: the Fish syndrome, one that assumes continuity and manageable transition, only to be surprised by unexpected turns of event; the Nairn syndrome, confident that history has a necessary and a predictable course of development; and the Lyttleton syndrome, sceptical about any claims to (advance) knowledge of political outcomes of any sort. However, surely something may be said about possibilities? Cannot one advance some view about where politics are going? To modify the Lyttleton syndrome, is it not the case that, to some extent, they *are* there already? Even a prominent conservative journalist appeared to have succumbed to the Nairn syndrome and wrote that the question which should be asked of all aspiring political leaders is: 'Who understands that everything has changed, changed utterly?' He was certain that 'Brexit is not, primarily, a negotiation, but a new path'[40].

Even cautious academics hint at qualitative transformation. According to Vernon Bogdanor, joining the EU had a profound impact on the British constitution and 'Brexit could prove just as revolutionary'. He thought this likely to be the case because 'it has created a state of uncertainty in three key areas of the UK constitution: the use and effect of referendums; the protection of fundamental rights; and devolution'. Brexit, he concluded, 'might prove a constitutional moment for the UK, leading to the creation and adoption of a codified constitution'[41]. The term 'constitutional moment' Bogdanor had adapted from Bruce Ackerman, who described it as an event which is a turning point, having a dramatic quality or being out of the ordinary[42]. He had previously likened such a political transition to a train moving along a different track, and quickly, into unknown territory. 'As the smoke clears, the folks on the caboose look back and begin to see familiar mountains from a different angle; new mountains come into view for the first time'[43]. Of course the analogy, though evocative, is less than satisfactory if only because there are no lines along which the train of history or politics is moving. As the Austrian novelist Robert Musil put the matter in Lyttleton terms, the notion of the train of events is a train unrolling its rails ahead of itself rather than following an established track[44]. Nevertheless, people have to make sense of the new terrain on which they find themselves. It is surely the case that Brexit, as one contemporary historian wrote, is one the consequences of which citizens – in the UK and Ireland – will live with 'for the rest of our lives'[45].

For unionists, in the course of the negotiations on the Withdrawal Agreement many Fish moments have emerged, the backstop being only one of them. Their expectation of a smooth withdrawal as an integral part of the UK has been replaced by anxiety at being cut off from Great Britain. They also fear that the Withdrawal Agreement intimates the possibility of their becoming that 'sacrifice' to the larger interest of the UK state they have feared, at least for as long as the first Home Rule crisis. For northern nationalists, the Nairn syndrome has become the dominant political mood. Their anxiety at 'being left behind' again exists side by side with an expectation that Brexit will unroll the rails of Irish unity before it. They assume knowledge of where things are going because unity is here already – and only a border poll away. Of course, these anxieties and expectations replay older themes in Irish history and this contest between unionism and nationalism is a familiar one. The referendum result changed the context of that contest but the Lyttleton syndrome still obtains. The year 2016 was the 400th anniversary of Shakespeare's birth and to paraphrase his own words, we are afloat on a full sea and where the present tide of affairs will take us, I fear we cannot tell.

Notes

[1]   Marshall Berman, All that is Solid Melts Into Air: The Experience of Modernity (New York, Simon and Schuster, 1982).

[2]   The Dictionary of Obscure Sorrows *http://www.dictionaryofobscuresorrows.com/*

[3]   John Gray, 'Liberalism: the other God that failed' *Unherd*, 2 April 2019, *https://unherd.com/2019/04/liberalism-the-other-god-that-failed/*

[4]   John Gray, 'Deluded liberals can't keep clinging to a dead idea' *Unherd*, 3 October 2018 *https://unherd.com/2018/10/deluded-liberals-cant-keep-clinging-dead-idea/*

[5]   Arthur Koestler (ed), *Suicide of a nation?* (London: Macmillan 1964).

[6]   Tom Nairn, The Break-Up of Britain: Crisis and Neo-Nationalism (London: NLB, 1977).

[7]   The Queen's Silver Jubilee address to Parliament, 4 May 1977 *https://www.royal.gov.uk/ImagesandBroadcasts/Historic%20speeches%20and%20broadcasts/SilverJubileeaddresstoParliament4May1977.aspx*

[8]   Richard Rose, Understanding the United Kingdom: The Territorial Dimension in Government (London: Longman, 1982).

[9]   See Rose's seminal work on Northern Ireland, Governing without Consensus: An Irish Perspective (London: Faber and Faber, 1971).

[10]   Norman Davies, The Isles: A History (Oxford: Oxford University Press, 1999).

[11]   Tom Nairn, After Britain: New Labour and the Return of Scotland (London: Granta, 2000), p.58.

[12]   Robert Hazell 'Britishness and the Future of the Union' in Andrew Gamble and Tony Wright (eds), Britishness: Perspectives on the British Question (Oxford: Blackwell, 2009), p.110.

[13]   Robert Hazell (ed) Constitutional Futures Revisited: Britain's Constitution to 2020 (Houndmills: Palgrave, 2008).

[14]   Mark Glover and Robert Hazell, 'Introduction: Forecasting Constitutional Futures', in Hazell (ed), op.cit. pp, 1-25.

[15]   Tom Nairn, 'Globalisation and nationalism: the New Deal?' The Edinburgh Lectures, 2008 http://www.scotland.gov.uk/Resource/Doc/923/0057271.pdf

[16]   David Mitchell 'Unionism since 1998: Five arguments', Paper presented Les Accords de Vendredi Saint, 20 Ans Après, University of Caen, France, 29 March 2019 https://www.academia.edu/38661033/Unionism_since_1998_Five_arguments.

[17]   Joseph McCarney, Hegel on Histor (London: Routledge 2000), pp. 215-6.

[18]   Michael Oakeshott, 'Political education', in Rationalism in Politics and Other Essays (Indianapolis: Liberty Fund 1991), p. 59.

[19]   C. Beckett The Making of Modern Ireland 1603-1923, (London: Faber and Faber, 1966), p. 461.

[20]   Cited in Peter Shirlow and Brendan Murtagh, Belfast: Segregation, Violence and the City (London: Pluto Press, 2006), p.56.

[21]   Lord Bew speech in debate Good Friday Agreement: The Impact of Brexit, House of Lords, 11 October 2018, https://hansard.parliament.uk/lords/2018-10-11/debates/AE10C27D-BBDC-445A-BC50-2CC27D85D36F/GoodFridayAgreementImpactOfBrexit

[22]   Marie O'Halloran, 'Varadkar clarifies 'offensive' remark on Northern Ireland' Irish Times 12 December 2017, https://www.irishtimes.com/news/politics/oireachtas/varadkar-clarifies-offensive-remark-on-northern-ireland-1.3325231

[23]   Malachi O'Doherty, 'Brexit: The same recklessness that has tipped us out of the EU could cause Northern Ireland's departure from UK', The Belfast Telegraph, 25 June, http://www.belfasttelegraph.co.uk/opinion/news-analysis/brexit-the-same-recklessness-that-has-tipped-us-out-of-the-eu-could-cause-northern-irelands-departure-from-uk-34830776.html

24 Siobhan Fenton, 'For the first time in my life, the prospect of a united Ireland is not only credible but inevitable' *The Independent* 27 March, 2017 *https://www. independent.co.uk/voices/northern-ireland-stormont-crisis-sinn-fein-dup-united-ire-land-credible-inevitable-a7615756.html*

25 Kevin Meagher 'A United Ireland: Why Unification is Inevitable and How It Will Come About' *Irish Times* 28 December 2016, *https://www.irishtimes.com/news/ politics/why-reunified-ireland-offers-best-outcome-for-north-s-future-1.2918645*

26 See the report of her speech 'Michelle O'Neill: Irish unity is within our grasp', *Belfast Newsletter*, 7 April 2019, *https://www.newsletter.co.uk/news/ michelle-o-neill-irish-unity-is-within-our-grasp-1-8881250*

27 Mike Nesbitt 'Brexit could be 'biggest own goal' for unionists in 100 years', *Belfast Telegraph*, February 26 2019 *https://www.belfasttelegraph.co.uk/news/ northern-ireland/mike-nesbitt-brexit-could-be-biggest-own-goal-for-unionists-in-100-years-37856043.html*

28 Steve Bruce, The Edge Of The Union: The Ulster Loyalist Political Vision (Oxford, OUP, 1995).

29 Paul Bew, *Ideology and the Irish Question* (Oxford, Clarendon Press, 1994), p. 47.

30 See Arthur Aughey, 'Learning from The Leopard', in Rick Wilford (ed) *Aspects of the Belfast Agreement* (Oxford, Oxford University Press, 2001), pp. 184-201.

31 Gavin Robinson, Oral evidence: Northern Ireland and the EU Referendum, HC 760, 7 March 2016, *http://data.parliament.uk/writtenevidence/com-mitteeevidence.svc/evidencedocument/northern-ireland-affairs-committee/ northern-ireland-and-the-eu-referendum/oral/30347.pdf*

32 Ian Paisley Jr, Oral evidence: Northern Ireland and the EU Referendum, HC 760 3 February 2016, *http://data.parliament.uk/writtenevidence/ committeeevidence.svc/evidencedocument/northern-ireland-affairs-committee/north-ern-ireland-and-the-eu-referendum/oral/28395.pdf*

33 Mike Nesbitt, Oral evidence: Northern Ireland and the EU Referendum, HC 760, 7 March 2016, *http://data.parliament.uk/writtenevidence/com-mitteeevidence.svc/evidencedocument/northern-ireland-affairs-committee/ northern-ireland-and-the-eu-referendum/oral/30347.pdf*

34 Sam McBride, 'Brexit peace fears are rubbish: Trimble', *Belfast Newsletter* 26 March 2016 *http://www.newsletter.co.uk/news/northern-ireland-news/ brexit-peace-fears-are-rubbish-trimble-1-7297554*

35 Ben Lowry, 'Despite what supporters of Brexit say, it might just blow the UK apart' *Belfast Newsletter*, 19 June 2016 *http://www.newsletter.co.uk/news/ben-lowry-despite-what-supporters-of-brexit-say-it-might-just-blow-the-uk-apart-1-7438171*

36   Richard Rose, 'Is the United Kingdom a State? Northern Ireland as a Test Case', in Peter Madgwick and Richard Rose (eds) *The Territorial Dimension in United Kingdom Politics* (London: Macmillan, 1981), pp 100-136.

37   Briefings for Brexit (2018) 'The Irish Backstop and UK Sovereignty' *https://brief-ingsforbrexit.com/the-irish-backstop-and-uk-sovereignty/*

38   Daniel Moylan, 'Why is Ireland the rock on which the Brexit talks could founder' *Brexit Central,* 29 September 2018 *https://brexitcentral.com/ireland-rock-brexit-talks-founder/*

39   Alastair Benn, 'The DUP is right to be worried that the backstop threatens the Union', *Reaction,* 17 December 2018 https://reaction.life/dup-right-worried-back-stop-threatens-union. See also James Forsyth 'Divide and rule: how the EU used Ireland to take control of Brexit', *The Spectator,* 20 October 2018 *https://www.specta-tor.co.uk/2018/10/divide-and-rule-how-the-eu-used-ireland-to-take-control-of-brexit/*

40   Charles Moore, 'The new Conservative leader must deliver the change that the country voted for', *The Daily Telegraph,* July 1, 2016.

41   Vernon Bogdanor, Brexit could prove to be Britain's constitutional moment, *LSE Blog, https://blogs.lse.ac.uk/brexit/2019/02/27/brexit-could-prove-to-be-britains-constitutional-moment/*

42   Bruce Ackerman, *We the People, Vol. 1: Foundations* (Cambridge, Harvard University Press, 1991).

43   Bruce Ackerman, 'Constitutional Politics/Constitutional Law', *Yale Law Journal,* 99: 3, 1989, pp 546-7.

44   Robert Musil, *Diaries: 1899-1941* (New York: Basic Books, 1999), p..318.

45   Dominic Sandbrook, 'As a historian, I can assure you this is the most tumultuous event of modern times, a people's revolt against the elite that's been brewing for years', *The Daily Mail,* 27 June, 2016.

9

The economics of nationalism and unionism: weighed in the balance and found wanting

J Esmond Birnie

Introduction

In recent decades exponents of Irish nationalism and republicanism have become much more self-confident in making a case for unity based on economic grounds. However, it is worth considering whether that confidence is well-placed. An assessment of the economics of Irish nationalism and republicanism forms the core of this consideration, but some observations about the economics of unionism are also included. Contemporary unionist views on the economy are by no means in a sound place.

The traditional economics of Irish nationalism and republicanism

Traditionally there was not that much economics in Irish nationalism and republicanism. Economic considerations were either dismissed as somehow unworthy or it was complacently assumed that independence by itself would be sufficient to guarantee prosperity. The exemplar of the view that the economy might not matter was given by *Taoiseach* Eamonn de Valera's famous (or infamous) speech on *Raidió Éireann* on St. Patrick's Day 1943: 'The ideal Ireland that we would have, the Ireland that we have dreamed of would be the home of a people who valued material wealth only as a basis for right living, of a people who, satisfied with frugal living comfort, devoted their leisure to things of the spirit'.[1] A colourful illustration of the contrasting growthmanship view was given by an associate of Wolfe Tone when he said in 1791: '... if Ireland were free and well-governed ... she would in arts, commerce and manufactures, spring up like an air balloon and leave England behind her at an immense distance'.[2]

Patrick Pearse represented a strange combination of Gaelic contempt for what he regarded as Anglo-Saxon commerce and mammon alongside a confidence that an independent Ireland would grow to contain a population of twenty million people.[3] His piece of Wellsian futurology published on 6 August 1906 in his newspaper *An Claidheamh Soluis* imagined an Irish utopia in 2006 where the British Empire had been crushed by the Russians and, 'It must be remembered that – as a result of draining of the bogs and the re-forestation of the country – the temperature of Ireland had risen several degrees within the last century'.[4] Pearse also envisaged that in the Dublin of 2006 everyone would speak Irish and no one would ever be drunk.

Much was made of the assumption that the union with Britain had been highly destructive to Irish well-being: all poor results regarding the economy were a consequence of an alien government.[5] The mid twentieth century Irish economic historian Professor George O'Brien sought to demonstrate just how harmful the 1801-1921 Union had been but modern economic historians such as Cormac Ó Gráda suggest his claims suffered from exaggeration.[6] Importantly, just as the prevalent assumption was that political union and hence free trade between Ireland and Britain had acted to stunt industrial and wider economic development in Ireland so it was felt that an independent Ireland should pursue protectionist economic policies. Such policies would achieve autarky and self-sufficiency relative to the former colonial master. An emphasis on tariffs and protectionism came to the fore in the 1930s that did lasting damage to the Irish economy. Independent Ireland was not unusual in international terms in applying protectionism in the 1930s nor in the intensity of those policies but what was unusual was how long those policies stayed in place which is suggestive of the ideological impact of nationalism and republicanism. As late as 1959 the Irish economist Patrick Lynch wrote:' The *Sinn Fein* myth, which has been a decisive influence on policy for more than two generations, has assumed that Irish political independence implied economic independence. The shadow of this unfounded dogma which identified political independence with economic self-sufficiency still remains'.[7]

In the aftermath of Partition in 1921 it was claimed that the creation of the border had imposed a substantial and ongoing economic cost on both Irish economies and especially on border towns such as Londonderry, Strabane, Newry and Dundalk and the wider border regions. Business hinterlands and labour markets may have been somewhat disrupted but it is implausible to argue that frictions imposed by the border were the main cause of the marked decline in, for example, the textiles and clothing industry in the north west of Northern Ireland or shipbuilding along Lough Foyle. In these sectors the main markets lay outside of the thirty two counties and in some cases ownership was also outside of Ireland. It is much more likely that changes in the broader UK and world economies during the 1920s and 1930s were driving the decline which happened in the border regions of Northern Ireland and the Irish Free State.[8] The economic historian David Johnston noted how in 1931 Northern Ireland's sales of textile and engineering products to Great Britain were about £10m or about twice the total Northern Ireland sales across the Border to the Irish Free State.[9] Even then the east-west trade flows far exceeded the scale of cross-border trade. There are parallels to contemporary debates about the potential impact of Brexit and any 'backstop' or other special arrangements.

The old themes have not entirely disappeared but they have been supplemented in recent decades by an apparently much more up-beat tune. Instead of the focus on how colonial victimhood produced poverty in Ireland the claim is now that Ireland has become 'Europe's shining light' implying the achievement of Irish independence has at last been vindicated.[10] It is notable that this approach waxes and wanes along with the economic cycle: it comes, goes and comes again depending on the strength of the Republic's economy. This kind of rhetoric became noticeable in the 1990s-early 2000s during the heyday of the Celtic Tiger. It was muted during the post 2008 banking crisis and bail-out period. It has only begun to reassert itself as the Irish economy recovered from 2012 onwards.

The performance of the two Irish economies

In order to ground consideration of the interaction between nationalist and republican ideology with the economy it is necessary to give a summary of the performance of the Republic of Ireland and Northern

281

Ireland economies. A lot hinges not just on the figures but also on how these data are interpreted.

Table 9.1: Comparative output per head of the population in Northern Ireland (NI), Republic of Ireland (RoI) and UK, 1924-2017

	NI/UK	RoI/UK
1924	62	56 (1926)
1947	71	49
1960	63	45
1973	73	66
1980	73	63
1985	71	67
1991	82	77
1995	83	91
2007	79	132
2009	78	119
2012	77	121
2014	75	125
2015	75	164
2017	77	173

GDP* per head of the population as a % of the UK average, UK= 100

Note: *: These data were adjusted for price differences between the RoI and UK. In other words, they attempt to compare the volumes for goods and services in the different areas at a constant or purchasing power parity price standard. From the 1980s onwards and especially in 2015 and after the RoI data were subject to distortions arising from particularly the behaviour of the international firms sector.

Source: For 1924-85: Kieran Anthony Kennedy, Thomas Giblin and Deirdrie McHugh, The Economic Development of Ireland in the Twentieth Century (Routledge: London, 1988), pp. 124-5. For 1991 and 1995: Esmond Birnie and David M.W.N. Hitchens, Northern Ireland Economy: Performance, Prospects, Policy (Ashgate: Aldershot, 1999), p. 17. For 2007-2017 Eurostat, accessed 28 March 2019, "Regional GDP (PPS per inhabitant), *https://ec.europa.eu/eurostat/web/products-datasets/-/tgs0006*, and Eurostat, accessed 28 March 2019, "GDP per capita in PPS", *https://ec.europa.eu/eurostat/tgm/table.do?tab=table&int=1&language=en&pcode=tec001148&plugin=1*

Since the 1950s economists have often used measures of national income per head of the population, mainly GDP per head, as perhaps their main summary measure of how well one economy whether national or regional is performing compared to another. Admittedly, such reliance on GDP measures has been criticised in recent years given a growing emphasis on attempts to measure and promote well-being. International or inter-regional comparisons of "happiness" are, however, subject to their own forms of unreliability. The GDP data have the advantage of being available for reasonably long runs of years.

The data in Table 9.1 suggest that during the first seventy or so years after Partition average GDP per head in Northern Ireland was comfortably ahead of that in the Irish Free State/Republic of Ireland. Two major policy failures contributed to the relative under-performance of the Republic of Ireland in the mid twentieth century: first, the protectionism of the 1930s was continued into the 1950s and early 1960s and, second, the promotion of state financed secondary and higher education lagged behind most of the rest of north western Europe by several decades.[11] At least the first of these policy failures could be partly attributed to the emphasis within Irish nationalist and republican thinking on the economics of autarky.

Table 9.1 also indicates that in the mid 1990s, GDP per head levels in the Republic of Ireland overtook those in Northern Ireland.[12] By the mid-2000s the Republic of Ireland had achieved a substantial advantage. Some though probably not all of that advantage could be explained as a statistical distortion arising from the transfer pricing behaviour of multi-national branches seeking to take advantage of the Republic of Ireland's easy regime in terms of corporate taxation.[13] Table 9.1 shows that the Republic's relative position did decline during the post 2007 recession (compare the figures for 2007 and 2009). However, the per capita output advantage relative to Northern Ireland remained very substantial and began to widen again from 2012 onwards. In 2015 measured GDP in the Republic of Ireland soared by just over one-quarter. A measured annual economic growth rate of 26 per cent must indicate very substantial unreliability in the data.[14] Nevertheless, even if a large part of the activities of the multinational sector are stripped out of the data it is likely that during 2012-17 Republic of Ireland economic growth was substantially higher than that in Northern Ireland and the level of GDP per head was also substantially higher.[15] Admittedly, the latter point can be qualified by recognising that, as was noted in a recent paper by two Dublin-based professors of economics Seamus McGuinness and Adele Bergin, levels of GDP per capita in Northern Ireland remain very similar to those in one region of the Republic of Ireland- the Border, Midland and West (BMW) region. In other words, the productivity superiority of the Republic of Ireland is very much concentrated in the greater Dublin sub-region and in the international business sector.[16]

Attempts to formally model the economic consequences of a united Ireland

In 2015 Dr Kurt Hübner and KLC Consulting used a macroeconomic forecasting model of the two Irish economies to consider the economic feasibility of a united Ireland and also to answer the question whether unity would be accompanied by an increase or decrease in prosperity in both economies.[17] Their model forecast that incomes would rise in both Irish economies in the 5-10 years following unification. Hübner rather boldly argued that it was possible to apply to Northern Ireland the type of economic modelling which had been applied to the experience of German unification after 1989 or one day might be applied to some sort of re-unification of North Korea and South Korea. Such exercises can be criticised at both a general level and at the particular level.

In terms of the more general criticism, one is reminded of Doctor Johnson's remark 'It is not done well; but you are surprised to find it done at all'. Economic forecasting models have often proven a not very reliable way of predicting what could happen in the economy especially when economies are undergoing very large structural changes: a united Ireland would certainly be a big structural change. Economists, collectively, do not have a good track forecasting record in terms of big structural changes. It is worth asking whether any economist predicted the upsurge in Irish economic growth which began around 1990 and continued through to 2007. With hindsight we see that the economies of the former Soviet Union and East Germany were on the brink of collapse in the 1980s but at that time many western economists were impressed by their apparent strengths. Not only did almost no one foresee the timing of German unification in 1990 but there was very little appreciation in 1990 that West Germany was committing itself to at least three decades of very substantial annual subsidies to the former East Germany.[18]

The particular criticism relates to the fact that importantly the forecasts were conditional. Hübner and KLC made certain assumptions and then forecast how the economy might respond. As the report itself concedes: 'The models are abstractions of reality, embodying many assumptions'.[19] The sensible thing to do, therefore, is to review KLC's assumptions. Four were particularly problematic:

First, that the exchange rate, the value of sterling, would depreciate. Hübner and KLC assumed a short to medium term boost to economic activity in Northern Ireland as unification replaced a high sterling exchange rate with a weaker one. Given the devaluation of the pound which occurred in the summer of 2016, this assumption now looks very inappropriate. To a large extent that adjustment has taken place without Northern Ireland leaving the UK.

Second, that there would be a big boost to trade. Hübner and KLC took a lead from economic research which suggests that borders are bad for trade. Given that, they look at how trade between Northern Ireland and the Republic of Ireland would grow if the Irish border disappeared. What they do not allow for is the fact that Northern Ireland's 'export' trade with Great Britain is about three to four times greater than that with the Republic of Ireland. If there was a border between Northern Ireland and Great Britain then surely, using their logic, that trade would be reduced? Indeed, it is very likely the loss in terms of less trade with Great Britain would exceed the gain in terms of greater trade with the Republic of Ireland. This is because in 2016 total sales from the Northern Ireland economy were £68.9bn, of which £44.7bn were to Northern Ireland itself, £14.0bn to Great Britain, £3.4bn to the Republic of Ireland, £2.3bn to the rest of the EU and £4.4bn to the rest of the world.[20] So, this assumption is probably wrong headed.

Third, that there would be a major economic miracle in terms of productivity growth in Northern Ireland. Hübner and KLC assumed that one consequence of unity would be that the Northern Ireland economy would suddenly start to look like the Republic's in terms of the rate of corporate tax, the structure of industry and, very importantly, the level of productivity. For Northern Ireland to close its productivity gap with the Republic of Ireland over fifteen years, as this report assumes, would require the sort of very rapid economic growth, perhaps of the order of 6 per cent annually, which the local economy has never sustained over any period since the Second World War. This assumption is therefore highly unrealistic. Northern Ireland could, of course, adopt policies to improve its productivity whilst remaining within the UK.[21]

Fourth, that the Republic of Ireland could without much cost to itself replace the fiscal transfer which the UK currently provides to Northern Ireland. Hübner and KLC's description of how the issue of the fiscal transfer would be dealt with is unclear. The existence of the fiscal transfer reflects the fact that government spending in Northern Ireland exceeds the value of tax receipts raised in the region. By implication, there has to be a transfer of resources from the UK Exchequer to the region. The figures for the transfer quoted in their text are much lower than the official estimate where this annual fiscal transfer to Northern Ireland is over £9bn.[22] In reality, possible scenarios include ones where the Republic of Ireland's taxpayers and citizens either pay more taxes or enjoy less public services so as to provide the resources to fund the fiscal transfer to Northern Ireland. Hübner and KLC may be assuming that the Republic of Ireland would simply borrow to make good this funding gap. Even, putting to one side the question of whether the EU would set aside its stated fiscal rules to let the Republic engage in this fiscal easing, this may not be a costless option. There is the danger than this would lead to public debt/GDP ratios rising. Admittedly, with the Republic of Ireland's GDP now totalling more than £280bn, and Northern Ireland's about £40bn, an annual outlay of about £9bn would equal about 3 per cent of a GDP of about £300bn. Given that, provided cash terms or nominal growth of the economy equalling about 3 per cent, which would be a fairly modest performance,[23] a post-unity Republic of Ireland could borrow an extra £9bn each year without any tendency for the debt/GDP ratio to rise. The threat of an upwards spiral in the debt/GDP ratio increases if the terms of unification included provision that the Republic or Ireland would assume the 'Northern Ireland's share' of the UK national debt.[24] If that share was about 3 per cent in line with Northern Ireland's share of UK population then about Euros 60bn would be added on top of the existing

Irish government debt of about Euros 200bn; a 30 per cent increase. Irish taxpayers would be obliged to pay at least Euros 1bn and perhaps considerably more every year in extra interest charges.[25]

The Hübner and KLC report has been much used as an intellectual prop by other proponents of Irish unification. One example of this is Kevin Meagher in his recent book on Irish unification, *A United Ireland.*.[26] This notwithstanding the fact that the recent track record of economic forecasts of large scale political-structural changes in the economy, notably the forecasts of the economic impact of Brexit,[27] has been a very chequered one. By implication, it is reasonable to be cautious about the Hübner and KLC report. Questionable assumptions produce questionable results.

Gerry Adams and the 'disappearing' transfer payment from the UK Exchequer

The former Sinn Fein leader, Gerry Adams has claimed that Irish unity had become more a question of 'when' rather than 'if'.[28] A critical plank of his argument was that Northern Ireland is not in fact as heavily subsidised by the UK Exchequer as is generally understood. The Adams claim is that the actual level of spending in Northern Ireland is lower than that stated by the statisticians and as a result the gap or deficit between public monies spent and revenues raised by taxes in Northern Ireland is smaller. If Adams is right, Irish unity could become more affordable. Adams's argument becomes something of a fiscal dance of the seven veils. With each sentence a few more billions come off!

Adams argued as follows. In 2015-16 of the public spending of £24bn which the UK Treasury attributes to Northern Ireland £3.7bn was actually Northern Ireland's "share" of UK spending on defence, overseas representation (for example, embassies) and payments on the national debt.[29] At the same time revenue raised was £16.7bn. So the true deficit was not £24bn minus £16.7bn but £20.3bn minus £16.7bn, given that Adams makes the assumption that all of the spending not 'in' Northern Ireland but assigned to it can be conveniently ignored. Adams went further, he said £1.8bn of spending in Northern Ireland is actually spending by UK (presumably London-based) government departments and 'may not be essential'. It is perhaps surprising to see the former leader of Sinn Fein become a proponent of caution regarding public spending but in any case it is unclear what the £1.8bn expenditure is which he was referring to. According to Adams' argument the fiscal transfer from the UK Treasury to Northern Ireland has shrunk to 'only' a few billions: namely, £18.5bn minus £16.7bn equals £1.8bn.

Adams claimed that HM Treasury produced figures which are 'deliberately misleading', but data are also available from the UK's official and independent statistical authority: the Office for National Statistics.[30] In 2015-16, total public spending attributed to Northern Ireland was £26bn and total revenues raised £15.9bn implying a fiscal deficit of just over £10bn. Incidently, in the estimate of revenue raised Northern Ireland was allocated a share of North Sea oil tax receipts- the former Sinn Fein President did not register any complaint about Northern Ireland appropriating some of Scotland's money![31]

Coming, then, to the nub of Adams's argument, within the attributed spending was Northern Ireland's share of the UK's common services (about £0.5bn), international services (£0.3bn), interest on the national debt (£1.0bn) and defence (£1.0bn). The crucial question is whether these sums of money can simply be written off as Adams implied. Membership of the 'club' of the UK implies making a contribution to the cost of those common services from which we all benefit. Perhaps Adams feels that global conditions are now so stable that we now have no need for defence spending? Perhaps he feels that Northern Ireland has derived no benefit from public spending funded in part from the borrowing which then added to the national debt? A number of other commentators (see below) have adopted a rather fast and loose approach to Northern Ireland's obligations in respect to UK national debt. In short, after Adams has finished his fiscal dance, the numbers still do not add up the way he would like. Adams has not allowed for the fact that after unification Northern Ireland would still require common services, international services and defence services and would probably still be making contributions to debt repayment. Perhaps, there would be some scope to use the existing central and international services provided by the Republic of Ireland state and "stretch" these to cover the Northern Ireland population though that could probably only be done to the extent people in the existing Republic of Ireland were willing to accept a reduction in the quality/quantity of such services received on a per head basis.[32]

Gunter Thumann and Senator Daly and The Irish Senate Report on a united Ireland

The German economist Gunther Thumann and the Republic of Ireland Senator Mark Daly present an argument rather similar to Adams' though they did spell out their assumptions more fully.[33] Along the way they try to argue that international experience, notably German unification in 1990, shows that Irish unity is eminently achievable. They note that whilst Northern Ireland received a measured fiscal transfer of £9.2bn during 2013-14,[34] in their view almost all of that transfer consisted of sums of money which a post-unity Republic of Ireland government would not have to spend. For example, £2.8bn consisted of pension payments. Since pension liabilities were built up during the period when Northern Ireland was part of the UK Thumann and Daly conveniently assume that the UK government would continue to pay even after Irish unity. This is not a reasonable assumption: why would the UK enter into a very long run arrangement involving substantial subsidies to another country.[35]

Thumann and Daly also argued that all of the £2.9bn assigned to Northern Ireland in 2013-14 relating to a combination of overseas defence spending and UK central services and interest payments on the UK public debt can be ignored. Like Adams, they are assuming a post-unity Ireland could simply free-ride behind the NATO/UK defence shield.[36] They are also assuming that the unity settlement would involve no share of UK public debt obligations transferring to the Republic of Ireland. Daly in his Irish Senate Report rather flippantly claimed much of the UK national debt had been created by wars as though that meant Northern Ireland had no obligation to share in its repayment.[37] Very importantly, Thumann and Daly smuggle in the assumption that one consequence of unity would be a very sizeable reduction public spending in Northern Ireland. They justify a reduction of £1.7bn annually to bring the proportionate scale of the public sector into line with its counterpart int the twenty-six counties. Given that total departmental spending in Northern Ireland was about £10bn in 2012-13 that would represent a reduction of about 15 per cent. By comparison, during the whole of the so-called "austerity era" 2009/10-2016-17 total identifiable public expenditure in Northern Ireland declined by only 2.8 per cent in real terms.[38] The likelihood that a sudden massive reduction of the scale envisaged in the Irish Senate Report would precipitate a crisis for the entire Northern Ireland economy and especially the private sector is discussed in a later section where the arguments of Paul Gosling who also proposes a substantial reduction in the public sector are considered.

Overall, the Thumann and Daly research report like some other pro-unity commentary (see the section on David McWilliams below) displays a tendency to be triumphalistic about the recent economic success of the Republic of Ireland: it is as if Irish economic history began in 1990 or perhaps even 2012! As noted earlier, recent Republic of Ireland economic growth has been commendable but it is worth remembering this was preceded by about 40 very difficult years (1921-60) and 30 very mixed years (1960-90). Thumann and Daly's research report is also very shrill or dismissive about the Northern Ireland economy's performance. One illustration of this is how they incorporate some *Oireachtas* Library and Research Services research based on UK and Republic of Ireland performance in terms of the UN Human Development Index (HDI).[39] The HDI attempts to summarise human development or quality of life using the average of three indicators: comparative GDP per capita, years of life expectancy, average length of schooling.[40] The Irish parliamentary research services paper recognised that the UNHDI is designed to use data sets relating to countries and as a result an attempt to include a region like Northern Ireland will face particular difficulties: no direct data on years in schooling in Northern Ireland were available and so the figures used in this research paper were inferred from a different source. It was indicated that in 2013 average school years in Northern Ireland were about four years lower (at 8.3 years) than the averages for the UK (12.3) or the Republic of Ireland (11.6). A discrepancy of such size is suggestive of some problem with the way the Northern Ireland result has been estimated. The *Oireachtas* Library and Research Service caveated their attempt to include Northern Ireland- unfortunately, when Thumann and Daly quote this research they fail to note any of the caveats.[41]

German lessons: Is German unification in 1990 a template?

Hübner and Thumann have both used the German experience in the 1990s as a sort of theoretical template for Ireland. Two former Professors of Dublin's Economic and Social Research Institute John FitzGerald and Edgar Morgenroth have compared Northern Ireland's comparative competitiveness performance to that of the East German regional economy since German unification.[42] More recently, the German Chancellor Angela Merkel in a visit to Dublin in 2019 pledged that her experience of the Iron Curtain and Berlin Wall gave her all the more reason to oppose any so-called 'hard border" between Northern Ireland and the Republic of Ireland: 'I have lived behind the Iron Curtain, so I know only to well what it means once borders vanish'.[43]

Inter-regional and international comparative studies can be a useful tool in the social sciences. This author was involved in matched factory comparisons of businesses in Northern Ireland with counterparts in the former West and East Germanys in the years immediately before and after the collapse of the Berlin Wall in November 1989.[44] Nevertheless, great care should always be taken when attempting to draw lessons from the experience of one country and then trying to apply it to another. We are now seeing something of a pattern in terms of attempts to use German unification as a model for Ireland but such comparisons are not necessarily appropriate for a number of reasons.

First, as noted earlier, rather abstract general models of the economy, especially Competitive General Equilibrium ones, may not have predicted accurately what actually happened in Germany post-unification and it has to be wondered how well they might predict the potential impact of a re-unification of North and South Korea. Application of such an approach to Northern Ireland is very question begging.

Second, the unification of East and West Germany in 1990 was based on majority consent as expressed by the results of elections in East Germany. No such majority consent exists in Northern Ireland in favour of a united Ireland.

Third, it is not necessarily clear what economic lessons East Germany provides for Northern Ireland. FitzGerald and Morgenroth imply East Germany compares well to Northern Ireland in terms of the extent of improvement in competitiveness and comparative productivity in the regional economy in recent decades: A sort of poster-child of "tough love" in that unlike Northern Ireland or the Mezzogornio of southern Italy the ill effects of a subsidy culture have been avoided. It is certainly true that East German productivity (GDP per worker) has converged rapidly on the level in West Germany: from about 45 per cent in 1990 to about 80 per cent in 2013. At the same time, East Germany achieved this in spite of (or because of?) a continued very substantial fiscal transfer from the West – the latter being variously estimated as between euros 68bn and euros 83bn annually.[45] Given that the current population of the former East Germany is about 13.6m or equivalent to about seven times that in Northern Ireland – by implication the fiscal transfer to East Germany has been broadly similar to that into Northern Ireland in per head terms. It is also of note that part of the reason why East Germany achieved so much economic convergence relative to the West since 1990 is that much of the "surplus population" has been exported to the West through migration: East Germany's population has declined by 3.0m since 1990. The existence of the fiscal transfer is one reason why Northern Ireland's population grew by 17 per cent during 1991-2018

Fourth, it might be claimed that if West Germany has sustained almost thirty years during which its annual fiscal transfer to East Germany has been equivalent to up to 5 per cent of West German GDP then surely the Republic of Ireland could sustain a transfer to Northern Ireland of up to £9bn annually or about 3 per cent of its GDP? However, West Germany has been paying to help a relatively poorer region whereas Republic of Ireland taxpayers would be asked to subsidise people in Northern so that the latter could continue to have a higher level of per capita consumption and government spending than is the case in the Republic of Ireland – FitzGerald and Morgenroth argue that there is little or no precedent within the EU for a less well off region subsidising a higher living standard region.

Fifth, leaving to one side the very important broader international factors (the fact that the four Allied Powers of 1945 all agreed that German unification could happen), what happened in Germany in 1990 was a case of putting back together again what had been a single, independent sovereign state before 1945. The thirty two counties of Ireland were under common administration when the island was part of the Union.[46]

Sixth, sadly, many people did die in the border areas of Northern Ireland during the Troubles. Those deaths can be attributed to the terrorist campaign rather than the border per se. According to recent research from the Free University in Berlin up to 327 people died attempting to escape from communist East Germany to the West.[47] At no point during the Troubles was any attempt made to prevent people in Northern Ireland moving to live in the Republic of Ireland or the reverse. It is likely that the Common Travel Area between the UK and the Republic of Ireland will be preserved post-Brexit. It is an insult to all those who suffered under the extremely harsh East German totalitarian system to compare the harsh experience of communism to the impact of the Irish border or the potential impact of any possible future "hard border".

The Gosling report

In a recent report, *The Economic Effects of an All Island Economy 2018* the journalist Paul Gosling argues the case for Irish unity.[48] He summarised his argument in an article in the *Belfast Telegraph* on 22 February 2018.[49] Gosling considers that Brexit will be devastating given the results of Treasury analysis which claims it could lead to a roughly 10 per cent hit to UK and Northern Ireland income – basically we might be less rich than we would otherwise have been. The evidence which implies that that Treasury analysis is likely to have exaggerated the negative economic impact of Brexit is considered in a later section. At the same time, he seems complacent about advocating unity that would, even in terms of his own analysis, bring with it a massive reduction in employment in Northern Ireland. He argues that post-unity the percentage employment in the public sector could be reduced to the rate which applies in the Republic of Ireland. This would be equivalent to a job loss of 50,000 employees. Once allowance is made for the extent to which total spending in the economy would be reduced, including spin-off effects such as the so-called "multiplier effect", the total job loss could be about 70,000. Much more serious than the worst predictions about Brexit; though with a lot more predictability and certainty about the scale of harm.[50]

There is a case for a re-balancing of the Northern Ireland economy under certain conditions, especially if this could be achieved via private sector growth rather than public sector contraction. What Gosling proposes would be a shattering blow to the Northern Ireland economy, to which it would be very difficult for the economy to adapt. He has to assume that unity and a marked reduction in public spending in Northern Ireland would itself spark some sort of private sector renaissance. But why would that happen? Gosling himself does not give any plausible reason.

Gosling underestimates just how challenging it would be for the Republic of Ireland, particularly its taxpayers, to absorb Northern Ireland. As one of the UK's poorer regions, Northern Ireland pays less in and gets more out of being a member of the club which is the UK economic union. As a part of the UK Northern Ireland benefits each year from a £9bn fiscal transfer from the Exchequer.

Like Adams and Thumann and Daly, Gosling tries to argue that post-unity, the Republic of Ireland would not need to find £9bn extra each year because some of the measured Northern Ireland public expenditure is in fact notional: Northern Ireland's share of certain UK-wide services or items of spending. According to Gosling, after unity Dublin would not need to pay for the equivalent amount of central services (e.g. embassies, investment promotion efforts, defence spending, payments on national debt) which is currently imputed to Northern Ireland.

In practice, unless the Republic of Ireland services suddenly become much more productive there would probably be some pressure to increase these spending areas after unity. He also assumes that the UK would impose no obligations on the Dublin government to pay for Northern Ireland's 'share' of UK national debt. Crucially, Gosling also seems to be assuming there are no problems of public order after unification.

Gosling does somewhat hedge his bets. Whatever the true scale of the fiscal transfer he wonders whether it could continue for a number of years, up to thirty, after unity. It has been said that sovereignty is like pregnancy: you cannot be a little bit pregnant. Somehow, Gosling envisages the UK's responsibility for Northern Ireland gradually fading away over the next thirty years. The UK could also, in his view, contribute into a fund to pay for Northern Ireland's infrastructure.[51] All this seems highly unlikely, a UK government making a very long term and expensive commitment to subsidising the dismemberment of the UK.[52] Would any London government really want to set a precedent which might also encourage Scottish nationalists?

Confronting Northern Ireland's investment deficit

Table 9.2: Comparative levels of per capita spending on different parts of the economy in Northern Ireland, Republic of Ireland (RoI) and UK, all as % of the level in the RoI, 2012

	UK	NI	RoI
Personal consumption	134	120	100
Government consumption	118	143	100
Investment (public and private)	62	31	100
GNI*	106	84	100

(numbers greater than 100 indicate a level of per capita spending in either the UK or NI greater than the level in the RoI)

Note: GNI = Gross National Income. A measure of total output which attempts to make some allowance for the statistical distortions generated by the international firms' sector within the RoI.

Gosling's point about how infrastructure could be funded post-unification matters because there is considerable evidence that Northern Ireland now lags considerably in terms of the amount invested per head and hence the amount of infrastructure and other capital available per head. Dublin-based Professors John FitzGerald and Edgar Morgenroth presented the data summarised in Table 9.2:[53]

The figures presented by FitzGerald and Morgenroth are now somewhat dated- recent economic growth in the Republic of Ireland would imply that the level of GNI per head was now substantially higher than both the UK average level and the Northern Ireland level. However, the broad points still stand. Northern Ireland is a very consumption orientated economy whereas the Republic of Ireland is very investment orientated. It might be claimed that it is the fiscal transfer itself which has allowed a situation to develop where levels of consumption per head are far above those in the Republic of Ireland and not that far behind the UK average and levels of government spending per head are considerably higher than those in the Republic of Ireland and the UK average. Alongside this, levels of investment per head are less than one-third the level in the Republic of Ireland and less than two-thirds the UK average.

The long term sustainability of this situation where levels of investment are so low might be questioned.[54] Proponents of unity might try to argue that it is an indictment of Northern Ireland's membership of the UK that this situation was able to develop. Nevertheless, advocates of unity also face the very practical challenge as to how any post-unity Republic of Ireland government would be able to afford to substantially increase investment spending in Northern Ireland.

The current position probably developed over a considerable period of time and whilst membership of the UK's public expenditure system was a permissive factor in allowing this situation to develop, there are probably other more direct explanations – for example, the extent to which during the Troubles public spending was diverted away from infrastructure and towards the maintenance of law and order. Northern Ireland's devolved administrations since 1999 and especially during 2007-17 repeatedly made decisions which favoured consumption over investment: attempts to protect health care funding in real terms, no domestic water charges, shifting departmental spending from the capital to current budget. The level of consumption may well impact on voting behaviour but there may be little electoral return to the politician who decides to shift resources towards investment and hence the longer term prosperity of the economy. Whilst it might be argued that the fiscal transfer helped allow this problem of the structural imbalance of the Northern Ireland economy to develop it does not necessarily follow that a sudden removal of that transfer in the context of Irish unity would by itself help to re-balance the economy towards investment and away from consumption. Much more likely is a situation where the sudden reduction in public spending reduces overall demand in the economy and depresses the private sector still further.

David McWilliams[55]

In essence McWilliams' approach is similar to other pro-unity advocates who have already been considered. He does have a tendency to engage in statistical shock and awe by trying to dazzle his audience as to just how well the Republic of Ireland economy is doing whilst, in his view, the Northern Ireland economy collapses. For example, he claimed that whereas the total exports of the Republic of Ireland equalled euros 282bn the equivalent sum in Northern Ireland was only euros 10bn.[56] Some of the 282bn figure in the case of the Republic of Ireland relates to the rather artificial intra-company transfers promoted by the relatively light corporate tax regime. Northern Ireland's total exports in 2017 were worth more than euros 10bn. According to NISRA's Broad Economy export and external sales figures, total Northern Ireland exports in 2017 were worth £10.1bn: equivalent to about euros 11.5bn.[57]

Similarly, McWilliams has tried to argue that the Republic of Ireland is a vastly more cosmopolitan and therefore more successful society than its Northern Ireland counterpart: in the Republic of Ireland one in six of the population are foreign-born compared to only one per cent in Northern Ireland.[58] In fact, according to the official data source the *Labour Force Survey* about 13 per cent of Northern Ireland's labour force are from outside the UK and the Republic of Ireland: no other UK region apart from London has a greater representation of migrant workers.

Brexit

Contrary to much other recent writing about the Northern Ireland economy and business prospects, what has been written here does not forefront the question of Brexit. There are two main reasons for this. First, the UK legally exited the EU on 31 January 2020 but until the long term trade relationship has been negotiated it is hard to say what the impact will be. Second, Brexit is far from being the biggest challenge facing the Northern Ireland economy (see below). Nevertheless, the commentators that have already been referred to – Hübner, Adams, Thumann and Daly and Gosling – have certainly suggested Brexit has made unity more likely if not inevitable. There are several strands to this argument and these will now be considered in turn.

First, that the Brexit process has transformed public opinion such that many people would now prefer a united Ireland as a means to ensure Northern Ireland does not leave the EU. In fact, a more careful reading of election results and opinion surveys such as the Northern Ireland Life and Times Survey indicate that this is not the case.[59]

Second, that Brexit has to imply a so-called 'hard Border", one characterised by many physical controls and hence frictions to movements of people or goods, which in turn will embolden republicanism and perhaps even provoke higher levels of violence.[60] In fact, both the London and Dublin governments have already confirmed that the Common Travel Area between the two Islands, which has existed since Irish independence in 1921, will continue. As regards the movement of commodities, we have the example of the Norway-Sweden border, which also happens to be a frontier between the EU and the rest of the world. Most of the movements of goods between the two Scandinavian countries happen without need for physical or document checks: 96 per cent of the flow into Norway and 87 per cent of the flow into Sweden. In the case of the Irish border, a combination of a comprehensive EU-UK free trade agreement, mutual recognition of standards, digital technology,[61] spot checks away from the border and some forbearance would make a hard border unnecessary.

Third (and there is an obvious inter-relationship with the first two points), that Brexit would inevitably deliver such a shattering blow to the economy of Northern Ireland that this would entail a massive blow to its position within the Union. It is worth considering this claim in some detail. There are in fact good grounds to argue that many of the most dire predictions as to the economic harm which will result from Brexit are likely to prove exaggerated.[62]

Those who argue Brexit will do immense harm underplay the extent to which Northern Ireland economy has long term, structural weaknesses – especially in terms of a competitiveness and productivity problem. Those weaknesses long pre-date the 2016 Brexit vote. Careful consideration of the data relating to Northern Ireland's comparative productivity in international terms suggests that membership of the EU's single market did not do all that much to improve our competitive position. By implication, ceasing to be a member of that single market would not necessarily have the very negative effect that some have implied. Table 9.3 below summarises the key data but given that the claims as to the negative impact of Brexit have been given such prominence it is worth going into this argument and counter argument in some detail.

At a UK-wide level HM Treasury attempted to project how much 'output would be lost' because of Brexit.[63] Those "big" Treasury numbers in turn formed the basis of the claim made by the Confederation of British Industry (CBI) that a 'no deal' Brexit would "cost £5bn" to the Northern

Ireland economy.[64] The validity or otherwise of such claims depends crucially on the reliability of the Treasury's analysis.

The projections produced by the Treasury and some independent economic commentators such as the London School of Economics (LSE) derive in part from a very old argument. Adam Smith in 1776 said that labour productivity would depend on the "division of labour" and that, in turn, would be increased if the extent of the market grew. However, notwithstanding the reasonableness of the case made in the eighteenth century about the manufacture of pins, the HM Treasury/LSE/CBI assumptions about the scale of the consequential impact from reduction in market access to reduction in productivity may represent Adam Smith on steroids.

Table 9.3 illustrates the United Kingdom's and Northern Ireland's comparative productivity performance (GDP per worker) using the most recent official statistics.

Table 9.3 UK and NI comparative GDP per worker since the mid 1990s: The elusive impact of the EU Single Market

	1995*	The year in the mid 2000s when UK comparative performance best	2016
Germany	115	105 (2006)	110
	130	*124 (2006)*	*127*
France	115	107 (2004)	114
	130	*126 (2004)*	*131*
USA	131	128 (2002)	138
	143	*151 (2002)*	*159*

(Top figures in each row show overseas country productivity as a % of the UK level, Figures in italics show overseas country productivity as a % of the NI level: *Numbers greater than 100 indicate productivity level in the overseas country greater than that in the UK or NI*)

Note* As ONS did not have NI/UK data for 1995 used NI/UK for 1997 to represent 1995.

Sources: ONS, "Industry by region estimates of labour productivity April 2018", Statistical Bulletin (ONS: Newport, April 2018). ONS, "International comparisons of UK productivity (ICP): 2016- The Database", Statistical Bulletin (ONS: Newport, November 2018).

The results in Table 9.3 show that after 1995 for about a decade the UK's comparative productivity did improve. This was consistent with the HM Treasury/LSE/Adam Smith argument that access to a larger market, in this case the development of the EU's single market from 1992 onwards, should be associated with improvements in productivity.

However, since the mid 2000s UK comparative productivity has been worsening again. A trend which is the opposite of that which might be expected if single market membership was really so positive in its effects. In fact, all of the earlier gains relative to France and the USA have been lost. A similar story can be told in terms of Northern Ireland comparative productivity with, in this case, the absolute size of the gap being bigger.

In fact, the greatest single threat posed by Brexit is that it could become the all-purpose excuse for various failings by policy makers and the Northern Ireland private sector.

Still an economic case for the Union – but the argument is weaker than it was

In economic terms the argument for the union remains but the real strength of that argument has declined. Over the very long run the Northern Ireland economy has not performed well even compared to a relatively poor standard of comparison: the UK average. Whatever may have been true in the 1950s-60s, the Republic of Ireland is no longer any sort of basket case economy. Gosling is one commentator who notes that in some ways the recent economic performance of the Republic of Ireland economy has been much more satisfactory than its Northern counterpart.[65] McGuinness and Bergin note how especially in recent years the Republic of Ireland's education and training system has been much more successful than its Northern Ireland counterpart in raising the average level of qualifications of the work-force.[66]

At the same time, the transfer payment is there and it is certainly substantial. It would still represent a substantial sacrifice for the Republic of Ireland tax payer to continue to pay it notwithstanding all the attempts by Adams, Thumann and Daly and Hübner and KLC to argue away most of the considerable sums of money. That there is a large and immediate fiscal obstacle to Irish unity has at least been recognised by FitzGerald and Morgenroth when they expressed some scepticism as to the assumptions which Thumann and Daly had made about how the size of the fiscal transfer might be reduced after unification.[67] Unionism is therefore deriving support from a position which is also potentially an economic embarrassment. Admittedly, there is a number of possible 'defences' of the fiscal transfer which pro-Union advocates might employ. There is some merit in each of these but perhaps none are wholly convincing.

First, the fiscal transfer is an automatic economic adjustment which to a large extent it is. As a relatively poor part of the UK, Northern Ireland tends to have more public spending per head and collect less tax revenue per person. Graham Gudgin amplifies this argument: Northern Ireland has had a relatively rapid growth in its labour supply. Possible adjustment mechanisms in order to prevent very high unemployment could be either a substantial decline in wages or substantial out-migration. Instead of adjustments in those ways the public sector and public spending expanded to absorb much of that supply.[68] If the transfer is largely an automatic mechanism then one would expect to see it in other UK regions and this is the case. All UK regions bar London and the East and South East of England receive a transfer. At the same time, it is not so much that there is a transfer which is notable. It is the scale of the transfer relative to Northern Ireland's regional output- about 20-30 per cent, which is much higher than the transfers to Scotland, Wales and the north of England.

Second, the fiscal transfer is a solidarity payment between UK citizens. If that was really the way that taxpayers in, say, South East England regarded it then there might be grounds to be confident that a large transfer payment was a sustainable position. Although there is a lack of evidence that the transfer is viewed that way, at the same time, there is probably a lack of awareness or visibility regarding Northern Ireland's fiscal transfer. Any resentment in the 'English' media or political classes against regional subsidies tends to be directed towards Scotland.[69] It may also be of note that £9bn annually whilst a large absolute sum of money is 'only' about 0.5 per cent of total GDP of Great Britain. In each year since 1990 the annual transfer from West to East Germany has on average been equivalent to about 5 per cent of the GDP of the former West Germany.[70]

Third, the fiscal transfer is a payment back to Northern Ireland to reflect some of the other contributions Northern Ireland makes to UK national life.

The 'value' of a region being part of a national unit cannot be reduced to a monetary flow. The territory of Northern Ireland certainly did have a strategic value to the rest of the UK in the past, notably during the Second World War's Battle of the Atlantic as was recognised by Winston Churchill, but probably less so today. Northern Ireland graduates often leave Northern Ireland and hence contribute to economic life in other UK region as say teachers or medical professionals, but it is very unlikely that the value of that type of contribution comes close to £9bn annually.

The Northern Ireland economy may in fact be stuck on the horns of a dilemma. It 'needs' the substantial transfer to keep consumption and activity, including in the private sector, at existing levels but unfortunately that position is also one associated with high consumption/low investment which works against the prospects for longer term growth.[71]

Unfortunately, there is little evidence that unionist politicians have fully grasped the ambivalent implications of the fiscal transfer: it is both a short term advantage but a possible long term disadvantage. Their recent behaviour suggests a tendency to prioritise short run advantage through maximising public spending in Northern Ireland whilst also holding down taxation. Such a policy combination is likely to increase the scale of the fiscal transfer. The DUP in particular has positioned itself as the party of low taxation- keeping rates down, reducing corporation tax below the UK average and certainly doing little or nothing to address the 'super-parity' issue: the extent that total taxes and charges in Northern Ireland are so much lower than in comparable UK regions.[72]

All the Northern Ireland political parties, and not just the DUP, if they are serious about wanting to return to regional self-responsibility in the form of stable and sustainable devolved government need to be thinking about how super-parity might be reduced and also about those measures which might slowly tilt the economy away from its consumption bias towards greater weight given to investment (see Table 9.2, and the discussion, above). The tragedy is that they may not do this. They may have very little electoral incentive so to do.

Similarly, there is the danger of complacency about the position of the health care system in Northern Ireland relative to the Republic of Ireland. As part of the UK welfare state and the NHS, the approach taken in Northern Ireland is undoubtedly much closer to universal access which is free at the point of use than its Republic of Ireland counterpart.[73] Importantly, this position is very dependent on the scale of the fiscal transfer and in terms of many performance indicators the health care system in Northern Ireland is struggling.

That the economic attitudes of the main political parties in Northern Ireland are not conducive to sustainable prosperity is not a new phenomenon. When Chief Secretary for Ireland in early nineteenth century Sir Robert Peel bemoaned the fact that, '... everybody in Ireland instead of setting about improvement as people elsewhere do, pester governments about boards and public aid. Why cannot people in Ireland fish without a board if fishing be so profitable ... [74] Peel summed up a society where there was much of what economists now call rent-seeking where individuals try to become rich through exploiting favours granted by government, the public sector or the regulatory system. Rent seeking remains a common activity in Northern Ireland and the political class, both unionist and nationalist/republican, seems happy to have collaborated in that outcome. The Renewable Heat Incentive (RHI) fiasco may be only the most recent example.[75] Another voice from the past which sounds quite contemporary is provided by Gladstone who scolded that in all his many years as Chancellor of the Exchequer in the mid nineteenth century he never once heard a Chief Secretary for Ireland come forward with any proposals to reduce public expenditure in Ireland.[76] To be fair to Northern Ireland, the Republic of Ireland is no stranger to rent-seeking and related problems: two Irish economic historians note how there was minimal financial regulation in the build-up to the 2007 banking crisis and also how 40 per cent of disclosed donations to the Fianna Fail party during 1997-2007 came from builders and property developers.[77]

A Northern Ireland which achieved greater prosperity through higher productivity and higher competitiveness would be one where the fiscal transfer would probably be smaller. That in turn would probably increase the real strength of the economic argument for the Union although, ironically, a smaller transfer would also imply that Irish unity would be more 'affordable'.[78]

303

Conclusion

Over the long run, notwithstanding the difficult years of the 1930s-50s, the comparative economic performance of the Republic of Ireland has improved very markedly compared to both Northern Ireland and the UK average. Pre-1921 advocates for the Union argued from a position of economic strength and could argue that Northern Ireland's membership of the UK contributed to economic growth and a measure of prosperity. In recent decades the economic case for the Union might appear to be a case of making a virtue out of weakness: Northern Ireland has been characterised by a substantial and longstanding fiscal transfer from the UK exchequer. Nevertheless, to the extent that it would be difficult for a united Ireland to replace that transfer then a movement away from the constitutional status quo faces a major obstacle.

There is no doubt that in recent years Irish nationalists and republicans are much more vociferous about making an economic case for unification. The volume of such claims has been strongest when the Republic of Ireland economy has been in a boom phase such as during the early 1990s to 2007 or, again, since about 2013. In particular, it is sometimes asserted that the recent macroeconomic performance of the Republic of Ireland is much superior to that of its Northern Ireland counterpart in terms of, say, growth of overall output, growth of manufacturing output, level of productivity and level of exports.

Although subject to various caveats, the statistics do suggest that this claim as to superior Republic of Ireland economic performance is largely correct but does this therefore mean that the challenge of the fiscal transfer has been resolved? No. Firstly, and contrary to some claims, the transfer remains a real phenomenon and one that is substantial in scale. Secondly, in the absence of a very large degree of fiscal forbearance from the rest of the UK either in terms of refusing to transfer any debt obligations to a united Ireland or in terms of continuing to subsidise Northern Ireland, it remains unlikely that the Republic of Ireland could afford Northern Ireland.

Notes

1   "The Ireland that we have dreamed of", Wikipedia. Accessed 15 May 2019.

2   James Francis Meenan, *The Irish Economy since 1922* (Liverpool: Liverpool University Press, 1970), p. 273.

3   The population of the 26 counties was 6.5 million in 1841, 3.1 million in 1911 and 3 million in 1926, rising to 4.9 million in 2018 (with Northern Ireland's population being 1.9 million). It is very unclear how Pearse envisaged a dramatic growth in Ireland's population could occur without the economy adopting the sort of high productivity agriculture and industry found in Great Britain and elsewhere.

4   For Pearse's 1906 article and his advocacy of Irish language education see Bryan Fanning, "Patrick Pearse predicts the future", *Blog*, 20 May 2013. *http://www.drb. ie/essays/patrick-pearse-predicts-the-future/*. Accessed 15 May 2019. Pearse was obviously writing before the issue of global warming came to the fore! To be fair to Pearse, during Terence O'Neill's period as Northern Ireland Prime Minister consideration was given to draining Lough Neagh.

5   Meenan, idem, p. 267.

6   Cormac Ó Gráda, *Ireland: A New Economic History, 1780-1939* (Oxford: Clarendon, 1995), p. 348. Also, Meenan, idem, p. 28. Even in the nineteenth century some nationalist leaders such as Daniel O'Connell conceded there could be a number of explanations for Ireland's economic difficulties- not just the 1801 Act of Union; R.D. Collison Black, *Economic Thought and The Irish Question 1817-1870* (Cambridge: Cambridge University Press:, 1960), p. 4.

7   *Irish Times*, 'The economics of independence', 25-27 May 1959. Quoted in Cormac Ó Gráda, *A Rocky Road: The Irish Economy since the 1920s* (Manchester: Manchester University Press, 1997), p. 226.

8   *Ó Gráda, 1995, op.cit., p. 402.* Kieran Anthony Kennedy, Thomas Giblin and Deirdrie McHugh, *The Economic Development of Ireland in the Twentieth Century* (London: Routledge, 1988), p. 101.

9   David Johnson, 'The Northern Ireland economy 1914-39' in Liam Kennedy and Philip Ollerenshaw (eds.), *An Economic History of Ulster* (Manchester: Manchester University Press, 1985), p. 189.

10   The idea that current prosperity vindicates the independence project runs throughout Gunther Thumann and Senator Mark Daly, 'Northern Ireland's Income and Expenditure in a reunification scenario', *Research Paper for the Joint Oireachtas Committee on the Implementation of the Good Friday Agreement* (Oireachtas: Dublin, 2018). The title "Europe's shining light" was used by the *Economist* newspaper in its edition 15 May 1997: *Economist*, 'Lessons and questions for an economic transformation', Leading article.

[11]   See Kevin Hjortshøj O'Rourke, 'Independent Ireland in comparative perspective", *Irish Economic and Social History,* vol. 44, no. 1, 2017, pp. 19-45. O'Rourke argues it is important not to exaggerate the extent to which the Republic of Ireland was unusually protectionist in the 1950s-60s. Nevertheless, the average tariff rate data he presents show that the Republic of Ireland did have a higher rate of protectionism than Austria, Finland, Germany, Norway, Sweden and Switzerland during 1950-72.

[12]   Ó Gráda, 1997, op.cit., p. 34.

[13]   The Republic of Ireland corporation tax system has three features which increase its attractiveness to international businesses when compared to the systems operating in the UK, much of the rest of the EU or the US: first, a relatively low stated rate of taxation (12.5 p[er cent in recent decades), second, a relatively low effective rate of taxation (estimated as even lower than 12.5 per cent) and, third, a capacity to shift on profits earned in the Republic of Ireland to tax havens in other parts of the world. That corporate tax system provides an incentive for international businesses to manipulate their internal transfers so as to maximise the stated profits earned in their Republic of Ireland operations. By implication, recorded value added and hence GDP in the Republic of Ireland is boosted without necessarily a correspond-ing level of 'real' output alongside the measured output.

[14]   The very high measured Republic of Ireland GDP growth in 2015 was the result of a combination of the introduction of a change in the definition of national income in the European system of national accounts alongside the strong representation of the international firm sector in the Republic of Ireland economy. Specifically, the jump in the 2015 level of GDP has been attributed to: (1.) contract manufacturing which is work done by Irish firms but overseas, (2.) tax inversion which is movement of profits by international firms into their Irish subsidiaries, (3.) allocation of patents to the Irish subsidiaries of international firms and (4.) the value of capital leasing by Irish based aircraft leasing firms. All of these four activities increased measured GDP but did not necessarily increase either employment or 'real' economic activity within the Republic of Ireland to any significant extent. See, *Irish Times,* "Ireland's GDP figures: Why 26% economic growth is a problem", 15 July 2016. Whilst the problematic nature of the Irish economic growth data for 2015 was obvious, as early as the 1980s-90s a number of Irish economists expressed strong doubts about the growth rates expressed in the official statistics. These sceptics included Jim O'Leary, Antoin Murphy, Paul Tansey and Raymond Crotty- see Ó Gráda, 1997, op.cit., p. 33.

[15]   For comparison of the growth rates including adjustment for the international firms in the Republic of Ireland see, 'Winter forecast 2019', *Economic Eye* (Dublin: EY, 2019). Importantly, it is not only the case that international firms operating in the Republic of Ireland have much higher productivity than businesses in Northern Ireland, but domestically owned businesses in the Republic of Ireland also now

have a productivity advantage compared to the Northern Ireland economy: Paul Goldrick-Kelly and Paul MacFlynn, 'Productivity on the island of Ireland- A tale of three economies', *Working Paper*, Number 2018/17 (Nevin Economic Research Institute (NERI): Belfast, October 2018). https://www.nerinstitute.net/research/productivity-on-the-island-of-ireland-a-tale-of-three-economies/

[16]   S. McGuinness and A. Bergin, 'The political economy of a Northern Ireland border poll', *Discussion Paper*, no. 12496 (IZA Institute of Labour Economics, Bonn, July 2019).

[17]   An economic forecasting model is a collection of a very large number of mathematical relationships or equations relating to the determinants of major economic variables such as output, employment, consumption and investment and the inter-relationship of such variables. This particular forecasting model was part of the sub-set of models called Competitive General Equilibrium (CGE) models. See, Kurt Hübner and KLC Consulting, *Modelling Irish unification* (Vancouver BC: KLC Consulting, 2015). Whilst Hübner appears to have updated his modelling in 2018 we have not been able to source this version: . Kurt Hübner and Renger H van Nieuwkoop, 'The costs of non-unification: Brexit and the unification of Ireland', *Report* (publisher unknown, 2018). See: *Irish Times,* 'Hard Brexit could cost island of Ireland euro 42.5bn over seven years', 7 November 2018. It appears Hübner remains very optimistic about the extent to which unity would provoke an upsurge in Northern Ireland productivity and that he continues to assume no trade frictions would develop between Northern Ireland and Great Britain.

[18]   These points were made by the German economist Gunther Thumann who was working at the IMF during the early period of German unification. See, Thumann and Daly, 2018, op.cit., p. 12 and p. 15.

[19]   Hübner and KLC Consulting, Idem, p. x.

[20]   See NISRA (Northern Ireland Statistics and Research Agency), 'Northern Ireland Broad Economy Sales and Export Statistics', *Report* (NISRA: Belfast, 2017). Admittedly, the most recent NISRA data indicate that in 2017 as compared to 2016 Northern Ireland sales to Great Britain fell very substantially by more than £2bn. If these data are taken at face value it has been suggested that the decline between 2016 and 2017 was partly explained by the closure of one cigarette manufacturing factory in Northern Ireland. The Northern Ireland sales figures for 2017 were: to Great Britain £11.3bn, to Republic of Ireland £3.9bn, to rest of EU £2bn and to rest of the world £4.3bn: See, NISRA, 'Northern Ireland Broad Economy Sales and Export Statistics', *Report* (NISRA: Belfast, 2018).

[21]   Such policies are recommended in David M.W.N. Hitchens, Karin Wagner and John Esmond Birnie, *Closing the Productivity Gap* (Aldershot,: Avebury, 1990), Birnie and Hitchens, op.cit. and Esmond Birnie, Richard Johnston, Laura Heery and Elaine Ramsey, "A critical review of competitiveness measurement in Northern Ireland", *Regional Studies*, online publication, March 2019.

[22] Department of Finance and Personnel, Net fiscal balance report 2012-13 to 2013-14, *Report* (Department of Finance and Personnel: Belfast, October 2015). Also, ONS, 'Country and regional public sector finances: financial year ending 2018', *Article* (ONS: Newport, May 2019).

[23] 3 per cent nominal GDP growth could be achieved by a combination of 2 per cent GDP growth in real terms and per cent % annual inflation. There is an argument that, to the extent that the Republic of Ireland's GDP measurement is exaggerated given the international firm sector and distortions related to the corporate tax system, a lower measure of Republic of Ireland income/output should be used (such as GNI: Gross National Income, see Table 9.2, above). By implication, the debt/income ratio would be higher.

[24] An assumption sometimes made by advocates of unity is that there would be no such obligation.

[25] In recent years borrowing costs for the Irish government have been as low as 1-2 per cent per annum but by historical standards those are very low rates. It might be prudent to assume that the next ten-twenty years will see some increase in long run interest rates: *Irish Times*, 'Think tank calls on Government to "borrow billions" to fund social housing', 9 October 2014. For the recent decline in the public debt/GDP ratio in the Republic of Ireland and the prospects for that ratio in the future see *Irish Independent*, 'On borrowed time: Ireland's deceptive debt numbers', 24 January 2016. In 2018 the level of public debt was euros 206.2bn, equivalent to 65% of the Republic or Ireland's GDP: *http://tradingeconomics.com/irelnad/government-debt-to-gdp*, accessed 8 May 2019.

[26] Kevin Meagher, *A United Ireland: Why Unification is Inevitable and How it Will Come About* (London: Biteback Publishing: London, 2016).

[27] For various forecasts of the likely impact of Brexit in the UK and interpretations of those forecasts and their accuracy see: Ken Coutts, Graham Gudgin and Jordan Buchanan, 'How the economics profession got it wrong on Brexit', *Working Paper*, no. 493 (Centre for Business Research: Cambridge University, January 2018).

http://www.cbr.cam.ac/fileadmin/user_upload/centre-for-business-research/downloads/working-papers/wp493.pdf

Graham Gudgin, Ken Coutts, Neil Gibson and Jordan Buchanan, 'The macro-economic impact of Brexit: Using the CBR macroeconomic model of the UK economy', *Journal of Self-Governance and Management Economics*, vol. 6, no. 2, 2018, pp. 7-9.

https://addletonacademicpublishers.com/conents-jgme/1164-volume-6-2-2018/3129-the-macro-economic-impact-of-brexit-using-the-cbr-macro-economic-model-of-the-uk-economy-ukmod

28   *Newsletter,* 'Irish unity makes economic sense', 31 August 2018. In June 2019, how-
     ever, the former *Sinn Fein* leader was reported as arguing unity and especially a
     border poll should only be progressed after sufficient planning. See *Irish News,*
     'Gerry Adams calls on Dublin government to plan for a united Ireland', 8 June 2019.

29   HM Treasury, *Public Expenditure Statistical Analysis* (London: HM Treasury,2017).

30   ONS (Office for National Statistics), 'Country and regional public sector finances:
     year ending March 2016', *Article* (Newport: ONS:, May 2017).

31   In recent years, given the decline in world oil prices and the run-down of North
     Sea production, the Treasury yield from oil and gas related taxes is much smaller
     than it once was.

32   *If* existing Republic of Ireland common and international services are characterised
     by some slack and could therefore raise productivity, or to the extent there are
     substantial economies of scale in their production, then the ability to service 1.9m
     extra people without increasing spending is more likely. However, there may not be
     much slack in the existing provision and these are usually service sector activities
     where economies of scale are not likely.

33   Thumann and Daly, 2018, op.cit.

34   There is some confusion as to which year is being referred to. In the earlier part of
     Thumann and Daly, 2018, idem, p. 4, 2012-13 is referred to but later on when the
     data are presented in more detail 2013-14 is used.

35   One of the tweaks made in the third Home Rule Bill of 1912 as compared to its
     nineteenth century predecessors in the attempt to make the proposed Dublin
     Parliament more viable was an undertaking that the London government would
     continue to fund old age pensions in Ireland. That proposal was never actually
     put into practice and related to a UK central government subsidy of a devolved
     government rather than a transfer payment to an independent, sovereign state.

36   Economists note that 'free riding' is a common problem- a situation where it is hard
     to exclude those who fail to pay for a certain service from continuing to enjoy the
     benefits of that service. In passing, it may be worth noting that differing views as
     to whether people in Northern Ireland should contribute to wider international
     defence obligations has been a persistent fault line between unionism and Irish
     nationalism/republicanism. The government of the Irish Free State opted for neu-
     trality in 1939-45, a neutrality which increased the difficulty of defeating Nazi
     Germany and yet it is doubtful if Ireland's freedom and independence could have
     been guaranteed if Hitler had won the war. Notwithstanding this, de Valera's neu-
     trality policy continues to be hailed as a success: See O'Rourke, op.cit. Post-1949
     the Republic of Ireland continued to free ride- this time on NATO. None of this
     is to downplay the fact that many individuals coming from the Irish nationalist or

THE NORTHERN IRELAND QUESTION

republican traditions in either Northern Ireland or the Free State chose to serve in the British Armed Forces during the Second World War. McGuinness and Bergin, op.cit, also imply that post-unification the obligation on Northern Ireland to allow for defence spending would be reduced.

[37] In fact, the bulk of UK public debt outstanding in 2019 can be attributed to borrowing to finance the post-Second World War welfare state. The share attributable to, say, spending on the Falklands and Iraq-Afghanistan Wars would be small. See Mark Daly, Brexit and the future of Ireland and its people in peace and prosperity, *Report by the Joint Oireachtas Committee on the Implementation of the Good Friday Agreement* (Dublin: *Oireachtas,* 2017).

[38] NISRA, 'NI in profilie: Key statistics on Northern Ireland', *Report* (Belfast: NISRA,14 February 2019).

[39] Oireachtas Research and Library Service, UN Human Development Index, *Research for Senator Mark Daly* (Dublin: *Oireachtas* Library and Research Service,February 2016), appended to Thumann and Daly, 2018, op.cit.

[40] That third indicator being itself an average of two variables: average number of years in school and average number of expected years in school for a recent school entry cohort.

[41] For caveats see Oireachtas Library and Research Service, op.cit., p. 3 and pp. 7-8. For the reference to this research and an inference that post-Brexit quality of life in Northern Ireland could be about to slump to levels seen in countries such as Belarus or Kazakhstan, see Thumann and Daly, 2018, pp. 26-7.

[42] John FitzGerald and Edgar Morgenroth, 'The Northern Ireland Economy', *Paper to the Dublin Economic Workshop,* Dublin, 14 September 2018. Paper available online at dublineconomics.com. My understanding is that a fuller version of their paper is forthcoming in the *Journal of the Statistical and Social Inquiry Society of Ireland.*

[43] Comments during visit to Dublin 3 April 2019: *Guardian,* 'Angela Merkel promises support for avoiding hard border in Ireland', 4 April 2019.

[44] David M.W.N. Hitchens, Karen Wagner and John Esmond Birnie, East German Productivity and the Transition to the Market Economy (Aldershot: Avebury, 1993).

[45] Thumann, 'Timeline of events in German re-unification', in Thumann and Daly, 2018, op.cit., p. 15.

[46] At one point, Thumann does recognise there are major differences between the German and Irish experiences: 'The only other major real life longitudinal study that comes anywhere near the same type of experiment is the partition of Germany. However, this was an entirely different political and economic experiment with the "control" being West Germany with democratic institutions versus the political and economic structure of communist East Germany. We are well aware how that

experiment ended. The situation on the island of Ireland was different because the fundamentals of democracy were the political structures on both parts of the border...', Thumann in Thumann and Daly, 2018, idem., p. 18.

[47]   BBC News online, 'East German border claims 327 lives, says Berlin study', 8 June 2017. Accessed 17 May 2019.

[48]   Paul Gosling, 'The economic effects of an all island economy 2018', *Report*, (publisher unstated, April 2018).

[49]   *Belfast Telegraph*, 'Unionists are facing a perfect storm of Brexit and demographic shift', 22 February 2018.

[50]   The Northern Ireland Civil Service produced an estimate of 40,000 jobs 'at risk' on account of Brexit. An economic forecasting model suggested in the worst, 'no deal', case 15,000-18,500 fewer jobs in the long run (in fifteen years time). The Executive Office, 'Northern Ireland trade and investment data under "No Deal"', *Report* Belfast: (The Executive Office, July 2019). Fraser of Allander Institute, 'The direct trade impact of EU exit scenarios on Northern Ireland's long-term economic performance', *Report* (Glasgow: Fraser of Allander Institute, September 2019).

[51]   Gosling may view the continuation of the fiscal transfer as an inducement which might make unionists more likely to consent to unification. Amongst other sweeteners proposed in his report he argues that some Orange parades could continue in a united Ireland just as some already happen in County Donegal and a physical connection (a bridge) might be built between Northern Ireland and Scotland. Regarding the proposal of a North Channel bridge, the Scottish Government has said they will give it some consideration and the DUP did mention the proposal in their 2015 election manifesto. Nevertheless, the financial cost of a bridge would probably be huge, upwards of £21 billion. It is hard to see how even over the long run, say fifty years, the economic benefits would come anywhere close to the costs: *Belfast Telegraph*, 'Economy Watch: Bridge to Scotland might have to stay as pie in the sky', 19 March 2019.

[52]   McGuinness and Bergin, op.cit., similarly recommend some sort of transitional period during which the UK would continue to pick up all or most of the fiscal tab.

[53]   John FitzGerald and Edgar Morgenroth, op.cit.

[54]   Current levels of investment per head and hence capital accumulated per head are likely to be a key determinant of levels of output per head in the future. A country or region (Northern Ireland?) which chooses to opt for a relatively high level of consumption now but that relatively low level of investment is likely to result in a relatively low level of income per head in the future. Unless, of course, there is some sort of outside intervention (continued high levels of fiscal transfer?).

[55]   As well as being a media commentator, McWilliams is also an adjunct Professor at the Business School in Trinity College Dublin.

56 *Financial Times*, 'Why the idea of a united Ireland is back in play', *Life and Arts Section*, 30 November 2018.

57 Using the average annual market exchange rate for 2017 as supplied by the HMRC website. Northern Ireland export data for 2017 in NISRA 2018, op.cit.

58 *Belfast Telegraph*, 'Demographics are shifting towards a united Ireland- we must have a plan', 26 June 2017.

59 See article by Graham Gudgin, 'A united Ireland is not inevitable and here is why', *Belfast Telegraph*, 19 December 2018.

60 Whilst there have been claims that Brexit will re-ignite physical force republicanism it is hard to assess the Brexit-related threat from the so-called "dissident" republican paramilitaries. Undoubtedly, such movements are opportunistic but they already existed before June 2016. In any case, the threat of more republican violence should not be allowed to exercise a veto over UK policy options. The available data on paramilitary incidents suggest a decline during 2008-March 2018 and especially during 2016-March 2018: Table "Ongoing paramilitary activity in Northern Ireland" on the website "thedetail. tv". Even in the most recent PSNI data the number of paramilitary-related shootings and bombings actually declined comparing September 2018-September 2019 to the previous 12 months, although there was an increase in the number of assaults: *Belfast Telegraph*, 'PSNI statistics show rise in paramilitary style assaults', 5 October 2019.

61 Policy Department for Citizens' Rights and Constitutional Affairs, DG for Internal Policies of the Union, Smart Border 2.0 Avoiding a hard border on the island of Ireland for customs control and the free movement of people, *Report* (Brussels: DG for Internal Policies of the Union,, November 2017). A range of technical and administrative facilitations exist around the world to handle tariff and non-tariff barriers *with reduced frictions at the border*, Prosperity UK/Alternative Arrangements Commission 18 July 2019, Alternative arrangements for the Irish Border, *Report*, London.

62 See Coutts, Gudgin and Buchanan, op.cit.

63 HM Treasury have produced three major pieces of analysis regarding the potential economic impact of Brexit:

HM Treasury, The immediate economic impact of leaving the EU, *Report* (London: HM Treasury, April 2016).

https://www.gov.uk/government/publications/hm-treasury-analysis-the-immediate-economic-impact-of-leaving-the-eu

HM Treasury, The long term economic impact of EU membership, Report (London: HM Treasury, April 2016). *https://www.gov.uk/government/publications/hm-treasury-analysis-the-long-term-economic-impact-of-eu-membership-and-the-alternatives*

UK Government, EU exit long term economic analysis, *Report* (London: HM Treasury, November 2018).

https://www.gov.uk/government/publications/exiting-the-european-union-publications Independent forecasters the Fraser of Allander Institute used a somewhat different approach to the Treasury- they did not make any allowance for any consequence from reduced market access to lower rates of productivity growth (see the argument in the main text, above, that there is a lack of evidence of a connection from UK access to the EU's single market to UK or Northern Ireland productivity growth). They produced a much lower forecast of the output reduction compared to the trend which might be attributed to a 'no deal 'Brexit after 16 years: 3-4 per cent in Northern Ireland rather than about 9 per cent : Fraser of Allander, op.cit.

[64] See, *Belfast Telegraph*, ' "No deal Brexit would cost NI £5bn a year", says CBI', 22 January 2019.

[65] *Belfast Telegraph*, 'If the Dublin government wants to indulge in rhetoric of a "new Ireland" then it needs to consider rejoining the Commonwealth', 25 March 2019.

[66] In 2015 for the 24-30 year old age cohort about 10 per cent in Northern Ireland had only primary level or the most basic level of qualifications. In the Republic of Ireland that proportion was only 3 per cent : McGuinness and Bergin, op.cit. Of course, the lower level of qualification in the Northern Ireland work-force is a product of two things – outputs from education and training and the extent of out-migration (especially of the highly qualified). A moot point is whether unification would help to root the highly qualified within the Northern Ireland region or would the traditional gravitation pool to London only be strengthened (together with an increase in the out-flow to Dublin)?

[67] FitzGerald and Morgenroth, op.cit. They doubted, for example, whether the UK government would continue to bear the cost of state pensions in Northern Ireland after unity.

[68] Gudgin was responding to some of the claims made by McWilliams in *Financial Times*, 30 November 2018, op cit. See, *Belfast Telegraph*, 'A united Ireland is far from inevitable', 19 December 2018.

[69] See *The Future of England Survey*: *Irish Times*, 'Post-Brexit Britain may not want to pay for Northern Ireland', 8 December 2018. Also, *Guardian*, 'English voters grow resentful of Scotland's privileges', 22 January 2012.

[70] Thumann and Daly, 2018, op.cit., p. 15.

[71] The transfer payment and some of the public spending it facilitates may even be detrimental to the efficiency, productivity and competitiveness of the economy. FitzGerald and Morgenroth op.cit. make this claim. This is an old argument: Hitchens, Wagner and Birnie, op.cit.

[72] The existence of super-parity was noted in a recent Department of Finance briefing document: in 2016-17 the average household in Wales, a UK region which is very similar to Northern Ireland in terms of average income and unemployment rates, was paying £600 more each year than its Northern Ireland counterpart in terms of the combination of Welsh council tax and water charges compared to Northern Ireland domestic rates (Northern Ireland does not have domestic water charges). Department of Finance, Briefing on the Northern Ireland Budgetary Outlook 2018-20 (Belfast: Department of Finance, November 2017). A more optimistic interpretation of the DUP's future behaviour might note that its pre-manifesto document in the December 2019 general election campaign did contain a commitment to adding increased productivity, infrastructure and skills to Northern Ireland's previously favourable performance in terms of jobs generation: *Our Plan Let's Get Northern Ireland Moving Again.*

[73] McGuinness and Bergin, op.cit.

[74] Meenan, op.cit., p. 273.

[75] S. McBride, *Burned- The Inside Story of the"cash-for-ash" Scandal and Northern Ireland's Secretive New Elite* (Dublin: Merrion Press, 2019), pp. 355-6: 'The scandal is likely to have immediate implications for the next time Stormont's politicians go to the Treasury with a begging bowl asking for more money. And at some point, if middle England realises it is paying for these sorts of scandals, there will be a day of reckoning'.

[76] "I do not recollect ever, during nearly 10 years for which I have been Finance Minister, to have received from a Secretary for Ireland ... a single suggestion for the reduction of any expense whatever": Simon Heffer, *The Age of Decadence: Britain 1880 to 1914* London: Windmill Publishing, 2017), p. 272.

[77] Andy Bielenberg and Raymond Ryan, *An Economic History of Ireland since Independence* (London: Routledge, 2013), p. 43 and p. 197.

[78] FitzGerald and Morgenroth (2018) hint at this ambivalent conclusion. For a similarly measured conclusion: 'Some speak of Irish reunification as the only way out of the Brexit conundrum. This may be so some time in the future but I am not at all convinced that either part of Ireland is ready for reunification now or soon economically, culturally or politically. Too much healing is needed and this will take a long, long time. However, we need to focus on what sort of society is possible and necessary both in the Republic of Ireland and Northern Ireland', Tom Healey, 'Brexit- an example of radical agnosis', *NERI Blog*, 5 April 2019. https://www.nerinstitute.net/blog/2019/04/05/brexit-an-example-of-radical-agnosis/

10

Buried lives: the Protestants of southern Ireland

Robin Bury

Personal recollection

I was brought up in various Church of Ireland parishes in Co. Cork: first in Skibbereen in west Cork where my father, Phineas Bury, was a curate from 1947 to 1949. Then Castletownroche and St. Mary's Church, Ballyhooly, 1950–52; and finally, Cloyne, Ballycotton and Whitegate where my father was first rector and later dean of Cloyne for eighteen years from 1954 to 1972.

In 1953 I was a day boy at the nearby boys' secondary school, Midleton College. Every day I left my bike in the shed by Cloyne cathedral before getting the bus from Cloyne to Midleton. The Roman Catholic curate lived in a large house across the road from the cathedral. One afternoon I collected my bike, to cycle home, and went to the little gate that opened on the pavement in front of the cathedral. There stood the Catholic curate outside the gate, holding it firmly closed. He had been waiting for me, the heretical son of a heretical Dean. He was dressed in black and, to a twelve-year-old boy, was very tall and threatening.

'Do you know who owns this cathedral?' he asked.

I was too stunned to reply.

'Go and tell your father it belongs to the Catholic church, not to his church. It was stolen from the Catholic church long ago at the time of the Reformation and should be returned to it.'

He then opened the gate to let me out and strode across the road to his house.

I cycled home to tell my parents. My father explained that hundreds of years ago the cathedral was owned by the Roman Catholic church but when the Henrician Reformation came in England, it became a Protestant church, or an Anglican one. He also told me the modern Roman Catholic cathedral in nearby Cobh was much larger and easier to maintain than the Norman one in Cloyne, where only a handful of Church of Ireland people attended. He chose to ignore the Catholic curate. Whether he told the Church of Ireland bishop of Cork I do not know. But that day, as a gentle person, he no doubt let it be, as was the way with southern Protestants.

About thirty years later I visited my father's grave in Cloyne cathedral. The cathedral was full of people, mainly Catholics, at his funeral on 7 November 1973. I met a parishioner visiting her parents' grave. I had just retired, and she asked me if I intended to retire to Cloyne. I told her I did not think so and she replied, 'You are right. There are few of us left here anymore. Most left, like you and your brothers and sisters.'

Why, I wondered, had Church of Ireland numbers declined so dramatically since independence? Why were they outsiders growing up in County Cork in the 1950s and 1960s, as my brother John asked me? This set me on a new course at the age of sixty-five, first doing an M.Phil. in Trinity College, Dublin in 2012/13, where I had studied the effects on southern Protestants of the violent, revolutionary period 1920–26. Later I researched by interviews attitudes of some Protestants in to-day's Republic of Ireland. This led to a book which was published in March 2016 called *Buried Lives: The Protestants of Southern Ireland*.

The myth of a Protestant sanctuary

The chapter is a summary of *Buried Lives* detailing the widespread intimidation and attacks on southern Protestants from 1920 to 1923, the enforced emigration of up to 48,000, the burning of 276 of their so called 'big houses,' further widespread sectarian attacks in 1935, the Church of Ireland's futile opposition to compulsory Irish in primary and secondary schools, their sharp drop in numbers until recent times and, finally, their position in modern, increasingly multicultural, secular Ireland where, however, Anglophobia is still dominant, as seen by the state's policy over

Brexit and the back stop border. The great crusading journalist Eoghan Harris, in articles in the *Sunday Independent*, has tirelessly pointed out Fine Gael's policy of isolating northern Irish unionists within the EU single market and customs union, emphasizing Fine Gael's Anglophobic approach to the Brexit negotiations.

The abandonment of southern Protestants by unionists in Northern Ireland needs to also be raised. Under Carson and Craig, before World War 1, Northern unionists rejected the third Home Rule bill in favour of Partition and this led to the prolonged isolation of southern Protestants. Historian Liam Kennedy muses about the refusal of southern unionist Carson and northern loyalists to accept the third Home Rule bill when writing:

> Nor is it obvious how a devolved parliament in Dublin, with limited powers and subject to the oversight of the Westminster parliament, could have seriously impaired the liberties of Ulster and Irish unionists, particularly as unionists would constitute a significant and voluble minority within a new parliament. The Home Rule legislation itself incorporated various safeguards to ensure an Irish devolved parliament would not interfere with religious freedom, while discrimination on sectarian grounds was also ruled out.[1]

The refusal of the Northern Ireland unionists to accept the third Home Rule bill, under the leadership of a southern Irish Protestant, Sir Edward Carson, left southern Protestant and Catholic loyalists abandoned, with no regrets by Carson and his followers, then, nor up to present times. They were left to their fate in a new Catholic, nationalist state. There they lived in isolated, vulnerable communities and in the early days of the Free State were often intimidated and attacked. Later, in the words of the Canadian historian Donald Akenson, '... the Protestants were tolerated and well treated as a religious minority but were penalised and ill-treated as a cultural minority' ... 'one of the cherished myths of Irish society has been that since independence southern Ireland has been a virtual sanctuary for the Protestants.'[2]

The book *Buried Lives* challenges the myth that the Free State and its successors was a 'sanctuary' for Protestants. The 1916 Proclamation made it clear that 'membership of the nation was not voluntary, but compulsory and hereditary, involving Ireland's claims on all its 'children' and resources and the rejection of all competing and contrasting aspirations. This did not bode well for the minority.'[3] The minority, with a few southern atypical Protestant exceptions such as Erskine Childers, Robert Barton, Constance Markievicz and later Douglas Hyde, was opposed to separation from the United Kingdom and the nationalist definition of Irishness as being Gaelic, Catholic and Anglophobic.

Why the sharp decline in southern Protestant numbers from 1920 to 1926? There had been a decline in southern Protestant numbers prior to the census of 1911. However, this decline conformed with the Catholic decline. From 1861 to 1911 Protestant numbers in the twenty-six counties went down by 30 per cent. But from 1911 to 1926 the decline in southern Protestant numbers was unprecedented, a fall of 33 per cent , while Catholic numbers remained almost static. After excluding Protestants in the British army and the Royal Irish Constabulary (RIC) who left, southern Irish men who fell in the First World War, estimated 'normal' emigration and fertility rate, I estimate up to 48,000 left, many as families.

Scarcely a county escaped incidents of intimidation and harassment, Carlow and King's counties (Leix) being exceptions. Dublin saw an exodus of the Orange Order and of many working-class Protestants: 'Practically the whole of the Protestant working-class—perhaps 10,000—fled from Dublin in the early 1920's.'[4]

'In 1920 at Mullingar in the then King's county, 'disgraceful scenes' were reported when business premises of nearly all Protestants were attacked … Furthermore, many the Protestants throughout County Westmeath got notice to quit.'[5] The *Church of Ireland Gazette* reported on 9 September 1921 that a rector in an urban area in the west had seen his congregation reduced by half and on 7 October: 'Over a large part of the country the already sparse congregations are being reduced to vanishing point … anyone who knows Southern Ireland knows also the undercurrent of feeling urging the elimination of Protestantism.'[6]

A relative of mine, David Hunt, whose family once lived near mine near Adare in county Limerick, sent me an email on 16 October 2017 describing vividly what happened to Annie Hunt, the widow of his great great uncle John Hunt, in 1920 when she was 82 years of age:

Anyhow, this old Protestant lady, Aunt Annie, then aged 82 and living alone at Friarstown, in the country side five miles out of Limerick, was repeatedly threatened by Republicans. On one occasion, ten tons of her hay were burnt. It may have been that some vindictive local committed this outrage rather than the IRA (Irish Republican Army). Surprisingly, the old lady was not frightened or disturbed by the incident. Another night while she was recovering from a bout of pneumonia and aged 80, a group of 18-20 armed young IRA men broke into the house and threatened to shoot her. She described the latter incident to her nephew Freddie.

'You know, Freddie, I can't help laughing when I think of those 18 or 20 scallywags marching into my room at that hour of the night, with revolvers in their hands. If you had only seen them! It looked like a burlesque out of one of Gilbert and Sullivan's operettas. A regular lot of gossons [boy servants] in military formation and taking themselves very seriously at that.

This account shows the dominant spirit of Protestant Annie who may well have been a character in a Sommerville and Ross novel.

County Tipperary was one of the counties worst hit by violence. Bishop Miller, Bishop of Cashel, Emly and Waterford said on 8 October 1922 during the civil war that: 'Many of our people were driven from their homes, many others left through fear of violence with the result that many of our parishes … were unable to meet their financial responsibilities.'[7]

There was a refugee crisis in London in 1922 post the treaty of December 1921, which saw the birth of the Free State. Some 20,000 people fled during the civil war, including Catholic policemen from the disbanded RIC.

There was a mini pogrom in the Bandon Valley in April 1922 when thirteen Protestants were murdered and a further sixteen targeted. The Canadian, Peter Hart, was the first historian to bring this to light in his book *The I.R.A. and Its Enemies*. A heated controversy followed involving the denial by some Irish historians of any sectarian motive but both Michael Collins and Erskine Childers had no doubt. They condemned the attacks as being sectarian which was in fact the case as Peter Hart cogently argues:

These men were shot because they were Protestants (sic). No Catholic
Free Staters, landlords or spies were shot or even shot at. The sectarian
antagonism which drove this massacre was interwoven with the political
hysteria and local vendettas, but it was sectarianism none the less[8]

Collins was pre-occupied with negotiations with opponents of the treaty,
including Childers, and in no position to put the murderers of Protestants
on trial. Also, he believed that the attacks were triggered by murders of
Catholics in Belfast at that time.

The reaction of Catholic bishops to the Bandon Valley pogrom was strong:

> We have seen too many instances … of barbarous treatment of our
> Protestant fellow countrymen. Not only has their property been at times
> unjustly seized, they have themselves occasionally driven from homes and
> their lives have in some cases been murderously attacked.[9]

Joseph O'Neill in *Dark-Blood Stain,* when writing about southern
Protestants murdered and targeted in April 1922 thinks they can be compared to the Armenians in Turkey, though the numbers of Armenians
who suffered was far in excess of southern Protestants:

> Both were minorities regarded as a fifth column of the foreign country;
> both suffered a demographic cataclysm unmentioned by dominant
> nationalist histories; and finally, both left a vestigial population in the new
> nation-state whose members instinctively understood that, whatever the
> political and constitutional affirmations to the contrary their citizenship
> was a matter of indulgence and not of right.[10]

O'Neill pointed out that the murderers 'who were members of the IRA,
were never identified or "brought to justice": not by the IRA which at the
time was effectively responsible for law and order in Cork, nor by history.'
O'Neill went on:

> Protestant opponents of the revolution, actual or perceived, were cast as
> informers or Orangemen or British agents and were liable to be 'executed' and,

in death, to be literally labelled as such. The April massacre, however, occurred during the Truce after the Anglo-Irish war. None of the military epithets could be applied to the victims, and their deaths could not be explained in the usual nationalist terms. What was startling that, in the absence of a conventional nationalist explanation, the Catholic community was struck dumb; it possessed no alternative vocabulary with which to speak of the dead.[11]

However, O'Neill is not correct in writing that 'the Catholic community was struck dumb'. Michael Collins, Daniel Colohan, Bishop of Cork, and Eamon de Valera all condemned the murders and thought that they were reprisals for northern murders of Catholics.[12] But the claim that the Protestant murders were 'reprisals' for the murder of Catholics in Northern Ireland is factually and morally problematic. Hart contests the factual status of the 'reprisals' claim and argues that the 'desire for vengeance [that led to the murders] went further back' than the Catholic murders in Northern Ireland.[13] The claim is also morally problematic because it could be construed as an attempt to provide some sort of moral exoneration of the IRA murderers.

One Protestant, John De Burgh in Drumkeen, county Limerick, was attacked. He was forced to leave his farm in September 1920. He returned in February 1922 but in September 1924 the IRA returned and attempted to kill him. De Burgh had a revolver and shot one insurgent dead. He got compensation from the Irish Grants Committee of £8,080 in February 1928. He went with his wife and sisters to Prevost Island, British Colombia and bought a farm there of 1,000 acres. The descendants of John believe he was attacked because he had been a Justice of the Peace. Many Protestant Justices of the Peace were attacked at this time.

In nearby county Clare seventy out of eighty 'Protestant landed families had left county Clare' since 1919.[14] This was an astonishingly large exodus.

Outrages, intimidation and murders of Protestants are dealt with in detail in *Buried Lives* and my research, as well as Donald Wood's, revealed new evidence that a large enforced Protestant exodus took place as mentioned. Irish historians are mostly in denial about this, including the late Professor David Fitzpatrick and Dr Bielenberg, seeking to explain that the large fall in the Protestant population was due to respectively, low fertility rate and, in the case of Dr Bielenberg, by economic depression post the Great War, both positions contradicted in a paper by Donald Wood.[15] He argues that there was a dramatic fall in numbers of Protestant marriages 1921–25[16] due to their exodus 1921–26: 'The loss of a significant part of the child producing age groups through migration, along with many of their dependents, seems a far more likely cause of the sharp Protestant fertility rate drop.'[17]

Further, Brian Walker has argued:

Elsewhere in the British Isles, there was also a sharp decline in birth rates and fertility in the years 1901 – 26, but this was more than compensated by a significant increase in life expectancy, resulting in a growing population in these places ... A fall in the birth rate of southern Protestants cannot be regarded as relevant for the decline in their overall numbers.[18]

The historian Robert B. McDowell thought southern Protestants and Catholic loyalists were the victims of history and there was an inevitability about their fate:

They had for centuries upheld the authority of the British Empire and 'flourished under its aegis', like 'Germans in Bohemia, Swedes in Finland ... Greeks in Asia Minor, Muslims in the Balkans. Among those abandoned adherents of a lost cause were the unionists in the south and west of Ireland.'[19]

The cause of southern loyalists was a 'lost' one, born out by ugly attacks over a geographically scattered area where their numbers were small. They were targeted not only because of their religion 'but as loyalists ... a matrix of religious, social, and political characteristics and to attack Protestants on any level was perforce to attack the entire constellation.'[20]

The British government eventually accepted responsibility for the losses suffered by its supporters over many centuries. The Irish Grants Committee was formed in 1925 to compensate loyalists in the twenty-six counties who suffered hardship or loss between 11 July 1921 (the truce) and 12 May 1923 (the end of the civil war). The names of two people were required for reference purposes. These had to be a bank manager, a solicitor or a minister of religion. It processed 4,032 cases between October 1926 and November 1930. Of these 2,237 were compensated and the total of the awards was £2,188,549. Nine hundred cases were refused many of which were 'try ons.'[21]

A major part of the outrages against Protestants involved the burning of their houses. A total of 276 so called 'big houses' were burnt from 1920 to 1923.[22] More were burnt later. The reasons varied. Some were burnt because of memories of past deeds seen as anti-Catholic, others as revenge for acts of the 'Black and Tans' against the IRA, others because they were to be occupied by the British army. County Cork was badly hit. Almost fifty were burnt before the Truce in July 1921. Six of these were burnt in May 1921, all around Innishannon, five owned by Protestants, all because the Essex regiment had been burning houses of IRA insurgents in that area.

In Cloyne, where I lived as a boy, Castle Mary was a fine castle owned by Colonel Longfield. The Longfields had come to Ireland from Wales after the English civil war, being Williamites. They held 10,813 acres in 1873, reduced to 670 acres in 1921 as Longfield had sold most of his land to tenants under various land acts.

In September 1920 two men arrived one night when the family was away and burnt the house to the ground, having taken some of the contents. Colonel Longfield was shattered. In the words of a relative, Jane Hayter-Hames, 'It was not just the material loss … it was the brutal statement of feeling; the flames said, "this is what your past here means to us" and the emotional bolt, like a burning arrow, went straight to Longfield's heart.'

Longfield wanted to leave but his English wife, Alice, persuaded him to stay on, not leave like his relatives the Bessboroughs in county Kilkenny, whose mansion was burnt. The Castle Mary stables and coach house were converted and years later that is where my parents went to play bridge with Rita Ponsonby, the daughter of Colonel Longfield. The new Irish Free State compensated them with a decree of £30,000.

It is uncertain why the castle was burnt. An ancestor was said to be responsible for hanging some rebels after the United Irishmen's rebellion in 1798. Some tenants were evicted during the Great Famine in 1848, but that was widespread in Ireland.[23]

The book, *Buried Lives,* details some of the burnings of these 'big houses' so I will mention only two more. One was owned by Lord Langford. It was one of the finest Irish Palladian houses where the Empress Elizabeth of Austria went to hunt on several occasions. The contents were stolen and ended up in local houses. The reason for the burning was that the IRA had been informed that British forces were about to occupy it to start a campaign in the area. However, this was not so. Lord Langford left never to return.

In the last month of the civil war, many country houses were destroyed by anti-treaty republicans. In December 1922 over twenty former unionists were elected or appointed to the new Senate by the Irish government. Republicans now targeted their homes as well as others. Also, the house of Horace Plunkett, in county Dublin, was burnt. He left for England, never to return. He was a patriot and worked to establish co-operative dairying and played a major role in the Irish convention in 1917. He was a senator in the new Irish parliament and the anti-treaty men opposed the Senate and burnt some of the senators' houses. Plunkett was singled out. In all, there were approximately 2,000 'big houses' in the twenty six counties and about 25 per cent were left in ruins. Of these, about thirty were rebuilt with compensation the owners got from the Irish Grants Committee and the Free State.

What was the fate of the vestigial Protestants who stayed on post-independence? The chapter will look at this in four ways. Firstly, the decline in their numbers up to present time and the reasons for the continued fall; secondly the widespread outrages in 1935; thirdly the reaction of Protestants to the imposition of compulsory Irish teaching in 1922; lastly, I will look at the position of Protestants in today's changed, multicultural and more secular Ireland.

Decline in Protestant numbers

First a few comments on the sort of Ireland that emerged post 1921. Don Akenson wrote:

> But the Protestants as a group were now as broken reeds. The Irish situation in 1922-23 was so debilitating that they lost their ability to operate as an effective political bloc. The campaign of intimidation, murder, and arson speeded the pace of Protestant emigration and weakened the determination of those who previously had been involved in political activity.[24]

> Now on the defensive, the minority became intensely aware of their
> isolation and withdrew into a kind of ghetto ... the most striking
> characteristic of the minority in the twenties and thirties, is the persistence
> of precisely this ghetto mentality.[25]

John Dunlop, a Presbyterian minister and former Presbyterian moderator,
wrote: 'The fact is that more than any other single factor, the observed
decline in the Protestant population in the Republic has confirmed northern Protestants in their prejudices and fears.'[26]

New legislation based on Catholic religious teachings was introduced
by the Cumann na nGaedheal government which almost certainly had
an influence on Protestant emigration:

Legislation for film censorship was introduced in 1923 and for book censorship in 1929. Divorce was prohibited in 1925. The Garda Siochana were
consecrated to the Sacred Heart of Jesus in 1923 and then to the Blessed Virgin
in 1930 ... All this, of course, reflected the fact that not only was the population
predominantly Catholic but that in the new state the Catholic church wielded
great influence in a wide range of social, educational and health issues.[27]

In 1911 there were about 226,000 Protestants in the twenty-six counties excluding the military. In 1991 there were only 89,000 native Irish
Protestants, a huge decline of 60 per cent. The overall Protestant population in 2016 increased to 122,000 but of these 33,000 were newly arrived
immigrants, many non-whites from Africa.

The historian Kurt Bowen wrote about the sharp decline in numbers
post-independence in his thorough analysis of demographic trends of
southern Protestants:

> The strong sense of isolation and insecurity created by their small numbers
> intensified in the years after 1926 as they saw their community diminish
> by a further 41% (up to 1971) ... they experienced substantial declines in
> all parts of the country ... although their heaviest losses tended to occur
> in the rural and remote counties of the west.'[28]

Why the fall in numbers? We have seen there was large enforced exodus
from 1920–23 but after that the decline continued. It has been suggested

that low fertility rate caused the decline brought on by the low esteem they suffered in independent Ireland. But Bowen points out that 'in 1946 the Church of Ireland rate was marginally higher than the rates for France, Sweden, and Switzerland, and it was considerably higher than the American or British.'[29] Bowen thought that '... emigration was the fundamental cause of this downward spiral.'[30]

The historian Henry Patterson thought that emigration to Britain was a major factor:

> While the pull of higher wages and salaries in Britain was one dimension of the problem, the fact remained that many had gone to serve in the Forces and ... the reality of low intensity unhappiness with what many southern Protestants saw as the anti-British and confessional nature of the Irish state ... aroused much resentment ... in Donegal, Cavan, and Monaghan with a Protestant population of nearly 15 per cent, there were virtually no Protestants on the public payroll.[31]

The *ne temere* decree of the Catholic church in 1908 was a major influence in lowering Protestant numbers and I will examine its severe imposition by the Irish Catholic church in some detail. It required that in mixed religion marriages the Protestant partner had to sign a document promising that all the children would be baptised as Catholics and raised as Catholics in order to get a dispensation to get married and only in a Catholic church. In addition, the Catholic partner promised to 'work prudently for the conversion of the non-Catholic spouse'.

According to O'Leary[32] the rate of mixed religion marriages was low from 1927 to 1973 at 12.9 per cent for the cohort of female partner. But after that the rate increased sharply to as high as 33.5 per cent by 1991. Bowen conducted research in six parishes in 1971–73 and discovered 'out of a sample of 164 Irish Anglicans, 39 per cent of the grooms and 34 per cent of the brides married Catholics'. His research was mostly from urban areas however and he concluded that: 'Considering this urban bias, we find that mixed religion marriages had risen to approximately 30 per cent by the early 1970s.'[33]

In 1970 *Motu Proprio Matrimonio Mixta* removed the requirement of the Protestant spouse to promise to bring up the children in the

Roman Catholic religion. Furthermore, after 1966 Catholics in mixed religion marriages no longer were to promise to seek the conversion of the Protestant partner. The Catholic partner, however, was required to do all that he or she could to have all the children baptized and brought up in the Catholic church. The non-Catholic partner was to be made aware of these promises made by the Catholic spouse. What we do know is that in Ireland the acceptance of the ending of *ne temere* was less than full hearted by a very conservative Catholic church. In county Cork, Bishop Lucey, insisted on ignoring the Vatican ruling throughout the 1970s but, according to Kurt Bowen, promises were not asked for in most dioceses. Significantly, Declan Deane, a Jesuit priest commented in 1974, when referring to mixed religion marriages, 'where the need for visible inter-church fellowship is most acute, we have seen perhaps the least liberal implementation of the papal instruction.'[34]

There were two high profile mixed religion marriage cases. In the 'Tilson case', the Church of Ireland father married Mary Barnes in 1941 in Dublin. Mary was only sixteen, but she was pregnant and unmarried. Ernest Tilson decided to marry her as at that time there was pressing morality that demanded marriage when the woman was pregnant, unlike in to-day's Ireland. Later, he removed three of his sons from the cramped family home in Dublin (the Tilsons shared the home with Mary Tilson's mother) and placed them in a home in Dun Laoghaire, a Protestant orphanage known as the Bird's Nest. The children were happy there, but the mother was very upset by their disappearance and started habeas corpus proceedings to get the boys back into her custody.

The case first went to the High Court where Justice Gavin Duffy wrote a judgement based on articles 41, 42 and 44.2 of the constitution. He emphasised that article 44.2 gave the Catholic church a 'special position' in the state and that article 42 stated that 'the primary and natural educator of the child is the family.'[35]

The previous legal position gave the father paternal supremacy under ancient common law inherited from Britain which 'ensured the absolute right of the father to determine the religion of his children.'[36] This paternal supremacy had been upheld in the *Frost* case in 1945. However, Justice Duffy overruled this judgement and argued that the prenuptial promise was legally binding.

Tilson appealed to the Supreme Court which supported the Duffy judgement, not on the 'special position' of the Catholic church but based on article 42.1. It ruled that as both parents had agreed to raise the children as Catholics then '… it is not in the power of the father – nor … the mother – to revoke the decision against the will of the other party.'[37] The decision 'sparked outrage in Protestant circles.'[38] The editorial in the *Irish Times* on 7 August 1959 criticised the Supreme Court's decision which 'laid no emphasis on its religious aspect.' The only dissenting judge was Mr Justice Black, Church of Ireland, who asked, 'whether the court would have ruled the same way had the mixed marriage promises favoured the Protestant party.'[39]

Gerard Hogan pointed out that later, in 1983, the Supreme Court ruled that 'a consent motivated by fear, stress, anxiety … cannot constitute a valid consent.' Hogan significantly goes on to write, 'The reality is very probably that Tilson felt by pressing social mores into marrying his wife and had thus little option but to give his consent to the undertaking that they would be raised in the Roman Catholic faith.'[40]

In Fethard-on-Sea in county Wexford in 1957 the Protestant wife of a Catholic farmer who had signed the *ne temere* decree, refused to send her two daughters to the local Catholic school and took them to first Belfast, and then Scotland. As Eugenio Biagini wrote, 'Instead of being regarded as a feminist hero resisting an act of unwarrantable oppression, she was promptly criminalized.'[41]

Protestant businesses were boycotted by Catholics, encouraged by the Catholic priest. There were two small Protestant businesses in the area, a hardware shop and a newsagent. Both suffered devastating loss of revenue as local Catholics stopped buying anything. The local piano teacher, a Protestant, lost most of her pupils and the Church of Ireland school closed because the Catholic teacher left. Eventually the brave mother, Sheila Clooney returned, and the children were educated in the home. Sheila stood up to the Catholic church bullies, unlike her fellow Protestants in mixed religion marriages.

The Taoiseach, de Valera, condemned the boycott which had been reported in *Time* magazine, but did not condemn the Catholic church for the mixed religion marriage promise the Protestant spouse had to take. He instead urged Sheila to 'respect her troth and to return' to her husband.

He had come under pressure to act because the Jewish Lord Mayor of Dublin, Robert Briscoe, had just returned from a visit to the USA and had portrayed Ireland as a tolerant state to minorities, as opposed to the bigotry of both Protestants and Catholics in Northern Ireland. But the boycott continued after de Valera called for it to end.

An excellent film was made about the boycott. Gerry Gregg was the director. He told me that: 'All aspects of the erosion of certain civil liberties are shown in microcosm in Fethard-on-Sea. It also showed the weakness of the temporal authorities which did not intervene and show leadership.' On the example that Sheila Cloney set, Gerry said:

> My contention is that she also revolted against the whole system that was destroying the Protestant community in the Republic at that time and undermining its sense of itself, its sense of equality, its sense of history. If Yeats said they were 'no petty people', by the 1950s they were. They were a poor, pathetic people.

No politician spoke up to oppose the *ne temere* decree with its harmful effects, its very denial of human rights to the Protestant community to choose the religion, with the Catholic partner, of the children in mixed religion marriages. As an orthodox Catholic, de Valera accepted this. So did local politicians and the one Fianna Fail Protestant politician in the Dail, Lionel Booth.

As stated, the two Cloney daughters were home educated. To-day, Eileen lives in Fethard-on-Sea but does not go to either the Church of Ireland church, nor the Catholic one. She told me that the locals are in denial and give the impression 'nothing had happened'. Gerry Gregg said in 1997:

> [T]he scary thing is that still forty years later, it is a challenge to call yourself Irish and not be of the Catholic faith, nor be of the Gaelic tradition, and not be of the political persuasion that look to nationalism as the panacea for the island's solutions.

Bishop Brendan Comiskey of Ferns apologised full-heartedly in 1998, forty one years later. He condemned the 'church leadership' at the time.[42]

Let Eileen have the last word on what two Catholic women she knows told her about Protestant children, no doubt getting their hate filled doctrines from the Catholic church. She emailed me on 2 August 2019 as follows:

> You asked about the lady who told me her parents warned her that " those kind of children in there do not go to heaven so keep away from them ". She was referring to when she was a child ... The reference was towards the Protestant children in Fethard school. She did not believe this to be the case at the time she told me. I hope! A Mayo woman told me the same thing, again she and I were the same age. She had been living in Switzerland and married to a Swiss. She said when they were children in Mayo, they were told 'Protestant children had no souls and when they met on the road they were not to speak to them and to turn the other way'.

Compulsory Irish

Compulsory Irish was imposed on all primary schools in 1922. This was highly unpopular with Protestants. In the words of Kurt Bowen:

> No other government policy provoked such widespread and sustained criticism from Protestants. For forty years, the annual reports of the Church of Ireland' Board of Education repeatedly condemned the compulsory and restrictive character of the regulations.[43]

Arthur A. Luce, a fellow of Trinity College, Dublin, thought Irish was 'eye wash, political window dressing, dope for Republicans, anything but a genuine educational experiment.[44] But such views were outside the unanimous nationalist dedication to reviving Gaelic, re-named Irish, through the schools. The first Taoiseach, William T Cosgrave stated: 'The possession of a cultivated national languages is known by every people who have it to be a secure guarantee of the national future.'[45] Akenson wrote: 'The Irish language came to have mystical, nearly magical properties ... we are dealing with a phenomenon which must be explained not by logic, but by psycho-logic.'[46]

There are two critical factors that were not considered. First, the number of people who spoke Gaelic in 1922, by which time the southern Irish had in effect chosen English as their national language. By 1922 only 17.6 per cent of the population were Irish speakers.[47] Reginald Hindley, who researched the state of the language in depth, wrote that those who opposed the imposition of Gaelic 'were up against lingo-fanatics who through ignorance, lack of perceptiveness, closed minds, excess of ide-alism refuse to accommodate the reality of an English-speaking Ireland.' Hindley also concluded that compulsory Irish was a fundamental error in social psychology by making language 'essential' or 'required by what the public sees as artificial means. "Loyal lies" are told about it for patriotic reasons. They 'honour it as a symbol.'[48]

In 1922 the new government required Irish to be taught for one hour a day in national schools and nature studies, drawing and science were eliminated. Teachers who spoke Irish were required to teach all subjects through it. However, Protestant schools in some rural areas had no teach-ers who spoke Irish and in the 1920s and 30s Irish was not taught. In secondary schools, in 1924 a bonus scheme was introduced for teaching through Irish. For teaching one subject other than Irish through Irish, a 2.5 per cent grant was given but a 25 per cent grant was given for teaching all subjects through Irish, which was simply impossible for Protestant schools.

It has been suggested by Reginald Hindley that successive govern-ments resorted to 'lingo-fascism'. They got stricter as time went on. In 1925 a pass in Irish was required for the intermediate certificate taken at age 15/16 and in 1934 for leaving certificate, the final secondary school examination. How did this effect Protestants? In the early days of the Free State, the lack of knowledge of Irish by Protestants in leading gov-ernment institutions was used to remove them. In the words of Myles Dillon:

All the cultural institutions of the country were in the hands of the Protestants: the Royal Irish Academy, the National Library, the National Gallery, the Royal Irish Academy of Music, the Royal Dublin Society, the Museum, the College of Science, the Botanical Gardens, even the Society of Antiquaries. All that must now be changed: a new administrative class was to be established, and the language was one of the means to be used. Lyster, Eglington, Praeger, Best, Armstrong, Westropp, Sir Frederick Moore, none of these men could have passed the test. None of them could stand a chance of civil service appointment now. I shall not dwell upon that painful subject: I believe that far from helping the language movement, this turning of the screws has destroyed its value as a form of allegiance.[49]

Tom Garvin wrote that compulsory Irish was:

[A]n ideological weapon for nationalist and fundamentalist Catholics, feared by Protestants' and 'used for moral superiority … The extremists confiscated the language much as they had confiscated Gaelic games with a particular political ideology – Protestants naturally excluded themselves (my emphasis) but so did most of the Catholic middle class.[50]

In 1928 a bill was passed that made it mandatory for those who were to qualify in future as Irish lawyers and barristers to pass an Irish examination. Protestant TDs objected but "the garrison must give place to the nation' according to the Fianna Fail TD T. Mullins. Since 2017 Irish is no longer mandatory for lawyers and barristers.

Protestants believed that the 'heavy emphasis on Irish reduced the amount of time available for other more important subjects … educational standards were being eroded by the misguided effort to teach through a language pupils did not understand.'[51] In 1966 a study by the Revd. John MacNamara found:

[T]hat the reasons for the Irish retardation in English language skills relative to British children was the amount of time spent in teaching the Irish language … Irish school children were about seventeen months behind British school children of the same age and background.'[52]

Clearly, the amount of time spent teaching Irish had a detrimental effect on English language skills.

In April 1973 the Fine Gael-Labour coalition government dropped compulsory Irish for the intermediate and leaving certificates but:

'Pupils did not have to offer Irish as an examination subject, but their schools would not earn grants unless the pupils followed the approved curriculum, which included Irish. Further, the bonus-points for writing various papers in Irish are to continue ...'[53]

It is compulsory for students to study Irish for the leaving certificate but it is not compulsory to sit the exam. The four national universities of Ireland require Irish at leaving certificate level. In 2005 the then Taoiseach, Enda Kenny, estimated euro 500 million a year was spent on teaching Irish though he did not specify the total costs to include grants to support the Gaeltacht areas and other ways of encouraging people to speak Irish. In the 2016 census, the number speaking Irish daily outside the educational system was 73,803, representing only 1.7 per cent of the population.

Outbreak of sectarian attacks in 1935

In 1935, there was an outbreak of widespread sectarian outrages against the southern Protestant community, as reported in considerable detail in the National Archives of Ireland. The trigger was an outbreak of violence in Belfast. Catholic frustration with their disadvantaged position led to violence at the end of an Orange parade on 12 July, when rioting broke out and continued to the end of August. Reportedly, eight Protestants and five Catholics were killed and up to 2,000 Catholics were driven from their homes.

Following these riots, there were outrages against Protestants in nineteen of the twenty-six counties of the Free State. A Church of Ireland church was burnt to the ground in county Limerick and attempts were made to burn others, as well as a Masonic lodge and Protestant halls. There were anti-Protestant riots in Limerick and Galway and some individual Protestants were targeted elsewhere. The police reported that these attacks were not 'organized by particular or central organization', though in Galway a trade union was involved. The events below are well recorded in the files of the Justice Department in the National Archives library in Dublin.

Very early on Monday 22 July, some men broke down the door of the Church of Ireland in Killmallock, County Limerick. They poured petrol on the wood inside and burnt the building to the ground. The rectory nearby where Canon Taylor lived was attacked and the windows were broken. The Circuit Judge awarded £4,555 to the Representative Church Body (Church of Ireland). Apparently four men were arrested but never tried, as the jurors 'were canvassed with a view to an acquittal of accused in this case'[54] and eleven refused to convict. A Garda report recommended that the trial be referred to the Central Criminal Court.

In Limerick and Galway, large mobs assembled and targeted Protestant premises and individuals. The plate glass window of a Protestant shop owner was broken on 20 July in Limerick. A large crowd gathered of some 600 young men. They attacked the Protestant mission hall, the Diocesan hall, Archdeacon Waller's house, the Masonic lodge, the Baptist and Presbyterian churches and tried to burn down the Church of Ireland church in Henry Street. The mob shouted, 'We won't leave a Protestant house standing.' The Gardaí decided to bring in military aid and it was reported that fourteen cases of malicious damage and attempted arson were brought. However, the Lord Mayor, District Justice and Catholic clergy sought to interfere, to stop the police making further investigations. A police report from the superintendent stated that 'further proceedings would tend to revive the bitterness and ill-feeling which have died down.'

On 23 July in Galway, dockers refused to unload a coal boat owned by a Belfast man by the name of Kelly. Later the SS Dun Aengus, which sailed to the Aran Islands, was not allowed to leave until the Protestant chief engineer disembarked. A crowd of about 500 assembled and marched with a band, demanding Catholic workers down tools in the Galway Foundry, Connaught Laundry and ESB centre, where the workers refused to leave, and a police baton charged the mob. They dispersed to Eyre Square, where they visited Protestant houses in the area with the band playing. The ATGWU union and two councillors led the way; a police report noted that 'all are of a poor type.'

Two Protestant men were targeted in Marlow, county Tipperary. Richard Pennefather, related to me, was a 70-year-old farmer with over 300 acres of land. He 'lived on very good terms with his immediate members [sic] and had 'a quiet and very honest disposition', according to the police report, and this was borne out by the fact that his two sons assisted in the farming. He had been attacked during the civil war, when his car was commandeered, and attempts were made to make him leave the area so that his farm could be taken. Joseph Abercrombie was Pennefather's secretary, aged 75. He was a retired RIC sergeant who did not take part in politics. He and Pennefather lived very near each other and their houses were shot at by a rifle or rifles on 26 July, but no damage was done. Police had suspicions of who the attackers were but, despite many attempts to find incriminating evidence, could not make any arrests. They believed that 'the real motive for underlying the attacks is agrarianism and that the conditions now prevailing in the North together with some incidents in An Staorstat (the Free State) are merely a cover up for restarting attacks – especially on Mr. Pennefather.'

Masonic halls were targeted in Kells, county Meath, and in Athlone, county Westmeath. In Clones, county Monaghan, the Masonic hall was destroyed, and the Pringle Memorial hall and Plymouth Brethren gospel hall were 'badly damaged.' An attempt was made to burn the Methodist church in Boyle, county Roscommon, in which petrol was poured at the end of pews and set on fire, but little damage was done. The Garda report stated: 'the general public in Boyle are [sic] not in sympathy with any demonstrations by way of retaliation for North of Ireland incidents.' There were a number of other incidents in which individual Protestants were targeted in Listowel, county Kerry, and in Castlepollard, county Meath, where the Church of Ireland church had a notice put up on 21 July warning 'people that attend this church – if this trouble in Belfast goes on much longer we will be compelled to make it hot for you and your friends. To hell with King William.'

In Clones, county Monaghan, the plate-glass windows of W.M. Meighan, a Protestant shop owner, were broken. Furthermore, a letter was sent to T. McDonagh's furniture factory, which read: 'God bless our Pope. Remember Belfast. Up de Valera. To hell with the King. We don't want you or your Orange Bastards in the Free State. We want revenge take a kindly warning you and your orange employees clear out. Beware the IRA.'

In Boyle, county Roscommon, an attempt was made to burn down the Methodist church on 26 July and in Fenit, county Kerry, fifty dockers refused to unload a boat containing coal owned by a Belfast man. The Taoiseach, Eamon de Valera, had no doubt that the riots in Belfast gave rise to these sectarian outrages yet did little to stop the sectarian behaviour. The Gardaí who thoroughly investigated these outrages laid no blame at the feet of any of the Protestants who were attacked. They had provoked no one but had been provoked themselves. It is hard to avoid the conclusion that the Irish Catholic people who were responsible for the attacks were motivated by a desire to remove Protestants from 'their' nation.

Some did leave. According to the unionist *Belfast News Letter*, in 1936, '... Loyalists were finding it more and more difficult to live in the Free State. During the past two or three-years, scores of Cavan and Monaghan families had crossed the border.'[55] Dennis Kennedy adds:

> The conclusive proof that Protestants were being "squeezed out" was that they were undeniably leaving the Free State. Between 1926 and 1936 another drop of roughly 12 per cent, or 25,000, had been recorded in the Protestant population.[56]

The new Ireland

How has the Republic of Ireland changed in recent decades? Put simply, since the fading away in the 1950s of the old nationalist elite of 1916, in the years up to 1973 the new political elite was more concerned about promoting trade and policies designed to attract multi-national companies to give employment to new university graduates and second-level educated youths (to-day these companies employ about 120,000 well-educated Irish nationals). The old emphasis on a protectionist economy, with high tariffs for local industries, was rejected following membership of the European common market in January 1973.

The most important influence on changing popular attitudes to the Catholic church were the many scandals, from the Magdalene laundry abuses of young women to the discovery of a mass grave of babies in Tuam Bon Secours Mother and Baby Home. In addition, many paedophilia scandals among Catholic clergy were revealed by the media. The once profound national obedience to Catholic moral teachings went in recent years. Less than 50 per cent of Catholics attend Mass on a regular basis in to-day's Ireland.

The Canadian historian, Kurt Bowen, is interesting on how the Republic of Ireland changed after Lemass became Taoiseach in 1957. Changes were made to the 'strongly Catholic character of the Republic's laws which have been subject to increasingly heavy criticism and resistance.'[57] The 'special position' of the Catholic church was removed in 1972, contraceptives were allowed in a bill Charlie Haughey, the Taoiseach, got through (though only for married couples) in 1972 and the censorship laws changed in 1967.

To-day the Irish state and its people constitute a liberal, multicultural democracy. Leo Varadkar was elected Taoiseach by his party, Fine Gael, in the public knowledge that he is a self-declared gay man. Same sex marriage and abortion were voted for in two referendums, respectively in 2015 and 2018. Irish Protestant numbers have stabilised and recently some Roman Catholics have converted to become Protestants. After years of chronic emigration, there is almost full employment and strong economic growth led by thriving transnational enterprises, mainly American, attracted by very low corporation tax rates.

Progress has been made in recent years on the recognition of the 35,000 Irish men who fell in World War 1. Thanks largely to the tireless work of writer and journalist, Kevin Myers, they are remembered on Armistice day by the President in St. Patrick's Cathedral, Dublin. In July there is a service at the Islandbridge Memorial Park in Dublin. It is ecumenical, is organised by the British Legion, and is held on the Saturday before the national day of commemoration which falls on the nearest Sunday to 11 July.

However, perhaps we need to know how the Irish-identified Protestants reacted to the still dominant nativist cult rooted in resentment and the promotion of violence as politics to end British oppression, or MOPE ('most oppressed people ever'), in the words of the historian Liam Kennedy.[58] In the centenary commemorations of the violence, self-immolation and human sacrifice of the unmandated 1916 insurgents, the Irish state celebrated the Rising as a reaction to British oppression over centuries. The birth of the Free State had its Easter 1916 foundation narrative 'as the birth moment of a risen Catholic nation.'[59] President Michael D. Higgins led by example, his father being supportive of the IRA.

Four Church of Ireland churches had no services in Dublin's inner city on Sunday, 27 March 2016, the day the commemoration parades took place. This was because of the traffic cordons put in place. One of these churches was St Audeon's and the rector, Canon Mark Gardner wrote:

> I feel no affinity with the commemoration of the Rising and my own memory of 1966 and what I have learnt about those events a hundred or so years ago convince me it was a series of ghastly mistakes compounded by one government after another. I feel the loss of the Public Record Office particularly keenly. In 1966, every school had to display a copy of the Proclamation and even as a child I felt it intrusive. [60]

The marginalisation of Protestants post-independence is reflected in the fall in numbers of Protestant TDs in the 1970s and 1980s. There were 144 TDs elected at each general election. In 1969 there were four Protestant TDs -Maurice Dockrell, Dublin Central, Henry Dockrell, Dun Laoghaire, Erskine Childers and Billy Fox, Monaghan. In previous decades there had typically been four/five Protestant TDs. In 1973 three Protestant TDS, James White, Donegal-Leitrim, Henry Dockrell, Dun Laoghaire, Erskine Childers, Monaghan. In 1977 one Protestant TD James White, Donegal. In 1981 two Protestant TDs James White, Donegal South West. Ivan Yates, Wexford. In 1982 (Nov) one Protestant TD, Ivan Yates, Wexford. In 1987 one Protestant TD, Ivan Yates. In 1989 (June) one Protestant TD Ivan Yates, Wexford. In the 1990s, following the election of Mary Robinson, the number of Protestant TDs increased again. To-day there are two Protestant ministers, Heather Humphreys from Monaghan and Shane Ross from Dublin.

What of the tiny numbers of southern Protestants to-day? Heather Crawford in her ground-breaking book, *Outside the Glow* found that as late as 1985 there was a tendency towards 'Protestant silence, even apparent pusillanimity, in the face of controversial issues; they were reluctant to say, face to face, anything contentious.' [61] The attitude was: 'Whatever you say, say nothing.'[62]

Deirdre Nuttall found in her extensive interviews with Protestants in the Irish Republic that many commented that their decline, and perceived loss of status, led to anxiety that prompted 'keeping themselves to themselves'. Where Protestants are few and not especially wealthy, some express that there has been a perception of public space as belonging to 'the other crowd.' In such areas, some describe the feeling their right to use public spaces, like parks or streets, where they were very much in a minority, was once conditional on 'keeping the head down.'[63] 'Irish Protestants nonetheless view themselves as sharing certain outlooks, stories, customs, and traditions that are integral to their identity.'[64]

A man from a small farm in the west commented: 'We were always conscious of the fact that we were a different religion.' He said that, 'It wasn't a nice feeling. It was a bad feeling, really it was, I think it's not good for young people to feel like that.' He and his brother complained about the bullying but were advised to 'keep their heads down' for fear that an intervention would damage the family's relationship with the neighbours in a small rural community with very few Protestants.[65]

Bernadette Hayes and Tony Fahy in their essay in *Irish Protestant Identities* wrote about Irish identity:

> More recent research, however, has questioned whether integration, much less assimilation, has in fact gone that far. For example, Fahey et al. found that although Catholics have a clear Irish identity, Protestants were more lukewarm and ambivalent in their attachment to that identity than were Catholics.[66]

On the question of the demographic decline Hayes and Fahy wrote:

> This decline persisted up to the 1990s and has only recently been reversed by the immigration of Protestant non-nationals. This suggests that Irish society has not provided as positive an environment for Protestantism as it might have with possible consequences for how Protestants might feel about that environment ... certain distinctive features of Protestant attitudes in the Republic that might be interpreted as signs of relative disengagement from core institutions in Irish life.[67]

However, they go on to questionably write that Protestants became 'greened' over time and completely integrated:

The overall conclusion, therefore, is to reinforce the thesis of complete Protestant integration into Irish society: Protestants have not become identical to the majority community in the way they relate to the Irish political system, but the ways they differ are within what might be called a normal range of diversion.[68]

The Irish sociologist, Joseph Ruane, questions these findings:

The big plus about Fahey and Hayes's piece is that they actually studied the Protestant difference, whereas most others simply ignore it. Its main limitation comes from the fact that they used standardised opinion data based on similar questions asked of Catholics. That kind of data doesn't allow one to get at subtleties of differences. They do not throw light on the question of how comfortable Southern Irish Protestants are with Irish society at present or how integrated into it they feel.[69]

The question of ethnic cleansing of southern Protestants has been an issue of debate. Joseph O'Neill wrote in *Blood-Dark Trail* that the southern Protestants 'suffered a demographic cataclysm unmentioned by dominant nationalist histories'.[70] The Welsh historian and author, Peter Cottrell believes ethnic cleansing did take place and the 'democratic cataclysm unmentioned by dominant national histories' is for Cottrell the Republic's 'elephant in the room':

[T]he ethnic cleansing of Protestants out of Southern Ireland is one of those elephants in the room. The Republic still has the temerity to deny that it happened, nor do they accept that whilst it may not have been official government policy, it was the closest thing to it an unofficial policy can get.

He added by way of explanation:

I think it is fair to say that there was no official policy of discrimination against Protestants, but the influence of the Catholic Church combined with the automatic association of Protestantism with Britishness ensured that the Protestant population were discriminated against during the early years of the State. The result was the decline in the Protestant population through choice and necessity.

Modern Ireland is a liberal democracy, but any state born out of bloodshed will always have a shadow cast over it by those who can look to the past to justify the use of violence to achieve their ends, regardless of whether they have any support or not.[71]

Yet in this 'liberal democracy', RTE, the public service broadcaster, relays the Angelus bell twice daily on radio and TV, arguably a sectarian act, since the Angelus prayer incorporates beliefs exclusive to the Roman Catholic church. RTE is the only public service broadcaster in the world to do this, unchallenged by the state, Protestant churches as well as the people.

There is little doubt the new pluralist, liberal Ireland has some distance to go, particularly under its present government, led by Leo Varadkar. The Brexit context did occasion a distinct display of Anglophobia on the part of Varadkar and Coveney and a nationalist orientated attempt to economically separate Northern Ireland from the rest of the UK.

The narrow and singular nationalist narrative about Irish history and the state's 'foundational mythology' is so ingrained in the minds of the general populace, that they may be 'deaf' to new perspectives on the historical place of the Protestant segments of Irish society. The narrative consists of the noble blood sacrifice and heroism of a small number of insurgents whose successors took control in 1922. Independence led to decades of poverty and emigration, mostly to the 'enemy' England and its ex-colonies, Australia and Canada. In April 2014, President Michael D. Higgins went on a state visit to London. In his speech at Windsor Castle, he did not thank England for welcoming the millions of people of Irish descent who had found a new home England, at a time when his country had failed to give them new lives, employment, free healthcare, as well as free secondary education.

The British Representative in Ireland, John Maffey, in his memorandum, *The Irish Question in 1945* addressed to the secretary of state for the Dominions expressed his view:

To-day, after six years' detachment, Eire is more than ever a foreign country. It is so dominated by the National Catholic Church as to be almost a theocratic State. Gaelic is enforced in order to show that Eire is not one of the English-speaking nations; foreign games are frowned upon, the war censorship has been misapplied for anti-British purposes, anti-British feeling is fostered in school and by Church and State by a system of hereditary enemy indoctrination. There is probably more widespread anti-British sentiment in Eire to-day than ever before … The Irish are a very distinct race, and their marked characteristics persist strongly … There still persist the dark Milesian strain, the tribal vendetta spirit, hatred and blarney, religious fanaticism, swift alternations between cruelty and laughter.[72]

Southern Protestants of British descent lived in 'almost a theocratic state' as Maffey makes clear. Many emigrated, others acquiesced, some prospered and adapted. The many Orange order lodges that were scattered all around the twenty-six counties closed. Perhaps it is best to let the Irish novelist and essayist, John Banville have the last word. In his introduction to James G. Farrell's book *Troubles* Banville wrote:

[I]n the South, the Protestants, some 5% of the population (note: in 1911 they were 10.4 per cent of the population, not 5 per cent) largely withdrew from public life, a matter of bitter regret to many of the more perceptive among them, from W.B.Yeats —'we are no petty people!' — to Hubert Butler, an essayist of genius, never ceased to bemoan the loss to the life of Southern Ireland of that energy, intransigence, and the fierce radicalism which marked the Protestant tradition.[73]

We can add to those Protestants of 'energy, intransigence and fierce radicalism' Swift, Goldsmith, Bishop Berkeley, Shaw, O'Casey, Wilde and Beckett. Their Protestant legacy rejects 'an authoritarian, centralist mindset: an unwillingness to make individuals accountable for performance; and an anarchic character with a mistrust of authority – frequently well founded.'[74] Arguably this legacy was pacified in the triumphalist, nationalist state that emerged characterised by the myth of a pure Catholic race persecuted for centuries and showing distaste for so called 'non Catholics'. The Irish constitution, after all, defines who 'the people of Eire' are in an unchallenged way to this day:

We, the people of Éire, humbly acknowledging all our obligations to our Divine Lord, Jesus Christ, Who sustained our fathers through centuries of trial …

Where is the Protestant legacy in this narrow constitutional definition of Irishness? It is arguably the unwanted legacy in the 'centuries of trial' of the real Irish people. A calculated and studied air of neglect applies to-day and since 1921, a neglect that fails to afford equal respect to all traditions and parts of the Irish community. Especially to the community that has all but disappeared.

Notes

1   Liam Kennedy. *Unhappy the Land: The Most Oppressed People Ever, the Irish?* (Sallins: Merrion Press, 2016) p. 137

2   Donald H. Akenson, *A Mirror to Kathleen's Face: Education in Independent Ireland 1922-1960* (Montreal: McGill-Queen's University Press, 1975), pp. 118-19 and 109.

3   Eugenio Biagini, 'The Protestant minority in Southern Ireland', *Historical Journal*, Vol. 54 (40), 2012, p. 1179.

4   Marcus Tanner, *Ireland's Holy Wars: The Struggle for a Nation's Soul 1500-2000* (London: Yale University Press, 2003), p. 313.

5   *The Witness*, 16 June 1920.

6   *Church of Ireland Gazette*, 9 September 1921.

7   *The Irish Times*, 9 October 1922.

8   Peter Hart, *The IRA and its Enemies: Violence and Community in Cork, 1916-1923* (Oxford: Clarendon Press, 1998), p.288.

9   Marcus Tanner, op. cit., p. 292.

10 Joseph O'Neill, *Bood-Dark Trail,* (New York: Vintage Books, 2010), pp. 326-7.

11 Idem.,p.330.

12 *Irish Times*, 13 May 1992; *Cork Examiner* 1,13 May 1922.

13 Peter Hart, op. cit., pp. 286-88, 291.

14 Enda Delaney, *Demography, State and Society: Irish Migration to Britain, 1921 -1971.*

(Liverpool: Liverpool University Press, 2000), p. 73.

[15] Wood, op. cit., pp. 13-14.

[16] Ibid.

[17] Ibid.

[18] Brian Walker, *Irish History Matters* (Gloucestershire: History Press: 2019), p. 218.

[19] Robert B. McDowell, *Crisis and Decline* (Dublin: Lilliput Press: 1977)), preface.

[20] Donald H. Akenson, op. cit., p. 112.

[21] For an excellent summary of outrages see Robert B. McDowell, op. cit. pp. 83-101.

[22] Terrence Dooley, *The Decline of the Big House in Ireland: A Study of Irish landed Families, 1860 – 1960* (Dublin:Wolfhound Press ,2001).

[23] I knew the Ponsonby children, Myles and Sarah. They had English accents and went to school in England, Myles to Harrow. Their father, Arthur, married a charming American, Patricia, who died young in Cloyne where she is buried in the cathedral graveyard. I sang the hymn, 'The Lord's my Shepherd' at her funeral. Eventually Arthur sold and went to live in England. I never discovered why. Sarah went to live in France where she died in 2010. Ireland was not her home, nor the home of her brother. But one thing I do remember about Arthur. He came to dinner one evening in the Deanery and did his best to get my father to stop praying for the British monarch during the Sunday service! After Ireland left the Commonwealth in 1949 and became a republic, the Church of Ireland bishops issued instructions that its clergy should stop praying for the monarch as part of the liturgy of the service. Clearly my father had gone on as a monarchist and empire loyalist. However, he did stop later on.

[24] Donald H Akenson, op cit., p. 112.

[25] Idem.,p. 115.

[26] John Dunlop, *A Precarious Belonging: Presbyterians and the Conflict in Ireland* (Belfast: Blackstaff Press, 1995), p. 34.

[27] Brian M. Walker, *A Political History of the Two Irelands: From Partition to Peace* (Basingstoke: Palgrave, 2012), p.16.

[28] Kurt Bowen, *Protestants in a Catholic State: Ireland's Privileged Minority* (Kingston; Dublin: Montreal : McGill-Queen's University Press ; Gill and Macmillan, 1983), p. 28.

[29] Kurt Bowen, op. cit., p. 30.

[30] Idem., p. 31.

[31] Henry Patterson, , *Ireland Since 1939: The Persistence of Conflict* (Dublin: Penguin, 2007), p. 104.

32   Richard O'Leary, 'Change in the rate and pattern of religious intermarriage in the Republic of Ireland', *The Economic and Social Review*, Vol. 30(2), 1999: p. 119.

33   Kurt Bowen, op. cit., p. 41.

34   *Irish Times*, 6 September 1974.

35   David Jameson, '*The religious upbringing of children in "mixed marriages": the evolution of Irish law*', New Hibernia Review / Iris Éireannach Nua, Vol. 18 (2), 2014, pp. 65–83.

36   David Jameson, op. cit., p.75

37   Tilson v Tilson (LXXXVI 1952) at 66.

38   Idem., p.76.

39   Idem., p. 80.

40   Gerard Hogan, 'A fresh look at *Tilson's* case', *Irish Jurist*, Vol. 33, 1998 p. 331.

41   Eugenio Biagini, op. cit., p.1179.

42   *Belfast Telegraph*, 1 June 1998.

43   Kurt Bowen, op. cit., pp.156-7.

44   Idem., p. 59.

45   Donald H. Akenson, op. cit., p. 36.

46   Idem., p. 35.

47   See, https://www.cso.ie/en/media/csoie/census/census1926results/volume8/C_1926_VOL_8_T1,2.pdf

48   Reginald Hindley, *The Death of the Irish Language* (London and New York: Routledge, 2005) p. 211.

49   Ernest Blythe, Myles Dillon and Cearbhall O. Dalaigh, 'The significance of the Irish language for the future of the Nation', *University Review*, Vol. 2(2), 1960, p. 24.

50   Tom Garvin, *Nationalist Revolutionaries in Ireland 1858–1928* (Dublin: Gill & Macmillan, 1987), p. 99.

51   Kurt Bowen, op. cit., p. 157.

52   Donald H. Akenson, op. cit., p. 58.

53   Idem., p. 154.

54   Department of Justice papers in National Archives, jus/2008/117.

55   Denis Kennedy, *The Widening Gulf: Northern Attitudes to the Independent Irish State, 1919-1949* (Belfast; Wolfeboro, N.H.: Blackstaff Press, 1988), p. 172.

56   Idem., p. 173.

57   Kurt Bowen, *op. cit.*, p. 72.

58   Liam Kennedy, *Unhappy the Land* (Sallins, Merrion Press, 2016). p.36.

59   Valerie Jones, *Rebel Prods: The Forgotten Story of Protestant Radical Nationalists and the 1916 Rising* (Dublin: Ashfield Press, 2016), p. 357.

60   Email to author 1 April 2016.

61   Heather Crawford, *Outside the Glow Protestants and Irishness in Independent Ireland* (Dublin: University College Dublin Press, 2010), p.96.

62   Eugenio Biagini, op. cit., p. 1179.

63   Deirdre Nuttall, 'Count us in too: wanting to be heard in independent Ireland', in Ian D'Alton and Ida Milne (eds), *Protestant and Irish: The Minority's Search for Place in Independent Ireland,* (Cork: Cork University Press, 2019), pp. 84 and 87.

64   Idem., pp 84-85.

65   Idem., p. 89.

66   Bernadette Hayes and Tony Fahy, 'Politics in the Republic of Ireland:is integation complete?' in M.A. Busteed, Frank Neal and Jonathan Tonge (eds), *Irish Protestant Identities* (Manchester: Manchester University Press, 2008), p. . 70.

67   Idem.,, p. 82.

68   Idem.,p. 82.

69   Personal communication to author 24 November 2019.

70   Joseph O'Neill, op. cit., pp.326-327

71   Personal communication to author18 April 2019.

72   CP. (45) 152. 7 September 1945 entitled "Relations with Eire" being a Memorandum by the Secretary of State for Dominion Affairs" and exhibiting a Memorandum by Maffey entitled "The Irish Question in 1945" dated 21 August 1945

73   John Banville, 'Introduction', in J. G. Farrell, *Troubles.* (New York: New York Review of Books, 2002), p. viii.

74   Conor Brady, *The Sunday Times*, 2 August 2015.

11

Political reality and the Belfast Agreement

Dennis Kennedy

The twentieth anniversary of the Belfast Agreement in April 2018 was marked by much general celebration, by a degree of self-congratulation by some of its architects, and much praise from a range of academics and media commentators. The Agreement was lauded internationally, frequently presented as a blueprint that could usefully be adopted by divided societies worldwide. The embarrassing fact that the key institutions set up under the Agreement were suspended leaving Northern Ireland without a governing Executive and a functioning Assembly was glossed over.

In the event the suspension continued for almost three years, and led, until well into the suspension, to surprising little questioning of the effectiveness of the Agreement as a mechanism leading to a political settlement. Assertions at the time of the anniversary that the Agreement was failing were dismissed. In the words of Richard English, Pro-Vice Chancellor of Queen's University and academic expert on conflict resolution, the twentieth anniversary was an occasion for remembering 'what an extraordinary achievement the peace process had actually been.'

> Yes, [he wrote] political progress in the North has rather stalled, and relationships have further soured. But the essence of the 1998 deal and of post-1998 progress – that goals should be pursued through a non-violent politics based on respect for rival perspectives – remains the impressive basis for a much less blood-stained political world in Northern Ireland than that which has preceded it.[1]

But it was almost two years from that optimistic pronouncement before suspension of the Executive/Assembly ended on 11 January 2020.. The immediate causes of the collapse of the institutions in January 2017 – Sinn Fein's demands for progress on an Irish language act and its call for the withdrawal from office of the First Minister, Arlene Foster, because of her involvement in the Renewable Heat Initiative -- were not in themselves insoluble problems, nor issues of such fundamental importance as to justify the disruption of the key mechanisms of devolved government. Rather they were symptomatic of the increased tribalisation of politics over the past two decades, and the almost total absence of 'respect for rival perspectives'.

Discussion of whether the Agreement has simply been a success or failure is likely to be unproductive. Certainly, it has brought a welcome and sustained reduction in terrorist-related violence. The statistics confirm this. In the twenty years since the Agreement about 160 people have been killed in security related incidents, contrasted with more than 1200 deaths in the two decades preceding it. In the ten years up to 2018 there have been twenty five deaths.

Since the Agreement, cross-border and cross-community projects have been created at inter-governmental, local authority, commercial and voluntary level. They include the all-Ireland electricity market, inland waterways, education, health and other fields. Much of this activity had been facilitated by the completion of the EU's single market in 1988, and many schemes were assisted by EU funding. The British and Irish governments pledged, in the Belfast Agreement, to develop still further 'the unique relationship between their peoples and the close co-operation between their countries as friendly neighbours and as partners in the European Union.'[2]

It is also true that political dialogue, even as conducted between parties representative of the more extreme varieties of nationalism and unionism, has been, for the most part, non-violent in that it has been verbal – in print, on the air and in debating chambers, rather than on the streets.

But has the Agreement proved to be 'the final resolution of what has for centuries been the most intractable source of political conflict in the whole of Europe.' as, in 2007, the then Secretary of State, Peter Hain, declared?[3] A dozen years after that grandiose claim, can it be said that significant progress has been made towards a political solution?

More than twenty years after the Agreement it is appropriate to ask why politics in Northern Ireland are more polarised than ever, why there are still factions on both sides armed and ready to use violence in pursuit of political aims, why there are still peace walls to keep rival communities apart, and why there is no real progress towards a 'settlement', that is no prospect of agreement between unionism and nationalism on what the constitutional position of the province should be -- within the UK, within an Irish state or within some other yet to be devised arrangement that will be, if not permanent, at least settled for the foreseeable future. Major decisions on education, on the heritage of the past, on social issues, on much else have been blocked by the ability of unionist and nationalist parties to veto each other's initiatives.

The purpose of this chapter is to discuss why the reality of Northern Ireland today, while certainly spared the awful violence of the Troubles, is still a divided society, politically even more divided than it was half a century ago.

- Is the Agreement itself flawed – in its language, in the institutional framework it created, in the way it has been implemented?

- Has there been a political failure at the level of the parties in Northern Ireland, and by the people who elect them?

- Have the two main guarantors of the Agreement, the British and Irish governments, been too ready to regard it as a peace settlement, a solid foundation leading to a political solution, rather than an armistice to stop the violence?

- Have the two governments given little consideration to the impact of national policy decisions on Northern Ireland and the 'peace process'?

- Has the context in which the Agreement has operated been altered by changing circumstances?

Does fault lie in the Agreement itself?

The Agreement secured the ceasefire, and eventually not the surrender of weapons but their 'decommissioning'. The IRA, instructed its 'volunteers' in July 2005 to assist in 'the development of purely political and democratic programmes through exclusively peaceful means'[4] and at Easter 2007, declared its 'firm belief' that the republican goal of a united Ireland 'is achievable through purely peaceful and democratic means'.[5]

That stops short of a renunciation of violence in principle, or of any acknowledgement that recent IRA violence had been unjustified. Supporters of the Agreement and the peace process indignantly dispute allegations of appeasement, but whatever the label, London and Dublin, plus Washington, and even John Hume, went to extraordinary lengths to facilitate IRA demands, not just in the language of the Agreement, but also in its implementation. President Robinson met and shook hands with Gerry Adams in Belfast in 1993, before any ceasefire; President Clinton gave Adams a hitherto denied visa to enter the USA resulting in a triumphant visit in early 1994. From being the public apologist for IRA violence Adams became a leading figure in the peace process, photographed in Downing, Street, Merrion Street and the White House.

The sanitisation of Sinn Fein thus begun, was carried forward in the Agreement itself, and in its implementation. Mo Mowlan initiated the process of installing the Executive long before the IRA had 'decommissioned' its arsenal, effectively forcing David Trimble and the Ulster Unionist Party (UUP) into [6]government with long-term defenders of the terrorist campaign and in some instances with the leaders of that campaign. This made nonsense of Blair's blackboard promise that there would be no place in government for those associated with violence.

Trimble and his party were denounced by Paisley and the Democratic Unionist Party (DUP) who vigorously opposed the Agreement. The general belief that the Agreement was endorsed by the great majority of voters in Ireland overlooks the detailed figures for the Northern referendum. The result was a decisive overall two-to-one majority for the Agreement, but more than a quarter of a million voters – 275,000 – said 'no'. In a contest that was, to most people, a vote for or against peace after decades of appalling violence, with the campaign for 'yes' having the backing of every political party except the DUP and the marginal UK Unionist Party, it was evidence of a significant, even large body of people determined to oppose the Agreement. It must be assumed that the 'no vote' came very largely from the unionist community – some estimates were that 47 per cent of unionists voting said 'no'.

So the Agreement began life with the formidable handicap of a large section of the unionist population resolutely rejecting it, and with Ian Paisley's DUP opposing the terms and implementation of the Agreement and severely criticising the negotiation of the Agreement by David Trimble and the UUP. This was the strong base upon which Paisley and his party were able to take over unionism in the Assembly election of 2003. Subsequent events, such as the defection of major figures from the Ulster Unionist Party to the DUP suggest that unionist support for the Agreement was fragile from the beginning.. As the release of prisoners, the disbandment of the RUC and other elements of the settlement were put in place, the DUP's standing with unionist voters rose dramatically, and Trimble and the UUP were sent packing.

On the nationalist side Sinn Fein had been transformed into peace-makers, indeed into media celebrities, and it became easier for many in nationalist community to welcome the new dispensation and do what they had steadily refused to do during the years of the Troubles – give their votes to those who had supported violence. John Hume and the Social Democratic and Labour Party (SDLP) were reduced to bit play-ers. Within a few years the political landscape in Northern Ireland was transformed. Following the Agreement, the unionist and nationalist com-munities dramatically switched their allegiances from the comparatively moderate to the extreme. The two politicians who received the Nobel Peace prize for their part in brokering the Agreement, John Hume and David Trimble, lived to see the side-lining of their once dominant parties, even seemingly at times to the point of threatened extinction.

In the 1997 Westminster election, the UUP had out-polled Paisley's DUP by more than two-to-one, and the SDLP were comfortably ahead of Sinn Fein by 24 per cent of the vote against 16 per cent. Twenty years later neither the UUP nor the SDLP was represented in the Commons at Westminster. In the June 2017 general election the DUP and Sinn Fein swept the board taking 17 of 18 seats allocated to Northern Ireland

THE NORTHERN IRELAND QUESTION

(DUP 10, Sinn Fein 7 and one independent.) In the Assembly elections of March 2017, the DUP had out-polled the UUP by more than two-to-one and Sinn Fein won twice as many votes as the SDLP.

The prolonged suspension of the Executive and Assembly which had lasted for three years by December 2019, had seen increasing public criticism of politicians in general, and of the DUP and Sinn Fein in particular as the main parties responsible for the deadlock. This criticism was reflected in the European election of May 2019, in the low turn out (45 per cent) and in the success of the Alliance party, winning a seat for the first time, at the expense of the Ulster Unionists. The Sinn Fein vote was down on the 2014 vote, but only by 3.0 percentage points and the DUP vote showed a marginal increase of 1.0 percentage point.

The two more extreme nationalist and unionist parties, despite the criticism levelled at them, maintained their dominance, and the tribal domination of Northern Ireland politics seem to be confirmed. The victory by the Alliance party suggested that public exasperation with politicians in general was more visited on the moderate versions of nationalism and unionism, the UUP and the SDLP. The structures of the Agreement still suit the two main parties, and help them feed off each other electorally.

The December 2019 general election produced major shocks, with the DUP losing two of their eight seats and their total vote down by more than 5 per cent , and while Sinn Fein held their seven seats, their vote was down almost 7 per cent. The big winners were the SDLP winning two seats, and Alliance one. While this did reflect some shift from the extremes to the centre on the part of the electorate, it still left the DUP and Sinn Fein the dominant players, by a considerable margin. Special factors came into play - tactical decisions not to split the tribal vote in some constituencies, and in the case of the SDLP in the form of a new young and articulate leader Colm Eastwood, who campaigned strongly against Sinn Fein's abstention policy, and who shrewdly covered his nationalist back by forming a link with the southern Fianna Fail party, countering Sinn Fein's claim to be uniquely an all-Ireland party.

The outcome of the 2019 Westminster election does not weaken the core thesis that following the Agreement the unionist and nationalist communities have dramatically switched their allegiance from the comparatively moderate to the extreme. There may be indications of some modification of that trend but the electoral situation in terms of the most recent results is still supportive of the core thesis.

The detailed provisions of the Agreement, and its overall facilitation of the cleansing of Sinn Fein, help explain this transformation of the political scene. The method of appointing an Executive in proportion to votes gained by political parties in the election of the Assembly, and not on voluntary agreement among parties, was defended as exceptional, and probably temporary. This way both communities, and even minor parties, would be involved in the running of the province, with the hope that that would foster cooperation and mutual understanding, and facilitate an eventual settlement.

The two decades of the Agreement have suggested the opposite. The system has resulted in pressure on each community to concentrate politically in one party in order to command most seats in the Assembly, and thereby gain maximum strength in the Executive. With the background and the legacy of the Troubles, and sharp divisions over policing, and many other issues, there were more votes for parties pushing harder for often narrowly defined unionist or nationalist interests or ambitions, and increasingly fewer for any party reaching out to some middle ground and thereby committing the unpardonable sin of splitting the vote. Tribal politics had already been enshrined by the requirement of all Members elected to the Assembly to declare themselves unionist, nationalist or other, and the use of these designations in Assembly decision-making. Did the architects of the Agreement, particularly the two governments, foresee this outcome – the dominance of the parties of the extremes and the near eclipse of the centre ground? Did the tailoring of the Agreement to meet the demands of Sinn Fein make it useful as an armistice, but a fatally flawed platform for a settlement?

Professor English, in the article cited above, almost assents, when he writes:

> In assessing the violence of a major group like the IRA, we need a layered understanding. They failed to secure their central strategic goals, but they did attain other goods through violence. They made a problem more famously urgent of resolution, but also more lastingly difficult to resolve. [7]

The Agreement contains one bizarre provision which may be seen as an acknowledgement that for all its declarations, promises and institutions the Agreement does not regard itself as a settlement. The only permanent end it foresees is a straight one-off referendum to decide – apparently even if only by the barest majority - whether Northern Ireland remains in the UK, or joins in a united Ireland. Unionists can argue that they have already won in an earlier referendum, or that successive elections since Partition have demonstrated majority support for membership of the UK. Nationalist rejection of that assertion as a solution is what the whole problem has been about, so why should one more vote work a miracle and provide a peaceful settlement? A vote either way would not solve the problem, it would either leave it unsolved where it is, or transfer it unsolved to a different battleground.

Have the politicians of Northern Ireland, and the people who elect them, failed to live up to the undertakings in the Agreement?

If the Agreement is as flawed as the above section suggests, it might be argued that both the politicians and the people were, and still are, to some extent prisoners of the Agreement. It is asserted above that the provisions of the Agreement regarding the Assembly and the formation of the Executive formed a quasi-democratic straitjacket within the politics post-Agreement were confined. The benign view of the Agreement and its convoluted mechanisms is that, whatever the long-term outcome, it would mean that unionist and nationalist would be obliged to share in government of the province and to do so mindful that they had agreed to do it, in 'partnership, equality and mutual respect as the basis of relationships within Northern Ireland, between North and South, and between these islands.'[8]

With the relatively moderate UUP and SDLP expected to dominate the Executive and Assembly it was possible to hope that the experience of having to work together, and to take on the responsibilities of a whole range of devolved matters vital to the people of Northern Ireland, would, perhaps, make a reality of the hopes embodied in the Agreement. These, from a British point of view at least, were neatly summarised by one prominent supporter of the Agreement, Professor Paul Bew (now Lord Bew):

'above all [it is] an agreement about the sharing of power within Northern Ireland and on a North/South basis.'[9]

But the Agreement got off to a rocky start with, as detailed above, a large (275,000) block of presumably unionists voting against it. The DUP nominated two members to the Executive in 1998 but continued to attack the terms and implementation of the Agreement – specifically the initial decision by Trimble to form an Executive with Sinn Fein without actual IRA 'decommissioning'. The DUP and Sinn Fein secured electoral dominance within unionism and nationalism in the November 2003 Assembly election but until 2007 the DUP refused to form an Executive with Sinn Fein. The Executive was restored in May 2007 under the terms of the 2006 St Andrews Agreement.

Much was made at the time of Ian Paisley's conversion from the 'Dr No' of Northern Ireland politics, to the smiling partner of Martin McGuinness in the 'Chuckle Brothers' act as First and Deputy First Minister. Was it a conversion or a change of strategy? His primary concern was to protect the real interests of Ulster, or his perception of its real interests. He could continue to thwart the working of the Agreement, but that could lead to direct rule from London, with, inevitably, an increasing input from Dublin – the worst possible outcome from his point of view. Better to be First Minister, a position from which he would be well placed to thwart the, as he saw it, machinations of Sinn Fein to exploit the working of the Agreement to pursue their ambition of a united Ireland.

Sinn Fein's main concern after the Agreement in 1998, was to secure the backing of the broader nationalist community, something it had failed to have during almost thirty years of the Troubles. To do that it had to rewrite history, portraying the IRA campaign not as one of terror, but as a struggle for the rights of nationalists. The Agreement was, as suggested above, a useful text book in this regard. It also set about making itself a very efficient political party, responding to local concerns, and after 2007, playing a full role in the operation of devolved government. In this it was successful.

But its ultimate over-riding goal was, as it never disguised, a united Ireland. As the Agreement left a final decision on that to a referendum, and as repeated opinion polls suggested that at least a portion of Sinn Fein's electoral support came from voters who, while broadly nationalist in background and outlook, had no desire to leave the United Kingdom, this meant Sinn Fein had no vested interest in a too successful operation of the Agreement.

Neither had the DUP. The party under Ian Paisley had shown its distain for, and profound distrust of the Agreement. The decision to do an about turn in 2007 and take a full part in the working of the institutions was not a sudden conversion to the Belfast Agreement, but a decision that from a position of power, guaranteed by its status as the biggest political party in the Assembly, it was better placed to counter Sinn Fein. There is no mutual trust or respect between Sinn Fein and the DUP.

The Agreement leaves the ultimate decision on the future of Northern Ireland to a border poll, with first past the post the winner. Neither the DUP nor Sinn Fein seem to have allowed such a prospect to impact on their policies and seem blind to their own long-term interests, and to evolving realities. The unionist goal of keeping Northern Ireland within the UK can be achieved only if significant numbers of non-unionists are content to be in the UK, and vote accordingly in a border poll. On the nationalist side it has long been recognised that Irish unification can be achieved only by persuasion, and that must mean persuading a goodly section of the broader unionist community that it is a good idea. Yet the DUP's policies and public utterances seem, at times, calculated to offend moderate nationalists, not to make them feel at home in the UK. DUP obduracy over flags, parades, and bonfires, plus the jeering dismissal of the Irish language on the part of some of its members all work against this. The appeal of the party's fundamental conservatism on moral and social issues may increasingly be confined to the traditionalist core of the DUP. The party's zeal in its support of Brexit since 2016 widens the political gulf between itself and the bulk of nationalist and middle-ground voters, and shows no awareness of the need, in its own interest, to make Northern Ireland a welcoming home for non-unionists.

Sinn Fein, is generally more careful about its public image and has gone to some lengths to emphasize its rejection of violence when republican splinter groups resort to it, but it seems to go out of its way to cause serious offence, not just to unionists, but to others, including many in the nationalist community, by its very public honouring of IRA terrorists. Both Michelle O'Neill and Mary Lou McDonald chose to make among their first public appearances after taking office, events honouring IRA men who had been killed in the act of carrying out terrorist raids. In January 2017 Michelle O'Neill addressed a vigil in Clonoe in memory of four IRA men who had been killed when they attacked Coalisland police station in 1972.[10] In February 2018, just after she had become Sinn Fein President-elect to succeed Gerry Adams, Mary Lou McDonald, on what was her first public appearance in Northern Ireland since her elevation, attended a ceremony honouring an IRA bomber who had died in 1972 when a device he was placing near Castlewellan police station exploded prematurely.[11]

There had been much comment that the choice of these two ladies to take over from Adams was an indication of Sinn Fein's new non-violent stance, and distancing of the party from the IRA of the Troubles. The choice of these two IRA commemorations suggests Sinn Fein was more anxious to emphasise its republican credentials and secure its hard nationalist base than it was to worry about the offence caused to many.

Both the Ulster Unionist Party and the SDLP, finding themselves having to compete for votes with the now much larger DUP and Sinn Fein, have felt forced to go some way along the same tribal path, lessening their ability to build anything like a middle ground in politics.

Have the guarantors – the governments in London and Dublin – too readily assumed they had solved the problem?

Northern Ireland has presented by far the most serious problem to both the United Kingdom and the Republic of Ireland in the past half century. It has imposed enormous costs in terms of public expenditure, damage to public and private property and, particularly but not only, in the case of the UK, loss of life unthinkable outside a national or civil war. But after the signing of the Belfast Agreement, until very recently, it has been far from the centre of political debate in either country. The problem for London and Dublin had been solved in 1998 by the tortuous negotiation of the Belfast Agreement; it was left to Northern Ireland and its people to take the solution handed to them and make it work.

The Northern Ireland problem was never just a Northern Ireland problem. It was the outcome of centuries of inter-action between the two islands, of claims and counter claims, of rebellion and repression.

It was the left-over business from the bloody transforming of what is known as the British Isles and from 1801 until 1921/22 as the United Kingdom of Great Britain and Ireland, into a British state and a de facto independent Irish one. The complication was that one quarter or Ireland, roughly speaking, opted to be part of the British state, not the Irish one. Since then neither the British state, of which Northern Ireland is a part, nor the Irish state which laid loud claims to it, showed much interest in it until its internal tensions burst into the awful violence of the Troubles in the early 1970s. The Belfast Agreement was the culmination of a joint British-Irish attempt to get together and devise a solution. Once it was agreed and approved of in referendums North and South, the problem was, in Peter Hain's words, finally resolved.

The key was to treat the issue as one of clashing identities, British and Irish, give everyone the right to be one or other or both, with equality all round, with all sorts of guarantees and assurances. If they could not manage to get on together then a simple head count via a referendum could decide whether Northern Ireland would remain in the United Kingdom or be absorbed into a politically united Ireland. The only difficulty was that was never going to be solution. There was also a fallacy at the heart of it. This was the equation of national identity with an existing state. As various commentators have pointed out, lots of people in Northern Ireland regard themselves as Irish, but have no wish to live in the Republic of Ireland and are, or would be, content to live as Irish in a British state.

Consider two examples of how Dublin and London can overlook the impact on Northern Ireland when taking policy decisions or declarations. The first example is the Irish Republic's celebration of the centenary of the Easter Rising in 2016 (the second is London's commitment to Brexit, which is dealt with in the next section). The Irish government promised the 2016 centenary of the Easter Rising would be an inclusive commemoration and not celebration, as the 1966 the fiftieth anniversary had been. But in the event, 'inclusive' meant an invitation to all to join in honouring the men and women of 1916.. The then Taoiseach, Enda Kenny, at the start of the commemoration proclaimed himself 'a man of 1916' and declared the Easter Rising 'the central formative and defining act in the shaping of modern Ireland'.

Nations develop a national narrative which defines their identity and their people. Usually more fiction than fact it is very useful for nation-building, for solidarity, in defining Irishness or Britishness or whatever. Until early last century the national narrative of Ireland was centred on people like O'Connell and Parnell, heroes of the long (peaceful) struggles for Catholic emancipation and self-government. It began to be rewritten after the executions of the 1916 leaders, but the Civil War complicated things, and Partition and the hard twenties and thirties slowed its development. The real transition came with the fiftieth anniversary in 1966, when all the main railway stations were renamed after the leaders of 1916 and the full panoply of the state was deployed in the celebration. Coming shortly after the violent IRA border campaign, it was the state's way of claiming to itself the heritage of 1916, and denying it to the illegal IRA. The 2016 commemoration was to some degree the political establishment's response to Sinn Fein's rising political power both North and South.

But this narrative, as former Taoiseach John Bruton forcefully noted, was 'a recipe for endless conflict' and he daringly attacked the Proclamation read by Pearse in O'Connell Street signalling the start of The Rising:

> The Proclamation, which our schoolchildren are now being asked to regard as the founding stone of our democracy, left no room at all for democratic negotiation ... The Republic was proclaimed already to exist, once declared outside the GPO, and to exist as a 'sovereign independent state' of 32 counties. No room for compromise there. Such a state does not even now exis[12]

When the government in Dublin in 2016 invited the leaders of the Northern Ireland political parties to be guests at the official ceremonies in Dublin – an attempt at inclusiveness – all the unionist parties, and the cross-community Alliance declined. The then Alliance Party leader at Stormont, David Ford, explained why. His difficulty, he said, was with the state putting such effort into commemorating those who engaged in violence, when there was a democratic way available. He agreed with the Northern Ireland Attorney General, John Larkin – a northern Catholic

– who wrote, in a contribution to a publication *1916-2016: The Rising and the Somme*, that the Easter Rising was 'profoundly wrong'. The Attorney General also wrote that the rebellion did not pass the test for a just war. The Easter Rising, he stated, 'wasn't justified in any way of the traditional just war criteria - there was no mandate for it … The 1916 Rising was a product of a secret revolutionary society, and an adventure that lacked any democratic or constitutional legitimacy'.[13]

David Ford, in declining the invitation was, in short, indicating he could not buy into the Irish national narrative. No party leader in the Republic seems to have had any bother with the national narrative placing the 1916 Rising at its heart, and at the same time decrying the use of violence to achieve political ends anywhere in Ireland which is required in explicit terms in the Belfast Agreement. There was, and still is, a disconnect between the centrality of an armed rising by a self-appointed small minority with no mandate in the formation and the ethos of an Irish state which is committed to a policy of unity by persuading the citizens of Northern Ireland to join it, particularly when most of them have had thirty years of terror inflicted on them by a small minority with no mandate.

The Taoiseach, Leo Varadkar, on a visit to Belfast in 2019 showed a refreshing and welcome readiness to step outside the normal limits of Irish nationalist orthodoxy when, in an interview, he talked of Irish unification as a distant possibility, not a certainty; he used the phrase 'if it ever would happen' and talked about it coming about in 'a generational context' which would suggest a much longer time frame than the imminent prospects aroused by Brexit among many politicians and media commentators. He also came closer than any previous Taioseach to stating that the founding fathers of the Irish state – 'those that fought in the GPO' – were wrong in envisaging a unitary 32-county republic, which, he said 'could never fully respect or embrace the million people here in the north who are British, who have a unique identity'. What's more, he suggested that this was not the only mistake they made by describing it as 'perhaps one of the flaws of the founding project of my state'.

Speaking at, of all places, the West Belfast *Féile an Phobail* he cited the current designation of Irish as the first official language as one of the things that would have to be considered in a new constitution in a united Ireland 'if there ever was one'. He was speaking about what might be needed if and when a united Ireland comes about, not of what needed to be done now to improve the chances both of that ever happening and of better understanding now between communities in Northern Ireland.[14]

Unionists in Northern Ireland experience and define their British identity in circumstances different from other regions of the UK. In Northern Ireland they are British on another island, and for many years Northern Ireland was the only component part of the UK to have a devolved government. It is the only part in which the main political parties of the state do not organise. Until the recent resurgence of Scottish nationalism it was the only part of the UK in which a large section of the population with whom unionists share the province do not see themselves as British. In the referendum of 2016 Northern Ireland, like Scotland, voted to remain in the European Union, while the bulk of the UK wanted to leave. Unionism's reaction to these different circumstances has been largely to become more stridently British, rather than contemplate their implications. They live, of course, in the only part of the UK which has had to withstand a thirty year massive terrorist campaign specifically aimed at a British presence.

The prime example of how London can overlook the impact on Northern Ireland when taking major policy decisions, is, of course, Brexit. In this case, London's decision to embark on the reversal of a policy supported by every UK parliament for more than half a century, and which, since 1973, has fundamentally altered the way in which the United Kingdom has been governed, was undertaken without any obvious consideration of the impact upon Northern Ireland. As the debates of the past three years have shown, Brexit has potentially transformed the whole context within which the Belfast Agreement was agreed and has been implemented; it is more appropriately dealt with in the following section.

Have events unrelated to the Agreement significantly altered the context in which it was framed and has been implemented?

London showed almost complete unawareness of the serious and distinct implications for Northern Ireland when the Conservative government embarked on Brexit in 2016. In the event Northern Ireland and its border occupied an inordinate amount of the negotiators' time and ingenuity, and the agreement reached has outraged the Tories' hitherto best friends in Belfast, the DUP, and left almost everyone mystified as to how it will work.

The UK legally exited the EU on 31 January 2020, but the final outcome at the time of writing (February 2020) in terms of, crucially, future UK/EU trade relations and the impact on Northern Ireland has still to be seen. But what is clear is that the three years of turmoil in the UK over Brexit have fundamentally changed the larger context in which the Belfast Agreement was negotiated and under which Northern Ireland has been administered for two decades.

Since 1973 Ireland has found itself sitting alongside the UK inside the multinational framework of the EEC, now the EU, and dealing with it as, in principle, an equal. United by a common language, and often enough by common interests, but free to seek other allies in debate in Brussels, the relationship between the two countries has never been so good. It has survived such shocks as the burning of the British embassy in Dublin, the assassination of the British ambassador, the murder of Lord Mountbatten, the murderous attack on Mrs Thatcher and her cabinet during the party conference in Brighton, and much else. It has withstood Ireland taking, and winning cases against the UK at the European Court of Human Rights over excesses by the British military and security services, and violations of the human rights of prisoners or detainees

Still, the two countries found common cause in fighting the IRA during the Troubles, even though the friendship was at times strained, and there was solidarity in the joint approach to finding an end to the killing. All this was the background to the negotiations which resulted in the Belfast Agreement. By 1998 the only border left in Ireland was the security one. The European single market had abolished frontier checks for commerce and people moved freely, duty free-allowances and other limitations were, in effect, confined to history.

As already noted, the Northern Ireland problem was presented in the Belfast Agreement as essentially one of identities, Irish and British, identities which had come, in the crucible of Northern Ireland, to be polar opposites, more sharply defined in the politics of the province than elsewhere. The remedy prescribed in the Agreement was to redefine those identities, showing how much they had in common rather than what divided them, to afford them equal legitimacy and equal respect, even to the point where they were interchangeable, or broad enough to be shared, even by individual citizens.

Such an approach surely drew much on the two governments' experience of the merging of national identities in the supranational European Union. The European integration project grew in its degree of integration and its membership without suppressing national identities – in fact it often had the opposite effect – but in adding the overall umbrella of a European identity not as a replacement for national identities, but as an added element to each. Thus most EU citizens, when asked their identity will automatically give their national one, but generally, if prompted, add 'European', not as an alternative identity but as an additional one they share with the citizens of now almost thirty other European states. This is not simply a geography-based identity, but one drawn from integration, the sharing in a unique system of shared governance.

EU membership has touched the lives of citizens and businesses on the island of Ireland through legislation at European level covering a large area of activities. Resentment of this in the UK partly fuelled the Brexit campaign to 'take back control' of its own affairs. In the 2016 referendum the people of Northern Ireland voted to stay in the EU by a margin greater proportionally than that by which the UK, as a whole, voted to leave.[15] That impinges directly on the core of the Belfast Agreement in that it changes the nature of British identity. This undermines the assertion in the Agreement that the two identities have so much in common that people of Irish identity can be comfortably accommodated in a British Northern Ireland, and that those of British identity can be equally at home in a united Irish state, if and when that comes about.

Another change in the context of the Agreement and its implementation is less of an event than a suddenly renewed excitement over what is a long known trend – the demographic pattern in Northern Ireland which has for many years shown a steadily growing Catholic population which, if sustained, would surely lead to a Catholic majority. In a recent interview Paul Nolan, an academic researcher based in Belfast, made the headlines with his prediction that Northern Ireland will have a Catholic majority by 2021. Based on already known figures from the 2011 census and a 2016 survey he estimated that at the level of schoolchildren, Catholic already outnumbered Protestant by 51 per cent to 37 per cent , and there would be an overall Catholic majority within two years, that is by 2021.

But as Nolan assured unionists, being a Catholic, real or perceived, did not necessarily mean supporting a united Ireland. He pointed out that although 45 per cent identified in the 2011 census as being from a Catholic background, only 25 per cent claimed an exclusively Irish iden- tity[16] The term 'Catholics' was, for many years a loose but useful synonym for 'nationalists'. It was applied to anyone from a Catholic background, or who attended a Catholic school and was assumed likely to vote nation- alist. More recently many such people might no longer be practising Catholics, but might still regard themselves as Irish and be deemed as 'perceived nationalists'. In the 2019 European Parliament elections total first preference votes in Northern Ireland showed a majority going to broadly unionist candidates over the nationalists of Sinn Fein and the SDLP, of 250,000 to 205,000 with both totals being well-down on the previous 2014 European Parliament election. However, other parties, nei- ther unionist or nationalist, polled, a substantial 120,000 votes in 2019, largely made up of the Alliance and Green party's increased votes.

Critics have disputed Nolan's conclusion that Catholics will inevita- bly form a majority in Northern Ireland, citing the decline in the Catholic birth-rate and the decline in practising Catholics, and the increasing num- bers who now declare themselves as of no religion. They also point to the large percentage of recent migrants, many of whom, notably from Nigeria, Poland and other Catholic countries, who help fill vacant Catholic pews but are presumed, perhaps too readily, not likely to vote for Irish unity, or perhaps to vote at all.[17] But that is a somewhat specious argument. The children who were Catholic in 2016 may in 2021 have outgrown religious belief and be happy no longer to be counted as Catholic. In a rapidly changing Ireland if to be Catholic does not mean to be nation- alist or Irish, then ceasing to be Catholic does not mean ceasing to be nationalist. The Belfast Agreement does not allow for such flexibility in the matter of identities.

Then there is the Brexit effect: A survey in 2018 for the Economic and Social Research Council, *The United Kingdom in a Changing Europe*, on voting intentions in Northern Ireland in a future border poll found that Catholic support for staying in the UK was strongly conditional on the outcome of the Brexit negotiations and the expected economic consequences. If there is no Brexit, 27.5 per cent said they would vote for a united Ireland in any border poll. In the event of a 'soft' Brexit this figure increased to 33.4 per cent and rose even further to 52.7 per cent if there was a 'hard' Brexit. Asked how they would vote if Brexit raised their cost of living by £3,500 per annum, that figure was 54.7 per cent.[18] Such a change in voting intentions among Catholics, presumably meaning people from a Catholic background, would not guarantee a border poll ending in favour of Irish unity, but it would certainly change the arithmetic, and strengthen the argument for amendment of the border poll clause in the Agreement. Will the DUP's pro-Brexit stance, and its support of Conservative Brexiteer governments be another factor persuading waverers to prefer a united Ireland in the EU to a UK outside it?

Since the referendum vote for Brexit in 2016 there has been a marked increase in the number of residents of Northern Ireland applying for Irish passports, and a decline in the number of British passports issued to residents of the province. In 2015 a total of 53,715 Irish passports were issued to Northern residents. That rose by about 12,000 in 2016 and last year, 2018, the total was almost 85,000. These figures do not include Northern residents who have gone directly to Dublin for a passport, not through the NIPX scheme run by the Post Office in Northern Ireland. In 2015 almost 130,00 British passports were issued to residents of Northern Ireland; in succeeding years the total has dropped modestly, and by last year was just over 119,000 – a drop of about 10,000 from 2015, and less than a third of the increase over the same period for Irish passports.[19]

These figures do not necessarily represent a switch in voting intentions in a Border poll – many people opting to change to an Irish passport might see that as a sensible measure, as a precaution against whatever difficulties might follow Brexit. But they do suggest more not from a nationalist background are happy enough to be Irish. The Irish identity that many from both communities in Northern Ireland claim is not necessarily related to the existing Irish state, but may be based on geography, history, culture, and even sport or church connection.

Conclusion

Northern Ireland, we are told, now holds the world record as the democratic entity to have managed longest without functioning democratic institutions. The intransigence of local politicians is usually blamed, but that is not the only explanation. The suspensions of the Executive and the Assembly from January 2017 to January 2020 were made possible by the terms of the Agreement. Sinn Fein was able, unilaterally, to call a halt to devolved government simply by withdrawing their nominee for Deputy First Minister, which collapsed the Executive, and the intricate linking of other institutions in the Agreement meant the Assembly along with other bodies had to be suspended.

In a normal parliamentary democracy the exit of one party might bring down a coalition government, but would not automatically suspend the whole governmental structure. A new coalition could be formed and a new government would carry on, or an election called. The Agreement does not create a normal parliamentary democracy and after twenty years of spasmodic malfunctioning, doubts about its provisions are increasingly heard, not only from critics of the Agreement, but from some of its strongest supporters.

In early 2017, Senator George Mitchell, formerly President Clinton's special envoy to Northern Ireland and one of the architects of the Agreement, said it might be time to review its structures. Speaking in the context of Brexit and on the eve of Assembly elections, he said he feared Brexit had reduced the prospect of compromise, and he hoped it would not hinder the establishment of a new power-sharing government at Stormont. On the possibility of reviewing the Agreement and the issue of changing the Executive from a mandatory to a voluntary coalition he said:

> We recognised at the time, that by itself, the Agreement did not assure peace or prosperity or reconciliation. It made them possible … I think everyone anticipated that these arrangements were established to meet the problems and the needs of that time … It is a normal part of the development of every society that over time institutions should be reviewed, processes should be reviewed.[20]

Seamus Mallon, the veteran SDLP politician who was much involved in the negotiations leading to the Agreement and who held the post of Deputy First Minister (1998-2001), identified the Agreement's promise of a border poll requiring no more than a bare majority to take Northern Ireland out of the UK and into a united Ireland, as a fundamental weakness: 'I would propose replacing the Sword of Damocles of a 50% + 1.0 Border poll vote with the doubly protective shield of Parallel Consent.'[21] The Taoiseach, Leo Varadkar, has also shown little enthusiasm for a border poll, particularly if it followed a hard Brexit and was held at a time when there might be no functioning Executive or Assembly in Belfast, and when the Republic would be sorting out its future relationship with the UK. Speaking in October 2017, he said that even if a vote resulted in a narrow decision for a united Ireland, that would not be an endorsement. He did not want a repeat in reverse of what happened after partition, with (this time) the unionists alienated from the state in which they found themselves.[22]

Later, Varadkar speaking in the Dail in October 2019, calling specifically for changes in the voting regulations for the Stormont Assembly, said the requirement for MLAs to declare themselves as nationalist, unionist or other should be removed:

> One of the real flaws in double majorities in a system of cross-community consent is not just that it allows one community or even one party within that community to have a veto, it totally discounts and reduces to nothing the votes of those who are designated as 'other. I think people find the term 'other' pejorative because it doesn't describe that growing identity in Northern Ireland, that centre ground of people who see themselves as being both British and Irish. [23]

On the 'Petition of Concern' he said he believed the Agreement should be reformed to change it. This was a flaw that had developed, and had been used in a way that was not anticipated when the Agreement had been signed.[24] The Taoiseach's comments followed a question from the leader of the Green Party in the Dail, Eamon Ryan, on the need to reform the voting mechanisms at Stormont. Ryan said the institutions and arrangements at Stormont were 'not fit for purpose', and that a meeting of the two governments and all the parties soon was probably essential to see a resolution of the deadlock that had caused the suspension of the Executive and Assembly. These talks, he said, should not be restricted to getting the institutions going again, but to a much wider consideration of why such little progress has been made in the two decades since 1998, and what provisions of the Agreements have not worked as anticipated and need to be changed: 'Stormont should not just be restored back to where it has always been, we should look at this as a chance to evolve the institutions.'[25]

Has that opportunity been missed in the agreement of January 2020 between the two governments and the Assembly parties which enabled the institutions to resume their functions? Does *New Decade, New Approach* meet the expectations not only of Taoiseach Varadkar or the leader of the Green Party, but also those of President Clinton, Senator George Mitchell, Seamus Mallon, John Bruton and many others?

Given the limited time available and the overriding concern with obtaining assent from the two main parties involved in the disputes that had led to the collapse of the Executive, this latest round could hardly be expected to meet Deputy Ryan's appeal for a much wider consideration of why there had been so little progress over two decades and what provisions of the Agreements have not worked as anticipated and need to be changed.

As it was a provision of the Agreement – the dual structure of the First Minister/Deputy First Minister post – that enabled Sinn Fein to collapse the Executive the talks could hardly avoid doing something about that, nor about the Petition of Concern which has been much abused. But what they have done in both cases amounts more to, if not sticking plaster, minor procedures instead of the major surgery that is called for. There is nothing on changing the mandatory coalition to a voluntary one, as the Taoiseach and Senator Mitchell have raised, nor on the classification of MLAs as unionist, nationalist or 'other', and the voting mechanisms based on it, which the Taoiseach has criticised. No concern is shown about the wisdom of a border poll as decreed in the Belfast Agreement. The changes that have been made to guard against one party collapsing the Executive or abusing the Petition of Concern mechanism may make the main parties – or others – pause before they do so. But it could still happen.

On the one issue that is most likely to provoke another existential crisis for the Executive and the Assembly – language, specifically the Irish language – may have been further complicated by the January 2020 *New Decade, New Approach* agreement institutionalising a division that is far more political than real in the lives of citizens. It has done this by decreeing the creation of a raft of new institutions or offices. In what seems a totalitarian approach, there is to be an Office of Identity and Cultural Expression at Stormont 'to promote cultural pluralism and respect for diversity, build social cohesion and reconciliation and to celebrate and support all aspects of Northern Ireland's rich cultural and linguistic heritage.' Its work of building 'social cohesion and reconciliation' may be made more difficult by the similarly decreed appointment of separate Commissioners for Irish and Ulster Scots. It is not too reassuring to be told that 'The First Minister and Deputy First Minister, supported by Junior Ministers in The Executive Office, will sponsor and oversee a new framework both recognising and celebrating Northern Ireland's diversity of identities and culture, and accommodating cultural difference.'[26]

With such a flourishing of linguistic diversity there is bound to be increased need of translation facilities. So there is to be a central Translation Hub in the Department of Finance 'to provide language translation services for the 9 Executive Departments, Arm's Length Bodies, Local Government and Public Bodies'. And a simultaneous translation system will be made available in an Assembly where everyone is fluent in English, to facilitate those members who wish to speak in Irish or Ulster Scots instead, and perhaps *vice versa* wish to hear translations of the English contributions.[27]

The *New Decade, New Approach* round table negotiations was the third time since 1997 that this device of bringing together the two governments and the Stormont parties has been used to break deadlocks in the Northern Ireland 'peace process'. Belfast produced the Agreement and restored devolution, St Andrews brought the DUP into the Executive and ended the suspension of the institutions. The *New Decade, New Approach* agreement of 9 January 2020 has restored regional government after a three year vacuum.

But we still have no sign of a solution. The saga of the Irish language act is illustrative of one fault at the heart of the round table approach. Each ends up by telling the devolved authority – Executive and Assembly – what it must do. Decisions at such summits mainly concern devolved matters, matters that have been devolved because regional assemblies are better placed to deal with them. That is the reason for devolution.

Sinn Fein's main reason for collapsing the Executive was the failure of the Assembly to introduce the Irish language act promised at St Andrews. The matter stems from the endorsement in the 1998 Belfast Agreement of the obligations deriving from the United Kingdom's adherence to the Council of Europe Charter for Regional or Minority Languages.

At the time of the endorsement in the Agreement the UK had not signed up to the Charter and did not do so until 2001. Countries adhering to the Charter opt for which of its many provisions they feel appropriate, which the UK did in 2004. The Belfast Agreement listed eight actions to be taken by the British government. All eight related generally or in particular to Irish and its use in Northern Ireland. They were promised by the British government, but clearly fell into the competence of a devolved institution in Belfast.

The UK government in the section Rights, Safeguards and Equality of Opportunity in the Belfast Agreement undertook to:

> encourage the parties to secure agreement that this commitment will be sustained by a new Assembly in a way which takes account of the desires and sensitivities of the community.[28]

That paragraph acknowledged that the new 1998 Assembly would have the power to make up its own mind on language diversity.

The 2006 St Andrews promise by the British government was to introduce an Irish language act 'reflecting on the experience of Wales and Ireland, and to work with the incoming Executive to enhance and protect the development of the Irish language.'[29] The UK government has never attempted to introduce an Irish language act by legislation at Westminster, presumably because such matters are for the devolved institutions in Belfast. Yet London had undertaken obligations directly affecting language policy in Northern Ireland under the European Charter in 2004 while the devolved institutions in Belfast existed but were in suspension.

The DUP opposed the Belfast Agreement, but participated in the St.Andrews negotiation. The party deny ever agreeing to the proposal for an Irish language act. It seems the agreement at St Andrews was never formally signed by anyone, but subsequent participation in the institutions was deemed acceptance by the British and Irish governments.

The designation of languages to be classified as 'minority' or 'regional' under the terms of the Charter depends on nomination from the member state according to guidelines in the Charter. Here again such a decision involving a devolved region would, presumably, need the approval of the regional government and Assembly.

At St.Andrews in 2006 London handed the Northern Ireland Assembly what was a highly sensitive and controversial issue of reaching agreement on an Irish language act, and it did so with demands as to what the act must contain. A decade later the matter brought down Stormont. Now the same task has been handed to the reconstituted administration in Belfast, with an increased list of demands involving new offices and agencies which, apart from adding considerably to public expenditure, have a greater likelihood of making a solution more difficult to resolve, not less.

The difficulty of finding a compromise necessary for the resolution of the Irish language issue is exacerbated by the rigid structures of the Belfast Agreement settlement, where power is shared in coalition , not because of shared policies or agreed objectives, but because those structures demand a mandatory coalition of political parties according to their election votes. It is more geared to preventing controversial decisions being taken than it is to fostering alliances and compromise.

Language has proved to be one of Europe's most divisive problems and is still capable of inflaming passions and dividing people and countries. In the century since partition Northern Ireland's problem has been seen by many as a conflict between Catholic and Protestant, or between an Irish identity and a British one, but never between Irish-speakers and English speakers. It is a tragedy now, when the bogey of 'Rome rule' has largely disappeared, that a theoretical, even fabricated barrier, should be erected.

Notes

1. Richard English, 'Belfast Agreement reflects an astonishing journey by republicans', *Irish Times*, 30 March 2018.

2. Agreement between the Government of Great Britain and Northern Ireland and the Government of Ireland, Belfast Agreement, 1998.

3. Political developments in Northern Ireland since March 2007, House of Commons Standard Note SN/PC/04513, 15 November 2007, p.5.

4. Text of the Irish Republican Army (IRA) statement on ending the armed campaign, 28 July 2005, www.cain@ulster.ac.uk

5. Text of Irish Republican Army (IRA), Easter statement, 5 April 2007, www. cain@ulster.ac.uk

6. https://europarl.europa.eu/election-results-2019/en/national-results/united-kingdom/northern-ireland-electoral-college/2019-2024/

7. Richard English, op. cit.

8. Declaration of Support, Par. 3, Belfast Agreement, 1998.

9. Lord Bew, 'What do we want from the next Prime Minister on the Backstop?', *The Policy Exchange*, 17 June 2019, p. 8.

10. 'Michelle O'Neill pays homage to IRA dead in home village of Clonoe', Belfast Telegraph, 17 February 2017.

11. 'Mary Lou McDonald tribute to IRA men at memorial angers unionists', *Belfast Telegraph*, 29 January 2018.

12. 'John Bruton: his full speech denouncing the Easter Rising', *News Letter*, 29 March 2016. See also, 'John Bruton says 1916 was a "recipe for endless conflict"', *Irish Times*, 6 August 2019.

13. '1916 Rising wasn't just or lawful, says legal chief Larkin', *Belfast Telegraph*, 19 March 2016.

14. 'A united Ireland would be a "different state" Leo Varadkar warns', *Irish Times*, 6 August 2019.

15. UK voted to leave by 52% to 48%, NI to remain by 56% o 44%.

16. 'Catholic majority in Northern Ireland likely by 2021',*Irish News*, 8 January 2020.

17. Graham Gudgin, 'David McWilliamsis wrong, Northern Ireland might never get a Catholic majority', *News Letter*, 13 December 2018. See also, 'A united Ireland is far from inevitable and here is why', *Belfast Telegraph*, 19 December 2018.

18. John Garry et al, 'Northern Ireland and the UK's exit from the EU', ESRC Report, May 2018, Figure 98, p.45

19   *Irish Times,* 12 August 2019.

20   Interview with Sky News. Reported in *Irish News,* 27 February 2017.

21   Seamus Mallon and Andy Pollock, *A Shared Home Place,* (Dublin: Lilliput Press, 2019), p.192.

22   'Varadkar says more than 50%+1 needed in a border poll', *Belfast Telegraph,* 17 October 2017 ... See also, 'Fianna Fail not planning a border poll, says Micheal Martin', *Belfast Telegraph,* 21 December 2019.

23   'Leo Varadkar calls for petition of concern reform in the event of a Stormont return', *Belfast Telegraph,* 16 October 2019. (The petition of concern gives a bloc of Assembly Members from either the nationalist or the unionist community a veto on some important decisions, even if they are a minority in the chamber.)

24   Ibid.

25   Ibid.

26   *New Decade, New Approach ,* 9 January 2010, Pars. 25-29, pp. 15-16.

27   Ibid.

28   Rights, Safeguards and Equality of Opportunity, Par. 4, Belfast Agreement,1998

29   St Andrews Agreement, October 2006, Annex B.

Notes on contributors

Arthur Aughey is Emeritus Professor of Politics at Ulster University. His books on Northern Ireland politics include *The Politics of Northern Ireland: Beyond* the *Belfast Agreement* (2005) and *The Conservative Party and the Nation* is his most recent book on conservatism published by Manchester University Press in 2018.

Brian Barton, graduated from Queen's University Belfast in modern history (1967) and was awarded an MA by the University of Ulster (1979) and completed a PhD in history at Queen's University (1994). He tutored in modern history with the Open University (1995-2013) and held research fellowships at Queen's University, Belfast and Churchill College, Cambridge and is a Fellow of the Royal Historical Society. He has authored or edited over twelve books on Irish history and politics. His most recent publications include *The Belfast Blitz: the City in the War* (2015); *The Secret Court Martial Records of the Easter Rising* (2010) and (co-authored with Michael Foy) *The Easter Rising* (2011). He co-edited with Patrick Roche and contributed to four published volumes on the 'Northern Ireland question' the most recent being *The Northern Ireland Question: The Peace Process and the Belfast Agreement* (2009). He also contributed chapters on Northern Ireland *to A New History of Ireland, Vol. VII, Ireland 1921-1984* produced by the Royal Irish Academy and published by Oxford University Press in 2003.

Esmond Birnie is a senior economist in the Ulster University Business School. He is a graduate of Cambridge University with a first class degree in economics and of Queen's University Belfast with a PhD in economics. Prior to 1998 he was senior lecturer in economics at Queen's University and in 1998 was elected to the Northern Ireland Assembly and was chair of an Assembly committee (1998-2007). He was a ministerial special advisor (2007-10) and PwC's chief economist in Northern Ireland and

Scotland (2010-2016). He is the author/co-author of twenty-one academic journal articles and of eleven books/book chapters regarding aspects of economic policy. He has written extensively for the *Belfast Telegraph, Irish News* and *News Letter* and his economic commentary has been cited by *The Economist, Irish Times, Daily Mail* and *Guardian*. His most recent publication, 'A critical review of competitiveness measurement in Northern Ireland' was published in the journal *Regional Studies* in January 2019.

Robin Bury is a graduate of Trinity College Dublin in modern history and political science and he taught at Downside School, Somerset and in Kenya before a career in export business based in Dublin. Following retirement he returned to his Alma Mater and completed an M.Phil, specializing in a study of southern Irish Protestants during 1921-1926 and his book, *Buried Lives: The Protestants of Southern Ireland* based on this research was published by The History Press Ireland in 2017.

Andrew Charles is a graduate of Queen's University, Belfast with a BA honours degree in politics and social policy (2006); an MSc in social research methods (2009) and a PhD in politics (2016) examining the development of community relations in Northern Ireland from 1969 to 2016.

Graham Gudgin is Honorary Research Associate at the Centre For Business Research (CBR) in the Judge Business School at the University of Cambridge and Chief Economic Advisor at Policy Exchange in London. He was formerly Director of the Northern Ireland Economic Research Centre in Belfast and from 1998-2002 was Special Advisor to First Minister David Trimble in Northern Ireland. He is a member of the DEXEU Commission on Alternative Arrangements for the Irish Border. Together with Professor Robert Tombs, he co-edits Briefings for Brexit a pro-Brexit academic website run from Cambridge University.

Dennis Kennedy graduated in modern history from Queen's University, Belfast (1958) and from Trinity College Dublin with a PhD in politics (1984). He has worked as a journalist in Northern Ireland, the United

States, Ethiopia and the Republic of Ireland mainly with *The Irish Times* (1968-85) of which he was deputy editor (1982-85). Subsequently he was Head of European Commission Office in Northern Ireland (1985-1991) and lecturer in the Institute of European Studies, Queen's University, Belfast. His publications on Irish affairs includes *The Widening Gulf: Northern Attitudes to the Independent Irish* (1988) and on Northern Ireland and the European Community his book *Living with the European Union; the Northern Ireland Experience,* was published by Macmillan in 2000. He contributed to three earlier Barton and Roche volumes on the 'Northern Ireland question'.

Cillian McGrattan lectures in politics at Ulster University. He is the author of numerous journal articles on themes of conflict, political violence and terrorism, conflict resolution, dealing with the past in post-conflict situations , trauma and peacebuilding, transitional justice, and Northern Irish nationalism and he has published a number of books on Northern Ireland politics including *The Politics of Trauma and Peace-Building: Lessons from Northern Ireland* published by Routledge in 2016.

William Matchett is a former detective inspector in the RUC Special Branch with a PhD from Ulster University (2014) on which his bestseller book, *Secret Victory: The Intelligence War that Beat the IRA* is based. He is an adjunct senior researcher at the Edward M. Kennedy Institute for Conflict Prevention in Maynooth University and his international lecturing to policy groups such as Policy Exchange (UK) and the Combatting Terrorist Technical Support Office (US) has extended to Washington DC, Auckland, Oslo and London. He works on capacity building police missions in challenging environments overseas and was central to making the BBC documentary 'Cops on the Frontline' along with contributing articles to newspapers and providing analysis on security matters on radio and television.

Patrick J. Roche graduated with a BA in economics and politics from Trinity College Dublin (1970) and an MA in political philosophy from University of Durham (1972). He lectured in economics at Ulster University (1974-1995) and was elected to the Northern Ireland Assembly in 1998. His publications on Irish nationalism include a contribution to Jurgen Elvert (ed), *Northern Ireland: Past and Present* (1994) and articles published in the *Salisbury Review* and since 1991 he has co-edited with Brian Barton four volumes on the 'Northern Ireland question' the most recent of which was *The Northern Ireland Question: The Peace Process and the Belfast Agreement* published by Palgrave Macmillan in 2009.

Graham Walker is Professor of Political History in the School of History, Anthropology, Philosophy and Politics at Queen's University Belfast. He works in the subject areas of the history and politics of Northern Ireland and of Scotland, and among his publications are *A History of the Ulster Unionist Party: Protest, Pragmatism, Pessimism* (2004) and *The Labour Party in Scotland: Religion, The Union, and the Irish Dimension* published by Palgrave in 2016.

Index

Markievicz, Countess C., 23, 318
Mason, R., 200, 203
Maxwell, Major General Sir J., 22, 23, 27
Mellows, L., 38-9
Mitchell, G., 366, 367
'Monaghan footballers', 45
Mullins, T., 332
Myers, K., 337
Ne temere decree, 326-9
New Decade, New Approach, 368, 369
Northern Ireland
    And Scottish and Welsh devolution,
        71, 75, 81
    Assessments of Northern Ireland gov-
        ernment, 79-81
    Demographic change, 363-4
    Discrimination in, 76-80
    Enduring legacy of the 'troubles' (1921-
        2), 58-61
    Finances, 72, 73, 75
    Nationalist attitudes to, 19-20, 28, 30,
        31-2, 37-8, 39-55, 78-9
    'step by step' policy, 72-6, 80
    'Under seige' (1921-22), 37-53
Northern Ireland Civil Rights Association,
    77, 78, 80
    August 1969, 133-5
    Early ideologues, 122-4
    Early marches, 128-31
    Partition, 119-22
    People's Democracy, 131-3
    Polarization, 127-32
    Wolfe Tone Societies, 124
Northern Ireland Labour Party (NILP), 76
Nuttall, D., 338
O'Bradaigh, R., 60
O'Brien, CC., 193-4
    Ghosts that call for blood, 100
    Mystique of the gunman, 100
O'Callaghan, S., 201, 216
O'Duffy, E., 48
O'Halloran, C., 86
O'Hanrahan, M., 24

O'Leary, R., 326
Oliver, JA., 158
O'Neill, J., 320, 340
O'Neill, M.,
    Commemoration of the IRA, 356
O'Neill, T., 72
Paisley, I., 350
Patterson, H., 326
Pearse, P., 17, 18, 20, 25, 27, 29, 35, 38, 100
Pearse, W., 24
Plunkett, H., 324
Plunkett, J., 18, 24
Pollock, H., 71, 72, 73
Protestants in Southern Ireland, 315-43
    'big houses' burnt, 323-4
    Causes of population decline, 317-43
    Continuing marginalization, 338
    Contribution to the state, 342-3
    Cultural alienation, 316-8, 324, 325-8,
        330-33, 336-41
    Intimidation of, 315-6, 318-24
    'mini pogrom', Bandon Valley (1922),
        319-21
    Ne temere decree, 326-9
    Sectarian attacks (1935), 333-6
    Statistics of population decline, 316,
        324-30
    'Tilson case', 327-8
Radio Telefis Eireann, 341
Redmond, J., 28, 34, 38
Renewable Heat Initiative, 348
Reports
    Cameron Report, 120, 129, 132
    De Silva Report, 207
        Handling of informers, 208
    Forum Report, 88
    Gardiner Report, 199
    Hannigan Report, 201
    Hunt Report, 196
    Richards Report, 209
    Scarman Report, 195
Republic of Ireland,
    IRA safe haven, 193